APARTMENT STORIES

APARTMENT STORIES

City and Home in Nineteenth-Century
Paris and London

SHARON MARCUS

University of California Press

Berkeley   Los Angeles   London

This book is a print-on-demand volume. It is
manufactured using toner in place of ink. Type and
images may be less sharp than the same material seen in
traditionally printed University of California editions.

University of California Press
Berkeley and Los Angeles, California

University of California Press, Ltd.
London, England

© 1999 by
The Regents of the University of California

Library of Congress Cataloging-in-Publication Data

Marcus, Sharon, 1966–
    Apartment stories : city and home in
nineteenth-century Paris and London /
Sharon Marcus.
        p.   cm.
    Includes bibliographical references and index.
    ISBN 0-520-20852-8. — ISBN 0-520-21726-8
(pbk.)
    1. Apartment houses—Social aspects—
France—Paris—History—19th century.
    2. Apartment houses—Social aspects—
England—London—History—19th century.
    3. Personal space—England—London—
History—19th century.   4. Paris (France)—
Social conditions—19th century.   5. London
(England)—Social conditions—19th century.
    6. Paris (France)—Social life and customs—
19th century.   7. London (England)—Social life
and customs—19th century.   8. Paris (France)—
Intellectual life—19th century.   9. London
(England)—Intellectual life—19th century.
    I. Title.
HD7287.6.F82P375   1999
307.3'36—dc21   98-40597

Printed in the United States of America

The paper used in this publication meets the minimum
requirements of ANSI/NISO Z39.48 (R 1997)
(Permanence of paper)

Contents

List of Illustrations   vii

Acknowledgments   ix

Introduction   I

PART ONE: OPEN HOUSES

1. Seeing through Paris, 1820–1848   17
2. Balzac's Spatial Relations   51

PART TWO: THE CITY AND THE DOMESTIC IDEAL

3. The Haunted London House, 1840–1880   83

PART THREE: INTERIORIZATION AND ITS DISCONTENTS

4. Enclosing Paris, 1852–1880   135
5. Zola's Restless House   166

Notes   199

Bibliography   281

Photograph Credits   314

Index   315

Illustrations

1. Elevation and cross-section of a Parisian apartment building on the boulevard St-Denis   20
2. Floor plan of a Parisian apartment building on the boulevard St-Denis   23
3. Karl Girardet, "Coupe de maison à Paris"   30
4. Cross-section of a Parisian apartment building on the rue de Marignan   31
5. Frontispiece to *Les Français peints par eux-mêmes*, vol. 4   35
6. Facing pages from *Le Diable à Paris*, vol. 2   36
7. Frontispiece to *Physiologie de la portière*   44
8. Illustration to *Physiologie de la portière*   45
9. Honoré Daumier, "Un Locataire qui a eu un oubli le 1er janvier"   46
10. Illustration to *Physiologie de la portière*   48
11. Illustration to *Physiologie de la portière*   49
12. William Young, project for model flats for the middle classes   89
13. Photograph of Park Crescent, London   95
14. Elevations of No. 1, Cornwall Terrace, and No. 2, Hanover Terrace, London   96
15. Photograph of terrace row, Fassett Square, London   98
16. Photograph of terrace row, Queensdown Road, London   99
17. Elevation of a Parisian apartment building   100
18. Perspective view of a double detached house, London   101

19. Elevation of a pair of semidetached houses   112
20. Elevation of a pair of semidetached houses   113
21. Elevation and basement floor plan of a pair of semi-
     detached houses   114
22. Panorama of the rue Vivienne   141
23. Photograph of the avenue de l'Opéra   142
24. A. Robida, "Pot-Bouille, ou tous détraqués mais
     tous vertueux"   195

Acknowledgments

INTELLECTUAL WORK IS FUELED first of all by money, and I am very grateful to the institutions that provided me with grants to write this book. In its initial phases as a doctoral dissertation, it was funded by a Bosanquet Bursary, a Gilbert Chinard fellowship, a Fulbright fellowship, a Woodrow Wilson Women's Studies grant, a National Endowment for the Humanities Dissertation Fellowship, and fellowships at the Johns Hopkins University Humanities Center. Additional research and writing have been made possible by a series of grants from the University of California at Berkeley, including a fellowship at the Doreen Townsend Center for the Humanities.

This work has also basked in the thoughtfulness and attention of people who have given me many reasons to be grateful. Without the support and example of my undergraduate mentors at Brown University—Karen Newman, Naomi Schor, Joan Wallach Scott, and Elizabeth Weed—I would never have come to writing. At the Johns Hopkins University I had the good fortune to work with Michael Fried, Neil Hertz, Mary Poovey, and Judith Walkowitz, who along with many other students and faculty there, generously brought their considerable scholarly knowledge and acumen to bear on several incarnations of this work. I am also grateful to the University of California, Berkeley, for providing this project with a welcoming and final home, as well as to readers from there and all over whose comments and queries changed it for the better, and whose words of encouragement gave me the energy to implement their insightful suggestions: Elizabeth Abel, Andrew Aisenberg, Ann Banfield, Jennifer Callahan, Margaret Cohen, Liz Constable, Kamilla Elliot, Charlotte Eyerman, Catherine Gallagher, Stephen Greenblatt, Dorothy Hale, Betty Hall, Dana Hollander, Jeffrey Knapp, Cathy Kudlick, Celeste Langan, Tom Laqueur, David Lloyd, Michael Lucey, Stephen Nichols, John Plotz, Bruce Robbins, Dan Rosenberg, Mary Ryan, Elaine Scarry, Vanessa Schwartz, Lynn Sharp, Katie Snyder, Peggy Waller, Alex Zwerdling, the fellows at the Townsend Center for the Humanities (1997–98), and the members of the British Studies and French History Groups at UC Berkeley. The expert research assistance of Sally Huang, Gia Kim, and Simon Stern helped to sustain both the book and its author, as did the staff members of the many libraries I haunted in search of materials. My warmest thanks also to Anne Cheng, Keith Crudgington, Tim Culvahouse, Carolyn Dinshaw, Paul Groth, Jamer Hunt, Cathy Jurca, Caren Kaplan, Rob Kaufman, Annie Levy, Sid Maskit, Susan Maslan, Leila May, Sam Otter, Don Palmer, and Eric Smoodin.

Two friends have lived with my apartment stories almost as long as I have: Charlotte Eyerman and Vanessa Schwartz, who were always willing to share so much with me, including their own work on urban and domestic culture in Paris. Betty Hall infused joy and affection into every day we shared. Finally, this book is dedicated to Jennifer Callahan, with the hope that it reflects at least some of the intelligence, originality, and care that she brings to her own reading and writing and has for many years lavished on me and on our friendship.

Introduction

PICTURE THE NINETEENTH-CENTURY CITY. If the image that comes to mind first is Victorian London, you probably conjure up people struggling with dire poverty in decrepit, filthy tenements. Members of an apparently content but secretly anxious middle class avail themselves of the latest in urban leisure while observing the poor from a safe distance as philanthropists, government officials, and amateur ethnographers. Turn to Paris: once again, dark images of an underclass vie with the vivid flashes of modernity provided by street lights, railway stations, department stores, and museums. Men freely stroll the boulevards, mingling with the crowd and collecting impressions, but women enter the streets only at the risk of being taken for streetwalkers.

Now picture the nineteenth-century home. The very word "home" evokes English prototypes. Perhaps the tenement and the mansion come to mind, emblems of the social extremes produced by unfettered capitalism. More likely to emerge is the ideal home associated with the middle ground of domesticity. An interior first and foremost, this home's many rooms abound in the furniture, decorations, and material goods that make it a self-contained world. Gathered around the inevitable hearth are women and children. Servants weave in and out, laboring intensively to maintain this domestic universe. Middle-class men enter this home only intermittently, spending most of their time in the competitive marketplace that funds the domestic oasis. This home is hard to situate in the larger spaces of street, city, village, or region, because it is by definition abstracted from external influences; it is enclosed, built to hold only one family and to stand freely on its own plot of land.

Yet even as you recognize this picture, its limitations and contradictions assert themselves. Servants cross the home's borders and breach its hermetically sealed walls. The sociability that forms a necessary part of women's domestic business makes their total isolation impossible and undesirable. In the heart of the city, clubs provide domestic oases designed exclusively for men. Young middle-class women like "Caroline B." make daily treks across Paris to visit friends and relatives and record their movements in diaries that celebrate their "adventures" in the city's "muddy streets." Caroline's diary even suggests that the single-family house was neither the only nor the most desirable type of residence. Upon arriving at her family's dwelling in Lille, Caroline sighs, "My Lord but this big house is dismal"; on returning to their Parisian flat, however, she exclaims, "Ah! finally, here we are in this delicious apartment!"[1]

What is the story of that "delicious apartment," and how might it change our view of the relationship between city and home, public and private, women and men? Throughout the nineteenth century, the apartment house dominated the Parisian urban landscape, inspired and worried domestic ideologues and urban planners, and provided fiction writers with settings for farces, melodramas, supernatural tales, and realist novels. As a then uniquely urban form of housing that combined the relatively private spaces of individual apartment units with the common spaces of shared entrances, staircases, and party walls, the apartment house embodied the continuity between domestic and urban, private and public spaces. Unlike the isolated single-family house and the barely livable tenement, which opposed the city to the home, apartment buildings linked the city and its residences in real and imagined ways, and nineteenth-century discourses about apartment buildings registered the connections and coincidences between urban and domestic spaces, values, and activities. For their inhabitants and observers, apartment buildings were miniature cities whose multiplication of individual dwellings both magnified domesticity and perturbed its customary boundaries; in Paris, wrote Jacques Raphael, "each apartment house is a small city; each floor, a neighborhood."[2] Like the city, but on a scale more easily grasped, the apartment house provided a unifying frame for heterogeneity, for the simultaneous enactment of several different stories.

Apartment Stories presents a history of the city written from the point of view of houses that were not enclosed cells, sealed off from urban streets, markets, and labor but fluid spaces perceived to be happily or dangerously communicating with more overtly public terrain. The discourses that praised, condemned, or neutrally accepted apartment houses often imagined them as sites for activities we now take to be exclusive to city streets. Apartment houses were vantage points for visual observation and exhibition, nodes of commercial and sexual exchange, and settings for the sensory overload and chance encounters associated with crowds. Attempts to separate the city and the home had to contend with powerful celebrations of the apartment house's capacity to make urban and domestic spaces continuous and often foundered on the impossibility of fully separating the city and the home. By dissolving the boundary between residential and collective spaces, the apartment house produced an urban geography of gender that challenges current preconceptions about where women and men were to be found in the nineteenth-century city, allowing us to see, for example, that the home was often a masculine domain, and that heterosexual imperatives demanded the presence of women in streets as well as homes.

The apartment stories told here supply us with new visions of Paris and London, the nineteenth-century home, and the location of men and women in public and private spaces. We recover the history of Paris from the 1820s through 1840s, when a city of permeable apartment buildings was supervised by female porters who became crucial representatives of urban knowledge and mobility. In Balzac's *Cousin Pons* (1847), we encounter an aged man who creates a secret museum in his apartment and a female porter who successfully schemes to expose her tenant's most private space. Haussmann's Paris comes into focus as a city where modernization and domestication went hand in hand, with planners, architects, and writers all striving to reconfigure urban spaces as enclosed, opaque interiors. In Zola's *Pot-Bouille* (1881) the drive to contain the family within the home faces multiple challenges from adulterous wives, cracking buildings, the noise and smell of neighbors, servants giving voice and giving birth, and authors who raid private life to write realist novels. A new London emerges in this book as well. Although the tradition of "An Englishman's Castle" may have led many a Briton to "boast to the Frenchmen that we do not pile our houses one upon another, to the eighth and ninth story," the simple fact that the Englishman did "not live . . . with a hundred people, and consign the key of his chamber to the hands of a prying porter" did not guarantee "that he enjoy[ed] more privacy or tranquility than the Frenchman." [3]

Rather, Londoners failed to materialize the domestic ideal of single-family houses—a failure encoded in popular stories of middle-class lodgings plagued by ghosts.

Apartment Stories concentrates on the middle decades of the nineteenth century, defined then and now as the "age of great cities," and takes up a pair of cities that have been opposed for centuries, Paris and London, not only in order to study their differences but also to highlight their points of intersection.[4] Paris and London contrast most starkly with respect to the apartment house: against London, a city that expanded enormously throughout the nineteenth century, but whose landowners and builders concentrated on single-family houses, stands Paris, a city that also increased in population and dimensions, but whose housing stock consisted mostly of apartment buildings. Paris, the capital not only of France but, in Walter Benjamin's formulation, of the nineteenth century, became an international symbol of urban modernity; London, despite its metropolitan status, was measured unfavorably against the idyllic rural images that defined the English nation. Parisians engaged in far more celebrations of their city than Londoners, who focused on how urban "slums" destroyed domestic life and suburbs redeemed it. Even in the scholarship of the past two decades, the major works on domestic ideology in nineteenth-century Europe have focused on England, while the paradigmatic studies of urbanism have converged on Paris.[5]

This book's comparative approach aims not to invigorate these oppositions but to undo them by bringing to light the domesticity of Parisian urbanism and the urbanism of London's domesticity. My comparative approach is not symmetrical; because my organizing device is the apartment house—typical of Paris but anomalous in London—the French material outweighs the British. But London does not operate here peripherally, as a foil or frame that by exemplifying the rule of separate spheres proves Paris to have been an exception. Rather, London appears at the center of this book because, in important and unrecognized ways, its residents failed in practice to sustain the domestic isolation they promulgated in theory. London also occupies a central temporal position in my overarching historical narrative because its investment in isolated domestic units played a pivotal role in both England and France, with Londoners reflecting on Paris and Parisians looking back at London. When London builders, residents, and architects commented on their city's suburban expansion after the 1840s, they explicitly opposed the homes of the British metropolis to Parisian apartment-house life. Few English critics seemed aware that the Parisian model they rejected had enjoyed its heyday only from the 1820s until the 1848 revolution. When France underwent a conservative backlash that lasted from 1851 through the 1870s, Parisian administrators restructured the city along lines they identified as those adopted by the British capital in the first half of the nineteenth century. Comparison thus reveals that statements contrasting the two cities were part of a larger dialogue connecting them.

Each of the book's three parts offers a new view of the relationship between urban and domestic life in nineteenth-century Paris and London. Part one, "Open Houses," shows discourses promoting urban mobility and legibility at work in Paris from 1820 to 1848, extending the visibility and fluidity of all urban space even to the homes and women who, in an ideology of separate spheres, would have been associated with sequestered private space. Those architectural and urban discourses made the apartment house and the female porter who managed it emblems of the continuity between the street and the home. Part two, "The City and the Domestic Ideal," argues that although the ideology of separate spheres infused almost all representations of Victorian London, and all the houses built there, it did not generate a corresponding set of dwelling practices in the metropolis. In the discourses that deplored those practices for leading to houses whose subdivision, flimsiness, and status as rental property prevented Londoners from realizing the British domestic ideal, the haunted house became the crucial emblem. Part three, "Interiorization and Its Discontents," demonstrates that from 1850 to 1880, Parisians became more receptive to English models for conceiving the entire city as a set of enclosed domestic spaces, built to retain not only women but also men within the home. For those new urban discourses, the apartment house posed the major obstacle to the creation of a private, domesticated city that would securely transmit patriarchal power.

Apartment Stories addresses itself to readers interested in feminist criticism and theory; geography; urban studies; architectural history; the novel; and interdisciplinary research on everyday life. Those fields set precedents for taking domestic life and architecture seriously: they place on several disciplinary agendas questions about how gender and class create unequal relationships to city and home, and they treat space, often relegated in philosophical discourse to the status of a passive background, as a fully historical and political dimension.[6] I also find polemical inspiration in landmark books that implicitly posit the city and the home as parallel realms incapable of coinciding. Take, for example, two of the most important recent studies of Paris and its representations, T. J. Clark's *The Painting of Modern Life* and Christopher Prendergast's *Paris and the Nineteenth Century*. The list of sites they identify as urban includes parks, boulevards, sewers, cafés, monuments, barricades, markets, world's fairs, department stores, restaurants, hotels, transportation, and of course, streets, but the houses that dominated the built environments of Paris do not enter their lists of urban locations.[7]

The absence of residential spaces seems to go without saying in accounts of modernity, which define city life as the public life that takes place in collective spaces of exchange or display and describe home life as private, concealed, and self-enclosed, often taking their cue from Walter Benjamin's notion of the home as a hermetically sealed "interior," isolated from its surroundings.[8] Scholarship on domestic architecture tends inversely to isolate the home from its wider spatial context, focusing almost exclusively on the evolution of room distribution and changing styles of facade decor.[9] More broadly defined studies of the relationships among interior decoration, high art, and social history still depict houses as interiors removed from their urban, suburban, or rural surroundings.[10] And even work that argues for the interdependence of public and private spheres can reinstate a hierarchical opposition in which the public trumps the private. For example, Leora Auslander's *Taste and Power: Furnishing Modern France* explains changes in the private, material spheres of consumption, taste, and household objects by referring to shifts in the public sphere, defined as political regimes, modes of production, institutional structures, and disciplinary forces. Although she notes the potential for resistance within the private sphere, that resistance reacts to and hence depends on the public sphere, which remains temporally, logically, and politically prior and dominant.[11] *Apartment Stories* joins forces with arguments for the relationship between public and private realms but seeks to reconceive public and private not as a temporal sequence of abstract causes and physical effects but as simultaneous and coincident entities, equally capable of taking conceptual or material form.

This book depends on and departs from a prior generation of feminist studies in history, political theory, and literary criticism that took the *gendered* separation of public and private spheres as an explicit topic of research and critique.[12] Feminist scholarship showed how a host of nineteenth-century discourses and practices defined the home as a private, cloistered space, advocated women's restriction to that space, and correspondingly excluded women from the easy commerce with the city's public spaces that was the privilege of many men. Crucial as that demonstration was, it anchored those divisions too securely and fixed their extent too widely. Although critics like Janet Wolff and Griselda Pollock took a critical distance from the separation of public and private realms, their descriptions of women's exclusion from the spaces of Parisian modernity adhered with surprising absoluteness to an oppositional relationship between the city and the home, between public and private spheres, and between men and women. These feminist critics and others clearly called for an end to gendered splits between public and private in the future, but in so doing they overlooked crossings that already undermined those divisions in the past.

Apartment Stories seeks out those crossings and aligns itself in particular with a shift in feminist studies from critiques of the public-private opposition as ideological rather than natural to a critical skepticism about the very hegemony of those oppositions.[13] That skepticism emerges most emphatically in studies of working-class family life and housing that illustrate the impact of state policies on domestic space; point to the fluid relations among dwellings, streets, pubs, and cafés; and highlight the gap between bourgeois prescriptions and the quotidian culture of working-class and poor urbanites.[14] *Apartment Stories* suggests that we question the hegemony of separate spheres ideology not only because it applied to only one class, the bourgeoisie, but because it may not even have applied to that class. Throughout this book, I uncover variations on middle-class prescriptions and gaps within the bourgeoisie itself. I show that the middle class did not always represent the city and the home as separate gendered spheres; that juridical and literary discourses aiming to establish the home as a guarantee of masculine property also registered the many fault lines traversing their version of the home; and finally, that middle-class self-representations often failed to correspond to their spatial practices.

Apartment Stories examines how nineteenth-century discourses interpreted spaces as public and private, masculine and feminine but refuses to assume any foregone relationship among the key terms of liberal politics (public/private), gender construction (masculine/feminine), and the organization of space (interior/exterior). By refusing to collapse theoretically autonomous domains, I seek to make visible the relationships that separate-spheres frameworks occlude and to question totalizing claims (which still have scholarly currency) that create oppositions between men and women, public and private realms, and exterior and interior spaces, then conflate the opposing terms of each pair.[15] My point

is not that "the public," for example, is an invalid concept, but that it is
neither intrinsically nor historically aligned in any consistent way with
a particular gender or spatial coordinate. Nineteenth-century discourses
that welded masculinity to exterior spaces and the public sphere, or femininity to interiors and the private sphere, did so only tenuously and after an arduous process. Many nineteenth-century writers saw no necessary relationship between spatial interiors and privacy and did not even
demarcate the home as a category distinct from the street. Contributors
to anthologies about Paris in the 1830s and 1840s qualified as urban
only those streets or buildings where women were present and available
to view. French and English writers insistently demarcated the home as
a masculine domain as well as a feminine one and enjoined both men
and women to stay at home, though for different reasons.

Identifying the domains of politics, gender, and space as theoretically
distinct and the relationships between their categorical terms as historically variable complicates our understanding of past and present initiatives to reform everyday life. Such projects often founder because they
attempt to effect political, social, and spatial change by rearranging only
one of those domains. The assumption of an interdependence tanta-
mount to equivalence among gender, spatial, and political arrangements
leads to the conclusion that radically altering one domain will automat-
ically transform the others. However, precisely because these domains
are distinct, the relations that obtain in one do not necessarily translate
into the others. Thus, for example, the fluidity between exterior and interior space that governed perceptions and constructions of Paris from
the 1820s through the 1840s did not produce a feminist city, because it
was not accompanied by any equally successful project to create political equality between men and women.

Apartment Stories uses the sources and methods of cultural history and
literary criticism to interpret the apartment houses of Paris and the subdivided homes of London. I discuss the effects of architectural styles, urban demography, rental markets, and property laws in shaping apartment houses, but my focus throughout is on the meanings that apartment
houses had for their builders, occupants, and regulators. I find those
meanings in architectural pattern books, urban encyclopedias, public
health surveys, and fictional discourses of everyday life, particularly realist novels and urban ghost stories. The book as a whole also presents
the story of those stories, the historical narrative of how the meanings

assigned to the apartment house varied over time, between national cultures, and even within apparently unified times and places.

As a cultural historian, I address writings by architects, doctors, government officials, journalists, and domestic advisors. I sift those texts for telling idiosyncrasies and representative patterns and show how the discourses they comprised were intertwined with economic and state formations and collective cultural fantasies. My focus throughout is on discourses about apartment houses, not on apartment houses themselves, and I assume that those discourses often produced the facts they claimed to describe.[16] I thus treat even architectural floor-plans and elevations as representations elaborated on the basis of institutional affiliations, rhetorical codes, and political objectives. Like many geographers, I view spaces such as the apartment house or the city as both social products and conduits for social production; I do not, however, consider them monolithic agents of social control.[17] Architectural determinism—the belief that spatial environments determine the social arrangements, daily behaviors, and political status of those who inhabit them—is here an object of historical critique, not a methodological assumption.[18] Hence, I provide accounts of the nineteenth-century arguments that attributed moral, psychological, and physical characteristics to environmental influences without replicating their belief in the intentional agency of space.

Apartment Stories follows many other critics in identifying the novel as a crucial discourse of everyday life and as a result takes literary criticism and cultural history to be entwined endeavors.[19] I approach literary works as discourses, articulating their institutional ambitions, audiences, and market positions and examining how they worked to define gender, domestic and urban space, and the relations between public and private realms. The conceptual frameworks of my literary interpretations emerge from my historical arguments, since the problems I analyze in the context of literature were equally problems for architectural manuals and works of metropolitan observation. The *portière,* the specter, and the insufficiently sealed interior appeared in works of urban fact and urban fiction alike. At the same time, I have deliberately selected literary texts with an eccentric relation to dominant cultural discourses, and in order to make good my particularizing claims about their divergence from discursive conventions, I use the tools of literary criticism: close reading; detailed attention to how texts engage literary precedents; and analysis of narration, characterization, and the internal structural relations produced by plot.[20] My choice of atypical texts is not an argument for literature's oppositional nature but rather a heuristic device for conveying the range and complexity of nineteenth-century debates on domesticity and urbanism: Balzac's novel *Le Cousin Pons* decried the fluidity between public and private space that his contemporaries promoted; the authors of urban ghost stories encoded the failure of London's middle-class houses to embody the British domestic ideal; and Zola's *Pot-Bouille* derided the futility of widespread attempts to isolate the home from external disturbances.

While I treat nineteenth-century fiction as one discourse among the many others that sought to demarcate public and private, I also focus on the novel's generic specificity, which I locate in its attention to topography and to plot. By topography I mean the ways that narration itself (and not simply the events narrated) inscribes spatial relations—the ways that narration establishes zones as exterior and interior, mobile and fixed, global and local, publicly open and privately opaque. While an imbrication of spaces now commonly assumed to be distinct (city and home, public and private) characterized the *content* of all the discourses studied here, the novel blended public and private in its *form*, its narration and circulation. The omniscient and often impersonal third-person narration that constituted a hallmark of nineteenth-century British and French realist and naturalist novels was, on the one hand, aligned with the public sphere because such narrators spoke from a generalizing point of view to a general public, and because those narrators' boundlessness and bodilessness paralleled the open structure of public spaces and the immateriality of the public sphere. On the other hand, omniscient narration consistently focused on the delimited, concealed, inaccessible spaces of private subjects and domestic spaces and relayed the stories it uncovered to readers who, while part of a reading public, often consumed novels in private.[21] Because many nineteenth-century discourses emphasized how apartments either created a domestic form of publicness or undermined privacy, the apartment house was an available and apt emblem for novelistic depictions of the paradoxical interplay of public and private that structured their narrative procedures. The readings of literary texts here show that the apartment-house descriptions, plots, and characters generated by realist narratives often mirrored the realist narrator's tendency to simultaneously dissolve and maintain, invade and secure, the privacy of spaces and of persons.

Given the number of literary texts that exploited the homology between the formal paradoxes of realism and those of the apartment house, I propose expanding previous typologies of realism to include the apartment-house plot. The apartment-house plot bridges the gap between novels identified with spaces of the home (the salon novel, the domestic novel) and with urban sites (the urban bildungsroman, the novel of the street and of the crowd).[22] I refer to the apartment-house *plot* and not the apartment-house novel because that plot was not exclusive to novels but also popular in short stories and plays, and because its characteristic feature was its concatenation of an apartment-house setting with a formulaic series of actions. Exemplified in its most schematic form by the popular plays and novels of Henry Monnier, Paul de Kock, and William Brough, the apartment-house plot took elements from comic and melodramatic modes—particularly random sexual encounters, cases of mistaken identity, and acts of voyeurism, eavesdropping, and spying—and situated them within a single apartment house or in neighboring and facing apartment buildings.[23]

Although highly episodic, apartment-house plots nonetheless followed a strict narrative sequence: the conversion of strangers into kin, either by marriage or the revelation of prior relationships, and the corollary transformation of randomness into structure. Thus, in Paul de Kock's *Les Bains à domicile* (1845), characters who initially seem unrelated and whose occupation of the same apartment building seems equally haphazard discover that they already know each other. The revelation of their prior relationship confers a metaphorical order onto their physical propinquity within the building. In de Kock's *La Demoiselle du cinquième* (1857), sexual liaisons among the tenants transform physical vicinity and social ties from casual distance into purposeful connection. The apartment-house plot thus combines the salon novel's emphasis on domestic interiors and microscopic social networks (think *Le Père Goriot*) with the urban novel's emphasis on chance encounters, the interplay between isolation and community, and the sudden transformation of strangers into kin (think *Oliver Twist*). As a result, the apartment house attached the city to the home as sturdily in literature as it did in architectural and urban discourse.

Although the apartment-house plot appeared most clearly in the now forgotten realisms of Monnier and de Kock, once identified it helps us to redefine what makes more canonical novels "urban." Novels that have been described as urban because they represent panoramas, streets, and crowds now can also be understood as urban because, in variations on the apartment-house plot, they situate the city's flow and multiplicity *inside* the home. Read with the apartment-house plot in mind, urban fictions such as Balzac's *Illusions perdues* and *Histoire des treize;* Zola's *La Curée* and *L'Assommoir;* and Dickens's *Martin Chuzzlewit, Little Dorrit,* and *Bleak House* emerge as city novels not only because they describe spaces conventionally associated with the city but also because they stage the eruptions of urban characters, actions, and events in the multiple and porous spaces of urban homes.

Apartment Stories focuses on fictional texts at odds not only with dominant cultural discourses but also with the conventional apartment-house plot. Balzac's *Cousin Pons* does not convert strangers into kin but makes kin into strangers; Zola's *Pot-Bouille* stages the dissolution of paternal and conjugal identities in the shared space of an apartment building; ghost stories depict one set of occupants driving out another. Because these texts focus on residential settings, they fail to correspond to our generic expectations of urban novels and have never before been proposed as epitomes of urban realism. Indeed, *Le Cousin Pons* and *Pot-Bouille* have received little critical attention relative to other novels by Balzac and Zola; *Pot-Bouille* is currently unavailable in English translation; and the British urban ghost stories I discuss, many of them out of print, are identified as a subgenre for the first time here. Their very lack of familiarity, however, endows these works with a capacity to surprise us and to complicate our received notions in ways that more canonical works by Balzac, Dickens, and Zola would fail to do.

The apparent obscurity of these texts does not prevent them from providing lenses through which to survey the novel in general. For example, the *portière* so central to *Le Cousin Pons* can help us to find other female characters who shuttle between public and private spaces and between immaterial and particularized narration, not only literal *portières* but also such ubiquitous and omniscient characters as Madame Defarge in *A Tale of Two Cities.*[24] Urban ghost stories provide a new framework for understanding why in many British novels, such as *Great Expectations* and *Bleak House,* spectral eruptions accompany domestic disruption. The apparitions who disrupt male proprietorship when they appear in the rented rooms of ghost stories also haunt sensation novels, which frequently align transgressive women, ghosts, and lodging houses; this distinctive motif recurs in Wilkie Collins's *Basil, Armadale,* and *No-Name* and in Mary Braddon's *Charlotte's Inheritance* and *The Story of Barbara.* Zola's use of the apartment house to mirror the process of storytelling prefigures recent postmodern experiments such as Georges

Perec's *La Vie mode d'emploi*, which analogizes the chapters of a book to the rooms of an apartment and implicates reader, author, and characters in the construction of novelistic space.

Studies of urban culture continue to draw on Walter Benjamin's seminal essays on nineteenth-century Paris, adopting some of his key terms (shock, the *flâneur*, the prostitute) in ways that secure the separation of the urban and the domestic.[25] But when Walter Benjamin returned from his first visit to Paris in 1913, he described a city "whose houses seem made, not to be lived in, but rather to be stone wings or scenery [*steinerne Coulissen*] between which one walks. I have become almost more at home . . . on the Grand Boulevard than I am . . . on the streets of Berlin."[26] Benjamin's metaphor seems clear, simple, familiar: the city is a theater, down to its very houses.[27] Yet the sentence generates contradictory spatial images. *Coulissen* can mean the wings of a theater, which in the sentence's ambiguous syntax would make either the houses themselves or the spaces between them into hallways leading to a stage. If the houses are the wings, they become passages to and from the stage that is the street; if the spaces between them are the wings, then the streets become enclosed spaces leading to a domestic theater. In both instances, Benjamin's metaphor reverses expected associations: homes are not sealed, interior spaces but theatrical ones, streets are not open, exterior paths but domestic, enclosed corridors where one feels so "at home."[28] The complications only increase when we note that the word *Coulissen* also refers to stage sets or scenery and to an outward show or front. The houses thus become both backdrops and projections in the urban landscape. Nestled in Benjamin's deceptively offhand remark is a dizzying series of substitutions that blur the usual distinctions between the city and the home.

A slight imbalance, however, offsets Benjamin's evocation of the city as interchangeable with its houses. His qualification that the "houses seem made . . . *not* to be lived in, *but* rather to be stone wings or scenery between which one walks" implies that when they coincide with the city's streets, Parisian houses cease to be habitats. Living in a place seems incompatible with performance and promenade. Benjamin suggests that while the street can be "homelike" and "cozy" and still be a street, homes can only retain their domestic character if they are enclosed, hidden, static. Within the confines of his brief impression, contradictory views collide: on the one hand, the city and the home resemble one another to the point of being interchangeable; on the other, the home can only be a home in opposition to the city, as its antithesis. This book gives those contradictory views a history—one that begins in the 1820s, in Paris, with the culture of the transparent apartment house that is the subject of the next chapter.

PART ONE

Open Houses

1

Seeing through Paris, 1820–1848

WHY DID APARTMENT HOUSES BECOME THE dominant architectural elements in the Parisian landscape during the last decades of the Restoration (1814–30) and throughout the July Monarchy (1830–48)? Their popularity owed much to two factors: they provided spatially compact housing in a city with a rapidly increasing population and offered an expanding middle class opportunities for investing in relatively inexpensive and profitable properties. Demography and economics, however, do not sufficiently account for Parisians' adoption of the apartment building as their chief residential form; as we will see in chapter three, although London's population also expanded dramatically throughout the nineteenth century, Londoners did not build apartment houses. In order to understand the Parisian enthusiasm for apartment buildings, we need to excavate the cultural beliefs about domestic and urban space embedded in the discourses of Parisian architecture and everyday life. Apartment buildings appealed to Parisians as a material figure of broad social conceptions of private and public life: the containment of social heterogeneity in a unifying framework; the imbrication of the domestic and the urban; and the transparency and fluidity of every component of urban space.

Paris in the first half of the nineteenth century reflected, in intensified form, the extreme social mobility that characterized France in the years following the fall of the old regime. Many of the aspects of urban modernity that marked Second Empire and fin-de-siècle Paris were already in place by the 1820s, including a culture based on commodification, spectacle, and speculation, and a legible urban space easily mapped and navigated by the upwardly mobile.[1] The premium on legible urban space was matched by a desire to decipher the exact social position and moral character of any Parisian in a glance, as a series of urban "physiognomists" claimed the power to do. Within the July Monarchy's capitalist democracy, the desire for transparent space and citizens, whose exteriors would be windows onto their interiors, emphasized reading people in terms of commodities and wealth; by the cut of a man's suit, you could assess his income.[2] Specific as it was to that new regime, however, transparency also had deep roots in French political culture, which from Rousseau through the revolution had decried obscurity, duplicity, and theatricality as antithetical to democracy.[3]

The historiography of an urban culture and space as open as the society that generated them coexists uneasily, however, with the historiography of nineteenth-century domesticity, which describes a segregated private realm that emerged in the wake of the French Revolution, a realm strictly separated from public spaces and functions. That separation was most evident in political and medical discourses that aligned women with the private space of the home and excluded them from a public sphere of abstract masculine political activity as well as from a set of collective exterior urban spaces (the street, the café, the theater).[4]

Scholarly assumptions about domestic space as a separate sphere have occluded more representative discourses about Paris, discourses so invested in the notion of a legible, transparent urban space conducive to easy circulation and observation that they actively incorporated domestic space into the city and even extended urban mobility to the emblematic figures of the private sphere—women of all classes, and especially the women who lived in the middle-class apartment building. The first section of this chapter studies both apartment-house designs and architectural pattern books to demonstrate how the apartment house embodied the cultural amalgamation of private and public spaces. The next section turns to the vast descriptive literature produced about Paris, particularly during the July Monarchy, and shows how the discourse of urban observation described the apartment building as a typical and integral physical feature of the Parisian landscape and, strikingly, as a figure for the objects and activity of urban observation itself. The apartment building's ability to unify its disparate residents within a single frame mirrored the efforts of urban observers to contain Parisian heterogeneity within a single text; its transparency illustrated the fluid relationship between apartments and the city's exterior spaces, as well as the accessibility of every space in Paris, even domestic space, to urban observers. The strength of the urban observers' commitment to mobility, transparency, and visibility can be measured by their insistence that even married women circulate within the city, and by their deployment of a female figure, the *portière,* to personify the apartment building and the activity of urban observation. At the same time, however, their resistance to the implications of their own discourse can be measured by the satiric distance they took from the *portière* who so resembled them.

Architectural Discourse and the Continuum of Street and Home

Historians tend to neglect the Paris of the first half of the nineteenth century for the city whose urban fabric altered dramatically after 1850. Viewed retrospectively through the lens of its eventual modernization, Paris from 1815 to 1848 is often reduced to the crowded, inefficient, and unsanitary city that Haussmann later claimed to have eradicated. The most influential scholarship on this period emphasizes the revolutionary turmoil and class anxiety of a "sick Paris" riddled with crime, death, and poverty.[5] Representations of a "dangerous and diseased city" in literature, medical reports, and fledgling attempts at demographic surveys attributed the city's social problems to its decaying environment of filthy streets and crowded, decrepit housing.[6]

Far less attention is paid to the more benign, even celebratory view of Paris prevalent in the architectural and urban literature that abounded during this period, a literature that concentrated on the quotidian pleasures afforded to the middle classes in the city's bourgeois spaces, particularly in the apartment houses constructed in large numbers during the 1820s. During the Restoration and the July Monarchy, from the 1820s through the 1840s, the characteristic Parisian house took on a new form, that of the modern six- to eight-story apartment building with shops on the ground floor and an imposing entrance supervised by a porter (fig. 1). In terms of both their form and the ways that their form was perceived, apartments embodied an urban domesticity that aligned them simultaneously with private homes and with public structures such as monuments, cafés, and streets.

The new apartment house represented a shift from earlier architectural articulations of private and public space. On the one hand, nineteenth-century apartment units were more self-contained and hence provided more spatial privacy than eighteenth-century housing for the

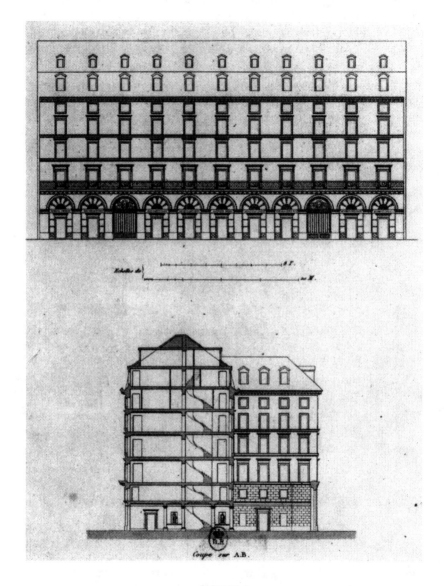

FIGURE 1

Elevation and cross-section of a Parisian apartment building
on the boulevard St-Denis. From [Louis-Marie] Normand fils,
Paris moderne (Paris: Bance, 1837).

middle and working classes; on the other hand, the increased size of nineteenth-century buildings, and their incorporation of vestibules, lobbies, and elaborate stairways, meant that these edifices brought more strangers into contact, in more places, than earlier ones had.[7] The apartment house partly owed its unique synthesis of publicity and privacy to its dual architectural sources, the *maisons à allée* and the *hôtels privés*. Most eighteenth-century apartment houses were *maisons à allée,* which lacked vestibules and were entered either through alleys off the street or through ground-floor shops. Internal apartments were formed by blocking off varying sets of rooms according to the needs of individual tenants and often consisted of suites of rooms distributed over several floors; this arrangement tended to multiply contact with other occupants, since one tenant might have to cross another's room to reach her own.[8]

Nineteenth-century apartment *units* were spatially self-contained and thus offered tenants greater seclusion within an individual apartment, but nineteenth-century apartment *buildings* maintained and even extended the public nature of the *maisons à allée,* since their larger scale (five to six stories) gathered greater numbers of residents together under one roof, while their inclusion of clearly articulated common spaces for entrance and egress formalized interaction among tenants. Like the *maisons à allée,* the new buildings had shops on the ground floor and thus continued to mix commerce and private life, though tradespeople and merchants were more common than artisans and manufacturers in more costly buildings.

The nineteenth-century apartment house did not evolve exclusively from earlier models of communal housing. Apartment house architects also drew on the aristocratic private townhouse, the *hôtel privé,* in their designs for the imposing double doors (*portes cochères*), elaborate vestibules, and porter's lodges that stood between the apartment building and the street. Some architectural historians have even identified the *hôtel* as the sole origin and model for the apartment house, but significant differences existed between the two building types.[9] The apartment brought public and private rooms into greater proximity with one another than the *hôtel* had. The *hôtel* separated reception rooms such as salons, which were open to strangers and designed for social occasions and display, from the bedrooms, studies, and cabinets intended for retirement and solitude. The apartment not only placed both types of rooms on a single floor but often placed them in direct communication with one another, so that one might enter an apartment's salon by passing through its main bedroom. Furthermore, the *hôtel* was divided into

separate wings for the husband and wife, which included separate bedroom suites for each of them, and thus created autonomous masculine
and feminine spaces; the more constricted bourgeois apartment usually
accommodated only a single conjugal bedroom and thus promoted a
greater degree of spatial heterosociality than the aristocratic *hôtel*.[10]

Apartment buildings and *hôtels privés* also differed in their orientation toward their urban surroundings. *Hôtels privés* occupied a space
distinct both from other buildings and from the street. As the historian
Roger Chartier points out, because *hôtels* were free-standing structures
set back from the thoroughfare by a walled courtyard, they "interrupted
the continuous ribbon of facades" that bordered the typical Parisian
street.[11] The *hôtel* turned its back to the street, since its primary, highly
decorated front and its most important rooms (dining room, salon, bedrooms) faced a private garden. The part of the *hôtel* facing the street, but
separated from it by a walled courtyard, consisted of service rooms such
as stables and the kitchen. Apartment buildings, by contrast, were situated directly on the street, entered from the street, made to be viewed
from and to provide views of the street. Builders constructed apartment
buildings with strong front/back axes, aligned facades with the sidewalk, and emphasized the importance of the street front by lavishing
better materials and more intricate designs on it. The most sought-after
apartments were those closest to the street, and the most prized rooms
of an apartment—living room, dining room, and main bedroom—faced
the street, while the kitchen, servant's room, and storage rooms faced the
courtyard (fig. 2).[12]

Apartment-house design also bore a conceptual similarity to urban
street systems. The ordered grid of the apartment-house facade, like that
of city streets, worked to abstract individual details into an aggregate
public form. Their unity and symmetry gave facades a decorative power
of generalization over the particularities of the rooms behind them in a
process related to the urban consolidation of heterogeneous individuals
into a public. The windows in a building's street facade often matched
one another in size, shape, and design, even when the rooms behind them
were different sizes or belonged to apartments separated from one another by vertical or horizontal partitions.[13] The apartment did have an
area whose external irregularities suggested internal dissymmetries—
the courtyard, carved out of the space where the undecorated, cheaply
constructed back walls of up to four different buildings met and were ir-
regularly punctuated by variously sized windows. Only the occupants of

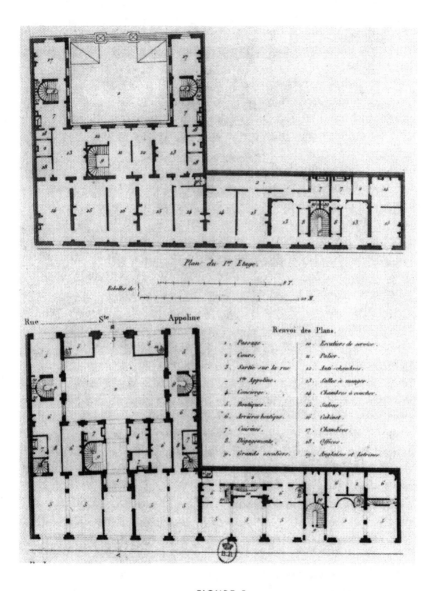

FIGURE 2

Floor plan of an apartment building on the boulevard St-Denis. The main bedroom [*chambre à coucher*] and living room [*salon*] are adjacent to one another, and both face the boulevard. From [Louis-Marie] Normand fils, *Paris moderne* (Paris: Bance, 1837).

neighboring buildings, however, could see the disorganization of the courtyard; the general public saw only the symmetry of a balanced, ordered facade.

Where *hôtels privés* allowed passersby mere glimpses of a circumspect, individualized image of domesticity, apartment buildings displayed and oriented a collective domesticity that communicated fully with the public street. Indeed, the building-street configuration characteristic of Paris from the 1820s through the 1840s—contiguous apartment buildings lining both sides of a street or wider boulevard—made streets and houses spatially interdependent. As the urban sociologist Chombart de Lauwe put it in his typology of the Parisian apartment, "the urban habitat invites . . . its users to turn toward the street."[14] Conversely, the July Monarchy street was oriented toward apartment houses and derived its shape from them; as William Ellis shows in "The Spatial Structure of Streets," when buildings constitute a "contiguous building pattern, [they] seem to form the spaces between them."[15]

The space of early nineteenth-century Parisian buildings mingled with the space of streets in concrete, quotidian ways. As prefect of Paris after 1833, Claude Rambuteau installed benches on all the major boulevards, a practice that made the comfort and stillness conventionally associated with the home available on the street; he also increased the number of public urinals on the sidewalks.[16] Apartment buildings began literally to enter the street when an 1823 ordinance of Louis XVIII allowed facades to project into the street, albeit in very restricted ways, for the first time since 1607. That ordinance also decreed that street widths would determine the height of a building and whether it could have balconies, thus deriving the facade's dimensions and design from those of the street.[17] Houses, like streets, became more rationalized, more subject to surveillance, better lit, and better marked; an 1824 police decree outlawed the defacement and obstruction of street names, house numbers, and streetlights.[18] And on a daily basis people threw their garbage into the streets, street sellers hawked their goods by yelling up into apartments, and merchants plastered building fronts with advertisements for their products.[19]

By the end of the July Monarchy, the apartment house was the most frequent and consistent element of the urban landscape. From the 1820s on architects, speculators, and landlords built small-scale apartments in central Paris and constructed new, largely residential neighborhoods just west, north, and east of the new Stock Exchange on the Right Bank, taking as their basic unit a row of apartment houses lining a street divided into a roadway and pedestrian sidewalks.[20] In response to this surge in building, publishers produced large volumes devoted to the new domestic architecture—pattern books designed to publicize individual architects, and to provide models for the many builders and contractors who bypassed trained architects. Most of those works consisted of brief introductions assessing and classifying the city's recent architectural productions, followed by architectural plates and explanatory text. The authors were either architects who had studied at the Ecole des Beaux-Arts but had not attained its highest honor, the prix de Rome, or whose more marginal architectural training gave them little access to the most lucrative and prestigious commissions for government buildings and aristocratic private mansions. Despite the relatively low professional status of their authors, compendia of apartment-house designs represented bids to exalt multiple-occupancy middle-class housing to the level of academic and aristocratic architecture, not by replicating the theoretical discussions of classical orders and perspective that filled architectural treatises, but by retaining those treatises' evaluative criteria and representational conventions. Their publishers adopted a large folio format and used expensive reproduction techniques that required the plates to appear separately from the text, thus distinguishing pattern books visually from popular architectural journals, whose woodcut illustrations could be inserted on the page along with type. Pattern books combined a canonical emphasis on architectural composition and the presentation of every building from three perspectives—cross-section, floor plan, and elevation—with a modern interest in construction techniques and the design of elements such as doors, cornices, and balconies.[21]

Architectural pattern books rarely used terms like "private" or "public" to describe the new residences; indeed, they barely distinguished the apartment building as a unique type at all, suggesting that its relative lack of privacy did not pose a problem for architects or their clients, and that urban homes were not defined in terms of privacy, nor in contradistinction to streets and other exterior spaces. Most architects simply called apartment buildings *maisons,* a general term meaning both "house" and "home," whose use emphasized the apartment building's similarity to other housing types, even more private ones, making the apartment house representative of the house in general. As late as 1850, Victor Calliat continued to classify any residence that was not an *hôtel* as a *maison*—whether it was a small single-family house or an apartment building of any size. Architects before 1850 thus positioned apartment buildings on a continuum with other kinds of houses and even took apartments to represent the generic "house." As we will see in chapter 4, only after 1850 did architects and writers in France promote the single-family house as the distinct ideal it was in England throughout the nineteenth century.[22] Indeed, the apartment house was so typical of Parisian domestic architecture, and its congruence with the term *maison* so established, that some Parisians perceived the single-family house as lexically indescribable: when Frédéric Soulié, the popular novelist and playwright, described a row of houses that would have been banal in London—"five or six buildings [*corps de logis*] . . . placed parallel to the street . . . followed by a garden"—he commented that "one could call them neither *hôtels* nor *maisons.*" [23]

Architectural texts linked the public spaces of the street and the private spaces of the residence by consistently associating apartment houses with the urban progress and modernity that twentieth-century historians have attributed only to public spaces such as boulevards and cafés. Victor Calliat, architect for the city of Paris from the 1820s through the 1870s, summed up three decades of Parisian building by announcing, "Never have so many private residences [*maisons particulières*] been built in Paris as during the last twenty-nine years. . . . An undeniably real progress has made itself felt. . . . Never perhaps have we built more, or better, as we have in the years since 1830." [24]

Others similarly associated apartment buildings with the modern qualities of contemporaneity and progress. In 1838 Jean-Charles Krafft, describing a recently built apartment house, complete with imposing entrance, ground-floor shops, and balconies, wrote: "This facade, taken as a whole and in its details, seems to conform perfectly to our modern practices and to fulfill all our current requirements for a residence; . . . everything in it could serve as a model for a rental house located in the city [*des maisons de ville dites à loyer*]." [25] And when L. Roux wrote that "the ground floor of a modern house is invariably left to commerce," he pointed out the links between modern consumer culture and contemporary domestic architecture.[26]

Over the course of the July Monarchy, architects identified apartments not only with an up-to-date, urban style but also with a financial potential redolent of modernity. Apartment buildings came to occupy an important position in a speculative Parisian real-estate market and provided opportunities for newly rich bourgeois to invest and generate income. The 1847 edition of Louis-Ambroise Dubut's *Architecture civile* referred to "*maisons à loyer,* consisting of several floors, otherwise

known as *maisons de rapport*," qualifying *maison* with a word that signified revenue and profit.[27] The term *maison de rapport* defined the apartment house from a property owner's perspective, as an investment and
source of income, and identified the apartment house with its economic
potential far more strongly than the term *maison à loyer,* which merely
indicated an apartment building's availability to potential inhabitants.
According to the *Statistique de l'industrie à Paris . . . sur les années
1847–1848,* "the rapid development of the population, the subdivision
of large urban estates, the development of new neighborhoods have all
encouraged building and thus turned house construction into a veritable industrial enterprise; there now exists a class of entrepreneurs and
merchants who deal in houses just as they do in any other industrial
product."[28]

As we will see in chapter 3, English observers often criticized Parisian
home life for its lack of privacy, not only because they took the single-
family house as an architectural standard, but also because they defined
domesticity in opposition to the marketplace, and the *maison de rapport*
brought economics close to home. French architects, however, did not
consider the apartment house's associations either with the street or with
urban speculation to disqualify it from a domestic function; they continued to call apartment buildings and units *maisons* or private houses
(*maisons particulières*) even after the late 1840s, when financial speculators had begun to build apartments on an almost industrial scale and
landlords were commonly depicted as impersonal administrators who
rarely lived in the buildings they owned.[29] François Thiollet, for example, in the third volume of a work that first appeared in 1829 and was
reprinted in 1838, classified buildings primarily in terms of their relationship to neighboring buildings and to the street, distinguishing among
hôtel, maison particulière, and *maison à loyer;* his use of the word *maison* in the two latter terms linked apartments to single-family houses.[30]
Maison particulière literally meant a private house for individuals (as opposed to government or commercial offices) and its primary architectural
and colloquial meaning was "single-family, owner-occupied house." Architects often stretched this meaning, however, to include multiple-
occupancy rental buildings. Krafft referred in 1838 to "maisons d'habitations particulières dites à loyer."[31] The text of Louis-Marie Normand
fils's architectural pattern book, *Paris moderne* (1837), stated that since
single-family houses had become "de luxe," the book would be devoted
to "habitations particulières" "dites de location"; the generic family

home had become a rental apartment, and the word *particulière*, far from denoting ownership and individual occupation, modified a multiple-occupancy rental building.[32]

Architects also placed apartment houses on a continuum with the imperial, royal city of imposing monuments and the modern, bourgeois city of boulevards, boutiques, and cafés.[33] Pattern books praised the ways that apartment houses combined public scale and private character. The apartment loomed larger than any residential building ever had, horizontally as well as vertically, and practices such as making the balconies of separate buildings continuous promoted the monumentality of apartments by emphasizing the mass block formed by their contiguity. The increased use of stone facades, often signed by stonecutters as artists would sign works of art, also contributed to the sense that the apartment building's exterior was, as one architectural historian puts it, "an enormous monumental sculpture facing the street."[34] Writers commented that the shift to five-, six- and even eight-story buildings brought apartment houses closer to public buildings and monuments.[35] Normand fils called *maisons à location* "veritable palaces raised to industry, commerce, luxury and the arts all at once"; Krafft called apartments the "monuments" of the "artistic renaissance of the nineteenth century," and in a medical work on *Des habitations et de l'influence de leurs dispositions sur l'homme* (1838), Dr. Pierre-Adolphe Piorry wrote that "in Paris . . . combined residences have reached such heights that they sometimes seem to dwarf nearby public monuments."[36]

Just as architects saw similarities between the monumental and the residential, between public and private building types, they also promoted designs that emphasized the similarity between a building's exterior, potentially more public face, and its interior, the space conventionally associated with privacy; indeed, architectural historians define Restoration architecture in terms of its "transposition of a building's indoor ornament onto its façade."[37] Authors of pattern books frequently compared apartment buildings to stores, cafés, and theaters and recommended incorporating elements from commercial and civic buildings into apartment-house decor. The stores, cafés, and restaurants that occupied the ground floor of most apartment buildings lent residences a commercial note, while the large sheets of plate glass that began to be incorporated into shops from the 1820s on made the apartment buildings that housed trade more physically open and transparent to the street.

Conversely, because café, restaurant, and shop interiors used the same decorating principles and materials as domestic ones, commercial spaces often resembled apartments, but apartments open to public view and entry. The mirrors commonly placed behind plate-glass store windows reflected pedestrians just as looking glasses on salon walls mirrored people at home. The Café de Paris "retained the appearance of an apartment in the grand style: high ceilings, antique mirrors, magnificent carpets," [38] and Thiollet's 1837 *Nouveau recueil de menuiserie et de décorations intérieures et extérieures* used the same criteria to evaluate stores, arcades, and apartments. Thiollet wrote that a "shop interior" possessed "the true character of a drawing room whose fireplace faces the entryway and whose principal ornaments are mirrors," and he praised the contemporary rapprochement of interiors and exteriors as a modern advance in decorating:

> today the least little vacation house [*maison de plaisance*], the most modest apartment [*appartement*] and even the fashionable clerk's attic room [*mansarde*] are decorated with care and often with taste. Not content with having transformed the interior of our cafés, restaurants, stores and bazaars into elegant salons, the decorative arts . . . strive each day to bring the exteriors of these same establishments into harmony with this richness and magnificence. . . . The time may not be far when . . . the facades of our houses [*maisons*] will be painted in oils from top to bottom and will offer trompe l'oeil, perspective effects, and so forth.[39]

Thiollet first comments on the similarity between the interiors of public and private buildings, between "cafés . . . restaurants . . . boutiques . . . bazaars [and] salons"; he then elaborates an architectural fantasy in which interior spaces coincide perfectly with exterior facades, by means of illusionistic projections (the "trompe l'oeil" effect) or false depths (the perspective effect).[40]

Thiollet's fantasy of the future was one that many architectural illustrators realized in their representations of contemporary buildings. Illustrators had the technical capacity to produce cross-sections with distinct foregrounds and receding, shadowy backgrounds, which conveyed the illusion of three-dimensional interiors with depth; indeed, the popular press occasionally used this convention (fig. 3). Instead, the architectural convention for cross-sections (*coupes*), which combined into a single image the walls of the facade and of the apartment unit, created the odd visual impression that the rear wall of an apartment was almost flush with the external facade by suppressing any visual suggestion of their difference in depth (fig. 4). This technique produced the illusion of an architectural impossibility: that the back wall of the apartment's interior coincided with its street facade. The image that expressed this

FIGURE 3

"Coupe de maison à Paris," by Karl Girardet. The use of
shadow and angle to suggest a receding background emphasizes the depth of the rooms shown in cross-section here. From
Le Magasin pittoresque 15 (1847).

FIGURE 4

Cross-section of an apartment building on the rue de Marignan. The mirrors and moldings located on the far walls of each room are drawn to appear flush with the exterior facade. From Victor Calliat, *Parallèle des maisons de Paris construites depuis 1830 jusqu'à nos jours* (Paris: Bance, 1850).

physical impossibility was legible to nineteenth-century readers, however, because it visually articulated their cultural equation of interior and exterior spaces. Far more marked in the depiction of apartment buildings than in those of *hôtels* or *pavillons,* the particularity of this convention will emerge even more clearly in chapter 3, when we juxtapose this type of cross-section with English architectural drawings. English architects adopted a more picturesque and textured approach to the representation of domestic architecture than French architects. Where English illustrators made abundant use of light, shadow, and composition to locate houses within a setting defined as "natural" by its irregularity and variety, French illustrators represented apartments in isolation from adjacent structures (although contiguous buildings were required by law to be directly attached to one another, with no gaps between them) and idealized buildings into a series of graphic, planar, blatantly two-dimensional lines that corresponded to the topographical conventions for representing the urban grid, creating yet another link between the city and its apartment houses.[41]

The *Tableaux de Paris* and the Apartment-House View

Beginning in the 1830s, an unprecedented number of books about Paris not only posited a continuum between the apartment house and the street but also presented the apartment house as an ideal framework for visual observations of the city. The texts that critic Margaret Cohen has identified as "a characteristic nineteenth-century genre for representing the everyday" were known as *tableaux de Paris* and were accompanied in the early 1840s by an important subgenre, the *physiologies.*[42] Authored mostly by professional writers who worked for the popular press and wrote criticism, prose, and plays, the *tableaux* and *physiologies* mapped the new types, places, and trends of contemporary Paris for a reading and viewing public eager to consume images of the city. As the critic Richard Sieburth has pointed out, "these illustrated anthologies of urban sites and mores responded to the public's desire to see its social space as a set or gallery whose intelligibility was guaranteed both by its visibility as an image and its legibility as a text."[43] Issued by various publishers, the *tableaux de Paris* conformed to certain generic conventions: they were usually multivolume, large-format books utilizing a variety of typefaces, lavishly illustrated by artists such as Daumier and Gavarni, and written by multiple authors who provided an encyclopedic overview of the city with fictional sketches and articles on Parisian history, geography, social types, and current events.

The authors of the *physiologies* often overlapped with contributors to the *tableaux*. The *physiologies,* however, were the work of only one author (and one illustrator); and where the kaleidoscopic *tableaux* aspired to a cumulatively exhaustive description of Paris, the *physiologies* adopted an overtly fragmentary approach, since each text anatomized, in a deliberately slangy style, an individual Parisian type (e.g., the grocer, the kept woman, the husband). Aubert published *physiologies* according to a standardized small, in-32 format of 120 pages, with copious but cheap illustrations. Priced at 1 franc each, the *physiologies* were considerably cheaper than the ordinary book, which cost roughly 3.50 francs, and much cheaper than the oversized, lavish *tableaux*. Their modish appearance and low price contributed to their popularity: more than 125 separate *physiologies* were issued between 1840 and 1842, and a total of approximately 500,000 copies were in print in the 1840s.[44]

Because the *tableaux* and the *physiologies* understood the city as a site in which events unfurled and as a decor within which character emerged, they frequently treated apartments as settings for the various episodes and types they recounted. Unlike architectural pattern books, which by convention eliminated all representations of people from their illustrations, the *tableaux* defined Paris as much by its population of *parisiens* and *parisiennes* as by its physical environment.[45] Apartment houses were seen as privileged settings for Parisians and their plots, as figures for "this big city where misfortune, good fortune, pain and pleasure frequently live under the same roof," and as sites of a narrative available only to the urban initiate, who with the aid of the urban observer would become aware of "entire novels hidden in the walls of . . . [a] house."[46]

In addition to privileging the apartment house as a descriptive object and narrative device, the *tableaux* also shared formal traits with apartment buildings. The visual arts represented apartment houses as both static objects and animated scenes, as pictorial, frontal planes to be viewed and as spaces through which to move, if only illusionistically.[47] The *tableaux* similarly set out to combine a static "store of information," including history, statistics, and geography, with lively anecdotal incident and narrative.[48] Updating long-standing equations between literary and architectural construction, the frontispieces of several *tableaux* explicitly represented their own volumes as elements of architectural construction (fig. 5), and, conversely, the *tableaux* frequently invoked the metaphor of buildings as books, pages, and lines, as if to endow readers with the ability to decipher a building as they would a text.[49] The visual presentation of the *tableaux* even mirrored the structure of apartment-house facades: innovative page layouts intercalated text and image so that illustrations were situated like windows in the space defined by the text (fig. 6).[50]

The writers who represented the city to itself thus not only emphasized apartment houses as elements of the Parisian landscape but also *saw through* the apartment house, treating it as a lens or as a point of view and not simply as an opaque visual object. In the process, they imagined apartment houses to be as transparent as they wanted the city to be. And by depicting the apartment house as though its facades and walls were transparent, Parisian chroniclers demonstrated that even the city's most private spaces posed no impediment to their vision. In a sketch called "Les Drames invisibles," which exemplified the *tableaux*'s representation of the apartment building, Frédéric Soulié, a frequent contributor to the genre, deployed the common device of describing Parisian society through a single apartment building. Even the most private events within the apartment house—what should be the "invisible dramas" of the title—become visible, with the narrator exposing blackmail and suicide on one floor and a concealed pregnancy on another. For Soulié, to reveal the secrets of the building's occupants makes possible a more general exposure of the Parisian social body; for example, he describes a tenant's concealed pregnancy as "teem[ing] beneath the social epiderm."[51] Initially hidden by the woman's body, then inevitably revealed by it, the increasingly visible course of conception, pregnancy, and birth mirrors the trajectory of the apartment-house narrative, which transforms facades, walls, and doors from barriers that keep secrets into transmitters of sounds and stories.

By containing the many stories of an apartment house's occupants in one narrative, Soulié displayed his ability to control the city's heterogeneity, just as the *tableaux* contained numerous and diverging views of the city within a single anthology. The multiply authored pieces collected within the *tableaux* replicated the collective form of the apartment building, whose separate compartments were united by a common frame.[52] In architecture, the multiplicity of a building's parts were gathered in a unity that made each part, as well as the whole, transparent. As the architectural historian David Van Zanten explains in *Developing Paris*, "all . . . parts . . . [were] interrelated, so that the whole . . . [could]

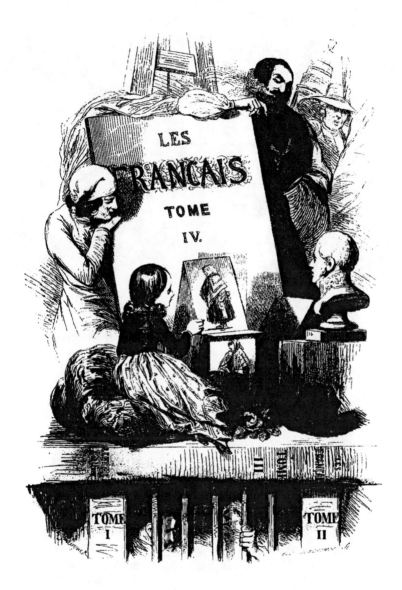

FIGURE 5

Frontispiece to volume four of *Les Français peints par eux-mêmes* (Paris: Curmer, 1841), depicting the preceding volumes as horizontal and vertical architectural supports.

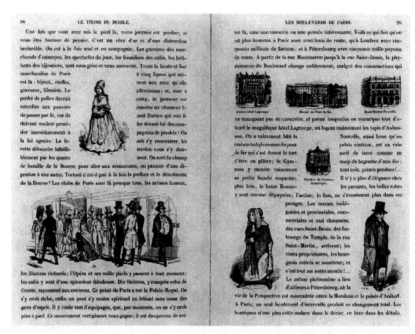

FIGURE 6

Pages from volume two of *Le Diable à Paris* (Paris: Hetzel, 1846). The rectilinear blank spaces surrounding the images create the impression of windows cut into blocks of text.

be reconstructed from a single element. . . . The ideal . . . was transparency . . . where the whole work of architecture . . . might be grasped by a glance at its exterior, as if one were conceptually seeing right through its walls."[53] Similarly, the *tableaux*'s collection of many disparate essays on Paris into a single book aimed to unify the "thousand facets" and "multiple aspect" of Paris, and to make that multiplicity more visible and legible by making it more manageable.[54]

The preface to the fifteen-volume *Paris, ou le livre des cent-et-un* (1831), one of the first *tableaux* to use multiple authors (the 101 of the title), emphasized that its multiple authorship and encyclopedic range encapsulated the heterogeneity of Paris itself and described the book's literary ambition to capture the city's multiplicity in terms of an architectural fantasy. Declaring that Paris has become so *multiplié*—"multiple" and "multiplied"—that one must "renounce unity in favor of a

multiple portrayal," the preface's author, Jules Janin, consolidated that
representational process into an allusion to a single figure, Asmodeus,
the devilish hero of Lesage's *Le Diable boiteux* (1707), who removed
roofs and peered inside houses. His reference suggested that Paris itself
was reducible to a series of domestic interiors, and that those interiors
were the primary objects of an ambulatory urban gaze: "whatever the
imagination of our contributors might be, it [*elle*] will have a place in
this book, it will temporarily put on Asmodeus's cloak and go everywhere, poor girl, everywhere where a man who fears nothing would
go." [55] For Janin, the book's multiple form engenders multiply gendered
figures who can roam the city at will: the male Asmodeus's cloak can extend even to the female figure of the imagination, which Janin deliberately personifies as a woman by referring to the grammatically feminine
imagination as "poor girl." The power of Asmodeus and his urban observation is so strong that it can even make a "poor girl" mobile, dressing a pitiful female figure in the garb of a male—one whose urban ex-
plorations know no limits. [56]

Janin's Asmodeus, faithful to the methods of the original, enters apartments by lifting off their roofs. His bird's-eye view perceives buildings as
a series of scenes and organizes the apartment house as a planar picture
to be observed, as a live, three-dimensional scene to be entered, and as
the narrative formed by movement from one scene to the next. Asmodeus's horizontal and aerial orientation, however, marks even Janin's
updated version of Lesage's viewpoint as premodern. A decade later, in
the 1840s, Asmodeus began to peel away apartment-house facades, and
even when he approached apartments from the sky, he aligned his viewpoint with a building's vertical front. Take, for example, the caption
to Karl Girardet's image of a *coupe de maison*—a cross-section of an
apartment—which appeared in the *Magasin pittoresque* in 1847 (see
fig. 3): "Asmodeus has borne you up above the big city . . . your eyes
have come to rest on an elegant three-story house. . . . Asmodeus has understood; he makes a gesture, and the walls that hid the interior from
you have become transparent. Everything that happens there appears
before you like so many moving pictures framed under glass." [57] This
Asmodeus's procedure resolved a sensory contradiction experienced by
apartment-dwellers, who could easily hear neighbors whom they could
not see from within their apartment unit's confines. [58] The peeled-off
facade translated the uncontrolled sound and visual inaccessibility of
contiguous apartments into a vivid and lucid pictorial composition—
"so many moving pictures framed under glass."

Representations of transparent facades also expressed their authors' desire to make the apartment building continuous with the street, where everything and everyone was visible and within reach. The apartment house was an important focal point for the *flâneur* who roamed the city's streets; while an article from the 1830s pointed out that "the *flâneur* scarcely has an interior of his own," the peripatetic Parisian observer frequently included the domestic interiors of others in his urban itinerary.[59] As a result, both streets and apartment buildings were equally described as areas of display and contact, open to effortless visual penetration.

In a landmark article on the *flâneur*, Janet Wolff argues that urban discourse gave men a monopoly on urban circulation and observation, and consigned women to the role of objects of a masculine urban gaze.[60] Many moments in the *tableaux* seem to support her argument but, as we will see, urban discourses also represented women as mobile urban observers, because to do otherwise would have been to acknowledge a limit to the transparency and accessibility of urban space. Indeed, even the most blatant examples of male voyeurism in the *tableaux* worked not only to constitute women as sexualized objects of a male gaze but also to liquidate the barrier potentially posed by the private space of the home. As a result, the objectification of women viewed either in the street or in their apartments had the unintended effect of bringing women into the city or bringing the city to women and did not, as Wolff implies, simply confine them to an impermeable private space.

In a contribution to *Les Rues de Paris* (1844), for example, Albéric Second attached his description of an entire Parisian neighborhood to a man who simultaneously observes an apartment building and its female tenants. In his story, a painter's ability to bridge the gap between facing apartment buildings becomes a device for depicting the Parisian neighborhood of Notre-Dame-de-Lorette: "it is in the person of his female neighbors that a painter indulges in observations of nature. His gaze pierces [*transperce*] windows and their light muslin armor; the couch [*divan*] and loveseat [*causeuse*] can hold no secrets for him; he deciphers at first glance all the hieroglyphics of the boudoir."[61] The painter's gaze takes on an ambulatory life of its own, and its remarkable capacity to penetrate is emphasized both by the verb *transpercer* and by the overstated opacity ascribed to the curtains: the painter does not merely catch a glimpse of something through parted muslin drapes but has a gaze that "pierces . . . armor." Once the painter's gaze has rendered the facade transparent and penetrable, it perceives the women's interiors as sexually legible. Second highlights the sexual connotations of the room and its furniture by using *boudoir,* the word for a woman's private bedroom, instead of the generic word for bedroom, *chambre,* and by singling out the loveseat; his claim that the painter deciphers "the hieroglyphics" of the bedroom "on first sight" underscores the immediacy of his access to the most intimate recesses of the woman's apartment.

For the young, unmarried male sexual adventurers featured in many of the *tableaux*'s sketches, access to women in the city's apartment buildings had all the hallmarks of the urban: it was deliberately transient, the result of a cultural understanding of the city as a place for fleeting, chance sexual contacts, yet all the more vulnerable to interference because of its very ephemerality. These texts conflated women with the city on the basis of rental, not ownership, and modeled men's temporary possession of women encountered in streets and buildings on their equally temporary rental of city property. At the same time, the *tableaux* also produced more stable configurations of women as the city and the city as a woman, suggesting that male property owners could own, trade, or rent out women as they did buildings and land. Various texts referred to the landlord's droit du seigneur over his female tenants, as well as to women's equivalence to real estate and to the money derived from it.[62] Apartment buildings were assimilated to female bodies: they were "girls of stone"; their faults could be covered up just as "an old coquette" would "conceal her wrinkles"; the For Rent signs hung outside apartments (white for unfurnished, yellow for furnished) would "glitter like a courtesan's ardent eyes"; and landlords renting apartments for the first time would feel like "unnatural fathers who sell their children," but children figured as nubile women—"virginal," "completely fresh," full of "innocence."[63]

The feminization of the apartment house clearly worked to adumbrate the status of both women and buildings as legible signs of male property, but at the same time, equations of women with apartment houses placed them in an open urban realm instead of in a sequestered private space. Not surprisingly, then, the *tableaux* often identified women with Paris, describing the city's regions in terms of the types of women who inhabited them and arguing that women were condensed expressions of the city's essence, so that one could understand Paris by studying *la parisienne.*[64] Contributors to the *tableaux* developed a sexualized topography that classified Parisian neighborhoods according to the types of women found in them and defined female types in terms of their urban locations and their relative sexual availability to men.

Examples of these types included the *lorette* who lived in and was named for the newly constructed quarter of Notre-Dame-de-Lorette and was a scheming, rapacious courtesan; the *grisette* who lived between the Bourse and the Palais-Royal (often on rues St-Denis and Vivienne) and selflessly helped support her student lover; and the *parisienne* who could be recognized by the unforgettable decor of her bedroom, to which all were welcome.[65]

The sexualization of Parisian streets, apartment buildings, and urban observers often had the surprising effect of enhancing rather than negating women's powers of urban locomotion and observation within the discursive world of the *tableaux*. Women's movement was essential to the urbanism and urbanity that issued from those texts, in which all women, including married *bourgeoises*, were required to be sexually available to men, in a city whose every space became an open heterosexual forum: one *physiologie*, for example, described the city's omnibuses as the "providence of lovers" and "hell for husbands."[66] Even the home became the locus of a compulsory Parisian heterosexuality that prevailed over any patriarchal urge to restrict women's forays into the city or to confine them to marital sexuality. Thus a humorous sketch entitled "Where Does A Woman Who Goes Out Go? A Riddle [*Où va une femme qui sort: énigme*]," although it posed the destination of the woman who "goes out" as a riddle, emphasized her ubiquity and legibility by offering ten ways to recognize her. The sketch regretfully admits that "it is as easy to recognize a woman who is going out as it is difficult to know where she is going" but implies that her destination is perfectly familiar, arguing that if men confess "loyally" to one another, her secret will be revealed; "a woman who goes out" is a woman engaged in adultery with one of her husband's friends. Her freedom of movement is delimited by the homosocial male circle that contains her, but the equivalence of going out and meeting a man exemplifies the *tableaux*'s vision of both street and home as heterosexual bazaars, and of the city as a network of interior and exterior bedrooms through which women constantly moved.[67]

The problem that the *tableaux* posed for women in the city was not how to gain access to the street but how to find any place, inside or out, where they could be left alone or with one another without incurring blame. The *tableaux* expressed little disapproval of female mobility that brought women into men's purview, defined variously as a heterosexual marketplace, a worldly heterosocial circle that met in salons and cafés, or a domestic niche based on the conjugal couple.[68] They did, however, censure women like the "spinster" [*vieille fille*] and the "bluestocking" [*bas-bleu*], who occupied negative positions vis-à-vis heterosexuality. Louis Couailhac's *Physiologie du célibataire et de la vieille fille* condemned the unmarried woman for her "selfishness" and ended with a remarkable vision of an association of wealthy, unmarried women who open up a boarding house "where one encounters only old maids. . . . There, these witches begin by disrupting the house and forcing everyone young and respectable to flee; then they undertake to do the same for the street, then they extend their malicious influence throughout the neighborhood; the entire city risks coming under their sway."[69]

Yet the *physiologies* and *tableaux* spoke glowingly of wives who haunted the city "amidst the movement and tumult of a market" in search of reasonably priced food for their husbands: "The ladies of Paris go to market, and that is to their credit, for it proves that they take care of their household [*ménage*] and of the interior details of their houses."[70] They also tolerated women who pursued economic gain through heterosexual transactions, if those women competed against other women and conformed to stereotypes of narcissistic and exhibitionistic femininity by acting out their "need to show off [*se faire voir*]" for a male audience.[71] Taxile Delord, an editor of *Le Charivari*, a satirical weekly established in the 1830s, and author of several *physiologies,* described the Parisian woman's sexual career as the development of a joint-stock company: "speculation is the genius of this century . . . and since she [*la parisienne*] is a woman, in other words a highly sought-after pleasure mine, she has taken it upon herself to issue stock in herself." Delord's language suggests an amused, tolerant, and somewhat admiring tone— the *parisienne* participates in the "genius" of her time, demonstrates "cleverness" in her choice of shareholders, and becomes a "young female industrialist" [*jeune industrielle*].[72]

When women banded together to pursue their own financial interests independently of men, however, the male observer could make little sense of the scene. In his article on "La Bourse," Frédéric Soulié wrote that "the oddest and most inexplicable group of gamblers at the Stock Exchange are the women. A police regulation has relegated them to the upper galleries." Women of all classes, from the "duchess" to the "dishwasher," mingle in this gallery and exchange information about the market, a cooperation that astounds Soulié: "that the woman dressed in velvet talks to the worker in cotton truly surprised me!"[73]

The *Portière* and the Personification of Urban Observation

The *tableaux* and *physiologies* directed their most concentrated animus against a female type whom they themselves associated with the power to see into apartment buildings—the *portière*.[74] By the 1840s the *portière* had become a standard presence even in buildings that lacked a formal entrance or porter's lodge. She often selected tenants for the landlord and collected rents; within the building, she distributed mail, cleaned landings and entrances, and did light housekeeping for some tenants (especially unmarried men); and she responded when tenants (who did not have keys to the main door) and visitors rang the bell.[75] The *portière* personified the passage between the street and the apartment because she let tenants into the building; because, as the historian Jean-Louis Deaucourt puts it, she "appeared everywhere, in the building's semiprivate spaces, in the open space of the street"; and because her *loge,* located off the building's vestibule or courtyard, was a "space both closed and open at the same time, eminently theatrical . . . propitious for exchanges, for comings and goings."[76]

The *portière* was a modern phenomenon, like the apartment house in which she worked, since only apartments constructed after the 1820s included a porter's lodge. Before then, only *hôtels* had porters (known as *suisses* or *concierges,* and exclusively male). During the July Monarchy, a *portière* signaled a modern building's bourgeois status and aristocratic pretensions, although her own body also brought into the building the working-class presence that both landlords and tenants sought to exclude.[77] The authors of the *tableaux* and *physiologies* underscored the contemporaneity of the *portière,* who in their view personified the modern apartment house. Taxile Delord, in a *physiologie* entitled *Paris-Portière,* wrote that "the *portière* is a very recent creation, a product of modern civilization."[78] She was a "modern creation," wrote James Rousseau in 1841, like the "houses populated by a large number of tenants . . . that people build nowadays."[79]

Urban literature characterized the *portière* as an adept observer: her duties as mail distributor, rent collector, and maid gave her an intimate and composite overview of the building's individual parts that perfected the totalizing yet local vision of the Parisian microcosm sought after by the authors of the *tableaux.* Skill at reading the city was not the only characteristic the *portière* had in common with the authors of the *physiologies.* They shared a liminal class position: the *portière* came from the working classes but lived among the bourgeoisie, worked as a servant but had the power to choose tenants and demand rents, while the authors of the *physiologies* were primarily lower middle-class men of letters who parlayed their skills at reading a range of modern types into cultural capital. Writers did not explicitly acknowledge their resemblance to the *portière*, but their satirical portrayals of her can be read as defensive attempts to distinguish between acceptable and unacceptable social climbing during a period of intense class mobility, as well as between their culturally endorsed interpretive activities and those of the *portière*, whose information gathering was denigrated as feminized prying and gossip—*commérages*.[80]

The *tableaux* made the apartment house into an object and means of urban observation and the *physiologies* made the *portière* a stand-in for the apartment house: the *portière* was thus both a prime object of urban observation and embodied the activity of observing. The *physiologie* of the *portière* situated her at the intersection of the exterior street and the interior home, while *physiologies* as a genre assumed that external activities penetrated an individual's soul and mind, then reemerged at the body's surface as a set of typed expressions, behaviors, mannerisms, and physical signs.[81] The *portière* was herself a type, whose labor marked her appearance, but her topographical situation (at the door, in the stairwell and vestibule, shuttling between the apartment and the street, and even peering out of the space of the page) also emblematized the key locus of physiognomy—the point where external and internal coincided (figs. 7, 8, 9).[82]

Physiologists represented the porter as a personification of their own project of rendering the city "legible" by describing her as an Asmodeus figure, a knowing urban observer and an expert reader of physiognomies. Rousseau wrote that in terms of her "topographical position," the *portière* is "first in the house" and "knows how to read physiognomies admirably."[83] Other writers similarly identified the *portière* as a figure for the processes of reading and writing. In Henry Monnier's play *Le Roman chez la portière*, the author identified himself with the *portière* by playing her in drag (reversing Janin's figure of a female imagination dressed in Asmodeus's cloak) and mocked the *portière*'s obsession with finishing her novel by contrasting her desire to read with the constant interruptions of tenants ringing the bell to be let in.[84] Writers endowed the *portière* with authorial omniscience, placing her in the allegorical ranks of destiny and the fates: "It's hard to believe how much occult power is attributed to the *portière*," wrote Rousseau; "she plays the role of destiny in our lives." He entitled his eleventh chapter "On the *Portière*'s

Physiologie

DE LA PORTIÈRE,

PAR

James Rousseau

(De la *Gazette des Tribunaux*).

VIGNETTES

PAR DAUMIER.

PARIS,

AUBERT ET Cᴵᴱ,   LA VIGNE,
Place de la Bourse.   Rue du Paon-St-André, 1.

1841.

FIGURE 7

The *portière* as voyeur and spy, examining the hidden contents of a letter. Honoré Daumier, illustration from James Rousseau, *Physiologie de la portière* (Paris: Aubert, 1841).

CHAPITRE II.

Des rapports de la Portière avec le Propriétaire et les Locataires.

e proprié-
taire et le
locataire
sont enne-
mis nés.
Celui - ci
veut louer
son appar-
tement le
plus cher
qu'il peut ;
celui - là
veut l'avoir au meilleur marché possible ; l'un
pense que des papiers qui ont dix ans de service , qui sont tachés de graisse et dont tous les
angles sont déchirés, pourraient bien être rempla-
cés ; l'autre ne trouve rien d'élégant comme des
bordures grasses et qui pendillent en loques ; le
locataire n'a aucune estime pour une cheminée
qui fume , le propriétaire ne voit pas le moindre
inconvénient à laisser sa fenêtre ouverte par un

FIGURE 8

The *portière* peers through a window and out of the page,
with her fingers grasping a letter illuminated as a window-
sill. Honoré Daumier, illustration from James Rousseau,
Physiologie de la portière (Paris: Aubert, 1841).

FIGURE 9

The *portière* on the stairs, sweeping dirt onto the tenant below
her, who has forgotten to give her the porter's customary New
Year's Day tip. Honoré Daumier, "Un Locataire qui a eu un oubli le 1er janvier" (1847). Plate 28 of the series *Locataires et propriétaires* (Tenants and landlords) from Delteil, *Peintre-graveur*
(Paris, 1926), plate 1622.

Influence on Everything in Life and on Lots of Other Things Besides
That" and began it, "I've said it once and I'll say it again: the *portière*
plays the role of Destiny on earth. She can, according to her whim, make
your life sweet or turn your existence into a premature hell." [85] Eugène
Scribe asked rhetorically in his one-act comedy *La Loge du portier*
(1823),

Who knows the news
Of the whole neighborhood?
In faithful accounts
Who will publish it all?
. . . .

It's our *portière*,
Who knows all, who sees all,
Hears all, is everywhere.[86]

Porters were not exclusively female, and Parisian chroniclers also attributed acute visual power to male *portiers*. Jacques Raphael, in *Le livre des cent-et-un,* used language almost identical to Rousseau's when he wrote that the *portier* "admirably possesses what we could call topographical knowledge of every apartment in the building [*maison*]" and labeled the *portier* "the Argus of the building. . . . [H]e knows your habits . . . he penetrates into the most secret folds of your private life."[87] The reference to Argus recalls Janin's characterization of the *tableaux*'s multiple authorship and the city's multiple scenes: here the *portier* has an eye in every apartment because metaphorically he has thousands of eyes.

Writers evaluated the ocular powers of male and female porters very differently, however, indicating that their uneasiness about the powers of working-class porters in general was inflected by a particular hostility to the female porter. Commentators suggested that the spying of her male counterpart was official men's work by linking it to despised but legitimate forms of government surveillance and to the invisibility proper to the police. A contributor to the 1839 *Paris au XIXe siècle,* for example, invoked the *portier*'s "occult power" and "shadowy power . . . to know everything and everyone, to be aware of every detail . . . to read the lives of ten families like an open book . . . to be feared like a god or like a police commissioner."[88] Such analogies to a deity or the police placed the male porter at the invisible center of a complex web of surveillance that could easily extend over the entire city.[89]

The female porter's dominion, however, was overt rather than shadowy, limited to the immediate realm of her apartment building and tied to her overwhelming physical presence within it. She entered the political arena only through a metaphorical miniaturization that transformed her apartment building into a small kingdom:

In all second- and third-class apartment buildings [*maisons de second et de troisième ordre*], the most influential person is without a doubt the *portière*. . . . She has the upper floors completely in her power [*sous sa domination immédiate*], is authorized to give people notice . . . if their political opin-

FIGURE 10

The *portière* and her female circle. Honoré Daumier,
illustration from James Rousseau, *Physiologie de la
portière* (Paris: Aubert, 1841).

ions aren't in sympathy with hers. . . . [and] reigns like a sovereign . . . she
has survived all the landlords who succeeded one another.[90]

The *portière* in this passage has a sovereign monarch's visible power
but lacks the police's invisible stealth, and she can exercise that power
only within the apartment building, within a *domination immédiate.*
The characterization of the *portière* as grotesque and almost monstrous
stemmed partly from the disparity between her quasi-divine powers and
the minuscule space in which she exercised them, since the *tableaux*
rarely showed the *portière* outside the vicinity of her apartment building
and described her own apartment, the *loge,* as hyperbolically tiny. The
portière's ambitions and powers strained the bonds of her location.

Like the "blue-stocking" and the feminists of the 1840s, the *portière*
became a figure for a female society that existed apart from heterosexual exchange, as well as for an inverted, "women-on-top" domestic sys-

FIGURE 11

The *portière* and her cats. Honoré Daumier, frontispiece to James Rousseau, *Physiologie de la portière* (Paris: Aubert, 1841).

tem.[91] The physiologists associated the *portière* with a powerful circle of women who transformed the apartment building into a space permeated and governed by a network of female servants, female tenants, the *portière*'s children, almost inevitably daughters, and her many cats, who emphasized the *portière*'s femininity by functioning as both generic symbols of women and as slang references to female genitalia (figs. 10, 11).[92] And the texts that showed the *portière* running her building with an iron hand and a sharp tongue also showed her dominating her husband, who typically made no sound, took up no space, and worked at home as either a cobbler or tailor, trades that had been feminized by the 1840s.[93] Monnier wrote, "she completely dominates her husband" and Rousseau emphasized the *portière*'s inverted conjugal relations: "When the *portière* has a husband, he's just another piece of furniture in her lodge [*loge*]. In the *portière*'s household more than in any other the scepter has been conquered by the distaff. The poor husband is a purely passive being . . . and if people call him a porter, it's only because he's the husband of one."[94] Whereas Rousseau earlier described the *portière* as personifying the entire building, her husband's person is an inanimate portion of the building, a piece of the *portière*'s property—"just another item of furniture in her *loge*." Rousseau's reference to the scepter and the distaff invokes classic symbols of male and female power, political and domestic rule. The distaff that prevails in the *portière*'s household, however, is not simply domestic. It casts its net over the public sphere, since the *portière*'s work within the apartment house defines her husband's public identity.

The authors of the *tableaux* and *physiologies* represented the *portière* as, like themselves, an adept practitioner of urban observation, but also as a barrier frustrating men's visual access to the apartment building, and by extension to the city itself. As we have seen, the literature of Paris ultimately suggested that their authors cared so intensely about keeping traffic fluid in both the home and the street that they extended fluidity to women, on the condition that women participate in heterosexual exchanges within those urban spaces. The *tableaux* depicted both the Parisian street and the apartment house as sites of display, voyeurism, and heterosexual exchange, whose open structures ensured women's availability to men, even in the city's potentially private apartments. The only significant threat to male enjoyment of the city was the *portière*, the apartment building's live-in caretaker. As a relatively independent woman who replaced heterosexual conjugality with powerful female homosocial networks and who controlled the commerce between domestic spaces and public thoroughfares, the *portière* came to symbolize an obstruction to men's heterosexual gaze precisely because she shared, even surpassed, their ability to penetrate and know the apartment building. In the next chapter, we will see how Balzac, a frequent contributor to the *tableaux* and the author of several *physiologies*, took up the *portière*'s challenge to the male observer's urban omniscience in one of his final novels, *Le Cousin Pons*.

2

Balzac's Spatial Relations

TO UNDERSTAND THE FULL RANGE OF cultural beliefs about the relationship between domestic life and urban life during the July Monarchy, we must turn to what was perhaps the most popular and influential discourse of everyday life, the realist novel. The realist novel emerged in its fully delineated form at the same time as the modern urban culture examined in the previous chapter, but the relationship among realist novels, urban discourse, and Paris went far beyond mere historical coincidence. First, a majority of realist novels were not only set in Paris but also took the description of the city to be one of their central narrative tasks, drawing on the referential status of Paris as a "real" city to bolster their mimetic project. Second, both the narrators and protagonists of many realist novels deployed the same discursive approach as the authors of the *tableaux* and *physiologies*: emphasizing the need to contain the city's multiplicity within a unifying narrative or narratorial viewpoint; mapping the city in terms of social types and topographies; assuming the transparency of urban signs; and representing the mobility made possible by the variety of exchanges that could take place in urban space. Third, as in the *tableaux*, Paris became in the realist novel a fluid conjunction of interior and exterior spaces, a point made most famously by the opening of Honoré de Balzac's *Le Père Goriot*, in which an omniscient narrator proceeds in a unidirectional vector from a boarding-house's outer envelope (the street, the grounds, the building's external facade) to the innermost layer of its landlady's clothing, then to the core of her subjective thoughts.[1]

The realist novel, like the urban discourses examined in the previous chapter, also converged on the apartment house as a sign of both the city and of its own representational procedures.[2] Although *Le Père Goriot* focused on a *pension*, not an apartment building, in numerous other novels by Balzac and other equally popular realists such as Paul de Kock, Eugène Sue, and Henry Monnier, the apartment house recurred as an object that, by virtue of its contemporaneity, signified the novel's participation in the world of the reader, and, by virtue of its real presence in the city, substantiated the novel's fictions. The apartment house also provided realist novels with an emblem of the reconciliation of multiplicity and unity, which in the apartment took the form of containing numerous units within a single building, and in realist works such as Balzac's *Histoire des treize* or de Kock's *La Demoiselle du cinquième* took the form of gathering the multiple threads of an urban narrative into a single yet multifarious plot. Finally, like the *tableaux*, realist novels were invested in making all aspects of urban life transparent, including its provisionally private domestic spaces; the realist novel incorporated the Asmodeus of the *tableaux* into omniscient narrators who move effortlessly through the city and peer into its apartments.

Despite their similarities, however, the *tableaux* and the realist novel had subtly different relationships to the private realm that both discourses rendered transparent. The *tableaux*'s interest in transparency derived from a desire to expose the city to view; because domestic spaces were part of Paris and no part of Paris could be hidden, domestic spaces would also be on view in the *tableaux*. The novel, on the other hand, made the exposure of private life its primary subject; because Paris consisted in large part of nominally private spaces, Paris would also be on view in the novel.[3] The novel had a more complicated relationship than the *tableaux* to the private sphere, because the value of its revelation of the hidden, secret aspects of characters' lives depended on maintaining the very category of "private life" that its narration necessarily breached.

From the realist novel's more ambivalent relationship to the category of the private followed a more complicated relationship to the apartment building and to the woman who represented it, the *portière*. This chapter will chart the vagaries of that relationship in the work of Balzac, whose novels epitomized French literary realism during the July Monarchy. I begin with an analysis of the *Physiologie du mariage* (1829), one of Balzac's first successful literary works, and then focus on one of his last completed novels, *Le Cousin Pons* (1846). The early *Physiologie du mariage* was not a novel but a parodic manual for husbands on how to keep their wives faithful. Unlike the *tableaux*, which argued that even wives could not be kept out of urban circulation and which amplified the apartment house's continuity with the street, the *Physiologie* attacked the apartment house for destroying the privacy derived from a husband's exclusive possession of his wife. Where the *tableaux* celebrated the apartment house for multiplying sexual opportunities and deplored the female porter for impeding men's access to women, Balzac suggested that a male porter might help a husband sequester his wife. Balzac's *Physiologie* represented the apartment house as an open domestic space but posed that very structure as a problem in need of spatial and narrative closure.

Balzac's late novel *Le Cousin Pons* similarly posed the apartment house's lack of privacy as a problem by sympathetically depicting the suffering of two aged bachelors whose apartment is invaded with unstoppable force by the building's *portière*. Unlike the *Physiologie du mariage*, whose narrator directly addresses the reader as a husband and thus lends his aphoristic powers to the preservation of uxorious marital privileges, *Le Cousin Pons* links the omniscient narrator—who has limitless mobility and vision—to the *portière*, a bounded character who nevertheless has a boundless point of view. The novel's plot develops the pathos of a situation in which a man cannot secure the integrity of his apartment, the possessions in it, and ultimately even his own body, and generates a corresponding antipathy for the *portière* who pervades the apartment with malignant force.

The novel's narration, however, cannot dismiss the *portière*, because she becomes identified with the narrator of the very novel we are reading: both enter private space without knocking, precisely because it is private. In the *portière*'s case, the privacy of a space suggests that it might contain an object worth stealing and putting into circulation because care has been taken to sequester it, while in the narrator's case, privacy signifies a story worth recounting because it is not already in the public domain. As we will see, the identification between the narrator and the *portière* ultimately works to neutralize the antipathy that could be directed at her within the plot when, at the novel's close, the omniscient narrator exonerates the *portière* for her crimes.

The *Physiologie du mariage*
and the Dangers of the Apartment House

Related in name only to the *physiologies* popularized in the 1840s, Balzac's *Physiologie du mariage* (1829) portrayed the vagaries of contemporary marriage by parodying analyses of sensation and sensibility, such as Brillat-Savarin's popular *Physiologie du goût* (1825), as well as domestic manuals, conduct books, and the Civil Code. In writing a parodic code, Balzac capitalized on a vogue for Horace Raisson's satiric *Codes* and *Arts,* published from 1827 to 1830, which caricatured the abstract language, formal scaffolding, and normative legislation of the Civil Code by applying them to areas outside the purview of legislation, such as sexual manners (the *Code des boudoirs*), eating (the *Code gourmand*), and sponging off friends (the *Art de ne jamais déjeuner chez soi*).[4] Balzac's *Physiologie,* however, focused on marriage, a subject already amply represented in the Civil Code, and its satire stemmed not from a gap between the law's high form and daily life's low subjects but from its claim to improve upon the law by succeeding where it had failed—in the prevention of female adultery.

Though the *Physiologie du mariage* satirized the impotence of the legal code that wrote patriarchal power into French law, its parodic stance weakened the law's authority only in order to substitute its own worldly commentary for the law's ineffectual prescriptions. The text opposed its enlightened persuasion to the law's coercion, but it also advocated physical enforcement of its tenets, by figuring itself as a building that excluded women and by arguing that patriarchal power could best be secured by physically isolating women in the home.[5] On the page preceding the introduction, the narrator warns any women who might pick up the book that "the author . . . has, in a way, inscribed on the frontispiece of his book the prudent inscription placed above the door of certain establishments: *No women allowed*" (34). The architectural metaphor makes these opening words into a partition between the text's interior and exterior; the narrator makes that spatial division into a gendered barrier by insisting, however impossibly and ironically, that women should be kept outside the space of the book, a space affiliated with a network of exclusively male "establishments."

Conversely, in a chapter entitled "On Apartments" the narrator urges husbands to keep their wives faithful by confining them within the space of the home—but not just any home. Alternating between a voice that propounds maxims on marriage and one that addresses the husband directly as "you [*vous*]," the narrator asserts that to be safe from cuck-oldry a husband must live in an *hôtel privé*, never an apartment. (The narrator does not address the high cost and aristocratic status of the *hôtel*; here and throughout he takes the wealth of his prototypical mar-ried couple for granted.) The narrator couches his advocacy of the *hôtel* in the language of war, titling the section in which it appears "Interior and Exterior Means of Defense" and prefacing his suggestions with a mock-heroic exhortation: "Do not weaken. There is a marital type of courage, just as there is civil courage and military courage" (162). The narrator's actual advice seems to contradict the bellicose character of his opening salvo, since he advocates a purely domestic and architectural solution to the problem of female infidelity. Yet by making the home a place of containment, a fortress or strategic camp built to prevent the in-vasion of other men, the narrator posits domestic space as a domain that contains women but is ruled by men.

The urban literature examined in the previous chapter imagined apart-ment buildings as continuous with the street and portrayed men cheer-fully acknowledging that women leave home to meet lovers. The *Physio-logie*'s definition of domestic space, by contrast, assumed that women were sequestered and thus received lovers only at home. A hierarchy of housing types results, in which the best house is the one most easily guarded by one set of men, and most effectively isolated from another:

> [H]alf the troubles come about because of the deplorable ease of entry [*faci-lités*] that most suites of rooms present.
>
> Above all, think about getting a concierge who is single and devoted en-tirely to your person. . . .
>
> You must cultivate a hatred like that between Atreus and Thyestes between your wife and this Nestor, the guardian of your door. This door is the alpha and the omega of an intrigue. Aren't all amorous intrigues reducible to this: entering, exiting?
>
> Your house will be good for nothing unless it is between a courtyard and a garden, and built so as to be in contact with no other.
>
> You will first of all suppress the slightest openings [*cavités*] in your recep-tion rooms. (162)

The "house" to which the passage refers bears all the features of the *hôtel*: it is free-standing, separated from the street by its courtyard and garden, with the concierge that July Monarchy terminology linked to the town mansion, as opposed to the porter attached to the apartment building. The *hôtel* is no simple guarantee against a wife's infidelity, since the passage produces a chiasmus in which architectural space takes on the anxiety-provoking characteristics of a sexualized female body and the wife's body takes on the structural deficiencies of an excessively porous space. The chiasmus converges on two double entendres—that the *hôtel*'s rooms and the wife's body might allow for too easy and too many "entrances and exits," so that a room's *facilités* might produce a *femme facile,* and that both a woman's and a room's overly receptive "openings" [*cavités*] must be walled up and jealously guarded. The only figure who can secure the integrity of the husband's marriage lies, paradoxically, outside the marital relation: only the single, male concierge, the wife's enemy and the husband's devoted servant, can effectively secure the husband's home and the wife's marital claustration.

The faithful male concierge constitutes one of the crucial differences between the *hôtel* and the *maison à loyer*. His presence makes the *hôtel*'s dangers remediable, while the apartment house, with its sheer abundance of potential lovers, its contiguity with other buildings, and a porter who serves many transient tenants rather than one fixed proprietor, cannot be made safe for marriage:

> Husbands condemned to live in apartment houses [*appartements à loyer*] are in the most horrible situation of all.
> What a fortunate or fatal influence the porter can have on their fate!
> Is their house not flanked right and left by two other houses? It is true that in placing their wives' rooms on one side only, the danger will be lessened by half; but aren't they obliged to memorize and ponder the age, status, fortune, character and habits of the tenants in the building next door [*la maison voisine*] and even to get to know their friends and relatives?
> A wise husband will never live on the ground floor. (166)[6]

This brief diatribe against apartment houses associates them with extramarital sexuality and a consequent disintegration of family identity and male authority. The hyperbolic addition of the neighbors' friends and family to the list of people whom the husband must know intimately suggests that the husband can only safeguard his own family's integrity by familiarizing himself with strangers. The adumbration of all the characteristics that the husband must "learn by heart" about his potential rivals carries a sexual charge that ascribes the danger of infidelity as much to the husband as to the wife; the passage neutralizes the threat that the husband's sexual interest in his neighbors might pose to the married couple by describing it as a defense of the couple and an attack on those who might attempt to dissolve it.

A preoccupation with a male homosocial rivalry that effaces women's sexual agency underlies the *Physiologie*'s departure from the conventional topography of apartment-house eroticism. In addition to locating sexual encounters in the space created by the traffic between the street and the residence, the *tableaux* often staged romances either within a building or between facing buildings. Balzac's passage gratuitously and counterintuitively specifies that sexual danger stems only from the *maison voisine*—the contiguous but separate building whose occupants would be least likely to see, speak to, or come into physical contact with neighbors in a building alongside their own. Where most apartment-house romances privileged visual, linguistic, and aural communication as the means of seduction, Balzac's passage locates the sexual threat in a male lover's phantasmatic power to eradicate the material barriers separating distinct buildings. The narrator's urgency suggests that merely by being next door to a wife's rooms, another man is already in them, and the passage equates the husband's sexual fear that the wife's body will be a conduit instead of a barrier with his architectural worry that party walls will link rather than separate those on either side of them.[7] The passage thus works to dismiss the possibility that extramarital liaisons might stem from within the building occupied by the couple or from the specular space that doubles and mirrors the couple's, the building opposite theirs. To the extent that the wife and the building have been previously identified with one another, this elision of the building's potential to instigate or abet the wife's adultery also serves to suppress the wife's agency in her own infidelity. The only human forces at work here are the husband, who maintains boundaries, and the lover, whose desire breaks them down.

Le Cousin Pons: The Apartment and the Museum

Almost two decades after publishing the *Physiologie du mariage,* Balzac continued to meditate on apartment houses and sexual relations, writing in his "Philosophie de la vie conjugale à Paris" (1846) that "in Paris, all lives are coupled." The apartment house is what conjugates all these lives, creating a specifically urban version of marriage that serves less to bind individual men to women than to link separate households. Apartment houses destroy private life by making each apartment simultaneously function as an observatory, theater, and mirror in which the residents of one apartment spy on those of another, provide unwitting spectacles for each other, and see their own lives reflected or inverted in their neighbors':

> in Paris, unless one lives in one's own townhouse [*un hôtel à soi*], between a courtyard and a garden, all lives are coupled [*toutes les existences sont*

accouplées]. On every floor of a house, one household faces another in the house opposite. Everyone plunges his gaze at will into his neighbor's household. There is a servitude of mutual observation, common visitation rights that no-one can avoid. . . . Oh! where is the sanctity of private life?[8]

The narrator's paean to lost privacy does not, however, prevent him from taking full advantage of the apartment house's transparency in the sketch's subsequent chapters, which chart in full detail the evolution of a typical Parisian marriage.

Balzac's last completed work, *Les Parents pauvres* (Poor Relations), provided a novelistic equivalent for the "coupled . . . existences" of facing apartment buildings, in the form of a textual diptych. *Les Parents pauvres* consists of two interreflecting halves, *La Cousine Bette* (1846) and *Le Cousin Pons* (1847), and Balzac's prefatory dedication explains the texts' duality in both gendered and architectural terms: "The two sketches that I am dedicating to you constitute the two eternal faces of a single fact. *Homo duplex,* said our great Buffon; why not add: *Res duplex?* Everything is double. . . . Hence my two stories are matching counterparts [*mises en pendant*], like twins of the opposite sex."[9] Balzac's reinscription of *homo* as *res* suggests that these two novels will enact the interchangeability of people and things, just as each sketch, identified by a gendered article, familial title, and proper name (*le cousin Pons, la cousine Bette*), becomes a "face"—a facet, a facade, and what critic Michel Butor calls a "volet"—a word that refers both to a panel in a triptych and the shutter of a window.[10] Similarly, Balzac's sexual metaphor for the novels' dual structure—"twins of the opposite sex"— relies on a spatial relation between objects that form pairs.

Though the title *Les Parents pauvres* encourages the reader to view the novels and their eponymous characters as a pair unified by similar familial positions, the phrase "twins of the *opposite* sex" also establishes an antagonism based on gender, which the preface's equation of gendered and architectural forms suggests will be worked out as differences in spatial relations.[11] Though Bette and Pons share a marginalized status within their wealthy families as poor, unmarried relations and though both form their closest affective and domestic ties with members of their own sex, each takes up very different positions relative to domestic space. Bette poses as a domestic angel in order to infiltrate and destroy several households, while Pons's constricted private space is invaded by female caretakers who dispossess him of everything he values; Bette can become a virtual *portière,* while Pons literally becomes the victim of one. Like the *Physiologie du mariage, Les Parents pauvres* depicts the loss of privacy as more dangerous for men than for women and makes those dangers even more pointed and poignant by focusing on a bachelor, whose privacy is not invaded indirectly, by the seduction of his wife, but in a frontal assault on his cherished art collection and on his very self.[12]

The novels' structural oppositions emerge most clearly if we compare their respective portrayals of the family and of the apartment house. Though this chapter will focus on *Le Cousin Pons*, the particularities of that novel will be clearer if we look briefly at those of its sister text, *La Cousine Bette*. Instead of focusing on a single apartment house, *La Cousine Bette* disperses its action over a series of residential interiors that provide a catalog of architectural types, making the unit of Bette and Valérie Marneffe into the nodal point uniting the novel's disparate characters and plots. Valérie represents the apartment house's potential for carefully staged sexual encounters, while Bette personifies the apartment house as an invisible network linking dispersed characters; the narrator refers to her as a "spider" weaving a dangerous web.[13] Bette, like a porter, always knows too much about what happens in each household, while the other characters always know too little.[14]

Together these two women form an almost invulnerable pair, and to enact their defeat the novel must not only eliminate their characters but replace the apartment house as well. The novel thus concludes with the image of the Hulot family united under one roof, in the *pavillon* of Hulot fils, a villa that mediates between the patriarchal *hôtel* of the old regime and the dissolute apartment house of the July Monarchy, between the private character of the single-family house and the commercial character of the neighboring apartment buildings and nearby Stock Exchange. The novel's final setting links a familial compromise in which the son heads the family to a spatial compromise that allots each family unit (parents, son, and daughter) its own floor and banishes the incompetent father to the third story.

The family has a clear identity in *La Cousine Bette*, and its strains, constraints, and eventual repair furnish the novel's plot.[15] Until its conclusion, however, *La Cousine Bette* lacks a unity of place that could contain the novel's interrelated households—it lacks, that is, a setting like the apartment house. *Le Cousin Pons*, on the other hand, focuses almost exclusively on one apartment building and represents the normative family only as a series of deformations. The novel's unity of place produces no corresponding familial unity. The family in *Le Cousin Pons* is

a structuring absence, present only as a long list of deviations and failures: the Camusots' failed attempts to marry their daughter Cécile; a
gratuitous and extended digression about a minor character's evil step-
mother; the truncation of familial obligations into aggressive "bile."
Pons's relationship to his family is both lacking and excessive, shrunken
and stretched: Pons, the parasitical poor relation, "reduced to making
the rounds among his family circle, had . . . extended the meaning of the
word family much too far" (28).

The consistent absence and distortion of the family in *Le Cousin Pons*
mark the ways that, despite its adherence to an apartment-house setting, the novel departs from what I will call the conventional nineteenth-
century apartment-house plot. By plot I mean a sequence of events that
structures the relationships among characters; by apartment-house plot
I mean sequences of events in which an apartment-house setting is not
merely incidental to the action but produces that sequence of events in
a way that no other site could (and still retain its cultural legibility as
that site). And by conventional nineteenth-century apartment-house
plot I refer to the ways that during this period the plot was standardized
in terms of content (the sequence of events tended to follow set patterns)
and form (the plot tended to attach itself to particular genres—novels,
plays, and fictional sketches).

Briefly—since my aim is to chart a divergence from this plot rather
than an adherence to it—the conventional nineteenth-century apartment-house plot was defined by a sequence of events (chance meetings
in the apartment building's common spaces, deliberate spying on other
tenants, visits between tenants, and other exchanges between individual
apartments) that worked to reconfigure the apartment building's characters from an urban assembly of strangers into a family circle, either by
having characters discover a preexisting relationship (the melodramatic
mode) or by uniting them through sex or marriage (the comic mode) in
an expansion of the erotic encounters deployed in many of the *tableaux*.[16]
In terms of generic affiliation, the apartment-house plot typically appeared in two genres. Theatrical vaudevilles such as Paul de Kock's *Les
Bains à domicile* and Henry Monnier's *Le Roman chez la portière* max-
imized the farcical possibilities of the apartment-house plot.[17] Prose
fiction, novels, and short stories used the realist technique of describing
in detail the apartment house and its inhabitants before setting in motion several parallel and contrasting plots, ranging from the bawdy to
the sentimental to the mysterious, but all tending toward the common

goal of transforming the apartment building's sets of strangers into a family unit.[18]

Le Cousin Pons is governed by an apartment-house plot in that it takes place mostly in one apartment building, focuses on the interactions of a (restricted) set of inhabitants—the *portière,* Mme Cibot, and Pons and Schmucke, two elderly musicians who share an apartment—and consists of a sequence of events possible only in an apartment building. But *Le Cousin Pons* departs from the conventional ending of the apartment-house plot because it forecloses the usual resolution of strangers into family, opting instead to maintain strangers as such by keeping Pons's neighbors invisible in all except two scenes and to make family members into strangers by demonizing Pons's biological relatives, and dissolving the novel's only disinterested relationship, the friendship between Pons and Schmucke, who live together at the beginning of the novel but are separated completely by the end.

Le Cousin Pons also departs from the apartment-house plot's typical affiliation with realist description by remaining strangely reticent about the building and the apartment that Pons rents within it. Standard realist narratives in general and Balzac's novels in particular often begin with a systematic topography that imbricates setting and character; *Le Cousin Pons,* however, offers no systematic, unified inventory of the building and rooms in which almost all its actions transpire. Instead it scatters fragmented information about their layout and furnishings throughout the novel, in the form of small kernels of descriptive prose, placeholders appended to dialogue, or information contained within characters' speech or accounts of their movements.[19]

If *Le Cousin Pons* lacks the introductory overview we would expect from a realist novel with an apartment-house plot, that is because another plot is also present in the novel—the museum plot. *Le Cousin Pons* is best known for its portrayal of Pons as a collector with a private museum; indeed, critics consider *Pons* to be the exemplary museum novel, in which the main characters are the valuable and extraordinary objects hidden in a secret room, the hero's task is to assemble and sequester the objects that confer value and interest on him, and the action consists, paradoxically, in preventing any action that would threaten the integrity and secrecy of the collection.[20]

The museum plot and the apartment-house plot thus follow diametrically opposed trajectories. The apartment-house plot represents the city in microcosm, exhaustively exploring a single residential setting that comes to stand for the entire urban fabric; in a usually comic register and toward generally happy ends, the apartment-house plot repeatedly stages exchanges between private spaces, so that the boundaries between individual apartments dissolve into a larger, more porous, and more public space. The museum plot, by contrast, transfers objects from public spaces into a private one and then details the efforts required to protect that space from invasion; in the case of *Le Cousin Pons*, the narrative even shields the museum from the novel's readers for most of the novel.

The museum plot should not be confused with the museum motif or episode, which appeared in novels such as Emile Zola's *L'Assommoir* and George Eliot's *Middlemarch*. In the museum *episode*, characters encounter art on public display and experience either a surplus or deficit of understanding, epiphany, or bewilderment, as well as a collision between past and present.[21] In the museum *plot*, the works of art are totally private, the hero is their only observer, has a uniquely apt understanding of them, and strives to maintain what critic Luce Abélès calls "the self-enclosed museum or the 'museum-as-sanctuary.'"[22] In *Le Cousin Pons*, enclosure extends even to the narrative that takes the museum as its subject, since the novel withholds a detailed account of the collection for many chapters, making it as inaccessible to the reader as it is to strangers.'

The privacy of the museum is always implicitly at risk in the museum plot; the hero's determination to keep his museum closed suggests an opposing desire to force it open—to make it, that is, more like a transparent apartment. The tension between a closed and open space for art objects has a genealogy specific to the historical tension between the provisionally private "collection" and the urban, monumental, and public "museum" in nineteenth-century France. *Le Cousin Pons* uses both terms to describe Pons's hidden art trove: the narrator designates it a "collection" when he is discussing its market value, and a "museum" when he refers to it as an inalienable ensemble inseparable from its location.[23] In so doing, the novel reversed contemporary usage, which treated the museum as public and the collection as private. The modern art museum, exemplified by the Louvre, was defined as "a state institution occupying center stage in the public life of the capital," a representative selection of the best types and examples of painting and sculpture, arranged carefully by school and chronology in order to best instruct and entertain the public.[24] It was opposed to collections in both the past and the present: to the princely cabinets of the Old Regime, which had been private rooms containing heterogeneous objects linked only by their

aesthetic value, arranged idiosyncratically or with a view to the effect of
the ensemble; and to the modern private collections of the newly rich,
made possible by the dispersal of aristocratic cabinets after the revolution, which were characterized primarily by their privacy but also by their
inclusion of art excluded from the Louvre—decorative objects, genre
scenes, religious painting, and the work of Regency and Pompadour
artists.[25]

Pons's museum resembles princely cabinets because it contains "curiosities" (155) in an elegantly decorated "salon" (154); it resembles private collections because it includes precisely what the Louvre rejected—
bric-a-brac and ornaments painted by eighteenth-century artists such as
Watteau; but it also resembles the Louvre because of its relative orderli-
ness, its emphasis on painting and sculpture, and its inclusion of four
"chefs-d'oeuvre" (155), among them a painting by Sebastiano, who, the
narrator points out, also has a painting at the Louvre (155).[26] Pons's collection thus incorporates several aspects of the modern museum—but
not its public accessibility. The spatial logic of the "sanctuary" (155)
that governs Pons's collection makes even the public museum private.[27]
The novel's museum plot thus defends (unsuccessfully) the very privacy
that its apartment-house setting erodes.

The Bachelor Versus the *Portière*

Le Cousin Pons's dramatic tensions stem from the conflict between the
museum plot its protagonist attempts to sustain and the apartment-
house plot that its setting threatens to inaugurate. The agent who transforms the museum novel's secrets into an apartment-house plot is none
other than the *portière* of Pons's building, Mme Cibot, whose idiosyncratic take on that plot involves not uniting all her tenants into one
happy family but rather, uniting them and their possessions within her
own person. Cibot's proximity to Pons enables her first to eliminate all
the characteristics that make him a collector and then literally to appropriate him. Like the *Physiologie du mariage*, the novel implies that
both Pons and his collection would have been safe as houses had he lived
in an *hôtel privé* with a faithful male porter instead of in an apartment
house, with its intrusive, maleficent, and self-interested *portière*.

The novel begins by generating the conditions necessary for a museum plot when it presents Pons as a composite of three types, the gourmand, the bachelor, and the collector, each of which depends in overdetermined ways on the divisions between the public and the private, the

commercial and the nonalienable, the visible and the invisible, the material and the abstract, and the familial and the extrafamilial. Each of Pons's characteristic traits acts, while intact, as a bulwark against Cibot's encroachments on Pons's territory. For example, because Pons is a gourmand, he never eats at home and does not depend on his *portière* to feed him, as his roommate Schmucke does. Pons's taste for fine food first appears as a sign of internal division: "Pons did not dare confess to Schmucke that for him [*chez lui*], his heart and his stomach were enemies . . . , that he needed at all costs to savor a good dinner" (22–23). *Chez lui* has two plausible meanings. It can mean "for" or "within Pons," but it also means "at Pons's home." Because Pons cannot stomach the dinners that Cibot cooks, his culinary desires (the psychologized *chez lui*) take him away from his home (the spatialized *chez lui*); his gastronomic tastes conflict with his desire to spend time with Schmucke, but they also prevent his domestication, the circumscription of his desires within his domestic location.

Pons's second trait is that he is a *célibataire*—an unmarried old man. Pons differs from the typical bachelor of 1840s *physiologies* and *tableaux* because he lives with another man, his equally aged friend Schmucke.[28] Pons's relationship with Schmucke shields his property from the depredations of his family and his *portière*, since their ambitions to inherit Pons's property must overcome Schmucke's claim to it. Schmucke and Pons establish an intimate domestic partnership that protects them from a hostile world: immediately after they first meet they develop "the economical idea of living together" (23) in order to pool their meager resources, and contrast the "happiness of their private life [*vie intime*]" with "the barbarism of society" (57). Pons calls Schmucke his family, his father, his mother, his wife, his lover, and finally names him as his "universal" heir. The narrator overtly describes the two men in the idealized terms of exclusive romantic love, the correspondence of souls, and a joint retreat from the external world. Schmucke says, in the German accent Balzac transcribes orthographically, "I luf only Pons" (120) and Pons concurs that "all my life only he has loved me" (147). When Pons's notary asks him if he has a wife, children, father, or brother, Pons replies "I have none of that, all of my affections are united in the person of my dear friend Schmucke" (255).[29]

Pons also constitutes a specimen of a third type, the collector who haunts the boulevards in order to transfer objects from the commercial spaces of shops to his private museum, which as we have seen is defined by its anonymity, secrecy, and recessed location in his apartment. Pons conforms in many respects to Walter Benjamin's account of the collector as a nest-builder who gathers together objects dispersed in the world and renders them "formidable" to others. For Benjamin, the collection is marked by its completeness for the collector and its absolute lack of utility: the collector "in effect liberates objects from the servitude of being useful" and assembles "shipwrecked matter" in order to effect "the elevation of the commodity to the rank of allegory."[30] Pons's collection similarly provides him with a potentially "formidable" shield against the world because he constructs it as an architectural secret and a secret object of desire; it protects him from his porter, Mme Cibot, because of its location in his apartment, its absence from circuits of commercial exchange, and its status as an idealized love object.

Pons's collection is located in one of the building's original salons, in a space that re-members a previous architectural era, when his apartment building was an *hôtel,* not yet subdivided or subject to a *portière*'s supervision: "The salon where the main part of the Pons Museum was located was one of those old-fashioned salons, like the ones designed by the architects hired by the French nobility, twenty-five feet long by thirty feet wide and thirteen feet high" (154). Typically, we discover this information about the architectural integrity of Pons's collection—its location in the one room of his apartment that dates from a time when the building would have had only one owner—at the moment that this integrity is being violated, since the narrator describes the room only in the course of describing Cibot's secret introduction of Rémonencq, Fraisier, and Magus into Pons's museum. Prior to their intervention, however, Pons's collection, like the salon that contains it, exists only as a spatial unity, an indivisible group, and he maintains its integrity by refusing to show it to anyone, particularly to other collectors who would recognize its value: Pons "hid his collection of masterpieces from everyone's sight," and even "the deceased M. Dusommerard, the Prince of bric-a-brac, died without having been able to gain entry into [*pénétrer*] Pons's museum" (13).

In the first sections of the novel, Pons's collection also remains unsullied by the alienating transactions associated with any form of exchange, including heterosexual marriage. Though the narrator describes Pons's love for food and for collecting both as substitutes for a female lover—"Good food and bric-a-brac were the equivalent of a woman for him" (19)—and writes that Pons loves his collection as a "lover" adores "a beautiful mistress" (14), Pons's collection exists in opposition to money and all the transactions associated with it, which include marriage: the chapter in which Pons's relatives attempt to marry their daughter, for example, is entitled "What a Woman Costs."[31] Pons's restricted income puts him in the magical position of always acquiring priceless treasures for next to nothing, and we learn in the opening pages that Pons would choose his "cherished collection" and "the possession of his curiosities" over personal fame and success (12), that he himself does not know how much his collection is worth, and that he is virtually unknown as a collector: "unknown in the field of Bricabracology, because he didn't frequent sales and never showed up at famous dealers, Pons did not know the venal value of his treasure," unlike "those illustrious rich people who put together collections in order to compete shrewdly with dealers [marchands]" (13–14).

In contrast to Cibot's domestic economy, which sustains the flow of goods as long as possible, Pons's collecting short-circuits exchange. Both Cibot and Pons revalue waste: while Pons salvages outmoded masterpieces that most people consider debris, Cibot sells Pons's and Schmucke's leftover food to her neighbors. But where Pons creates value by taking remaindered objects out of circulation, hence reducing their utility, Cibot creates value by keeping scraps in circulation and maximizing their use. The novel glorifies Pons's collecting as an aesthetic alchemy that endows material objects with transcendent artistic value and contrasts his aesthetic sensitivity to an image of architectural transience: "The genius of admiration . . . the only faculty by which an ordinary man can become the brother of a great poet, is so rare in Paris, where ideas resemble travelers passing through an inn, that one must grant Pons respectful esteem" (12).[32] The reference to an inn metonymically suggests Cibot, who has worked in a restaurant as well as in an apartment building, and the novel explicitly insists several times on Cibot's inability to see paintings except as brute matter or money. For Cibot, a painting is either "forty sous of canvas or 100,000 francs of painting!" (184). When Cibot contemplates "a sublime little picture by Metzu" that she has stolen from Pons's apartment, she asks herself uncomprehendingly "how could such a small painted board be worth so much money?" (271).[33]

The result of the collision that Le Cousin Pons stages between the museum plot and the apartment-house plot is that Cibot appropriates and annihilates Pons as a *character*. She does so by subsuming the traits, inner appetites, and affections that define him as a spatialized subjectivity within the novel and initially protect him against her overwhelming presence. The former gourmand becomes a virtual anorexic who depends completely on Cibot for the little nourishment he takes; the collector who shuttled between his private museum and the city's boulevards becomes a bed-ridden invalid who lies helpless while his porter helps rival collectors rummage among his prized objects; and the devoted *célibataire* is thwarted in his attempts to make Schmucke his sole heir and thus preserve his collection's integrity and his companion's security.

When Pons's family first banishes him from their table, Cibot responds by saying "proudly" "Monsieur will dine here every day!"; she sees this addition of Pons's daily meals to Schmucke's as "the realization of her dream" (58). This "dream" refers initially to the increased revenues she expects to receive but rapidly also becomes the fantasy of dispossessing Pons and Schmucke that will propel her through the rest of the novel. Cibot announces at the chapter's close that she will consult the neighborhood fortune-teller that very evening, and the next chapter explicates what she wants her fortune to be:

> In seeing no heirs for either Pons or Schmucke, Madame Cibot had been flattering herself for about three years that she would obtain a mention in *her gentlemen's* will. . . . By dining out all the time, Pons had, up until now, escaped the complete servitude in which the *portière* wished to hold *her gentlemen*. The nomadic life of this old troubadour-collector had scared away the vague ideas of seduction that flitted about in Madame Cibot's brain and that became a formidable project on account of this memorable dinner. (58–59)[34]

Cibot's "vague ideas of seduction" revolve around her new position in Pons's life, her domestication of his former "nomadic life." Once Pons becomes ill, after a second rejection by his family that fatally repeats the first one, his gluttony disappears completely from view as a rival for Cibot's domestic influence. Confined to his apartment and to Schmucke's and Cibot's care, Pons loses all appetite and his doctor warns that giving him food or drink would kill him. When Pons can no longer deploy his taste for fine dining as a shield against Cibot, the field is clear for her to replace *La Table* and win a place in Pons's heart and will. In Schmucke's absence, Cibot becomes "mistress of the apartment and of the invalid. . . . [L]a Cibot no longer left her bachelor's side, she brooded [*couvait*] on him like a mother hen!" (142). The phrase "mistress . . . of the invalid" suggests that Cibot both supervises Pons and becomes his lover—but *couvait* transforms her sexual ambition into an image of bestial (s)mothering. Though Cibot bases her claim to Pons's property on her years of nurturance, *couvait* suggests that she is trying to transform him into food for her own consumption, trying to lay her own personal nest egg.[35]

Although Pons's and Schmucke's relationship is precisely what blocks Cibot's attempts at seduction, it also renders the two men dependent on her planning and labor. The novel thus pits the female porter's control over Pons and his apartment against the platonic virtues of his spiritual, romantic friendship with Schmucke. Cibot places herself so centrally in Pons's life because Pons is unmarried and has neither mistress nor heirs. She thus has two fantasies about his property: that he will leave it to her as compensation for loyal service, and that she will provide the heterosexual relations Pons lacks. Cibot interrogates Pons about his past heterosexual history and thrills at the news that he has no illegitimate offspring but then is crestfallen that he intends to make Schmucke his sole heir. In response to Cibot's indignant protest that no other woman would take care of Pons as she does, he yells, "But—goddamnit! listen to me! . . . I wasn't talking about women when I was talking about my friend Schmucke!" (149). Cibot's claim to Pons's property thus depends on her blindness to Pons's exclusive relationship with Schmucke, on her inability to imagine any relations of alliance and inheritance outside heterosexual reproduction; in her conflict with Pons, Cibot comes to represent the apartment house as a site of heterosexual material relations, while he stands for the home as a sanctuary for a domestic partnership between men.

It is thus Pons's uncharacteristic engagement in the world of heterosexual commerce that proves his downfall as a collector. His attempt to arrange a marriage between his cousin Cécile and Schmucke's rich friend Brunner inadvertently enables Cibot to appropriate his collection. In order to allow the two to meet without incurring any obligations, he invites Cécile, her mother, and Brunner to peruse his collection, an action that inspires him to replace the secrecy and privacy of his objects with their theatrical display: "Everything shined in its own particular way and sent its theme [*jetait sa phrase*] into the soul in this concert of masterpieces" (86). Both parties to the marriage deploy the subterfuges of drawing-room comedy: Cécile and her mother keep their backs to the door and pretend not to notice when Brunner enters, although they have been using a mirror to determine the precise moment when he will; Brunner feigns romantic enthusiasm for Cécile in her presence, then says to Pons after the women leave:

"Oh!" replied Brunner, "the little one is worthless, the mother is somewhat pinched . . . we'll see."

"A great fortune on the way," Pons noted. "More than a million . . . "

"Until Monday!" repeated the millionaire. "If you wanted to sell your picture collection, I'd definitely pay five to six hundred thousand francs for it. . . ."

"Oh!" cried the good fellow, who had no idea that he was so rich, "but I couldn't part from what makes me happy." (89)

Brunner is far more interested in spending money on the collection than in acquiring money by marrying Cécile. The collection is more valuable than Cécile because Pons cannot separate from his collection or alienate it in any way from himself, whereas Cécile is nothing but alienable, both from her parents and from her husband-to-be.

Brunner's offer allows Pons to affirm that his collection lies outside the circuits of heterosexual exchange and commercial valuation, even as it apprises him of its precise value. Pons's new knowledge about his collection's value coincides, however, with a redefinition of his private space as a marriage market and commercial theater for displaying his art, and the narrative underlines that the private museum has become wide open to view by revealing a few chapters later that Cibot and her friend Rémonencq (who runs a secondhand goods store across the street from her) have overheard Brunner's conversation with Pons and thus learned about the collection's value at the same time that Pons did. "The Auvergnat had listened to the last words that Brunner said to Pons at the doorstep, the day of the interview between the phoenix-fiancé and Cécile; he thus wanted to get into Pons's museum. Rémonencq, who was on good terms with the Cibots, was soon introduced into the two friends' apartment in their absence" (109).

The first intimation that an outsider has been privy to Pons's conversation occasions a cautionary homily about the vulnerability of thresholds: "In Paris, where the sidewalks have ears, where the doors have tongues [où les portes ont une langue], and where the crossbars on windows have eyes, nothing is more dangerous than to talk in front of entryways" (108).[36] The narrator's personification of the streets and buildings of Paris as capable both of absorbing information with metaphorical eyes and ears, and then actively communicating it with a figurative tongue or actual language (langue means both) of their own, suggests that the apartment house itself, particularly its porte, and the woman who represents it, the portière, pose the greatest danger to the integrity of Pons's collection and by extension, to his self as embodied in his collection, his apartment, and his partnership with Schmucke.[37]

The narrative underlines that the apartment house and its *portière* threaten to destroy the museum by offering a counterimage of a collection rendered perfectly secure by virtue of its location in an *hôtel privé* guarded by a male porter and male dogs. A lengthy description of the *hôtel* of Pons's rival collector, Elie Magus, represents his *hôtel* as everything that Pons's apartment building is not. Magus and Pons both own art collections, but Magus's townhouse fulfills all the criteria that the *Physiologie du mariage* established for a patriarchal residence: "located between a courtyard and a garden," it is an inviolable, impenetrable space that perfectly protects Magus's virginal daughter and valuable art collection, both described as female possessions that must be kept safe from other men: Magus's daughter is "his chief treasure," she and the collection are both "idols," and he lives "in a seraglio of beautiful pictures" (136, 138, 135). Most significantly, Magus has a male concierge and three male dogs who guard and guarantee the integrity of his dwelling, art collection, and family:

> This concierge, of herculean strength, adored Magus as Sancho Panza loved Don Quixote. The dogs, locked up during the day, were allowed no food; but, at night, Abramko let them loose, and they were condemned by the old Jew's shrewd strategy to stand guard, one in the garden, at the foot of a post on top of which hung a piece of meat, the other in the courtyard at the foot of a similar post, and the third in the big room on the ground floor. You understand that these dogs, who, by instinct, already guarded the house, were themselves guarded by their hunger; they would not have left, for the most beautiful female dog, their post at the foot of their greased pole. . . . This devilish set-up had an immense advantage. The dogs never barked. (136–137)

Every detail in this passage reflects, negatively, an aspect of Cibot's character as a *portière*. The passage describes the concierge's and dogs' devotion to Magus in terms of unbreakable masculine bonds: the legendary relationship of Sancho Panza and Don Quixote, the male dogs who would not desert their post even "for the most beautiful female dog." The dogs' hunger binds them to their task as guards and, most remarkably, they perform their work silently. No one could be further from these guards than Cibot, who has a possessive, maternal, and exploitative attitude toward Pons, who wants only to steal the desired objects she glimpses, and who is a figure of unstoppable garrulity with a verbal tic that makes her add extra *n*s to words, prompting the narrator to comment that finding "the means of stopping up a *portière*'s tongue will exhaust the genius of inventors" (151).

The difference between Cibot and Magus's porter and dogs stems less from any intrinsic difference in their characters, however, than from the spatial differences in Magus's home and in Pons's apartment; in the case of the dogs, on whom the passage lavishes a disproportionate attention, that spatial difference *is* the difference in character between them and Cibot. Magus lives in an enclosed *hôtel* with several floors; the dogs can occupy a space external to Magus's own rooms and thus exercise their restrained greed and bloodlust outside the house, in the service of the house. Nothing can be external to the apartment house—Pons's building is a former *hôtel* whose original courtyard has been filled in with a second building—and hence nothing is external to the *portière*'s appropriative desires, not even separate subjectivities.

Between Space and Place: The Omniscient *Portière*

The narrative of *Le Cousin Pons* underscores Cibot's boundlessness by using her as the point of departure and point of return for the lengthy description of Magus's *hôtel* we have just examined. Cibot's first interest in Pons's collection, expressed in directly reported dialogue, leads, with no transition, into the six-page omniscient description of Magus and his *hôtel*. At the end of this classic description, in which habitat corresponds to inhabitant, the narrator returns to Cibot, who has been transported with no exposition from the street in front of her apartment to the interior of Magus's *hôtel*, as though the narrator's motion were connected to hers. This almost magical shift in Cibot's location consolidates the impression that she has produced the description of the *hôtel*, even though the information contained within the passage and the narratorial voice in which it is delivered bear little connection to her character. The description's wealth of detail and information (disproportionate to the locale's minor diegetic importance) aligns Cibot with the omniscient narrator by attaching the narrator's mobility to her own and by retrospectively suggesting that her physical presence generated a description that nevertheless seems independent of, even antithetical to, her consciousness.[38]

Cibot's unexpected accompaniment of the omniscient narrator recurs throughout the novel. For example, everywhere we expect a description of Pons's apartment from Pons's point of view, we find Cibot instead.

Even the narrator's description of Pons's apartment building emerges from Cibot's presence, contributing further to Cibot's appropriation of Pons's place as a central character whose point of view should focalize descriptive passages. *Le Cousin Pons* never provides a description from either Pons's or Schmucke's point of view; indeed, the apartment house itself seems to occlude their vision, since the narrative never shows either man looking out or in, suggesting a curiously windowless apartment.[39] Pons's and Schmucke's relationship to their home consists of a narrative dispossession, a discursive, exegetical dispossession that precedes the literal, diegetic eviction that ultimately occurs.

The narrator defers any description of Pons's apartment until the end of chapter 11, which prepares the reader for an account of Pons's apartment from his point of view. Pons returns home unexpectedly early, and his approach sets the stage for a description of his building and rooms. The narrator, however, breaks off into a new paragraph and announces: "Now, in order to understand the revolution that Pons's early return was going to cause at his house, we need to provide the explanations about Madame Cibot promised earlier" (47). A chapter break follows, and in a new chapter called "Specimen de Portier (Mâle et Femelle)," the narrator provides a description of what until this point the reader would have called *Pons's* apartment building but now sees in the context of the Cibots (Mme Cibot is married, but her spouse's irrelevance throughout most of the novel aligns him with the ineffectual type of *portière's* husband encountered in the previous chapter).

The reader already knows that Mme Cibot is "the pivot on which the two nutcrackers' household turned" (indeed, Cibot and *pivot* rhyme) but has no detailed information about her, having been told earlier that "she plays such a large role in the drama that undid this double existence, that it would be best to reserve her portrait until the moment when she comes onstage [*de son entrée dans cette Scène*]" (23). Pons's entry onto the scene of his apartment is displaced by Cibot's entry onto the *Scène* of the novel. Only under the sign of "the promised explanations about Madame Cibot" does the omniscient narrator provide a history of the apartment, the topography of its relationship to the street, the organization of its external surfaces and internal volumes, information about its owner and the porters, and a history of Cibot's relationship to Pons and Schmucke. Thus only in the context of a description of *Cibot* do we learn that Pons and Schmucke have lived on the second floor of the apartment for eight years (since 1836), and only by narrating Cibot's domestic work does the narrator provide us with an inventory of Pons's and Schmucke's domestic habits—how much they spend on food, laundry, rent, and tobacco (52–53).

Le Cousin Pons's metamorphosis from a museum novel into a variation on the apartment-house novel thus entails Cibot's replacement of Pons as the central consciousness of the narrative and the driving force of the plot. The way that Cibot takes Pons's place reflects both on the narrative consequences of the novel's architectural setting and on the spatial dimensions of its narrative.[40] As we have seen, Cibot displaces Pons by virtue of her material presence in his house and room, and by inflecting the novel's mobile, omniscient narrative with that material presence. These two modes of action resonate with the Foucauldian distinction D. A. Miller makes in *The Novel and the Police* between domination and surveillance, but in Cibot's case the distinction founders, since her character simultaneously practices the overt, self-displaying, material force associated with an unreconstructed police force and sets into motion the less visible, tentacular, disciplinary power that Miller sees creeping, exhaustively, into every aspect of "private" life. Cibot's omnipresence, her hypervisibility as the apartment house's guardian and representative, her overt references to her own physical force, and her outright control of Pons's freedom of movement line up with "the direct and quasi-instantaneous ceremonies of physical punishment" and with a police power that "theatrically displays its repressiveness."[41] On the other hand, Cibot's interrogation of Pons's past sexual history enforces a confessional mode, one of the "various technologies of the self and its sexuality" that attempts to institute "a regime of the [heterosexual] norm," and she introduces practitioners of medicine, the law, and a bureaucratic state into Pons's most private domestic space, thus performing what Miller calls "the working-through of an amateur supplement" to the police.[42] Miller associates disciplinary power in Balzac with the omniscient narrator: "On the side of perspicacity, Balzac's omniscient narration assumes a fully panoptic view of the world it places under surveillance. . . . On the side of impenetrability, this panoptic vision constitutes its own immunity from being seen in turn."[43]

In Cibot, however, an invisible knower who exercises an abstract disciplinary power is combined with, not separated from, a concrete physical presence whose primary force is movement, not vision.[44] The amalgamation of an invisible knower with a fully embodied and visible one takes place in two passages where Cibot focalizes descriptions of an apartment. One apartment is occupied by the doctor Poulain, the other by the lawyer Fraisier, both of whom come to play vital roles in the plot against Pons. Like Magus's *hôtel,* however, these apartments exist in the novel only to be described, since no further action takes place within them. As in the description of Magus's townhouse, Cibot's physical presence motivates the descriptions of the two apartments, but the information that the narrator provides the reader quickly exceeds what Cibot could be presumed to see or to know. The description of Dr. Poulain's apartment, for example, offers us a complete overview of its layout although Cibot sees only the antechamber and living-room; Cibot also could not know that "the doctor's apartment had not been changed for forty years" (166).

These descriptions ally Cibot's physically circumscribed presence to a powerful and invisible intelligence whose range and scope go beyond Cibot's limitations in space and time. The narrator identifies this combination of the abstract and the concrete with the power to set the novel itself in motion. When Cibot is about to leave Poulain's apartment for Fraisier's, the narrator interjects, "Here begins the drama . . . of the death of a bachelor delivered up by the force of things into the rapacity of the greedy natures grouped around his bed, which, in this case, had as their auxiliaries the passion . . . of an art fanatic, the avidity of M. Fraisier . . . and the thirst of an Auvergnat capable of anything . . . to amass capital" (176–177). Just as this passage collapses endpoints and middles, declaring the story's beginning as it reveals its ending halfway through the text, it suggests both that Cibot is the foremost member of the conspiracy, hence an agent with a locatable body, and effaces her guilt by referring to her only in terms of disembodied generalizations. The narrator asserts Cibot's priority in the plot against Pons by making this declaration immediately after transcribing Cibot's decision to consult the doctor and Fraisier, but at the same time the passage differentiates Cibot from her partners by identifying her only obliquely: "the rapacity of the greedy natures grouped around his bed" seems to include Cibot, while "the force of *things*" might allude both to her and to the apartment house she superintends. Taken as a whole, the two descriptions and the metacommentary that intervenes between them characterize Cibot as an abstract, dematerialized power with the novelistic ability both to set a "drama" in motion and to describe apartment houses in minute physical detail on the strength of her physical presence in them.

Cibot's effect on Pons is so lethal because as a *portière,* she can produce effects by means of her bodily presence in a specific *place* and can also deploy an abstract power that extends into a diffuse *space.*[45] Cibot not only has a unique command over the circumscribed locale of her apartment building and street, she is known in her *quartier* and can use her collective identity as a *portière* to gain access to other apartment buildings and private offices. Cibot can thus maneuver in the city as though it were simply a series of "private" locales, which resemble her own apartment building in being anything but private. As a *portière*, Cibot constantly transforms private sites that she should not be allowed to enter or should prevent others from entering into places that she can enter freely or can permit others to enter. The novel feminizes Cibot's power to transform urban spaces into accessible places by attributing it to her membership in a female network of *portières*. When Cibot wants to place Pons and Schmucke in her debt in order to force them to sell paintings to her for less than they are worth, she visits their employers to tell them that the two men can no longer work. To do so, she must try to enter a series of increasingly inaccessible private places:

> La Cibot put on her Sunday best and left in a carriage . . . and promised her-self that she would do justice to her role as the two nutcrackers' trusty maid in all the boarding schools and in all the households where the two musicians had female pupils.
>
> It is useless to report the different gossip sessions [*commérages*], executed like variations on a theme, in which La Cibot indulged with the school-mistresses and in the hearts of the families, it will suffice to report what tran-spired in the director's office of the "Illustrious Gaudissard," which the *por-tière* penetrated, though not without unheard-of difficulties. Theater directors, in Paris, are better guarded than kings and ministers. . . .
>
> La Cibot covered the distance [*franchit toutes les distances*] by means of the sudden intimacy which she established with the female concierge [*la concierge*]. Porters can recognize one another, like all people of the same pro-fession. Every profession has its *shibboleths*, just as it has its curses and its stigmata. (199)[46]

This passage underlines Cibot's appropriation of Pons's character (now she, rather than the musician, "executes" her schemes "like the varia-tions on a theme"), multiplies signifiers of femaleness—*femme de con-fiance, écolières, commérages, maîtresses, la concierge*—and puts the weight of all those women behind Cibot's supernatural powers. With their help she "cover[s] the distance," overcoming even those barriers associated with the masculine public sphere of the "illustrious" theater director who is "better guarded than kings and ministers."[47]

The plot also links Cibot's abstract power over space to a curious form of agency, in which Cibot unintentionally realizes her desires. Throughout the novel Cibot generates powerful effects in the absence of any intention or intentional action, as though she were not a character herself but a narrative force. Cibot herself understands her ability to have effects without meaning them in terms of her abiding faith in chance and providence. She thus aspires to a place in Pons's will after a fortune-teller, Mme Fontaine, confirms Cibot's wish to inherit his wealth. The novel continually raises the expectation that Cibot will kill Pons outright (by feeding him the wrong food, for example), but instead gives her only an indirect and inadvertent role in the event that precipitates Pons's death (Pons's discovery of Cibot and her cronies in his museum). The narrator displaces Cibot's harmful intentions onto those of her accomplices; thus in the chapter that describes their invasion of Pons's museum, the narrator continually refers to Cibot either by name or as "the porter" but calls Fraisier, Rémonencq, and Magus "the three birds of prey" and "Pons's three executioners" (236, 238). Conversely, Cibot is not the agent of Pons's or her husband's death, but the novel takes pains to implicate her in both. She becomes associated with Pons's death by desiring it, and with her husband's death by marrying Rémonencq, his murderer. The novel implicates her in Rémonencq's actions by explaining that Rémonencq administered poison to M. Cibot every time Mme Cibot left their *loge* to nurse Pons. The discovery that M. Cibot was murdered gives the retrospective impression that Pons was murdered too, since both men die and then are buried on the same days. Cibot's involvement in both deaths is *inadvertently* lethal: in neither instance does she *intend* to kill or *plan* to kill, but in both cases her absence and presence are equally fatal.

Cibot's role in the plot against Pons resembles that of his building—essential to its unfolding, but not as a bearer of intentions or of a penetrating gaze. Like the apartment house, Cibot is a catalyst, an influence that shapes a plot without intending to; where the *physiologies* and *tableaux* ascribed a phantasmatically powerful and intentional will to the *portière*, the realist novelist, perhaps for the sake of personifying the reality effects that emerge when the writer's hand is effaced, assigns the *portière* an agency that, like that of a building, can only be involuntary. Because Cibot's agency is involuntary, critics either ignore her role in the plot against Pons or assimilate it to a familial fantasy of the devouring mother. In his study of conspiracy in Balzac, James Mileham responds to the peculiarly inanimate form of Cibot's agency by relegating her to the role of "mediator" in the plot against Pons. Yet his own structural analysis of the conspiracy plot points to Cibot as its leader, since he argues that the subject, originator, or agent of a conspiracy is the person whom its victim imitates when resisting the conspiracy—and when Pons tries to foil the plot against him, he begins to act like a *portière*.[48] His discovery of three strange men in his museum comes to him in a dream-like state whose semiconscious clairvoyance resembles the prophetic trance of Cibot's fortune-teller (236). Once Pons perceives the plot against him as primarily female, he acquires the ability to act at a distance that until this point has been associated mainly with Cibot the *portière*: "This virginal man . . . penetrated too late into the reserves of bile that made up the *présidente*'s heart. . . . In his tenderness for Schmucke, Pons was trying to protect him from the bottom of his grave" (254). The narrator describes Pons's enlightenment in spatial terms as a penetration that has until then been Cibot's specialty and couches his love for Schmucke as the power to act at a distance ("from the grave") that until this point has been Cibot's province.

To counter the conspiracy, Pons begins to exploit his apartment's spatial relations—its partitions, passages, doors, common landings and entryways, its public and secret spaces—and to manipulate the physical structure of his apartment and the social rules that govern its inhabitants. He mimics Cibot's "espionage" by staging a false will-writing, deliberately letting her know that he is summoning a notary and allowing her to leave his door half-open so that she can observe him. As he dictates his will, he is armed with "a curiously worked little hand mirror," but Cibot cannot see that he is watching her watch him, mirroring her action by spying on her with a mirror of his own (255–256). Pons uses elaborate theatrical ruses to prove to Schmucke that Cibot plans to open Pons's will: he feigns sleep, has Schmucke make a hidden entrance through a secret passageway, and spies on Cibot's spying by "parting the little muslin curtain of a . . . glass door" (263). Cibot falls into the trap set for her when the two men hide on either side of a doorway to catch her trying to destroy the will: "when [Cibot] . . . came back into the bedroom and advanced toward the fireplace, she felt herself seized by both arms! . . . She saw herself between Pons and Schmucke, who had both flattened themselves against the partition, one on each side of the door" (269).

The porter is thus deported, caught at the door, the site of her conspiratorial power, by tenants mimicking her own comportment. Pons and Schmucke disarm Cibot by duplicating her domestic espionage and expelling her from their apartment—though she deftly steals one more painting before being thrown out. Pons then enlists another conspiratorial force on his side by making a false will to divert Cibot—a will that is unassailable because it leaves all his property to the State, the only entity against which Cibot and her cohorts cannot act, since it is all-encompassing: "one cannot bring the State to trial!" (267). Pons then manipulates the publicity and sexual theatricality of the apartment building when he invites Héloïse Brisetout, a dancer from his theater, to come to his apartment at night: all the neighbors turn out on the landing to observe her, particularly "the first-floor tenant, who . . . was as dazzled as his wife to find such a get-up and such a beautiful creature on their staircase" (257).[49] Pons uses this diversion to obtain enough privacy to call in a notary and witnesses so that he can make a new, genuine will unobserved.

Pons's renascence in *portière*'s guise, however, proves short-lived. Although he learns to manipulate mirrors, hidden spaces, and the apartment house's public character, the novel's final mirror scene proves Pons's demise:

> Madame Sauvage [Pons's nurse], probably accustomed to this kind of scene, went toward the bed holding a mirror, which she put in front of the dead man's lips, and since no breath darkened it, she forcefully separated Schmucke's hand from the dead man's. (280)

This passage represents the story's final turning point, after which everything and everyone turn against Schmucke (and by extension Pons, who lives on in the intensive mourning that Schmucke performs until his own death soon after). With the mirror back in the hands of a female caretaker, the stage is set for Schmucke's complete dispossession, which Sauvage initiates by physically separating the two men's hands. Sauvage finishes what Cibot began, since unbeknown to Schmucke (though the reader has known all along) Sauvage is part of the conspiracy against Pons, hired by Fraisier to act as Pons's nurse after Cibot has been discredited. Sauvage, "accustomed to this kind of scene," is well equipped to undertake the theatrical maneuvers required of her, to divide the spiritually self-enclosed couple into two separate men, and to control Schmucke by ministering to the material needs that make him vulnerable. Thus Schmucke falls victim to what at this point in the novel become the insufficiencies of bachelorhood (as opposed to the independent bachelorhood Pons enjoyed at the novel's outset): because he does not know how to cook or keep house, he must allow Mme Sauvage and another woman to stay in his apartment: "Schmucke began to cry; the two women left him and went to take possession of the kitchen, where together they quickly set up all of life's necessities" (283).[50]

The women's takeover is only the first stage of Schmucke's dispossession; immediately after Pons's burial he finds, as the chapter title puts it, that "to open up an estate, one closes all the doors" (302) and that he is no longer *chez lui* (312). Schmucke faints as he watches Pons's coffin drop into the grave, and he reacts with a similar loss of consciousness when clerks come to seal the apartment after Pons's family has contested his will: "The four men of the law closed off the salon. . . . Schmucke mechanically watched this operation, which consists of affixing a ribbon of thread with the seal of the Justice of Peace on each leaf of the doors, when they have two leaves, or of sealing the openings of cabinets and simple doors by sealing the two lips of the partition" (313). This activity belatedly provides the apartment with what it has lacked throughout the novel—the privacy of impregnability and the capacity to transmit knowledge to its occupants, since the seals close the apartment's rooms to potential invaders or register any invasion. The apartment becomes an invulnerable shelter, however, only in the service of a nexus of familial and state interests. From Schmucke's perspective, the placing of the seals becomes a figure for Pons's death and the effacement of their relationship, since the officials seal everything that represents an architectural couple—the "two leaves" and the anthropomorphized "two lips" of the partition.

The novel ends by taking Schmucke's and Cibot's relative positions to their logical conclusions: Schmucke can do nothing but lose, even when he is in full possession of knowledge, and Cibot can do nothing but win, even in ignorance. Pons's legal family designs a document that names Schmucke as a conspirator against Pons: "the will is the work of an odious sequestration . . . the will was wrested from a weak and helpless testator. . . . Monsieur Schmucke, in order to be declared sole heir, held the testator captive. . . . [O]nce he obtained the desired result, he gave himself over to infamous acts of ingratitude that scandalized the entire building" (326–327). This document accusing Schmucke inadvertently names all of Cibot's criminal actions: claustration, undue influence, an effort to substitute an extrafamilial legatee for the legal family, and outrageously callous behavior toward a dying man. Schmucke, "stupefied," only belatedly understands that he has confessed to harming Pons, and that knowledge kills him.

Throughout *Le Cousin Pons*, Balzac's narrator has dissociated himself from the invasions of privacy required by realist narration by attributing them to the *portière*. Cibot's demonized status as a ubiquitous, all-knowing, meddling woman, compounded by the audacity and cruelty of her intrusions, distracts the reader from her resemblance to the equally omnipresent and omniscient narrator. The narrator, after all, not Cibot, is ultimately responsible for all the characters' fates, and the narrator provides the textual precedents for the acts of spying, inventorying, and tale-telling carried out by Cibot. Yet much as the novel strives to project those acts onto the discredited *portière* and onto the apartment-house network that makes her activities possible, the narrator's investment in realism's publication of private life ultimately impels him to redeem both Cibot and the apartment building. Thus, after a rapid account of Schmucke's death and of the fates of secondary characters, the novel concludes with a paragraph recounting the triumphs of the former Mme Cibot, now married to Rémonencq:

> Madame Rémonencq, struck by Madame Fontaine's prediction, does not want to retire to the country, she remains in her magnificent shop on the boulevard de la Madeleine, once more a widow. As it happens, the Auvergnat [Rémonencq], after having drawn up a marriage contract in which all possessions would go to the last surviving spouse, put a glass of vitriol in his wife's path, counting on an error, and his wife, having with a perfectly good intention moved the little glass somewhere else, Rémonencq swallowed it. This end, worthy of this rascal, finds in favor of the Providence that painters of morals are always accused of forgetting. (334)

True to her conspiratorial ability throughout the novel to act as a minimal cause of maximal effects, Cibot rids herself of an unwanted husband and inherits his property without exerting any malicious volition—indeed, "with a perfectly good intention." The narrator's identification with Cibot emerges in his diction: the offhandedness of his "as it happens" matches the inadvertence of her action. Indeed, Cibot secures the narrator's admiration when, by accidentally killing the murderous Rémonencq, she becomes a stand-in for a punishing Providence that by all rights should have also marked her for retribution. But Cibot herself remains disidentified with Providence in one respect—she will never own the country house that lay at the root of her desire to inherit from Pons. The fortune-teller predicted that this house would be hers but also predicted it would be the death of her—"You will die assassinated by two escaped prisoners . . . in the village where you will retire with your second husband" (131). The apartment house remains an inescapable structure for all the novel's actors: a fatal structure for Pons and Schmucke, who attempt to combat its dissolution of privacy, but a sustaining structure for the narrator and the *portière*, who thrive as they mimic and exploit the apartment house and its all-encompassing spatial relations.

PART TWO

The City and the Domestic Ideal

3

The Haunted London House, 1840–1880

ADDRESSING THE ROYAL INSTITUTE OF BRITISH ARCHITECTS in 1878, the architect William H. White used his lecture "On Middle-Class Houses in Paris and Central London" to make a controversial, idiosyncratic, and ultimately ineffective argument: that London's architects, developers, and residents should stop building the "interminable lines of thoroughfares . . . bordered with equally interminable lines of houses . . . each inhabited by one and the same family," which had flourished in London since the 1820s, and should instead start to construct apartment houses in the Parisian style.[1] White's plea for the apartment building assumed knowledge of a fact that his audience would indeed have taken for granted: the enormous increases in London's population since the beginning of the nineteenth century did not translate into purpose-built apartment houses but instead into the urban and suburban expansion of single-family housing stock. Just as most Parisians in the first half of the nineteenth century took the apartment house for granted as the basic unit of the urban landscape (see chapters one and two), so did most Londoners accept without question the pervasiveness of the single-family house in their metropolis. Considerable cultural work was necessary to produce such a seemingly effortless acceptance of the single-family house as the Victorian architectural ideal, an acceptance so powerful that it persisted even in the face of several discourses that protested the actual deviation of London's homes from that ideal.[2]

White's lecture gives us a valuable point of departure for an analysis of Londoners' devotion to the single-family house because in the process of arguing against that attachment he had to enumerate its terms. Seeking to persuade his listeners that apartment buildings were the best urban residences, White began by demystifying common British ideas about how Parisian apartment life inverted proper domestic regimes. When he explained that in Parisian apartments "[i]ntimacy between superposed neighbors not only does not ripen, it does not grow" because the different occupants of a building "rarely meet," or when he assured his auditors that Parisian dining rooms were used only for dining, White was promising that the Parisian apartment building did not violate two chief tenets of British domestic architecture, which we examine below: the separation of different households into noncommunicating buildings, and the separation of different household members and functions into distinct rooms.[3]

White audaciously went on to argue that Parisian apartment buildings, not London's private houses, best realized the British residential ideal—but he qualified his advocacy of apartment houses as pragmatic by conceding the theoretical superiority of the single-family house: "A system which gives to each family not only the superficial area of a plot of land but also the whole cube of space above it, reaching, were it possible, to the nearest heaven must be a right system. Anyone . . . will freely admit the advantages of a system that grants to the head of a household the partly poetical license of breathing his native air on his own household."[4] White made here a common claim: a spatial structure that created autonomy by horizontally isolating a family on its own "plot of land" should ideally also mark its isolation from other families vertically, by means of the void above the house, whose emptiness made present the absence of other households. Because that cube of space also linked the family's male "head of . . . household" to the stuff of the nation by granting him unobstructed access to "native air," that empty space simultaneously defined his membership in the nation and demarcated his separation from the other members of that nation. White articulated here what we will see to be a persistent topos: England as a nation whose collective identity consisted in the secure isolation of its members from one another.

White's allegiance to the single-family home as an indisputable ideal may seem to challenge his advocacy of the apartment house, in which access to the open areas above and below one household's unit must pass through spaces occupied by other households. White, however, reconciled the apartment house to the British ideal by accepting that ideal's content (isolation of families from one another) while shifting his discussion to the question of which architectural structure would best approximate that ideal within the constraints of London's urban setting. No nineteenth-century city could consist solely of single-family houses occupying their own plots of land; and when White compared the dwelling practices of Parisian apartment-dwellers with those of Londoners living in terraced houses, he concluded that in a city like London, the single-family house considered emblematically English departed from the domestic ideal even more than the apartment building deemed irrevocably French.

To prove his point, White cited topographical and statistical maps showing that although London's homes displayed the facades of private houses, internally they were divided into apartments: within central London "the great mass of the residents are lodgers. The neighbourhood of the Strand is almost entirely rented by tenants and sub-tenants, who occupy a storey, a set of rooms, or a single room" of a building that was "originally a private house." [5] Those subdivided London houses created the very problems of social and spatial blending that the British incorrectly attributed to Parisian apartments: "in such a lodging-house the different groups are all day and hourly encountering each other; and the children perforce mix. The lodgings are not let by floors or even by sets of rooms; they are dovetailed into each other." Where Parisian buildings had "solid vertical divisions" separating each unit, the walls that separated London buildings only appeared distinct from the outside but were in fact "sham party walls pierced and mutilated." [6] White's description of the walls confusingly directed his auditors both to pity the walls because their organic unity had been violated ("pierced and mutilated"), and to mistrust them for being "sham party walls" impersonating real ones; the contradictions in his language about the walls reflected the material instabilities he ascribed to the walls themselves.

White's suggestion that Londoners renounce the single-family house as the ideal building type contradicted decades of writings to the contrary—in housekeeping manuals, government documents, architectural journalism, and social commentary. To be English was to live in a house, and to live in a house was English. In their *Encyclopaedia of Domestic Economy* (1844), Thomas Webster and Mrs. Parkes insisted that "[i]n England it is generally the desire of every one whose finances can afford it, to have a house of his own. . . . This feeling is peculiarly characteristic of England."[7] In his introduction to the 1851 census, the registrar general wrote that "[t]he possession of an entire house is . . . strongly desired by every Englishman; for it throws a sharp, well-defined circle round his family and hearth."[8] The 1851 census had recorded extreme disparities in housing conditions among British nationals, but the registrar general's comment offered to equalize those differences by positing that at the very least, the desire to own and occupy a self-contained house linked all Englishmen.[9] *The Builder,* England's leading architectural periodical from the 1840s on, published an unsigned article two years before White's lecture that asserted, "it may be at once conceded that the sentiment of independence and of personal responsibility, which is so marked a feature in the character of the Englishman at home, is better . . . expressed architecturally, by the separate residence than by the 'flat' system." For that author, the risks of the apartment were the risks of standardization: "at a time when individual character is more and more in danger of being merged and lost in the complicated social machinery of modern life," the English could not "afford to accept inconsiderately any mode of living which may seem to tend towards its further effacement."[10] According to this paradoxical logic, Englishmen were both differentiated and conjoined by their shared allegiance to identical forms of personal individuality ("independence") and architectural individuation ("the separate residence").

The English residence also became a powerful symbol of national identity in architectural discourse when writers singled out English houses as the only branch of architecture that embodied a distinct national style. A series of lectures on architecture published in 1843 in *The Builder* argued that the villa, the common term for a small, fully detached single-family house with a garden, "may be said to be peculiar to England," despite the word's overtly foreign provenance.[11] Architects responded to those who complained " 'Classic' one day, 'Gothic' next— when shall we have ENGLISH?" by pointing out that the *"national* character attaches itself far more to domestic architecture than to . . . public buildings, ecclesiastical or civil."[12]

White was as singular in his praise of the apartment building as he was in his criticism of the private house, for if the English house signified English nationality, decades of English discourse about the home had consistently marked the apartment house as French (alien, immoral, and prone to revolt), Parisian (urban, cosmopolitan, commercial), or simply foreign.[13] For example, when the public health inspector Hector Gavin advocated legislation in 1850 that would bring about "the possession by the industrial population of the modest comforts of an English home," he specified that he did not mean "houses . . . built in the French fashion, [in which] . . . a family only occupies one of many rooms," but "houses . . . chiefly built in what may be termed the English fashion, that is small houses, with two, three, or four rooms." [14] Articles in *The Builder* identified living in apartments as "the Parisian mode of life," and the journalist T. H. S. Escott, commenting in 1879 on the large set of luxury flats built at Queen Anne's Gate, wrote that "[n]o arrangement can be imagined more diametrically antagonistic to the tastes with which Englishmen are generally credited." [15] In Escott's hyperbolic formulation, the apartment building was not merely incidentally un-English, but perfectly anti-English.

In addition to condemning the apartment house as a deviation from national standards, writers on urban housing warned of the dire moral effects apartments had on their inhabitants. While White's speech tried to neutralize that warning, other writers expressed their fears of the apartment house's ill effects in increasingly strong terms over the course of the nineteenth century. At best, dwellings built to house more than one family were perceived as "not . . . a satisfactory ideal" and viewed with "general distaste and suspicion"; at worst, they were seen as morally corrupting influences or monstrous, unspeakable structures possessing the characteristics that the historian Nicholas Taylor, paraphrasing Edmund Burke, attributes to the "awful sublimity" of the Victorian city: obscurity, terror, power.[16] In 1843, a group of "landowners, householders, and builders" commented in a petition to Parliament that "the system of erecting large tenements or barracks, and of letting them out in floors . . . [was] highly prejudicial, not only to the health and comfort, but to the morals of the inhabitants." [17] Octavia Hill, a philanthropist and investor who purchased several houses in London in order to renovate the buildings and reform their tenants, strongly advocated small buildings over large apartment blocks. In "The Influence of Model Dwellings Upon Character," written in 1892, when large blocks had become more common than they had been in previous decades, Hill argued that "the block becomes a sort of pandemonium" and warned that "what life in blocks is to . . . less self-controlled [tenants] hardly any words of mine are strong enough to describe." [18]

The daring and futility of White's appeal for apartment buildings in London become even clearer when we turn to the evidence of the built environment. Almost no purpose-built apartment houses were constructed in London before the 1880s: there were sets of chambers for single men, a moderate number of "model dwellings for the working classes," and fewer than ten buildings offering "luxury flats," which were usually rented only for the duration of the London social season.[19] Not only did architects build almost no apartment houses, whether for the rich or the poor; in their designs for the few that they did build, architects deliberately eradicated the elements that distinguished apartment buildings from single-family houses: shared entrances, staircases, landings, and courtyards (see chapter one). Architects of luxury flats and of housing for the poor drew apartment blocks with several small entrances rather than a single central one and even developed external stairways that provided each unit with an individual door leading directly to the exterior, "disconnecting the apartments" from one another and "rendering the tenements completely distinct" (fig. 12).[20] Thus, far from anticipating or responding to White's 1878 exhortation to build more apartments in the Parisian style, architects made sure that the few flats they built departed as much as possible from the Parisian type advocated by White.

Why did White's recommendations fail? To put the question positively, why did London architects, real-estate speculators, and inhabitants respond to increasing urban density and rising land costs by promoting the single-family home both within the central city and throughout its rapidly expanding suburbs? To answer these questions, I begin by making explicit the definition of the house within domestic ideology, then analyze British architects' commitment to realizing that ideology in built form. In the particular case of London from the late 1830s through the 1870s, when discourses of public health reform and urban observation began to purvey distinctly Victorian representations of the city, I analyze the terms in which those discourses singled out the homes of the London poor as deviating, architecturally and morally, from the middle-class domestic norm. Those discourses consistently occluded the housing conditions of the middle classes of London, but not because middle-class houses realized the ideal and thus required no commentary. Rather, as we saw already in White's description of central London as a neighborhood of rented lodging houses masquerading as private single-family houses, and in what I call the discourse of domestic complaint, the middle-class house in London failed in multiple ways to embody the domestic ideal.

The third section of the chapter traces how the discrepancy between domestic ideology and the dwelling practices of Londoners came to be inscribed within the literary subgenre of the haunted-house story, which

FIGURE 12

William Young, project for model flats for the middle classes,
The Builder 7, no. 356 (December 1849). The proliferation
of doors on every story of the apartment building helps to
eliminate the single common entrance and vestibule typical of
the Parisian apartment house.

flourished from the 1850s through the 1870s. That form's combination
of supernatural content and realist form allowed its authors and audience to represent life in London's houses, and, at the same time, to de-
realize both the content and formal procedures of their narratives. I con-
clude by turning briefly to the medical and popular literature on burial
reform, in which the movement of dead bodies from the central city to
the London suburbs resolved the problems of urban housing, making
the cemetery the site where the city and the home could be reconciled.

"An Englishman's Home Is His Castle":
The Domestic Ideal and Its Architectural Realization

The central tenet of British domestic ideology is a familiar one—the celebration within the middle class of separate spheres of home and work,
divided along gendered lines that assigned a domestic realm to women

and a public realm to men. Victorian authors of conduct and house-keeping manuals, essays on domesticity, and treatises on domestic architecture interpreted a "sphere" as an abstract set of moral attributes, as the range of behaviors and actions proper to wives and husbands, and as a physical space. Domestic ideology dictated that women were to be self-sacrificing and virtuous, men enterprising, protective of their families, and susceptible to women's softening influences. Women were to guarantee the neatness, order, and comfort of the home by managing household finances and supervising servants; men were to earn the money with which women created the domestic comfort that would restore their husbands at the end of each working day. The home was to be a physically enclosed refuge that isolated its inhabitants from contact with other households, the street, and the city's public spaces and institutions.

We have come to be increasingly skeptical of this vision of Victorian everyday life among the middle classes, largely because of feminist scholarship that has revealed the internal contradictions of domestic ideology. Leonore Davidoff and Catherine Hall have shown that the term "separate spheres" masks the asymmetry of a division in which men had full access both to the public realm and to the comforts and pleasures of the home. If public men were well ensconced in the private realm, private women also ventured into public space: Judith Walkowitz and Deborah Epstein Nord have explained that despite the construction of public terrain as a site of female danger, women of all classes circulated in many spaces outside the home. Other works have questioned the very division between public and private: Catherine Gallagher has noted the extent to which novelists and social theorists simultaneously linked and disassociated the public and private realms; Nancy Armstrong has argued that the domestic woman's management of a household and of servants provided the template for the political power exercised in public by middle-class men; and Mary Poovey has demonstrated the extent to which the division between public and private spheres relied on gender differences that could never be sustained.[21]

This scholarship does not explore how the domestic ideal took architectural form in mid-Victorian London, where urban conditions conflicted with the essentially rural ideal of home generated by domestic ideology.[22] To begin to fill that gap, this section explains first, how proponents of the domestic ideal enlisted the physical house in the project of realizing the attributes they assigned to the private sphere; and second, how architects working for the middle classes attempted to give the domestic ideal a material form.

"An Englishman's home is his castle." When Edward Coke first uttered a version of this statement in a seventeenth-century legal treatise, he used the castle as a metaphor for the right to be free from undue invasion of one's home: "a man's house is his castle," he wrote, and "[t]he house of everyone is to him as his castle and fortress, as well as for his defense against injury and violence as for his repose."[23] His phrase was cited frequently throughout the nineteenth century, but with two important differences: it was evoked primarily in domestic contexts that transmuted its original political and legal import; and it was commonly modified to emphasize its national component—"an *English*man's home is his castle." The conjunction of the two changes shows the extent to which nineteenth-century discourses shifted the terms of Englishness from men's enjoyment of political liberties (keeping authorities out) to their engrossment in an impregnable space (keeping themselves in).[24]

Proponents of the domestic ideal invoked this aphorism throughout the nineteenth century as a way of encapsulating the qualities they attributed to the house, and particularly to a man's enjoyment of that house. The aphorism signaled male dominion over the house with its casual reference to an "English*man*'s" possession, and amplified that Englishman's power by equating him with a feudal lord, thus replacing a lord's authority over serfs with a man's authority over a wife and children.[25] This maxim's most familiar rendition in Victorian literature, Wemmick's home in *Great Expectations,* seems to parody both the castle and its Englishman by emphasizing the castle's miniaturization into a mere home, since Wemmick's suburban abode is simultaneously a "Castle" complete with moat, battlements, and Union Jack flag, and "the smallest house" the narrator ever saw.[26] Dickens's joke worked, however, precisely because it reversed the far more common tendency to read the aphorism as magnifying the house. The domestication of the castle made every English dwelling, no matter how humble, an instance of national glory and distinction and made every English man a conduit for what W. R. Greg called the "veneration . . . conveyed by the name of the first and oldest English institution—the name of home."[27]

Domestic ideology and architectural theory subordinated the spatial implications of the home's status as castle to temporal ones: the castle represented durability, the persistence of the past into the present, and the timelessness that domestic ideologues conferred upon the Victorian middle-class house. In domestic discourse, the house's physical qualities mattered as a bulwark against the losses effected by the passage of time and as an embodiment of a persistent, unchanging version of the past that could be transmitted to future generations. The architect Francis Cross, in *Hints to All About to Rent, Buy, or Build House Property,* (1854) described the home as a container of memories, "the place in which all our best associations are to be found."[28] For John Ruskin, the home became a literalized memory; in "The Lamp of Memory," one of the *Seven Lamps of Architecture,* he wrote that "it is in becoming memorial and monumental that a true perfection is attained by civic and domestic buildings."[29] Ruskin enjoined his readers to believe that "when we build, let us think that we build forever." At the very least, architecture had to mean "command . . . over . . . modes of decay," but all good architecture should possess "unchangeableness," so that buildings could be lasting "witnesses" to and "record[s]" of the work of past generations, a capacity that Ruskin also associated with property.[30]

Paradoxically, the ideal home was required to concretize memories *and* to dissolve them, by acting to make men forget everything that lay outside their homes. The historic associations that pervaded the house mediated between past and present and created familiarity by virtue of being unchanging and familial; in turn, that familiarity promoted the forgetfulness and ease inspired by habit. The home's comforts thus produced an amnesia specific to domestic space; in her manual of *Domestic Duties, or Instructions to Young Married Ladies* (1825), Mrs. Parkes wrote:

> Every man . . . meets with numerous circumstances and disappointments which harass and distress him. For the painful effects of these, a happy home provides an instantaneous antidote. Everything beyond its walls seems for a time forgotten, while the mind is relieved, and its powers renovated for future exertions in the world, by the healthy air of cheerfulness which he breathes in the domestic circle.[31]

In this passage, the house absorbs the agency of its occupants: the "home," not the women and servants who work in it, "provides an instantaneous antidote," and the man's inspiration of the domestic "air of cheerfulness" allows his mind to expand to match the perimeters, and content, of the home: what the house keeps outside its walls, he can place outside his head.

Both the home's retention of past memories and its dissolution of present cares resonated with its status as property (a status underlined by the double possessives of "an Englishman's home is his castle"). In an article on "Cottage Economy" (1840), John Loudon, who more than any other individual popularized the suburban house as a domestic ideal, praised the "sense of property, the possession of a comfortable house, and the social affections and local attachments thereby produced." [32] Although as White's lecture suggested, and as we will see in greater detail below, Londoners were tenants, not owners, the English domestic ideal nonetheless envisioned the house as a freehold property occupied by one family for generations. [33] The ideal attached houses to land, and land signified durability; Francis Cross, a popular expert on the sale and lease of property, explained to the readers of Landed Property (1857) that land was even more valuable than houses: "It is not liable to destruction; nor is it, like house property, constantly requiring the 'healing' processes of restoration and 'repairs,' to ward off decay." [34] Property ownership helped solidify the house's metonymic investment with the qualities of the land on which it stood: resistance to decomposition, persistence in time, and the transcendence of the corporeal vulnerability and eventual death to which individual owners were subject.

While architects could not make buildings that would stand forever, they did publish designs for middle-class homes intended to realize many other aspects of the domestic ideal. Architects rarely built houses in London to clients' specifications, since their fees prohibited middle-class clients from hiring them. As architects began to professionalize, from the 1830s on, they sought out large-scale public commissions (churches, government buildings, monuments) and indeed differentiated themselves more and more from the builders, surveyors, and engineers who developed London's residential suburbs by constructing houses on speculation. [35] Architects influenced house design indirectly, by providing developers with prototypes in pattern books consciously directed at nonarchitects. Thus, for example, the subtitle of Richard Brown's Domestic Architecture (1841) described his book as providing "the principles of designing public buildings, private dwelling houses, country mansions, and suburban villas," and William Young addressed his luxurious volume of plans for Town and Country Mansions and Suburban Homes (1879) to "the few who build houses . . . the many who buy them, and . . . the multitude who lease them." [36] Pattern books ran the gamut from expensive, lavishly illustrated folios to cheap, "practical guides" for carpenters and builders, while architectural journals also offered illustrations and informative articles to a general audience at a moderate price. [37] Architectural publications flourished, fueled by a vogue for architectural literature of every variety that began at the end of the eighteenth century, when it was largely inspired by readers' desire to cultivate their taste, and sustained during the nineteenth century by builders' need for architectural models, especially in a rapidly expanding metropolis.[38]

Developers and architects worked to make the new built environment materialize the domestic ideal. Builders guaranteed that suburban dwellings would be sequestered from the public activities of trade and work by enforcing zoning rules that eliminated commercial and industrial activities in residential areas; architects promoted the domestic ideal of privacy through their designs for middle-class houses and their commentary on what constituted a house.[39] Throughout the nineteenth century, architectural discourse defined the house as an impenetrable, self-contained structure with distinct and specialized rooms. Doors and windows, necessary breaches in the house's impenetrable walls, were given treatments that reflected the English architectural view that, in one historian's paraphrase, "openings in the walls are not in the least desirable and can only be considered necessary evils."[40] Each room within the house was designed to secure occupants from observation and intrusion. Whenever possible, main rooms faced the back, not the front entrance, and all rooms became emblems of what architect J. J. Stevenson called "isolation," by the use of corridors that guaranteed "separate communication to each room."[41] A room entered only from a corridor, and not from other rooms, would also circumvent the danger that the people or purpose of one room might mix unexpectedly with those of another. Robert Kerr, whose *Gentleman's House, or, How to Plan English Residences* (1864) equated "progress" in architecture with the increasing recognition accorded to "the claims of privacy," defined proper room distribution as the isolation of bedrooms on their own floor, the separation of men's and women's rooms, and the separation of servants' and employers' quarters, "so that what passes on either side of the boundary shall be both invisible and inaudible on the other." Other writers insisted on the importance of separating kitchens from other rooms to prevent the apprehension of smells.[42] Kerr's use of linguistic fiat ("shall be") to create absolute sensory blockage ("invisible and inaudible") compensated for the physical impossibility of his "boundary," which had to allow the passage of servants and simultaneously impede the communication of all sights and sounds.

The house envisioned by architects was also a free-standing structure designed for one family, a demographic and economic impossibility in an increasingly dense metropolis whose developers compromised between

FIGURE 13

Photograph of Park Crescent, built circa 1812 near Regent's
Park; designed by John Nash. The continuity of the cornices,
balustrades, and columns subsumes the individual houses into
a single monumental row.

ideal and real conditions by building single-family houses attached in
rows called "terraces." The contiguity of houses in a terrace contradicted
the singularity that each house was meant to symbolize, but that contradiction only manifested itself as such during the Victorian period.
The builders of the Georgian era, working in a climate that celebrated
urban improvements on a grand scale, constructed houses in rows and
squares, and thus made groups of houses, not individual houses, the basic units of urban construction. In the 1810s and 1820s John Nash laid
out the Regent Street area in long rows of houses with unbroken flat
walls, shared cornices, and continuous porches that emphasized the
overall unity of the terrace line (fig. 13). The result was a monumental
effect in which many houses gave the impression of forming "a single
large mansion," an impression often accentuated by topping the two

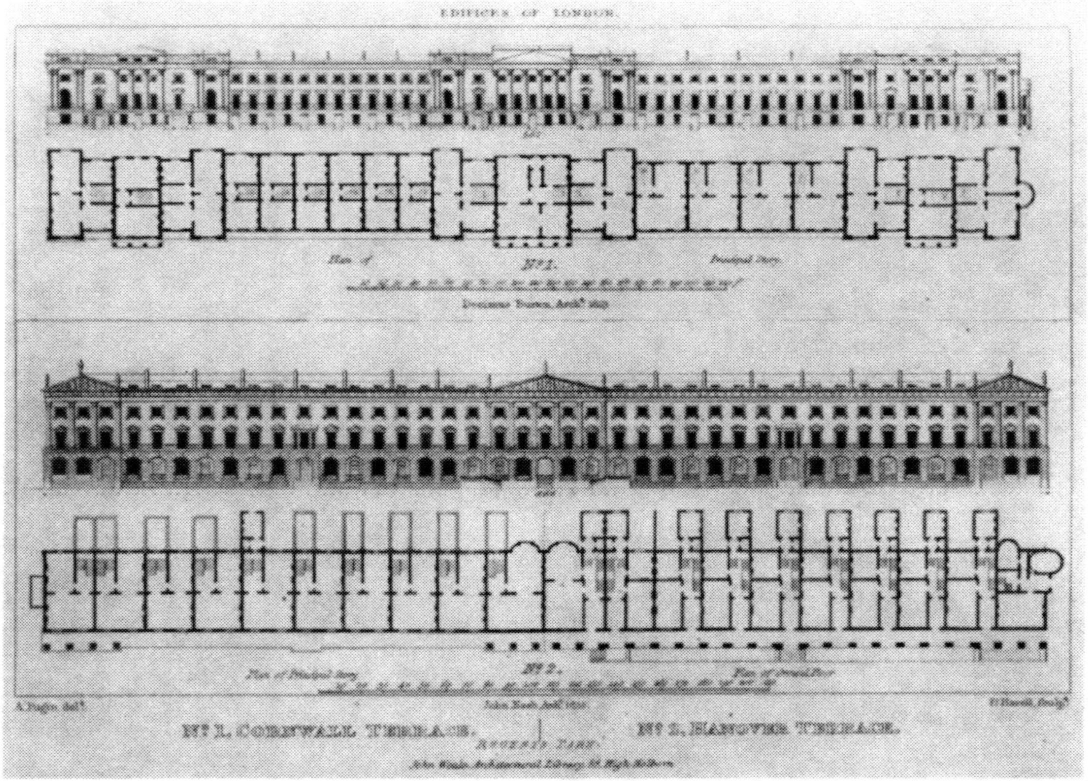

FIGURE 14

No. 1, Cornwall Terrace and No. 2, Hanover Terrace, London. Designed by John Nash, 1825. By topping the houses at the center and ends of the row with pediments and giving their cornices and facades more ornate decorative treatment, Nash treats the individual houses as elements of a much larger building. From W. H. Leeds, *Illustrations of the Public Buildings of London*, vol. 2 (London: John Weale, 1838).

center houses with an extra story and a pediment so that the houses on either side appeared to be the symmetrical wings of one large building (fig. 14).[43]

Victorian developers designed terraces that conformed more to the new ideals of social and spatial privacy: they gated and locked formerly communal gardens in squares, set terraced houses far back from the road, and used architectural treatments that rendered the individual houses within a row more distinct.[44] Those treatments included the repetition of each facade as an entirety (rather than the assignment to each facade of a part in a larger whole); individual gables and pillared porches on each house to emphasize its self-contained unity; iron railings demarcating the "area" in front of each house; recessed doors to break up the terrace into units defined by changes in volume; and protruding bow windows, or, as Kerr put it, some other "projection in the Facade" that separated one house from another by more than "a mere boundary-line between two shades of paint on one flat surface" (figs. 15, 16).[45]

Architectural illustrations of suburban villas deployed techniques that emphasized, on paper, the three-dimensionality that Kerr associated with a house's ability to stand apart from the houses connected to it. Alfred Cox, a real-estate agent, wrote in *The Landlord's and Tenant's Guide* (1853) that architectural draftsmen should depict houses in terms of strong "lights and shadows."[46] In opposition to the graphic, linear, and frontal style of French architectural drawings, English illustrations of villas used shading and perspective, which accentuated depth and contours and suggested that houses were situated in three-dimensional space. And where French architectural illustrators removed a building from its site in order to emphasize two-dimensional symmetry, English illustrators typically surrounded villas with shrubbery and gardens whose picturesque irregularity drew attention to the space surrounding the house (figs. 17, 18).[47]

The vegetation drawn and often actually planted around houses also connected dwellings to the cultivated version of nature prized by the suburban domestic ideal. John Loudon argued that "no cottage ought to be built without some land being attached to it" and even subordinated dwellings to grounds: "The enjoyments to be derived from a suburban residence depend principally on a knowledge of the resources which a garden, however small, is capable of affording."[48] The association of house and garden helped mark the house's privacy, not only by acting as a verdant screen, but also by linking the home to the garden's

FIGURE 15

Photograph of terrace row, Fassett Square, London, built circa
early 1860s. The projecting bay windows demarcate individual
pairs of houses. Doors recessed within decorative arches and the
low brick walls distance houses from the sidewalk and street.

symbolic inwardness, and promoting its resemblance to the rural cot-
tages and country mansions that emblematized the English domestic
ideal.[49] Real-estate agents and builders applied rural names to suburban
dwellings, even those that lacked gardens, in an effort to increase their
value. The author of an article on "Cottage Economy" redefined any domestic unit, including a city "tenement," as a cottage: "The word cottage is not confined to merely rural dwellings, at least we choose not to
confine it so, and we prefer it to the inexpressive terms tenement or
dwelling-house"; commenting sardonically on such nominalism, an article on "Houses to Let" in *Household Words* noted that advertisements
for dwellings used the "agrarian title[s]" of "villa" and "cottage" to designate any house.[50]

The cultural attachment to the domestic architectural ideal was so
strong that even Londoners preferred to build suburban miniaturizations

FIGURE 16

Photograph of terrace row, Queensdown Road, London, built
1869–70. The builders used projecting windows, staircases,
and white quoins to distinguish individual houses within the
row. The differences in height, style, and facade treatment between the houses in this single row indicate that this street was
divided into smaller lots and developed by at least three separate builders.

of country houses, complete with rural nomenclature, whose appearance
evoked the harmonious, organic social unity associated with the small
country town.[51] As a result of that preference, London's residential
neighborhoods exhibited a paradoxical symbiosis of the rural and the urban: paradoxical because, despite their identification as rural and even
antiurban, those suburban villas were also specifically and indelibly
metropolitan, just as the song "Home, Sweet Home" (1823) invoked a
prelapsarian village abode but was written for a melodrama set and performed in London.[52] As the architectural historian Geoffrey Tyack puts
it, "the middle-class suburb [was] perhaps the most original contribution of nineteenth-century London to urban civilisation," yet at the same

FIGURE 17

Elevation of a Parisian apartment building, from [Louis-Marie] Normand fils, *Paris moderne* (Paris: Bance, 1837). The two-dimensional linear style and the abstraction of the building from its surroundings are typical of Parisian architectural pattern books.

FOURTH-RATE GARDENS.

FIGURE 18

Elevation of a London semidetached suburban villa, by
E. B. Lamb (1837), from John Loudon, *The Suburban Gardener and Villa Companion* (London: Longman, Orme, Brown,
Green and Longmans, 1838). Executed in the same year as
Normand's elevation, Lamb's illustration emphasizes the villa's
privacy and closeness to nature by depicting trees and shrubs
so lush that they hide part of the building's facade. The perspective view and use of shading emphasize the house's depth;
the foreground accentuates its distance from the viewer.

time, "the fascination with suburban life went hand-in-hand with an
anti-urban prejudice." [53] Mid-Victorian architects strove to materialize
domestic ideology by designing urban homes apparently unmarked by
their urban locations—yet that very effacement of the urban *within the
urban* defined the metropolitan character of those homes, and of London
itself.

London's Deformation of the Domestic Ideal

If domestic ideology and architectural discourse tried to suggest that
even in London, homes could exist without reference to the city, the discourses of urban investigation that developed in the 1840s argued that
especially in London, the city had overtaken and destroyed the home.
Journalistic and statistical inquiries into the moral and physical dangers
of London equated the city with a particular type of home, the lodging

house, which exemplified the ills of both London and its inhabitants.[54] Furthermore, while the discourses of urban observation remained silent on the subject of London's middle-class dwellings, invoking them only tacitly as the standard by which they condemned the homes of the poor, another discourse—the discourse of domestic complaint—deplored the extent to which almost all homes in London, including those of the middle classes, deviated from the domestic ideal.

The discursive tendency—prominent after 1840 and through the 1870s—to emphasize the city's dangers, and to locate those dangers in domestic spaces, represented a pronounced shift from prose depictions of London through the 1830s. Since the eighteenth century, publishers had profitably supplied readers with cheap guidebooks to London as well as topographical volumes of prints depicting the city's chief sights, and in the early nineteenth century Charles Lamb and Thomas de Quincey published essays on London life in the *London Magazine* (1820–29).[55] By far the most popular book about London, however, was Pierce Egan's *Life in London* (1820), which was reissued and imitated many times.[56] As the literary critic Deborah Epstein Nord points out, *Life in London* typified the urban discourse of the 1820s, which "celebrated" the "metropolis as a stage on which to perform," privileging distanced, panoramic views of the city.[57] *Life in London*'s popularity can be ascribed to its innovative conjunction of text and illustrations (by the Cruikshanks), along with its use of a fictional framework to present guidebook information; *Life in London* depicted the peregrinations of a city sophisticate named Tom as he introduces the city to his country cousin, Jerry. As the critic Carol Bernstein shows, Egan's work described London in terms of an episodic "contrast between high life and low life" that proceeded as a catalog of urban types and urban slang.[58] Egan's narrator, characters, and readers move easily between aristocratic and criminal realms whose differences become as slight as those between homonyms: the high life at Almack's aurally becomes the equivalent of the low life at All-max.

As in Victorian urban discourse, crime, prostitution, and poverty figure prominently among the scenes that Tom and Jerry enter, but the text justifies those scenes as lessons about avoiding the dangers of the metropolis. Egan's distinctly pre-Victorian belief was that those dangers *could* be avoided; he adopted an essentially euphoric view of London as a city where those pursuing urban pleasure could easily learn to avoid pain. Egan's *Life in London* also differed significantly from Victorian discourses of the city by virtue of its relaxed incorporation of all types of domestic spaces into a larger urban setting. Rather than confine its narration of Tom and Jerry's adventures to their forays into streets, taverns, and other public settings, it combined those scenes with a detailed description of their house. Similarly, while Egan was one of the first writers in English to use the word "slum," his narratorial stance toward the houses of the poor displayed none of the prescriptive outrage of the Victorian commentators discussed below.

The urban discourse typified by Egan found an echo even in early Victorian texts, such as Charles Dickens's *Sketches by Boz* (1833–36), which extended Egan's interest in contrasts, slang, and urban euphoria to a London dominated by an expanding middle class; the narrator of *Sketches by Boz* also moved easily between streets, house facades, and domestic interiors, as did the contemporaneous *tableaux de Paris* examined in chapter one.[59] Even as late as the 1840s, writers such as Albert Smith combined Egan's strategies of urban representation with explicit adaptations of the *tableaux* and *physiologies*.[60] After living in Paris from 1838 to 1841, where he was introduced to the French *physiologies,* Smith returned to England and published a series of "physiologies" and "social zoologies" that, like their French models, were cheap, small, and copiously illustrated. Smith's efforts to import the urban discourse of Paris into the English metropolis culminated with *Gavarni in London* (1849). That volume's title placed a famous illustrator of the Parisian urban scene in London, and its format imitated the multiple authorship and panoramic viewpoint of the Parisian *encyclopédies;* like those works and other texts by Smith, *Gavarni in London* depicted the home and the city as both continuous and homologous spaces.[61]

Smith's physiologies were popular but atypical representations of Victorian London.[62] The dominant discourses of London were produced by journalists such as James Greenwood and Henry Mayhew, government investigators such as Edwin Chadwick, and philanthropic reformers including George Godwin and Ellen Ranyard, who all, despite their political differences, deployed a consistent set of rhetorical gestures and imagery in texts directed largely at middle-class audiences concerned about newly visible urban poverty. The producers of that urban discourse posited themselves as collecting and conveying detailed information about London's poor, using interviews and observation. They both aggrandized and undermined that work of observation by ascribing a labyrinthine, mysterious, and even dangerous character to the people and sites they aimed to observe; frequently they compared themselves to explorers investigating foreign, "savage," and uncharted territory.[63]

Victorian urban discourse represented London through a series of metonymies whose final term was the lodging house. While the urban discourse of Paris tended to isolate its *maisons garnies* from the rest of the city, the urban discourse of London reduced the city to one part, a homogenized composite of all the areas inhabited by the very poor, and then represented that part in terms of an even smaller unit—the lodging houses and tenements that came to stand both for their occupants and for the city as a whole.[64] The anonymous author of *Sinks of London Laid Open*, for example, after promising in his title to reveal the city's obscurities, pledged to fulfill the promises roused in an "Age of Inquiry" and to develop the reader's "powers of observation"—all of which would be achieved merely by offering a "correct account" of lodging houses.[65] On the basis of a similar equivalence between the lodging house and the city, proponents of acts to regulate lodging houses argued that regulation would not only solve the local problems of lodging houses but also eliminate all the nefarious consequences attributed to urban overcrowding: the spread of contagious diseases, dirt, immoral and criminal behavior, high mortality rates, and insurrection. The wording of the legislation defined lodging houses as synecdoches for the overcrowding of the entire city and as the origins of all its evils—"the great source of contagious and loathsome diseases, the hotbeds of crime and moral depravity."[66]

Almost every book about London published between the 1840s and the 1870s singled out lodging houses and lodgings as exemplars of urban dirt, disease, crowding, and promiscuity. (Lodging houses offered beds by the night or week, while lodgings consisted of a room or rooms rented for longer periods; although they served very different residential purposes, urban observers often conflated them.[67]) What one American historian terms "the demonology of boarding" can be traced through British texts that called lodging houses and the multiple-occupancy homes of the poor a "festering mischief," the "common" sites of "horrors," of "gross acts . . . which cannot be detailed in print," of "crimes . . . not fit to be mentioned," and of "scenes . . . far too gross and revolting to be described," the "details" of their "Filth, Dishonesty, and Immorality . . . too gross to be more than alluded to."[68] Its epitomization of urban ills made the lodging house thoroughly antidomestic, both because it typified the city (which we have already seen was opposed to the home) and because the imagery of dirt and contagion contradicted the domestic ideal's emphasis on cleanliness and order.

Architects pointed out that the lodging house lacked the permanence attributed to the middle-class home. An anonymous contributor to *The Builder* in 1878 explained that "[w]e have always looked upon . . . a [London] lodging-house . . . as a calamitous medley of extemporal divisions and subdivisions." [69] The reference to an "extemporal" lodging house represented it as ephemeral, the product of little planning before its construction, productive of scant permanence after being built. Such attributions of impermanence to lodging houses were common; in *Lectures on Architecture and Painting* (1853), Ruskin attributed the failures of contemporary domestic architecture to the tendency to "look upon our houses as mere temporary lodgings" and noted that the "wandering habits" fostered by lodging houses undermined the stability necessary for great architecture. [70]

The reference to lodging houses as a "calamitous medley of . . . divisions and subdivisions" underscored their distance from two other important aspects of the domestic ideal: the separation of households (vs. a "medley") and the assignment of an entire house to each household (vs. "divisions and subdivisions"). Urban observers deplored that in lodging houses, the conventional dwelling unit (a house) was segmented into several parts (sets of rooms, a single room, a single room divided by a screen); that several household members were crowded into one room; and that several families were crammed into one house. Thomas Beames, a London clergyman interested in replacing extant lodging houses with model dwellings, provided a typical description of tenements in *The Rookeries of London:* "stories piled on stories . . . not each floor, but each room tenanted by a family." Beames used the term "rookery" to link the spatial resemblance between slum housing and bird's nests (both were "for the most part high and narrow") to a social resemblance— neither rooks nor the poor lived in separate families. [71]

Crowding not only represented the pressure of many bodies on too small a space (several urban observers even calculated that lodgings provided an insufficient number of cubic feet of air per person); by bringing family members and distinct families into close proximity, crowding also broke down social units and hierarchies and as a result, led to indiscriminate mixing. Middle-class urban observers focused particularly on the sexual promiscuity that they believed resulted from spatial proximity, obliquely referring to the widespread occurrence of incest, prostitution, and sodomy among poor people in lodgings. [72] Writing generally of *The Manufacturing Population of England* (1833), Peter Gaskell set the tone for subsequent discussions of London homes when, after condemning the separation of work and home for making the family "a body of distinct individuals . . . lodgers merely," he commented on families crowded into one room: "the promiscuous way in which families herd together . . . prevents all privacy, and . . . destroys all notions of sexual decency and domestic chastity."[73] Writers concentrating on London identified the lodging house as a key location in narratives of the urban corruption of city youth and rural emigrants. Charles Kingsley attributed premature sexual knowledge to the overcrowding associated with lodging houses and tenements: "the child's mind is contaminated, by seeing and hearing, in overcrowded houses, what he should not hear and see."[74] Thomas Archer, a magazine writer whose work focused on the London poor, wrote that London's young women "are lost in the tide which sweeps them into the broad stream of crime, and takes them from the common lodging-house to the common brothel."[75] Archer's statement linked the lodging house to the brothel rhetorically, by qualifying both as "common"; spatially, by situating both within the same "broad stream of crime"; and narratively (that is, both spatially and temporally), by designating the brothel as the terminus of a trajectory whose starting point was the lodging house.

Narratives of degradation extended to the buildings themselves, in a personification that worked not to endow lodging houses with productive life but to associate them with decay (and, as we will see in the last section, with death). Lodging houses and tenements were described as the final stages in the fall of buildings and neighborhoods, in their "degenerat[ion]" into "a nest of lodging houses."[76] One of John Hollingshead's many works of urban observation, *Ragged London in 1861*, personified St. George's in East London in terms that charted the growing distance between lodging houses and active, "struggling" human beings: "From being occupied by struggling householders they sink gradually through all the phases of lodge-letting until they are reduced to the condition of being divided into tenements . . . and the unfortunate street is doomed."[77] Initially propped up by the agency and syntactical proximity of the "struggling householders," the lodging houses lose agency as they submit to sinking, an action that resonated with the noun often used to designate them, "sinks." A *Quarterly Review* article used a similar image of nautical descent when it claimed that "[m]ore of rustic innocence and honest purpose . . . has suffered shipwreck in these *lodging-houses* than from any other perils."[78] The lodging house, in these views, substituted the fluid, receptive states of an open sink or a ship succumbing to gravity for the solid, deflecting walls of an upright house. While the model house was depicted as actively protecting its inhabitants from external dangers, the lodging house was too passive even to be an agent of immorality—"purpose" suffers *in* it rather than *from* it, and the house itself experiences the same deterioration as its inhabitants.

Urban observers singled out the ills of lodging houses for exhaustive description—and marked lodging houses as the cause of descriptive exhaustion. Almost all urban observers spoke of lodging houses as unspeakable, collapsing hyperbole and ellipsis in statements that claimed that the dirt and immorality of lodging houses were so extreme that their referents had to be or already were obscured. *Knight's London* stated "OUR LONDON IS PICTORIAL" and aimed to depict "things which *can be seen*" but called the "sights and smells" of lodgings in the St. Giles district of London "indescribable." [79] Archer qualified his description of the homes of the East London poor by demurring, "I have written the word 'home,' but it is almost impiety to associate it with any meaning which can attach to the dens of Bethnal Green." [80] The conditional locution—"any meaning which can attach"—implied the unlikelihood of either a name or a meaning adhering to such a corrupted housing type, defined as altogether resistant to signification. Indeed, Archer's use of the word "impiety" warned that using "home" to refer to the houses of Bethnal Green risked degrading the word itself, making even the sign "home" literally unspeakable.

The obsessive attention that urban observers paid to the lodgings and lodging houses occupied by the poor corresponded inversely to their lack of interest in describing the homes of the middle classes. Middle-class houses were negative objects of observation in urban discourse, in two senses: a discourse premised upon thorough description of London never described middle-class houses, allowing lodging houses instead to represent the city as a whole; and middle-class houses constituted, albeit tacitly, the negative ground against which the homes of the poor stood condemned as domestic failures. To subject middle-class houses to first-hand observation would have undermined the discursive difference between those homes and lodging houses, since the urban investigators who entered and exposed working-class houses to their reading public enforced the very lack of privacy they claimed to describe. By securing middle-class homes from their own intrusions, urban observers discursively made those homes the private, nonurban counterpoint to lodgings.[81]

Urban observers occasionally acknowledged that the distinction between the homes of the poor and the middle classes was liable to collapse, particularly because a literal proximity made respectable houses complicit in the veiling of a criminality that writers considered it their duty to expose. "The most lordly streets," wrote John Garwood, "are frequently but a mask for the squalid districts which lie behind them."[82] The force and scandal in the revelation of a connection between "lordly streets" and "squalid districts" depended, however, on their opposition. For representations of the middle-class house that articulated its *internal* opposition to the ideal it was meant to embody, we must turn to a different discourse: that of domestic complaint, which showed how legal conventions, building conditions, and dwelling practices all prevented London's homes from coinciding with the domestic ideal.

Legal reformers protested the conditions that prevented the middle-class house from sustaining its ideal status as property, particularly objecting to the English patterns of landownership that prevented individual home ownership from becoming widespread. Works with titles such as *English Land and English Landlords: An Enquiry into the Origin and Character of the English Land System, with Proposals for Its Reform* (1881) provided indignant overviews of a problem whose factual outlines have been confirmed by recent historical studies: a majority of the middle class leased rather than owned homes, because English land remained concentrated in the hands of a very small percentage of proprietors, most of them either aristocrats or institutions. In London, for example, the descendants of the earl of Southampton owned and developed much of Bloomsbury, and the College of Eton owned large tracts of Hampstead.[83] Such landowners were called "freeholders," which meant they had the right to dispose of their land as they pleased (although settlements often prevented them from selling it outright). J. T. Emmet, in an article on "The Ethics of Urban Leaseholds" (1879), estimated that only a thousand men in London lived in their own freehold houses.[84] Most freeholders in London owned very large blocks of land, called "estates," which they usually leased in smaller lots to individual speculators, who installed roads and sewers and supervised house construction. The freeholder could dictate the nature of all of those structures through restrictive covenants in the leaseholding agreement.[85] In London, the lease between a freeholder and a speculator typically lasted for ninety-nine years; the freeholder remained the owner of the land, and the leaseholder paid a nominal annual ground rent plus an initial lump sum for the lease itself. Most leases stipulated that the houses built on freehold land either be returned in good condition or that "dilapidation" fines be paid.[86] At the end of the ninety-nine-year lease period, the ownership of every structure built on the freeholder's land reverted back to the freeholder, and the land itself remained the freeholder's property throughout the tenure of the lease.

The speculator, as the initial party contracting to a ninety-nine-year lease with the ground landlord, was usually only the first in a chain of lessors; as one advocate of reform put it, "the population generally are mere tenants in the fourth or even fifth degree," while the primary leaseholder, "as if in mockery, is called the 'owner.'"[87] Some speculators developed and leased entire tracts themselves, but most sold portions of their leases to others, who in turn often sold their leases in even smaller increments. Not untypically, then, a row of terraces set in a parcel of land that had recently been sold comprised houses in various states of construction, some fully finished and occupied, some standing for years as unfinished "carcasses" because their individual developer had temporarily run out of funds.[88] Once developers had completed construction of a house, they might lease it again to a small-scale investor interested in managing, maintaining, and collecting rent on one or several properties or they might lease it directly to a household for a period ranging anywhere from a few months to ninety-nine years; that household could in turn sublet portions of the house to lodgers, usually for periods less than a year.

Legal reformers focused on the restrictions that the leasehold system imposed on generalized property ownership, particularly in London, "a city in which comparatively few people lived in their own freehold homes," and "temporary tenancies of furnished houses" were frequent.[89] According to Frank Banfield's *The Great Landlords of London* (1888), small freeholds and 999-year leases were the custom in northern cities and many rural areas, making the "shackles imposed by the present leasehold system" most constricting in London; and Emmet commented that "the bad influence of leasehold tenure is most evident in metropolitan and urban buildings."[90] Legal reformers argued that while other European countries, particularly France, had "released [land] from its feudal fetters" and extended property ownership to those who could afford it, the English leasehold system made property the monopoly of a privileged few and deprived Englishmen of the national liberties that were supposed to inhere in their homes.[91] That deprivation became even more unjustifiable when it took place in the nation's capital: "Boasting that she carries freedom everywhere together with her flag, she [England] should scarcely endure longer in the heart of her Empire a most vile oppression," wrote Banfield, transposing the conventional comparison between London's poor and "savages" to middle-class Londoners, in order to show that their geographic centrality to imperial England belied their economic and political exclusion from the freedom attributed to imperial English subjects.[92]

Banfield's association of political freedom with the ability to buy property led to a corollary insistence that aristocratic ground landlords be forced to sell their land; indeed, most advocates of what Joseph Kay called *Free Trade in Land* (1885) in effect called for the completion of the economic shift from a feudal system of land tenure to a capitalist one with a free market in commodified land.[93] However, Banfield, Kay, and others were less overtly interested in making land more mobile through potentially endless exchanges than they were in creating a temporary market that would give the majority of Londoners access to permanent property. Their complaints about the leasehold system focused not on the barriers it posed to the alienation of property, but on the multiple ways it prevented a majority of people from enjoying fixed, absolute possession. First, they deplored the facts that, because few leases ran longer than ninety-nine years, even the most stable tenant could at best bequeath only a portion of a long lease to his or her inheritors and that, because inheritance law defined leaseholds not as "real" property but as personal property, heirs could not directly inherit leases.[94] Second, not only did leaseholds themselves lack the defining characteristic of property, "indeterminate duration"; according to legal reformers, the very existence of leaseholds compromised and diluted the absolute status of freehold property: "the freehold . . . bec[omes] by action of the lease depreciated to mere leasehold," and the resulting "transmutation of the freehold is in every way an injury to the proprietor."[95] Third, reformers claimed that leases undermined property and its holders physically by producing flimsy houses and transient tenants. Emmet, for example, unfavorably contrasted "possession of a freehold house," which "confers upon its occupier social freedom and political importance," with leasehold, which made tenants "unsettled, apprehensive, constantly expectant, never satisfied"; resulted in "increased mobility among the London population"; and produced "domiciles [that] reflect the weakness and the want of individuality of those who occupy them."[96]

Architectural journalists elaborated on Emmet's claim that the lease-hold system produced tenants and houses lacking the permanence crucial to the domestic ideal, arguing that the system of ninety-nine-year leases encouraged builders to construct houses that often barely lasted for the duration of the lease. A contributor to *Building News* commented on "the ephemeral character of all our middle-class dwellings" and identified "the very origin of the gigantic evil we are speaking of . . . [as] this horrid system of short leases," while Charles Eastlake wrote in *Hints on Household Taste* that "[a]ccording to the present system of tenure adopted for house property, the rule is to build residences which are only intended to last a certain number of years."[97] Several articles criticized the poor construction of speculatively built London housing and frequently related stories of decaying, "falling houses" whose lack of permanence also threatened the longevity of their occupants. An 1843 *Builder* article on "Falling of Houses," for example, reported a child burned and a father killed by falling timber, and a later issue provided increasing evidence of falling houses.[98] The very walls and floors that were supposed to provide a secure framework for private space were perceived as liable to gape, sag, and cave in, as though "prepared expressly for premature decay and ruin."[99]

Complaints about the transience and instability of London's houses also appeared in semifictional articles in the periodical press that cataloged moves from one disastrous house to another, using a first-person narration that underscored the reliability and pathos of the stories' anecdotal testimony. In a humorous sketch on "Apartments, Furnished," the independently wealthy narrator changes lodgings several times over the course of a few years.[100] The narrator of "How to Build a House and Live in It" tells the readers about a Mr. Johnson, who loosens his next-door neighbor's shelves when he hammers on his own wall; he comments on that fact with the statement "so much for the substantiality of Johnson's townhouse" and invokes the proverbial castle to underline the incompatibility of an urban location and the domestic ideal: "the idea of a man living in his own castle is applicable only to that state of society when large towns do not exist."[101] A sketch with the peripatetic title "Scamping" (1879) featured a narrator whose house "had been erected on speculation" and who gradually suspects "that all is not right. There is a screw loose somewhere, or rather a great many screws." Using the serial intensification typical of a form that often moved from domestic complaint to domestic disaster, the loose screws become smells, spots,

FIGURE 19

Semidetached houses, from T. L Walker, *Architectural Precedents* (1841). Called "semidetached" because they are free on one side but attached on another, these two houses appear to be one, particularly because the individual doors leading to each house are located at the side of the building rather than in front.

and finally a set of broken pipes that pour back into the house the only substance it should not retain—sewage.[102]

The discourse of domestic complaint saved its most heartfelt laments for the ways that middle-class houses in London failed to be insular structures that kept households separate. Even the external separation and individuality of middle-class houses was compromised by the widespread practice of building semidetached houses, in which two internally independent units were connected under a single gabled roof to

FIGURE 20

Semidetached houses, designed circa 1855, from Samuel Hemming, *Designs for Villas* (n.d.). The shared roof and the doorways spanned by a single overhang convey the impression of one house.

give the appearance of one house that on closer inspection proved to be two (figs. 19, 20). Ruskin emphasized the deindividuation and even the potential monstrosity of the duplicate structure of semidetached houses by describing them as "fastened in a Siamese-twin manner together by their sides." [103] And despite architectural attempts to differentiate houses attached in long, terraced rows, the problem of deindividuation emerged in representations of those houses as well; the identity of each house was compromised by being an exact replica of the others in the row, even in terms of the features (bow windows, recessed doors) that set it apart from them spatially. Each adjoining house became a less substantial, less distinct, more spectral semblance of the other, as in the illustrations of a pair of terraced houses in *The Builder's Practical Director* (1855). The image represents two neighboring terrace houses with identical layouts, but the floor plan identifies the rooms in only one house; the blank spaces of the corresponding rooms in the adjoining house create an apparitional effect, as though the internal contents of its rooms had been rendered less substantial and less identifiable by virtue of its contiguity with, or replication of, its twin (fig. 21).

The problem of deindividuation became even more obvious in comments on internally subdivided houses. Although, as William White observed in remarks on London's houses, "such is the force of custom, [that] no 'family man' likes to admit that he occupies only part of a house,"

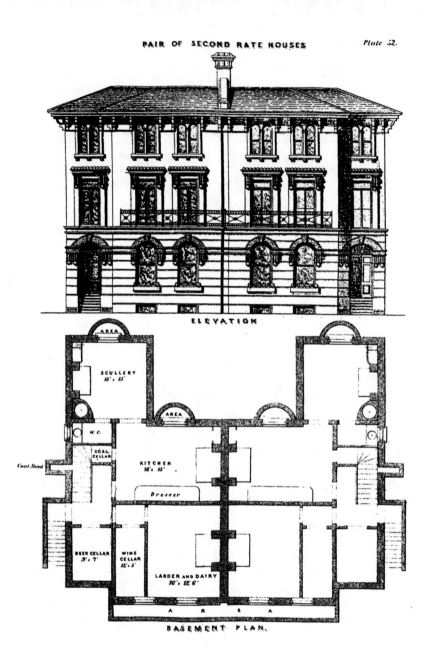

FIGURE 21

Elevation and basement plan of a pair of semidetached houses, from *The Builder's Practical Director, or Buildings for All Classes* (London: Hagger, 1855). The floor plan of the house on the left is the mirror image of the house on the right; the rooms of only one house are marked on the floor plan, making its attached neighbor appear to be its spectral reflection.

most single people, couples, and even families with children and servants rented only the fraction of a house—the original drawing room and dining room, for example, or a set of what had been designed as bedrooms, grouped together on the top floor.[104] The rooms in which people slept adjoined the rooms in which they ate and entertained, an arrangement that ran counter to the principle of separate communication to each room. Arthur Ashpitel and John Whichcord commented on this situation in 1855 by calling middle-class houses in London "strange anomalous places. . . . Planned for one family, they are inhabited by three or four, who are perforce in some degree associated, however opposite their elements may be. With thin partitions and thinner doors . . . where any one can pry into each other's movements . . . there can be no privacy, no comfort, no home." [105]

For some writers in the architectural and periodical press, the subdivision of houses built for one family meant that middle-class houses had become, like lodging houses, crowded, dirty, and immoral.[106] Indeed, in real-estate advertisements, the middle-class house and the lodging house became interchangeable terms. A "moderate-sized but elegant house close to the Park" on Little Stanhope Street, in Mayfair, for example, could be "suitable for either a private family or as a lodging-house." [107] The authors of an article on "Architecture" for a collection on *Our Homes, and How to Make Them Healthy* (1883), wrote that "[t]he discomfort, the want of privacy, the absence of adequate sanitary appliances, and the consequent loss of decency and lowering of the moral tone, involved by such a state of affairs [subdivided houses], are at once obvious defects." Emmet linked urban leaseholds both to ethics and to hygiene, arguing that "the leasehold tenure tends to home neglect and dirtiness, and propagates disease," and an article on "Modern House Building" rued "the sins and weaknesses" of middle-class houses.[108] Like lodging houses, subdivided houses were understood as corrupted and corrupting, and moral effects were attributed to their structural design.

While the discourse of urban observation excluded the middle-class home from the purview of the urban and opposed vivid descriptions of actual lodging houses to the implicit standard set by an unvisualized single-family house, discourses of legal reform and domestic complaint trained their gazes directly on London's middle-class houses and found that the middle-class house was also opposed to the ideal it was supposed to realize. In their attempts to figure that lack of identity, those discourses had recourse to an equation between London's suburban villas and its lodging houses and registered by their words of outrage that such an equation should not be. Occasionally, those discourses also expressed the middle-class house's failure to coincide with itself by using metaphors of the supernatural, of a world in which appearances no longer followed the dictates of "natural" laws. Emmet, for example, called the middleman in the leasehold system an "incubus" and asserted that the lawyers who administered the system had "bewitched house property."[109] A parallel discourse, within the bounds of fiction, portrayed the middle-class house as literally haunted.

London's Haunted Houses

Representations of London as a city of haunted middle-class homes were not confined to oblique references in legal pamphlets and the architectural press. Nor were references to a haunted London limited to the odd supernatural moment or metaphor in realist novels. From the 1850s through the 1870s, scores of short stories formulated a popular and distinct subgenre, the urban haunted-house tale, which has received no attention in the scholarship on literary representations of London. That scholarship has focused primarily on the realist novel, arguing for an affinity between realist form and urban content, while simultaneously observing that the British novel's manifest commitment to domestic ideology either prevented novelists from depicting London at all or led them to depict the city in terms of an antithesis between a tumultuous, dangerous space of urban crowds, streets, and slums, and a serene, restorative space of middle-class domesticity, an opposition exemplified in novels such as *Oliver Twist* and *Bleak House*. The many ways that realist novels often failed to sustain those oppositions have also been demonstrated by critics with a persuasiveness that reduces the urgency of any need to rehearse that deconstruction anew.[110] My aim instead is to define and interpret a set of texts that showed a crowd already present within the middle-class home and represented the home as simultaneously urban and domestic. Those stories constitute a significant intertext for the realist novel (and thus provide future levers for understanding that form's relationship to domestic ideology and urban discourse) and add significantly to our understanding of how the Victorians represented the relationship between domestic life and London.

Ghost stories flourished in the 1850s and 1860s, precisely the period when even London's suburbs began to replicate the urban conditions they had been designed to circumvent (crowding, subdivision, transience), and when suburban houses became more likely to be subdivided into lodgings.[111] A majority of ghost stories were haunted-house stories, with titles like "A House to Let," "The Ghost at Laburnum Villa," "The Haunted House in Westminster," and "The Haunted Lodging House."[112] A large number of those haunted-house stories were set in London (as opposed to the isolated country estates that readers now commonly associate with the ghostly tale), and the mode in which they represented supernatural events was a surprisingly realistic one. In 1889 Vernon Lee underscored how her psychological ghost stories broke from the Victorian ones of "our fathers," precisely because that previous generation of supernatural writers had believed that "ghosts have an existence outside our fancy and emotion." Indeed, she qualified their belief in the authenticity of ghosts, and their corresponding investment in realism, as domestic and suburban: in Victorian fiction, ghosts "stumbled and fumbled . . . among the arm-chairs and rep sofas of reality" and writers invoked the supernatural only to "land us in Islington or Shepherd's Bush."[113]

The taste for supernatural tales set in London's suburban houses was not an isolated phenomenon; indeed, both the cultural purchase and historical specificity of those stories become clear only when we place the works in the traditions and conditions that shaped their production: representations of London as haunted; figurations of homes as haunted; the literary market created by the periodical press; and the literary history of supernatural fiction.

During much of the eighteenth and nineteenth centuries, haunting was perceived as both particularly extraneous and endemic to London. As representatives of superseded eras and modes of thought, ghosts were seen by some as antithetical to a metropolis conceived of as a modern seat of rational enlightenment.[114] For example, when John Ingram noted in a book on England's haunted houses that "more buildings hav[e] a reputation for being haunted . . . in towns and cities than in sparsely populated places," he qualified that "circumstance" as "curious" and, in his following sentence, contradictory: "The British metropolis, despite its gas-lamps and guardian police, contains many residences that even now are left to the mercies of those spectral tenants who alone inhabit them."[115] Ingram's "even now" underscored the contradictions between ghosts and modern London; ghosts represented a drag on modernity, an exception in a regime defined by new technologies of visualization and surveillance designed to abolish all hidden dangers, including specters. Compton Mackenzie simply assumed that ghosts could not exist in London; of a suburban house reputed to be haunted, he remarked "by what such a comparatively recent building without any kind of history attached to it should be haunted, nobody explained." [116] Conceived as the persistence of the past, haunting seemed antithetical to a city whose recently constructed buildings belonged only to the present.

At the same time, other writers saw ghosts as proper to London, either because they emphasized the city's antiquity, or because ghosts too could be modern. Once some parts of London had been renovated, other parts seemed "ancient," producing a distinctly modern appreciation of London as a historical city whose own embodiment of the past made it hospitable to ghosts. [117] Alternatively, a modernizing city could make even ghosts contemporary. As the literary critic E. J. Clery shows, the heightened sense of London as a modern metropolis of consumption and spectacle effected an "urban relocation of the supernatural," which removed ghosts from the sphere of belief and inserted them into "the fashion system of the city" as "metropolitan diversions." [118] As "The Latest Thing in Ghosts" (1862) put it, "Modern readers must have modern ghosts," and "progress is the word for ghost stories. . . . Ruined castles have given place to railway stations; trackless forests to the streets of cities." [119]

If Victorian London was particularly likely to be haunted, so were Victorian houses. Architectural theory frequently invoked the ontological confusions caused by spectrality's tendency to animate the inanimate when they invested physical space with human attributes and ascribed imaginative influence and moral determinacy to homes. As Ruskin put it in *The Seven Lamps of Architecture,* "All architecture proposes an effect on the human mind, not merely a service to the human frame." Ruskin insisted that powerful buildings commanded "sympathy," that is, produced sensible effects in their viewers; and he suggested in turn that buildings themselves were also sensible, by evaluating architecture in terms of vitality or "deadness" and saying of "Living Architecture" that "there is sensation in every inch of it." [120] The imputation of agency to architectural structures contributed to the ease with which they could become personified as subjects that spoke to or influenced human beings. Articles in *The Builder* made the same argument specific to dwellings, stating that "the standard of mechanical and moral excellence must be raised at the same time" and that "a tidy, well-arranged dwelling leads to observances of better manners and feelings of self-respect, induces neatness and industry, and elevates in tone the character of all its occupants." [121] The article personified space by sliding from the loose causation of "leads to" and "induces" to the direct agency predicated by "elevates"; its syntax suggested that dwellings were active subjects working on inhabitants who were malleable objects.

A literal claim for the haunting of houses was promulgated by the spiritualist movement that flourished during the second half of the nineteenth century, a period one historian terms "the heyday of the middle-class ghost."[122] Recent histories of spiritualism focus on mediumship, possession, and gender, but the common belief that the dead manifested themselves in the houses of the living constituted an equally salient aspect of the movement.[123] Spiritualists understood spectrality in spatial and temporal terms, interpreting the dead who seemed to belong to an irretrievable past as being merely at an accessible distance. F. J. Theobald updated biblical language to report that "[s]piritualism has come to throw down the partition that has so long been raised up between the natural and the supernatural worlds," and asserted "the power spirits possess of conveying messages to different friends at a distance."[124] That insistence on translating the difference between the dead and the living into spatial terms contributed to the spiritualist focus on the home as a privileged site for apparitions.[125] C. Maurice Davies, a chronicler of religious life in London, noted that people "have been accustomed to associate this subject [spiritualism] . . . with dancing tables and locomotive furniture"; "table-rapping" and "table-turning" became common terms for seances in which furniture became animated by the presence of the dead; messages from beyond took the form of writing on the walls of rooms; and volumes that documented the existence of haunted houses included floor plans showing exactly how ghosts navigated domestic spaces.[126]

Thus, while the premises grounding supernatural fiction may seem to us culturally marginal, for the Victorians they were in fact culturally central. Haunted-house stories, however, differed from architectural and spiritualist writings in their emphasis on the dire consequences of haunting: not the pleasures of animate buildings, nor the comforts of dead family members returning to their old homes, but the terror and damage inflicted by malevolent, disruptive ghosts, who, in many narratives, drive families out of their houses and in some cases even kill them. Nevertheless, the pervasiveness of haunting in Victorian culture helps explain one of the defining features of haunted-house stories—their popularity, attested to in part by their sheer numbers: at least a hundred ghost stories were published in the years between 1850 and 1870, throughout the year and in the special Christmas numbers that some periodicals devoted to ghost stories. Their popularity can also be inferred from their publication in the periodical press, whose scope expanded vastly in the 1830s and again in the 1850s and 1860s, as a result of new technologies and tax repeals that led to cheaper prices; increased leisure time and higher literacy rates that created more interest in reading material; and improved distribution made possible by railways. When Charles Dickens founded *Household Words* in 1850, he helped launch a market for numerous magazines and journals, mostly monthlies, which published entertaining fiction for middle-class readers. *Household Words* was followed by *All the Year Round* in 1859, *Temple Bar* in 1861, *London Society* in 1862, *Argosy* in 1866, *Belgravia* in 1867, and *Tinsley's* in 1868.[127] All had circulations in the thousands and all published numerous ghost stories, written by some of the most popular male and female authors of the day: Charles Dickens, Edward Bulwer-Lytton, Elizabeth Gaskell, Margaret Oliphant, Charlotte Riddell, Dinah Mulock Craik, Wilkie Collins, Sheridan Le Fanu, Rhoda Broughton, and Mary Braddon.[128]

Formal and thematic features distinguished Victorian ghost stories from other types of supernatural fiction, including contemporary French tales of the uncanny and the earlier Gothic novel. French supernatural fiction was never a particularly popular genre and almost never concentrated on ghostly dwellings; instead, French ghost stories were usually written in a romantic, subjective strain and focused on themes of doubling, necrophilia, hypnotic influence, mysticism, and dream states.[129] The Gothic English novels that flourished during the late eighteenth century often included ghosts but differed in several ways from Victorian supernatural tales. Although both the Gothic novel and Victorian ghost stories mobilized architecture to create supernatural effects, architecture in the Gothic novel set a fairly constant mood, while architecture in the Victorian supernatural tale changed over the course of a narrative. The Gothic novel focused on labyrinthine, secret, even ruined spaces in ancient aristocratic castles, so symbolic of the past and of mystery that they appear haunted even before any ghosts literally appear. By contrast, Victorian ghost stories concentrated on contemporary middle-class houses whose initial coziness, mundanity, and legibility get disrupted and altered by apparitions; "A Night in a Ghost-Chamber" (1872), for example, is set in "the most unromantic, unghostly-looking house possible, being, in fact, nothing more nor less than a perky cockney 'villa,' of the £35 or £40 a year class, abutting on the main thoroughfare of an equally cockney suburb."[130] Gothic novels were set on the Continent and in the distant past; they featured vulnerable heroines persecuted by male villains; in some cases, they undercut supernatural devices by offering rational explanations for them; and, in almost all cases, their third-person narration used deliberately vague evocations of apparitions to evoke terror and the sublime.[131] Victorian ghost stories, by contrast, tended to be set in nineteenth-century England, often in London, and almost exclusively used first-person narrators, usually men, whose gendered associations with rationalism supplemented the realistic precision with which they documented both their sightings of and responses to ghosts (spectrality, on the other hand, was not particularly gendered, since ghosts in Victorian fiction were as likely to be male as to be female).[132]

Realism constituted the formal hallmark of the Victorian ghost story, which often explicitly announced its status as truthful testimony; Mrs. Henry Wood's "Reality or Delusion?" opened by emphasizing the first term of its title: "This is a ghost story. Every word of it is true." [133] Victorian ghost stories also used the more seamless realistic techniques commonly deployed in novels. Their narratives usually opened by invoking the "hermeneutic code" Barthes deemed characteristic of realism, providing coherent, suspenseful accounts of a mystery and its resolution.[134] Instead of modalizations such as "seems" or "perhaps," which emphasize the narrator's subjectivity and uncertainty, their first-person narrators used objective language, even when describing their emotions. Frequent use of proper names and references to familiar places and current dates certified the tales' fidelity to conventional descriptive coordinates and furthered the impression of a correspondence between their words and the empirical world they claimed to represent.[135] Finally, many stories engaged in the exhaustive description typical of nineteenth-century realism, usually taking a house as the object to be described.[136]

The realistic narration and settings of Victorian ghost stories coexisted, however, with events that readers experienced as less real. Although we have seen that quite a few Victorians believed that they saw ghosts and many more had recourse to haunting as a vehicle for expressing the tenor of a dwelling or city, even those who credited the existence of spirits did not accord them the same ontological status as living beings or real objects. The Victorian ghost story thus amalgamated realism and unreality in ways that compromised the absolute status of each mode. Realistic technique conferred materiality and plausibility on supernatural events, but that plausibility was circumscribed by its location within a fiction, as well as by the representation of events whose supernatural character offset the narrative's referential gestures. Victorian supernatural fiction thus oscillated between the real and the unreal, the solid and the evanescent, the visualizable and the imperceptible—an oscillation that both derived from and extended to the ghosts and haunted houses they described. That oscillation enabled them simultaneously to dramatize the middle-class house's distance from the domestic ideals of tranquillity and insularity and to blunt that revelation by couching it in terms of the supernatural.[137] Haunted-house stories made manifest the contradictions between the middle class's domestic ideals and its dwelling practices in sensationally heightened ways; at the same time, however, they rendered that manifestation of contradiction oblique, vague, and hence more tolerable, by routing it through a figure. And by making that figure a ghost, they blurred the revelation even further, since ghosts were figures for immateriality at the same time as they metaphorically materialized the noisy, dangerous presences plaguing the middle-class home.[138]

Haunted-house stories broadcast the urban deformation of the domestic ideal. They concentrated on houses that were rented, not owned, and on the inconveniences that collected around renting; they depicted homes that were uncomfortable, riddled with noise and dirt; and they set in motion ghosts who attacked the middle-class home's status as an insular, individuating single-family structure.[139] The first event in a majority of haunted-house stories consists of renting a house, and the stories link the fact of rental to the existence of ghosts: either a house can't be rented because it is reputed to be haunted, or it rents below its value, or its rental status is accentuated because ghosts lead to high turnover among tenants.[140] The narrator of Charlotte Riddell's "The Uninhabited House" (1875) is a clerk at the law firm in charge of renting the eponymous "residence, 'suitable in every respect for a family of position,'" but in which, as the title suggests, no tenant will stay for long.[141] In Bulwer-Lytton's "The Haunted and the Haunters" (1859), one of the founding stories of the genre, an initially skeptical narrator sets out to investigate reports of "a haunted house in the midst of London . . . [i]n a dull but respectable thoroughfare," complete with a sign advertising "Apartments Furnished." Because the house is haunted, its tenants keep fleeing, reducing it in effect to the most transient of lodging houses. The house can be rehabilitated only by tearing down a secret room that was the site of a crime, but even in its renovated state, its owner simply "let[s] it out to advantage" to a new "tenant" whose claim on the property remains no better than that of the apparitions—called "vagrancies"—who had occupied it before.[142] Rhoda Broughton's "The Truth, the Whole Truth, and Nothing but the Truth" (1868) presents the correspondence between two fashionable women, one of whom finds "season" lodgings in West London that appear to embody the dream of every domestic economy, "a palace at the cost of a hovel," but which turns out to contain a terrifying vision that literally kills a man who confronts it.[143] The anonymous "Story of Clifford House" (1878) tells of the nefarious consequences attendant on a woman who has "grown tired of my lovely country home" and writes to a London "house agent" in order to locate a "town residence" that will epitomize metropolitan luxury. Though she and her family are the exclusive tenants of the house they eventually rent, her initial impression of "unseen inhabitants" is borne out by the appearance of two tenacious ghosts who persistently haunt the apartment, attack her husband, and eventually drive them "out of . . . house and home." [144] Rather than use spectrality as a figure for the vagaries of paternal property transmission and the dilution of aristocratic power, as stories about haunted country estates did, stories of rented urban houses emphasized an utter lack of property and the inability of London lodgers to assume even the temporary stability of a well-ensconced tenant.[145]

In most Victorian haunted-house stories, apparitions manifest themselves as noises before they appear visually, and hearing them usually causes as much annoyance and fear as seeing them. The translation of ghosts into noises within the house resonates with a recurrent motif of the discourse of domestic complaint—the compromise of the middle-class house's insularity by the noises of neighbors, both within a subdivided house and in neighboring houses. Indeed, in some haunted-house stories, the rational explanation of loud neighbors precedes the supernatural rationale of clamorous ghosts. Charles Dickens's "The Lawyer and the Ghost" (1836) tells the story of a lawyer occupying a "set of chambers, in one of the most ancient Inns," who hears a groan in his room after he threatens aloud to turn a wooden press into firewood. At first he takes the noise to be "some young fellow in the next chamber," but after a pale figure emerges from the press, he realizes that he already has a neighbor within his apartment. The apparition asserts a prior claim to the rooms, as though they were real property: "The apartment is mine: leave it to me!" Though the new occupant cleverly persuades the ghost to travel elsewhere, the ghost's presence permanently redefines the lawyer as an ephemeral "tenant," the only word the narrator uses to designate him after the ghost appears.[146] In "The Story of Clifford House," a woman tells how upon viewing her "first town residence" after marriage, the rooms appeared odd, "as if unseen inhabitants were stealthily crouching behind them." Her husband tries to understand the suspiciously low rent by inquiring about "unpleasant neighbours"; although the house agent's clerk denies that there are any, the story reveals that the apartment does have "unpleasant neighbours" *inside* the house, in the form of two noisy and violent ghosts, loudly audible through what another story called "the thin walls and floors of a London house." [147] Even a parodic commentary on contemporary ghost stories whose intention was to demystify ghosts confirmed the equivalence between ghosts and neighbors. The narrator of "The Latest Thing in Ghosts" (1862) explained:

> I am not a believer in ghosts, and it is a happy thing for me that I do not, for, according to the ghost-story tellers, I live in a thoroughly haunted house. I hear in the stillness of the night the wailing of a child. I am often disturbed in my sleep by a heavy footfall on the stairs. . . . Now, all these things are said to be certain signs that the spirits are about. . . . But . . . [w]hen I hear the wailing of a child, I put it down to Mrs. Jones's baby, next door. . . . When I hear the footfall on the stairs, and the trampling of feet overhead, I might shudder and think it a ghost, of course—but I don't. I conclude at once that it is the man who lodges above me, who comes in very late, and wears shamefully thick boots. [148]

While in haunted-house stories, neighbors turn out to be ghosts, in "The Latest Thing in Ghosts," ghosts turn out to be neighbors.

The ghosts in haunted-house stories invade apartments not only through sound but also through a physical presence that in effect compromises the insularity of dwellings, deprives them of domestic comfort and privacy, and ultimately crowds human tenants out of their homes. The narrator of another Dickens story, "To Be Taken with a Grain of Salt" (1865), reads about a murder site in a newspaper and sees "that bedroom passing through my room" as he sits "in chambers in Piccadilly, very near to the corner of St. James's Street." The story culminates with an apparition entering the narrator's apartment through a heavily locked door that leads from the dressing room within the apartment to the house's common staircase, shifting the question of crowding from the supernatural superimposition of rooms spread out over two different buildings to the actual dissolution of privacy within a single building. [149]

As noisy, intrusive strangers inescapably present within the middle-class home, ghosts figured the many ways that the middle-class London house failed, in practice, to secure the qualities advertised in the domestic ideal. At the same time, references to ghosts as criminal and even diseased brought the haunted house in rhetorical proximity to the lodging house described by the urban explorers. Simply by exposing the problems of middle-class houses to view, the haunted-house story eliminated what in the discourse of urban exploration was a crucial differentiation between the homes of the poor, always available for investigation, and the homes of the middle classes, carefully screened from any scrutinizing gaze. Haunted-house fiction made the connections between lodging houses and middle-class houses even stronger, by emphasizing that once haunted, even respectable houses took on the characteristics attributed to the lodging houses of the poor. The landlord of "The Haunted and the Haunters," who has fully refurbished an already genteel house, finds that haunting has made it as transient as a lodging house: "I never had one lodger who stayed more than three days." [150] Ghosts also conferred on middle-class houses the contagion and illness that urban investigators like Chadwick had associated with the housing of the poor. "Everybody knows how contagious fear is," explains the narrator of Le Fanu's "An Account of Some Strange Disturbances in Aungier Street," and in many stories illness and death follow as consequences of seeing a ghost. [151]

Just as lodging houses had been described in terms of narratives of social fall (degeneration from upper-class single-family houses into tenements) and moral decay (associated with the corruption of their tenants), the middle-class houses of haunted fiction became subject to similar narratives of descent. In "The Haunted and the Haunters," the investigating narrator discovers that the guilty secret of the house and of its ghost lies in the story of a former tenant who started out "the daughter of very respectable tradespeople" but sank "lower and lower" after committing a murder, to the point where she was "placed in charge [as a porter] of the very house which she had rented as mistress in the first year of her wedded life." [152] Being forced to haunt the house after death represents the logical culmination of the domestic social slide she had begun there during her life. Ghosts also transformed locales into places of ill repute; the hero of "The Wraith of Barnjum" (1884), assiduously followed by the ghost of a murdered friend, is asked to leave his lodgings by his landlady, who "would not have such nasty things in *her* house" and then gets expelled from his club for "introducing an acquaintance of questionable antecedents and disreputable exterior into the smoking-room." [153]

In Victorian ghost stories, haunted middle-class houses in London become, like the lodging houses of the poor, scenes of crime and familial dissolution, with specters often replaying the murder of a spouse, sibling, or child. Indeed, corpses litter middle-class houses in supernatural fiction as they did the houses of the poor in public health investigations. The ghosts in "The Haunted and the Haunters" have a "corpselike aspect," and in "To Be Taken with a Grain of Salt," the vision of a murdered man with a face "the colour of impure wax" persists in the narrator's rooms.[154] In Mary Braddon's "The Shadow in the Corner" (1879), both the house and its owner possess "the same faded complexion, the same look of slow decay," which culminates with the appearance of "a shadow in . . . the shape of a dead body hanging against the wall."[155] Sometimes the corpse made death itself contagious; when the hero of Le Fanu's "Strange Disturbances" sees the dead judge who has become his ghostly "fellow-lodger," he feels "that I had no more power to speak or stir than if I had been myself a corpse."[156]

The deployment of ghosts in haunted-house fiction was realistic by virtue of its adherence to realistic techniques and by virtue of its mimeticism: even for readers who did not believe that ghosts were real, the effects produced by ghosts in haunted-house stories corresponded point by point to the material conditions of middle-class life in London deplored by the discourse of domestic complaint. Attributing those effects to ghosts helped offset the affront to class identity caused by exposing the middle class's failure to live up to its own ideal, as well as its failure to fully differentiate itself from the poor. The ghosts in haunted-house stories, however, did double duty: not only did they simultaneously materialize and dematerialize a troublingly accurate picture of the middle-class home but, by driving away the narrator and reader who peered too closely into the house that should be private, they worked to block the very processes that generated supernatural fiction.

The pressures exerted by the ghosts, narrators, and readers of Victorian supernatural fiction on houses that should have been private point to a contradiction between domestic ideology, which as we have seen, advocated a privacy that required concealing the home from view, and realism, which paradoxically attempted to put private life on display *as private*. The contradiction between a privacy that by one cultural definition had to remain hidden, and yet by another cultural imperative had to be displayed, flickered throughout the British realist novel but was constantly visible in haunted-house stories, where the narrator's and reader's entrance into a house inevitably leads to an eruption of invasive presences (the ghosts) who simultaneously mirror and repel the narrator's and reader's breach of the home. Not for nothing is the ghost who drives a family of middle-class tenants out of the house they lease in Le Fanu's "The Ghost of a Hand" (1861) represented by a disembodied hand, which first appears "stealthily placed upon the stone window-sill outside," then begins "striving to force [its] way in." When the skeptical husband goes to the "hall-door" to drive it away, he inadvertently finds he has "actually given admission to the besieger." [157] The hand's immense speed and powers signify, of course, the spectral powers of the judge who used to inhabit the house, but the hand that leaves an "impression" in dust to show that he has "established himself in the house" also stands for the shaping, invasive hand of the author, who can write the story that exposes the family's house faster than they can hide, as well as the hand of the reader, who turns the pages of the text much more quickly than the characters within it experience the events it recounts. [158] Similarly, the hero of Dickens's "The Lawyer and the Ghost" exorcises the ghost who haunts the wooden paper press in his rented chambers by highlighting the powers that the apparition shares with an omniscient narrator: "I suppose space is nothing to you," he tells the ghost, advising him that since he can go anywhere he wants, he should seek out better quarters than the apartment he is currently haunting. [159] When ghost stories concluded, as they usually did, by chasing the reader and narrator out of the house, along with the protagonists, they in fact restored an extreme version of the privacy whose invasion they had depicted—a privacy that could never be documented, because it excluded the presence of any recorder or observer.

Coda: The Englishman's Castle as His Grave

Was there any space in London that could materialize the domestic ideal? Although haunted-house stories exposed the ways that the ideal failed to materialize in homes filled with ghosts, they also suggested an affinity between dwellings and death that was susceptible to reversal: if the homes of the living were disrupted by the dead, perhaps the dwellings of the dead could be redeemed for a tranquil domesticity. Indeed, from the 1840s on, debates about "interment in towns" developed the urban explorers' notion of the lodging house as a metonym and metaphor for urban crowding and contamination and at the same time echoed architectural discourse with proposals that vaunted the domestic pleasures of suburban cemeteries. No Victorian discourse analogous to that of domestic complaint emerged, however, to protest that the new cemeteries had failed to realize the ideals of property ownership, individuality, and rural serenity; rather, numerous commentators celebrated the extent to which London's new suburban burial grounds had finally provided the city with a site that realized the domestic ideal so often contradicted by its houses.

Both the discourse of urban exploration and the discourse of domestic complaint equated London's houses with the presence of dead bodies, assimilating them to the urban graveyards that were perceived as dangerously crowded and even productive of infectious vapors. Public health literature commonly associated high-density housing forms such as lodging houses and tenements with high rates of mortality or explained high urban death rates by describing cities as enormous and crowded dwelling places, lodging houses writ large.[160] To live in a lodging house or tenement was to live with death. A contributor to *Knight's London* personified the houses of the poor as murderous agents, "wretched dens, hidden in back courts and alleys, where the poor are smothered," which if they did not kill their "inmates" outright, reduced them to a mechanical state of life-in-death: in the lodgings of St. Giles, "thought, and hope, and exertion . . . seemed dead in the human bodies which moved mechanically about amid its pestilential effluvia."[161]

Sensational anecdotes recurred throughout the literature of urban exploration concerning dead bodies that moldered in tenements and lodging houses and made those residences "tainted" sites of "decomposition," transforming lodging houses into what a *Quarterly Review* article called, quite simply, "haunts."[162] John Knox cited a London medical officer's lurid description of "a woman suffering in travail, in the midst of males and females of different families that tenant the same room— where birth and death go hand in hand—where the child but newly-born, and the corpse waiting for interment, have no separation from each other, or from the rest of the inmates."[163] A twentieth-century historian of cemeteries has called this enclosure of corpses a domestication of the dead, but for nineteenth-century observers of rotting corpses, tenements failed to be domestic spaces at all.[164] Truly domesticated dwellings maintained distinctions between life and death, health and taint, and the presence of the dead within tenements undermined their functions as habitats.

The discourse of domestic complaint similarly linked London's middle-class houses to death. Articles in the architectural press pointed out that speculative "jerry-builders" often constructed houses out of materials derived from decayed houses, even old graveyards, to erect what critics described as veritable death-traps—"painted sepulchres."[165] A reporter on new houses in Camden Town described "bricks . . . dug out

of the foundations of the old buildings now disappearing from Bloomsbury, literally rotten," an internal rot belied by the attractive "exterior
of these sepulchres of decayed brick." [166] Filled with decomposing matter, subject as a result to a flimsiness that turned their occupants into
corpses, suburban middle-class houses once again failed to distinguish
themselves fully from the lodging houses of the central city, sharing with
lodging houses an inability to be distinct from graveyards.

During the 1840s, public health reformers and concerned citizens began to argue that London's burial grounds and cemeteries should be removed from the city to less populated suburban districts. Like lodging
houses, the graveyards attached to churches in the central city were seen
as sources of contagion, repeatedly condemned as overcrowded, and
rhetorically designated as unspeakable and indescribable. Edwin Chadwick's report on interment in towns identified the decomposing bodies
in cemeteries and burial grounds as contaminants of London's atmosphere and water supply and warned against the ill effects of layers
of dead bodies, "imperfectly interred" and "closely surrounded by the
abodes of the living"; his report on the state of health in towns criticized
the equally contagious power of those "abodes of the living" to kill their
inhabitants. [167] Just as books on London routinely drew attention to
overcrowding in tenements and in the "million-peopled" city generally,
the polemic against urban cemeteries—"cities of the dead"—repeatedly
drew attention to the excessive number of bodies contained in dispro-
portionately small spaces. [168] *Payne's Illustrated London* commented on
the "crowded state of the present insufficient and improper receptacles
for the dead" throughout London, and Thomas Miller called cemeteries "these ever-changing and common lodging houses" because of the
transience and crowding of their inhabitants: "in the very heart of our
close and over-crowded cities . . . the dead of to-day are crammed
amongst the remains which have been disinterred to give them a short
lodgement . . . they again in turn are cast out . . . in so unfeeling, heart-
less, and brutal a manner, that we dare not shock our readers with the
revolting details." [169] Miller's inability to convey details about cemeteries echoed the frequent designation of lodging houses and tenements as
disgusting beyond description, peopled by the "unheard-of human horrors" that G. A. Sala termed "ghoules." [170]

Writers who sought to reform London burial grounds advocated so-
lutions that resembled those that philanthropists and government investigators sought to apply to lodging houses: regulating them; transferring
them from the city to the suburbs; and restructuring them along the lines

of the miniature English castle by enclosing them completely, surrounding them with cultivated nature, and securing them as property that
would connect past and future generations.[171] As opposed to Paris,
which was able to incorporate the cemetery into the city by making the
cemetery itself more urban, in London reform worked to make the
houses of both the living and the dead more suburban, modified copies
of a rural ideal.[172] It proved easier, however, to halt the burial of the
dead within city limits than to demolish or renovate all unsanitary urban housing; an 1852 act simply empowered the Privy Council to prevent interment in any place of burial within the metropolis.

The new cemeteries of the 1830s and 1840s were not only literally situated in the suburbs but also featured architectural styles and irregular,
curved landscaping that "might well be taken for . . . suburban *tea-
gardens*." [173] Indeed, before the General Cemetery Company, formed in
1830, chose its Kensal Green site, it seriously considered the Eyre Estate
and Primrose Hill, which later became important suburban developments. John Loudon, the great advocate of suburban homes and gardens, also promoted the garden cemetery, and the London Cemetery
Company was founded in 1836 by a landscape gardener and an architect. At the first meeting of the new company, its chairman declared that
the new suburban cemetery would be "an honour to the country," attributing the same national identity to the suburban cemetery that architects had accorded to idealized versions of suburban homes.[174]

Just as the ideal home was meant to concentrate lasting memories
within its physical and imagined borders, the new "suburban cemeteries would become spots filled with solemn associations," wrote Thomas
Miller in *Picturesque Sketches of London* (1852).[175] The domesticated,
suburban cemetery would facilitate *controlled* haunting, in which memories pleasantly resuscitated the dead: in suburban cemeteries, "[t]he
dead seem to belong to us. . . . [W]hile gazing over the landscape, they
seem to accompany us, and to live again in our thoughts; or we stand,
as it were, in a great picture-gallery, surrounded with portraits of the
dead. . . . We believe that the dead will again rise." [176] The author of this
reverie begins by contemplating an external field ("gazing *over* the landscape"), an activity that conjures up images of the dead within the mental interior ("in our thoughts"); the writer then relocates this process
within one of the aristocratic manor's most important rooms, the picture gallery containing portraits of previous inhabitants. In the ghost
story, such portraits often enabled protagonists to identify an unruly,
usually guilt-ridden ghost as a former inhabitant and proprietor of the

building it haunted. In the controlled, pleasurable haunting that Miller envisions for the suburban cemetery, however, the apparition of the dead confirms a reassuring vision of the afterlife and provides the occasion for transforming the cemetery from an exterior space shared by many strangers into a grand house that embodies the transmission of property, names, and familial images from one generation to the next.

The reform of city churchyards led to cemeteries that successfully embodied stately suburban manors and, in the form of freehold purchases of graves, offered prospective clients the real property ownership that was lacking in both the burial grounds of London's churchyards and in London's houses. As one historian has written, "[t]he leases on the best houses [in London] . . . were beyond the pockets of most of the middle class; at Kensal Green, however, the availability of burial plots in perpetuity offered a permanent stake in a development that consciously expressed a cognate gentility."[177] The ability to own a family plot meant that the one place where the London paterfamilias could realize the national and domestic implications of the phrase "the Englishman's home is his castle" was the grave: "Ownership of land, what English politicians liked to call 'a stake in the country,' could extend itself beyond the grave, because the grave itself could become real property. . . . Perpetual possession ensured that, just as the individual body would remain undisturbed, so the larger body of the bourgeois family would remain intact."[178] A sense of property could be developed simply by visiting a suburban cemetery; just as the Englishman attained a special relationship to the stuff of his nation when he inhabited a house that contained only the sky of England above him and the ground of England below, so "[w]hen the Englishman wanders among the tombs of his forefathers . . . he is then, in a peculiar sense, a denizen of the soil on which he stands."[179]

Octavia Hill, who devoted most of her energies to improving housing for poor tenants, proposed to use the urban graveyards made defunct by the suburban cemeteries to help even London's poor move closer to the domestic ideal and to provide them with "a stake in the country." In an essay on "Our Common Land" (1877) that invoked many of the elements of the domestic ideal examined earlier in this chapter, she began by advocating the protection of common public lands (such as Clapham Commons) so that "the small shop-keeper, . . . the hard-working clerk, who will probably never own a square of English land" might continue to enjoy "those few spots which are [the] . . . common birthright in the soil . . . of their native England."[180] In Hill's vision, commons afforded the lowest echelons of the middle class with the same genealogical glue that freehold plots in suburban cemeteries offered to those higher in England's social ranks: "It will give a sense of a common possession to succeeding generations. It will give a share in his country to be inherited by the poorest citizen. It will be a link between the many and through the ages . . . which neither time nor outward change can destroy—as people are bound together by any common memory." [181]

Hill also outlined a plan to increase the number of open spaces within the poor, densely built areas of central London that lacked even commons: her proposal was to renovate the now inactive graveyards. The embellishment of defunct burial grounds, Hill argued, would provide poor Londoners with a better relationship to English soil and to English domesticity. Just as Miller envisioned the cemetery as a picture gallery, Hill imagined transforming city churchyards into the kinds of private, interior spaces that cramped tenements lacked. She advocated "laying out and opening small central spaces as public gardens . . . which might be used by [poor people] . . . in common as sitting-rooms in summer" and pointed out that "[t]here are, all over London, little spots unbuilt over, still strangely preserved among the sea of houses—our graveyards. They are capable of being made into beautiful outdoor sitting-rooms." [182] The disquiet caused by the insufficiencies of London's homes was thus laid to rest only in the homes of the dead. In the suburban cemeteries converted into ideal estates, in the urban graveyards recreated as domestic interiors, both London's crowded burial grounds and its crowded houses could be redeemed, and the relationships among memory, property, and national domesticity could be properly realigned.

PART THREE

Interiorization and Its Discontents

4

Enclosing Paris, 1852–1880

IN MAY 1855 AN ARTICLE BY FERDINAND SILAS in a short-lived newspaper, *Le Bourgeois de Paris,* playfully exhorted its readers to rebel against landlords and to "break with your effeminate, citified habits . . . return to the savage, patriarchal nature of your ancestors the Gaul. . . . [A]s long as you revel in the hybrid existence that the nineteenth century has set up for you, you will be nothing but dressed-up automatons—serving at best as tenants for your landlords."[1] With this statement, the article dismissed urban modernity as a historical and social degradation that reduced the bourgeois male tenant to a feminized machine. Rejecting any positive view of progress, Silas contrasted contemporary Parisian men unfavorably with their stronger, more masculine forebears.

Silas's article was one of many similar protests against the changes in the Parisian housing market triggered by the developments known as Haussmannization—the construction, by Napoleon III and his prefect of the Seine, Georges Haussmann, of an imperial capital city of monuments and public buildings, broad boulevards, and new infrastructure (sewers, gas and water networks). Haussmann and Napoleon III aimed to improve hygiene, facilitate traffic circulation, and prevent workers from building the barricades used so effectively in older, narrow streets during the 1848 revolution.[2] In so doing, they explicitly took London as a model, in ways that the English themselves rarely registered; as we saw in the previous chapter, most British writers starkly contrasted the two capitals.[3] Yet from 1850 to 1880, French urban planners adapted Paris to London's characteristic urban configurations of squares and parks; generated plans for model workers' housing, which included a translation of Henry Roberts's writings on the subject, commissioned by Napoleon III in 1850; and initiated state-sponsored public health investigations and street improvements similar to ones undertaken in England.[4] Indeed, French officials, who benefited from the powers of a dictatorial, centralized government, were able to institute many of the changes they associated with England on a far grander scale than anything undertaken in London, where a byzantine system of municipal administration made coordinated, wholesale transformations of the urban landscape almost impossible.[5]

French writers also began to take the English house as the prototype of a newly private domesticity, frequently referring, as we will see throughout this chapter, to the need to create a sense of *comfort* and *home,* citing those words in English and often glossing them as having no exact equivalent in French. In a lecture on housing at the 1878 International Exhibition, for example, Charles Lucas praised the suburban villas of London: "The Londoner . . . has all the advantages, all the charms of property, along with a dwelling that provides all the hygiene of the country, and he realizes the dream so dear to the English, and which should be so dear to everyone, of the 'at home,' the home of one's own [*la maison à soi*], in which to raise a family."[6] The internal political shifts effected by the French reactions to the revolutions of 1848 and 1871 made urban observers, domestic advisors, public health reformers, and architects newly amenable to viewing Paris through an English lens that brought into focus a proprietary, masculine domesticity. Under the notoriously conservative regimes of the Second Empire and the early Third Republic, urban and architectural discourses began to oppose what the preceding era had celebrated—the apartment building's capacity to create continuity between the street and the home.

Opposition to the apartment house did nothing, however, to eradicate its role as the predominant Parisian building type. Indeed, by defining every Parisian as either owning or occupying an apartment, the heated and voluminous literature about conflicts between landlords and tenants defined every Parisian in terms of the apartment house. So universally current did the conflict between landlord and tenant become that by 1865 the newly revised edition of François Sergent's *Manuel complet du propriétaire et du locataire* (first issued in 1826) stated in its introduction: "Everyone is either a landlord or a tenant. These two in-

terests are opposed and their contact is constant."[7] That new antagonism stemmed from the dramatic economic shifts in apartment living
triggered by Haussmannization: increases in land values and rents (between 1851 and 1857, rents doubled in the city's central arrondissements) promoted an expensive, competitive housing market that pushed
poor people to the outskirts of the city, encouraged real-estate speculation, and promoted the construction of larger, more expensive apartment buildings.[8]

The debates about landlords and tenants did not simply register a series of empirical changes, however; their rhetoric also suggested that the
cultural understanding of the apartment house had shifted significantly.
Thus, even though historical evidence suggests that the sociological
profile of landlords did not radically alter between the 1820s and the
1850s (in both periods most landlords did not live in the buildings they
owned), the debates of the Second Empire attacked contemporary landlords for no longer being properly paternal; and even though the *portière* continued to be a real presence in apartment houses during the
Second Empire, she became far less visible in representations of those
buildings.[9] Whereas in a July Monarchy novel like *Le Cousin Pons*, the
portière had eclipsed both the proprietor and his tenants, in the 1850s
writers began to focus on landlords whose failure to be "good family
men [*pères de famille*] . . . [and] wise administrators, husbanding the future" induced a corresponding breakdown of familial masculinity in
tenants presumed to be exclusively male.[10]

The debates about Haussmannization's effects attributed to both
tenant and landlord a shared deviation from newly asserted masculine norms. In a discussion of Haussmannization's ill effects on tenants,
Alexandre Weill wrote that "no one lives anymore according to the pre-
cepts of the ordinary wisdom and good sense of the family man [*père de
famille*]," while Victor Bellet, in a text defending landlords, argued that
"today not a single Parisian landlord can deem himself certain of con-
serving and transmitting to his children the house that he has purchased
or received from his forefathers [*pères*]."[11] Writing from different political poles about opposed groups, both Weill and Bellet invoked a breakdown in the attributes of the *père*, particularly in the paternal ability to
preserve the qualities of "wisdom and good sense" along with quanti-
ties of property.

The emphasis on paternal masculinity as the measure of the apartment house's effect on Parisian life erased women from the debate about

Haussmannization's consequences, yet polemicists drew on a metaphorical femininity to explain what ailed the modern apartment building. When Weill opposed the "honesty" of older buildings to new ones whose luxurious facades belied an interior parsimony, he described that architectural artifice as particularly female: "All these petticoated houses are covered with makeup. . . . But as a result the interior is as it were dishonest. . . . Nowhere is there an honest row of large square rooms, with vast courtyards, as the architects of our forefathers used to make them." [12] Weill attacked the facade for the way its attractive exterior masked the truth of its deficient interior; by personifying the facade as female—dressed in women's undergarments and daubed with cosmetics—he folded his architectural critique into a misogynist commonplace about the deceptiveness of women's appearances.

Weill's use of clichés about femininity diverted attention from, by naturalizing, a surprising aspect of his complaint: its deployment of a new criterion for evaluating the apartment house. In the first half of the nineteenth century, as we have seen, Parisian architects and observers understood the apartment house to be a relatively transparent structure. That transparency meant that the apartment house's facade worked less as a boundary between an external, public surface and its internal, private depths, and more as the frame for a series of views into and out of the building. Weill's 1860 lament about dissembling facades implied that the exterior and interior of the apartment house should form a coherent unit but also made clear that the interior should prevail over the facade in any contest between the two: if the facade was more lavish than the interior, both would be corrupted, but for the interior to be more luxurious than the facade would pose no problem.

A new emphasis on the interior became widespread during the period from the 1850s to 1880—years that spanned the Second Empire and the first decade of the Third Republic, forming a unit because the Third Republic's conservative reaction to the Paris Commune uprising of 1871 created significant continuities between the two regimes with respect to urban planning. The new configuration of the interior as a hermetic, concealed, and strictly demarcated place, and the valorization of the involuted domesticity that accompanied that innovation, involved changes in both architectural practices and cultural values. Taken together, those changes produced what I call the interiorization of Paris, the creation of enclosed, private spaces through both physical and discursive means. This chapter traces the course of interiorization in architectural practice and in urban literature, public hygiene reports, domestic manuals, and architectural criticism, focusing on how those discourses advocated the convergence of interiorization and masculinity. Because the proponents of urban enclosure assumed women's domestic sequestration, they did not have to insist on it; rather, they expended the bulk of their energy on urging *men* to return and adhere to a domestic space. As Eugène Pelletan put it in *La Nouvelle Babylone* (1862), in order to "save the fatherland," it was necessary to "regenerate *men at home*"—a home increasingly conceived of along the English model examined in the previous chapter, a home more and more prescribed as antithetical to the apartment house.[13]

Haussmannization and the New Urban Landscape

My claim that Paris became interiorized after 1850 challenges the received interpretations of Second Empire Paris as a city of spectacle, *flânerie,* and circulation, a Paris making the transition, as the historian Jeanne Gaillard puts it, from an "introverted" to an "extroverted city," a Paris about which the Goncourt brothers famously wrote, "the interior is going to die. Life threatens to become public."[14] My purpose is not to dismiss those understandings of the city, but to complicate them by showing that during the Second Empire, the very notion of a public realm based on mobility, exchange, and visual display developed alongside articulations of urban space as a private realm of intromission and seclusion. The commercial spaces promoted by Haussmann contributed to the formation of a mass, consumer public, but they also produced a reaction against that very notion of the public, a reaction implicit in the Goncourt brothers' comments, which touted interiorization as a nostalgic alternative to an alienating modernity.

Private life did not emerge only as the nostalgic and belated antidote to an expanded public realm; rather, Haussmannization itself directly promoted the containment of urban spaces. Haussmann literally interiorized many of the city's common areas by enclosing activities and sites that had formerly been open and coextensive with the street. Street sellers, artisans, and mechanics were moved from the street into restricted, specialized locations. The open central markets of Les Halles, where women had been highly visible workers, were rebuilt as covered structures. Women had formerly done laundry at various points on the banks of the Seine; after first being restricted to delimited areas of the river, they were then encouraged by Napoleon III's building program to do their laundry indoors, in purpose-built *lavoirs*. The carnival festivals that had periodically overtaken Parisian streets were moved into dance halls.[15]

Haussmannization has historically been associated with a series of *percements* (literally, piercings) that opened up the cramped medieval city to a streamlined, rational network of wide boulevards, but it also consistently filled in open spaces. As the architectural historian David Van Zanten explains,

> A series of existing open spaces that had been markets . . . or street crossings . . . had their centers filled with curbed islands of grass, trees, and flower beds, protected with a grill . . . with traffic channeled around them. . . . [T]here was a tradition of transforming city spaces into interiors on special occasions. . . . [T]he delimitation, enclosing, planting, and manicuring of these spaces made . . . this permanent. . . . [P]ublic space [was] . . . subdivided, differentiated, and furnished. The voids in the plan of Paris, as they broadened under Haussmann, filled with something new.[16]

Pedestrian sidewalks newly lined with trees, kiosks, newspaper stands, and urinals became physically and visually isolated and protected from the road and its vehicular traffic. By contrast with the adjoining, newly widened roadways, the embellished sidewalks appeared to be relatively interiorized spaces out of doors.

The spatial relationships between buildings and streets also changed in the areas reconfigured by Haussmann, whose emphasis on long, straight boulevards with perspective views of monuments at either one or both ends meant that the majority of new streets were built to direct the pedestrian's view straight toward a statue, column, or civic building. By focusing the pedestrian's gaze on what lay at the end of the street, perspectival organization placed the apartments that lined streets in a peripheral space that dissolved on the edge of vision. That peripherality visually distinguished lines of contiguous apartment buildings from the free-standing monuments that anchored the perspectival vanishing point. At the same time, apartments began to occupy a different plane from the street—a weak vertical plane as opposed to the strong horizontal axis that directed the flow of the street and the pedestrian's gaze. In illustrations of Paris, perspectival views down streets began to replace frontal views of apartment houses, with the perspectival view shifting attention from the mass of the building to the space of the street (often represented as empty) and to the impression of motion along it (figs. 22, 23).[17]

The newly wide boulevards did not form a continuous unit with the apartment buildings that flanked them; rather, boulevards and apartment

FIGURE 22

Panorama of the rue Vivienne, circa 1835. In this frontal view, the buildings dominate the
street and the picture plane. The viewer's eye travels predominantly along the horizontal
axis defined by the building facades, moving with the flow of traffic.

FIGURE 23

Photograph of the avenue de l'Opéra, by Fiorillo. Conceived in
the late 1850s during Haussmann's tenure as prefect, the avenue
de l'Opéra (originally the avenue Napoléon) and the opera
house were completed in the 1870s. Once again guided by the
direction of traffic, the viewer looks down the boulevard at the
monumental opera house, while the majority of the buildings
recede into the peripheral spaces that frame the boulevard.

buildings seemed to occupy distinct spaces, which in turn facilitated perceptions of streets as exterior spaces, apartment buildings as interior
ones.[18] Other changes in apartment-house construction and design separated apartment buildings from the spaces external to them, despite
the fact that under Haussmann, individual apartment buildings became
more tied to urban infrastructure by virtue of improved links to sewage,
gas, and water networks. Apartment buildings constructed under Haussmann no longer reserved the ground floor for shops, and Haussmann's
zoning practices isolated residential neighborhoods from businesses,
thus promoting a view of domestic space as separate from commercial
exchange.[19] Second Empire architects also discouraged decorating practices that made domestic interiors resemble streets. In an article whose
title—"Des voies publiques et des maisons d'habitation à Paris"—

signaled a conceptual separation between roads and houses, Charles Gourlier noted that within houses, wood parquet floors were replacing "pavement" [*dallages*]. Formerly, slabs of concrete, stone, or marble had been used to cover floors inside apartments and to pave streets, but now they began to be confined strictly to the street. The street thus became a mineral realm whose hard, unyielding durability was perceptibly distinct from the more delicate, vegetal ground of the home.[20]

In and of themselves, however, none of these physical changes in the city's streets and apartment buildings necessarily determined how Parisians would interpret their experience of them. Physically enclosed spaces can promote a sense of privacy, even outdoors, but that sense can be altered by the perceptions of those who occupy them. The equation of interior spaces with the political, social, and subjective characteristics of privacy does not inhere in the spaces themselves but constitutes a possible interpretation of them. It thus remains to be seen, through readings of key prescriptive and descriptive discourses on the structure of Parisian space, whether the users of the relatively enclosed built environment that Paris became after 1851 experienced it as subjectively interior and socially private.

Contracting the Urban Subject and Separating Street from Home: The Discourse of Urban Observation

The literature of urban observation in the Second Empire and Third Republic aimed explicitly to combine objective descriptions of Paris with subjective reactions to it. Some works exhibited continuities with the *tableaux* and *physiologies* of the July Monarchy, but much urban literature after 1850 differed from that of the July Monarchy in two ways that illuminate the experience of Parisian interiorization.[21] First, many books about Paris deployed a poetics of contraction—to single authors from multiple ones, to the space of an enclosed, individualized consciousness, to smaller and smaller units of time—that they mapped onto their representations of the city. Second, those works began, on a widespread basis, to demarcate the city's streets from its houses by means of a vocabulary of public and private that broke significantly with the urban literature of previous decades.[22]

In contrast to the *tableaux* of the 1830s and 1840s, which had emphasized heterogeneous authorship and an ambitiously global view of the city, works of urban observation written during the Second Empire effected a radical individualization of the urban observer, whose claim to describing the city was now based on an individual consciousness that could interiorize the city subjectively, then reproduce it through the prisms of memory, affect, and imagination. The titles of various works suggested that interiorization often took the form of contraction: contraction to a literal interior, to a single domestic space—*Paris chez soi* (1854), *Paris dans un fauteuil* (1855), *Paris intime* (1859); contraction to a single subjectivity or an individualized point of view—"Paris à vue de nez" (1867), *Mémoires du boulevard* (1866), *Mes Souvenirs: les boulevards de 1840–1870* (1884); and contraction to a single span of time, either a day or an hour—*Les Heures parisiennes* (1866) and *Entre minuit et une heure: étude parisienne* (1868). The titles of those works often belied their content, creating a contradiction between the interiority implied by a text's descriptive label and the exteriority that its content ascribed to the city. Most of the sketches in Léo Lespès's *Spectacles vus de ma fenêtre* (1866), for example, required the narrator to venture beyond the purview of his window and into the street.[23] Just as during the 1830s and 1840s, the words *Paris* and *ville* provided book titles with marketable cachet, during the Second Empire words that connoted individuals and interiors became equally profitable when applied to books about the city.[24]

The interiorization of the city in urban literature transformed the cataloging euphoria of the July Monarchy observer, who had shuttled from streets to theaters to apartments, into the elegiac melancholy of an enclosed and isolated narrator, whose contact with the urban crowd never claimed to transcend his own omnipresent subjectivity. Such narrators remain familiar to us through the urban lyricism of Baudelaire's *Les Fleurs du mal* and *Petits poèmes en prose* and through the spatial fantasies of Decadent works of the 1880s, such as Huysman's *A rebours* and *Là-bas*, but they were not unique to canonical texts.[25] Emile Souvestre, for example, in *Un Philosophe sous les toits: journal d'un homme heureux* (1850), moved his urban narrator into a garret room, from which the city appears as a distant, impressionistic blur of the allegorical and the banal: "our philosopher gazes upon society from the heights of his garret, as though upon a sea whose riches he does not desire and whose shipwrecks he does not fear." Unlike Balzac's Rastignac, who vows from the heights of Père Lachaise to conquer Paris, or the narrator of Victor Hugo's *Notre-Dame de Paris*, with his bird's-eye view of the city, Souvestre's narrator is both above the city yet still contained within it. The space that he occupies, a garret room, does not differ significantly from the space he observes, since when he looks out, he sees only reflections of his own inner dilemmas. His vantage point emphasizes the urban landscape's disarray rather than its organized legibility. Souvestre's narrator describes "the perspective that opens up in front of my window":

> Overlapping roofs whose peaks entwine, cross, and are superimposed on one another; on top of them jut the pylons of tall chimneys. Yesterday I thought they had an Alpine look to them . . . today all I see are tiles and pipes. . . . [T]he smoke that rises up in light drifts, instead of making me dream of the barred windows of Vesuvius, reminds me of cooking and dishwater; and the telegraph that I make out in the distance over the old tower of Montmartre puts me in mind of the vile gallows whose arms stand up over the city.[26]

The narrator turns this description of Paris into a display of his own subjective powers of perception, and hence into a display of his own interior imagination, by describing the city in terms of images of poetic reverie and contemplation—the ocean, steam and smoke, mountains—and by reminding the reader that his subjectivity has created these images out of the unpromising materials of urban and everyday life—dirty dishes, telegraph poles, and roof tiles. Even the most banal elements of the city are not presented as simple causes (cooking) of an effect (smoke), but instead as products of the writer's subjective associations, as memories and metaphors: "the smoke . . . *reminds me* of cooking and dishwater." He then uses the figure of the voyage to show how his imagination enables him to travel further and see more, within a confined space, than tourists who move freely through the streets: "How many times have my days of rest drifted away in the contemplation of this marvelous spectacle, in the discovery of somber and charming episodes, in seeking, that is, in this unknown world, the travel impressions that opulent tourists seek further below!"[27] By incorporating his views of buildings as he sees them in the present into memories of them in the past, the narrator achieves an even greater mental interiorization of the city that lies outside his room.[28]

Urban literature also contracted the city's sexual topography, considerably reducing the field of erotic encounters. The July Monarchy network that had relayed numerous apartment buildings and streets shrank in Second Empire narratives to the space of a single building. Louis Jacquier's *L'Amour à Paris* (1862), which sorted types of couples, romances, and marital arrangements according to neighborhood, recounts an anecdote about telegraphic communication between lovers who hold up different letters of the alphabet at the windows of facing buildings but subtly associated that practice with an earlier era by noting that such correspondence could now take place only in "certain streets . . . those

that are not excessively wide," that is, the streets built before Haussmannization.[29] In Emile Villars's *Le Roman de la parisienne* (1866),
whose title attempted to confer an illusory unity on an eclectic collection of poems and stories, two neighbors whose balconies adjoin can
successfully seduce one another in "Un Roman par la terrasse," but in a
lyrical evocation of "Ma Voisine: impression parisienne," a man fails to
make contact with a woman he spies in a building across the street, as
though the field of Parisian sexual vision had narrowed to the perimeter
of an individual apartment building.[30]

The strong desire and easy ability to see from one building into another that had so marked the July Monarchy literature began to retract
into itself to the point of obfuscation. In an 1855 apartment-house romance in which a man falls in love with a woman in the building opposite, Léo Lespès devoted the most space to elaborating *obstacles* to the
hero's vision and to detailing the instruments and techniques that pain-
stakingly allow him to incrementally increase his visual access to the
woman's apartment. Despite his efforts, however, the story presents the
failure of his attempt to penetrate visually an interiorized and feminized
space; the hero meets his neighbor only through the intervention of his
mother, who brings the woman to him after he falls ill. The street no
longer serves as a heterosexual copula that bridges facing interiors, as it
did in the *tableaux;* in this text, only a maternal, domestic agent from
one interior can link it to the other.[31]

Where a writer like Lespès presented visual penetration of the apartment house as desirable but difficult, other urban observers began to
denigrate the value of seeing into apartments altogether. In a *Tableau de
Paris* singly authored by Edmond Texier, editor of the leading bourgeois
weekly *L'Illustration,* several passages foregrounded the urban observer's inability to penetrate Parisian private life and made female modesty
a figure of privacy. Near the beginning of a chapter on "Private Life," his
narrator praises buildings whose "modesty" impedes his view of their
interiors:

> the observer strolls through the streets in vain, no hospitable breach exposes
> the houses' varied ramparts to his gaze or gives passage to his curiosity; in
> vain he scales a height and contemplates this immense and teeming hive of
> rooftops . . . hoping that a helpful genie will come to unhat all these impen-
> etrable sanctuaries of private life; nothing of the sort! Paris modestly con-
> serves her domiciles; it doesn't let its intimate acts be seen, and at most, it lets
> itself be guessed at.[32]

Texier insists here on the impossibility of both frontal and aerial views of what lies inside apartment buildings. The very act of describing an interior opens it up to view and signifies the entrance of an exterior agent who makes it accessible to an equally exterior reader/viewer; Texier's highlighted visual impasse, his inability to see inside, *produces* what lies within the apartment building as an interior.

The new opacity of the interior, perceived as a private space impervious to an intrusive gaze, corresponded to a newly emphatic equation of the exterior with the public, defined in terms of theatrical display and spectatorship. In *Ce qu'on voit dans les rues de Paris* (1858), Victor Fournel portrayed the familiar urban figure of the *badaud,* similar to the *flâneur* but defined less by walking than by an almost automatic, involuntary, vacant gawking. The *badaud*'s inner being, according to Fournel, becomes completely identified with the external objects at which he stares; the *badaud* "is no longer a man; he is the public, he is the crowd." [33] Fournel's emblematic public man of the street, characterized as an indiscriminate viewer who absorbs and projects himself into all he sees, does not once enter a house or even observe a house facade from the street. His failure to do so suggests the extent to which writers had begun to equate the public realm with a thoroughfare through which one moved forward, and to distinguish the street from the houses situated directly on it.

As the apartment building's interior came to be seen as less available to external vision, and as the street came to be the sole space in which public life was possible, a new sense arose of a division between the inside and the outside, newly defined as opposed and *competing* public and private spheres. Using pronouns like *on* and *nous* to designate a collective unit that rhetorically included men and women of all classes, writers sketched either an unbalanced economy in which resources that they considered proper to the interior were being disastrously transferred to the exterior, or an ecology in which one system, personified as an aggressor (the exterior) subsumed another (the interior). In an economic narrative that traced the imbalance between interior and exterior resources, Dr. Robinet expressed the fixed proportion of interior to exterior existence with an emphatic formula: "the more one provides air and light outdoors, the less there is on the inside!" [34] The implausibility of this statement is highlighted by Robinet's mathematical locution, derived from the public hygienists discussed later in this chapter, and suggests the extent to which the opposition of interior and exterior was a

matter of metaphor, not physical reality. Théophile Gautier, in a contribution to *Paris et les parisiens au XIXe siècle,* argued for ecological destruction by pointing out that the modern valorization of limitlessness
and speed had made the street more important than the home, and that
as a result, houses were being destroyed to make space for roads: "[Mod-
ern] civilization, which needs room for its frenetic activity and perpetual motion, carves out large avenues for itself in the black maze . . . of
the old city; civilization knocks down houses." [35] By moving the relatively literal spatial distinction between "avenues" and "houses" into a
more metaphorical antagonism between "civilization" and "houses,"
Gautier translated spatial difference into a temporal one and transferred
houses to a more distant, archaic, fragile era—the time of the "forefathers" often invoked, as we have seen, by critics of Haussmannization.

In the course of designating interior and exterior as spatially separate
and opposed, writers also came to construe them as attached to distinct
social spheres. Nestor Roqueplan's 1853 *La Vie parisienne* achieved this
simply by using the word "and" to link the "interior" to the "familial,"
and by contrasting "domestic duties" to "exterior ambitions." [36] The
"interior" no longer marked a space whose physical difference from the
exterior was neutral, obvious, and thus trivial; it became identified with
le foyer, the family home and hearth.[37] The language of a slightly later
work, Alfred Delvau's *Histoire anecdotique des cafés et cabarets de Paris*
(1862), highlighted the difficulties of aligning the spatial category "exterior" and the sociopolitical category "public." Delvau invoked "Paris,
where one gladly exteriorizes one's self. We find it tiresome to live and
die at home. . . . We require public display, big events, the street, the
cabaret, to witness us for better or for worse . . . we like to pose, to put
on a show, to have an audience, a *gallery,* witnesses to our life." [38] Cafés
and cabarets were primarily interior spaces, as were galleries (which referred to sections in the theater, salons, and semienclosed porticoes), yet
Delvau labeled them public by virtue of their theatricality and their opposition to the domestic space of "at home" [*chez soi*]. Social exteriorization ("public display, big events") logically and syntactically precedes and grounds the physical exteriority of spaces ("the street, the
cabaret").[39]

Writers began to vehemently articulate the qualities and resources
they believed should be exclusive to the home, often using a negative
logic that condemned the presence in the street of what was absent in the
home. In *Les Dessous de Paris* (1860), an anthology of articles originally

published in the newspaper *Le Figaro,* Delvau argued that the street had become more homelike than the home:

> As soon as it awakes, Paris leaves its abode and steps out, and doesn't return home until as late as possible in the evening—when it bothers to return home. . . . Paris deserts its houses. Its houses are dirty on the inside, while its streets are swept every morning. . . . All the luxury is outside—all its pleasures walk the streets.[40]

Delvau couched his argument for populated, clean, luxurious houses as a reproach against the streets that had those amenities when houses lacked them. In *Paris nouveau et Paris futur* (1865), Victor Fournel hyperbolically argued that the street offered better shelter than modern apartments: "One doesn't live in them, one perches . . . always in a rush to leave and seek out a little air, a little peace and rest in the street—yes, really, a little rest. . . . Where is a home of one's own [*le chez-soi*] possible in Paris?"[41] Fournel himself provides an answer to his rhetorical question—a home is possible in the street—but the opposition between street and home had become so strong that even his attribution of domestic comforts to the street could only serve as an accusation against both the advantages of Parisian boulevards and the deficiencies of the urban residence.

Domestic Manuals: Keeping Men in the Home

A tendency to conceive of the city as divided into distinctly separate interior and exterior spaces also emerged in the sizable corpus of Second Empire and Third Republic prescriptive domestic literature, which warned readers of the need to isolate dwellings from outside influences, both moral and material, and which counseled women not only how to create that privacy but how then to keep their families, and particularly their husbands, within the confines of that delimited residential space.

The domestic manuals of the second half of the nineteenth century, which emphasized the need to maintain a hermetically sealed home, represented a drastic shift from earlier prescriptive literature, which had understood domestic interiors as analogous to the sphere of political administration. The 1821 edition of the *Encyclopédie des dames: manuel de la maîtresse de maison, ou lettres sur l'économie domestique,* for example, defined both the woman and her home in relation to abstract qualities such as comfort and order; a woman's domestic work consisted in realizing those idealized concepts.[42] Pariset's 1821 version of female domesticity argued that the foremost beneficiary of domestic order was the woman herself, and that women became tied to their homes because they designed them to cater to their own comfort and pleasure.[43]

The 1852 reedition of Pariset's work, however, no longer commanded women to stay at home in order to enjoy themselves; it told women to stay at home to clean. At a time when the city was being reconfigured as a more sanitary structure from which excrement and corpses would be efficiently removed, the 1852 domestic manual reformulated the home as a tenuously isolated space from which the housewife had to constantly expel dirt. Hygiene replaced comfort in new appendices on specialized techniques for cleaning silver, parquets, iron, wood, and ivory. The authors advised women to cover stair landings with carpets to keep dirt from the street from spreading into the house, recommended shutters to keep out the sun, and gave advice on how to fend off the atmospheric humidity that could corrode objects and bodies alike.[44] Women were now charged with protecting the interior from the exterior, a task to be carried out in the service of the family unit: "the care one must take to preserve the family's health . . . is one of the most important and dearest duties of a housewife."[45]

The domestic manuals of the Second Empire and the Third Republic constituted a popular and profitable genre directed primarily at a Parisian audience; they offered a guide to cultivating a privacy whose precariousness urban observers highlighted, and they shared with works of urban observation a tendency to posit a competition between an isolated conjugal home and commercialized urban leisure. Louise d'Alq, the founding editor of several magazines and the author of numerous treatises on daily life, wrote in *La Vie intime* (1881): "private life, life in the interior of the family, that is what can really be called life." The comtesse de Bassanville's *Trésor de la maison: guide des femmes économes* (1867), written for families with moderate incomes, argued that the city was a dangerous place because its inimical effects on domestic "regularity" and "order" led women to depart from fixed schedules and fall ill. To shelter the home from the city, de Bassanville urged her readers to create a decor that would mark the difference between urban locales and the domestic interior, as in the following advice about wallpaper: "don't ever use red, unless you want your living-room to resemble a restaurant or a café."[46]

Writers of domestic manuals linked the security of the home's spatial enclosure to a social organization based on the difference between men

and women. In a manual called *La Science de la vie*, d'Alq advised that
women were made to be mothers, not politicians, and should base their
identity and that of their homes on their contrast to the men whom their
husbands could encounter outside the home: "Man does not need to
come back home [*rentrer à son foyer*] to find a second self; that he could
find at his club or at a café."[47] D'Alq's use of the verb *rentrer* constituted
the home as an interior and origin for the husband, the place that he entered and to which he "returned." She thus defined the home in terms of
two conflated differences: the spatial difference between a central point
of return and its peripheral but dangerously attractive satellites; and the
gendered difference between the wife and the husband, whose very dis-
similarity formed the basis for a complementary marital unit. The spatial difference became gendered by making the home both feminine, in
the wife's charge, and conjugal, a place in which husband and wife mingled; de Bassanville articulated the imbrication of space and gender in an
appositional chapter title, "De l'intérieur, de la famille."[48] Gender difference in turn became spatialized not only because the wife's difference
pulled the husband inside, but also because the wife was defined by her
anchored presence in the home, the husband by his ability to stay in that
home or leave it, according to where his desires could best be fulfilled.

The verb *rentrer* recurred in many domestic manuals, anchoring
an ideology that historians have imprecisely termed one of "separate
spheres," a nomenclature that implies a symmetry between men and
women that did not exist. Domestic manuals envisioned a system in
which men could move between the home and its outside, but women
could not; men needed to be persuaded to return to the home, while
women had to solicit their desire to do so. Manuals from the early 1860s
on taught women "to want, thanks to your efforts, your husbands to
be happy to return home, after the preoccupations and exhaustion of
days laboriously employed."[49] De Bassanville wrote that "an even more
valuable result of establishing clear order in one's home is that it keeps
one's husband in the house" and that "with know-how and worldliness,
not only will your house be good, but furthermore it will be pleasant,
and your husband and children will desert it as little as they can."[50]
Guillaume Belèze wrote that the married woman must "cultivate . . . [and]
encourage in her husband a taste for family life" and Adolphe Puissant
stated that "a woman's greatest point of pride is the cheerfulness of her
interior, of the place that most closely reunites the different members of
a single family. Our best companions are those who know best how to
keep us in our homes."[51]

The conceptual distinction between domestic interior and urban exterior ultimately collapsed for men, since manuals advised women to lure men into the home by making it resemble, in function if not in form, the very spaces against which they initially defined that home. The home resembled a club by becoming a site of homosocial contact for men, a place where men would "take charge of everything that requires contact with other men," and became like a brothel by becoming a place where women catered to men's desires. As far as women were concerned, however, the home remained a consistently interiorized and even carceral space whose oppressive qualities d'Alq barely bothered to dissimulate: "the domestic hearth, the *at home* [in English in the original] . . . occupies such an important place in life . . . that it always deserves . . . to be taken into serious consideration, especially by a woman, for whom it is her prison, or rather her nest, to use a slightly less harsh term." [52]

The Public Health Movement and the New Privacy of Housing

Just as d'Alq had recourse to the English term "at home" to evoke a domesticity marked by enclosure and isolation, the professional discourse of public hygiene in France similarly took its inspiration from England, often citing as exemplary England's statistical inquiries and model workers' housing. While domestic manuals focused on bourgeois life and public hygiene focused on the dwellings and families of the poor, both were preoccupied with securing the unity of the family by appointing women to safeguard the physical purity and isolation of the home.

Public health had been a matter of serious governmental concern and an arena for professional and political activity since the 1820s. Public health investigators took the interactions between humans and their physical environment as their theoretical object of investigation and assumed that those interactions provided reliable indices of social, moral, and political order. As the historians Catherine Kudlick and Andrew Aisenberg explain, public health reformers subscribed to Enlightenment beliefs in rationality, progress, and transparent, objective, and universally beneficial knowledge; they used empirical observation and the compilation of statistics as the basis for improving the health of a public created by those very measurements, diagnoses, and inspections. [53] Their researches focused on the living conditions of the poor, nearly always described as pathological and potentially infectious by proponents of the miasmic theory of disease.

The various institutions concerned with public health, such as the Conseil de Salubrité, the Commission des Logements insalubres, and the prefectures of the Seine and police, also depended on a postrevolutionary political regime in which the state sought to carve out legitimate spheres of governance by soliciting the expertise of middle-class professionals.[54] The field of public health brought together increasingly systematized government administrations such as the police and civil service with increasingly professionalized social investigators such as doctors, architects, and engineers. Yet while French hygiene reform was made possible by governments rooted in liberal individualism, it also risked violating (far more so than its English equivalents) the rights of private property so crucial to that political system.[55] Landlords complained that their rights were jeopardized by laws mandating building standards and inspections, and working-class occupants resisted the threats to privacy posed by health investigators who entered their domiciles, made observations and inquiries, and tried to impose new living standards. As Aisenberg argues, the public health movement's answer to such protests was that the violation of privacy and autonomy by regulation and inspection was necessary to create the proper homes and socialized individuals for whom privacy might be claimed. Using the term *foyer* to refer both to the domestic hearth and to the domestic site of disease and criminality, hygienists working for the government believed that "[t]o discover, explain and remove the danger of the foyer constituted by the criminal would require a relaxing of the inviolable boundaries of the other *foyer*— the 'home'—in favor of administrative prerogative."[56]

The writings of public health reformers during the Second Empire and Third Republic thus had to open up to view the very interiors whose greater insularity they prescribed, a paradox that had not been posed as acutely for their predecessors in the first half of the nineteenth century. Before the 1850s, treatises on hygiene and government-sponsored hygiene reports often excluded domestic interiors from their discussions of urban salubrity, both because they assumed that the condition of a dwelling simply matched and followed from the condition of the street in which it was situated, and because they lacked the authority to inspect them.[57] Before the 1840s, writers on public health who found fault with domestic buildings did so on strictly physical grounds, without distinguishing a building's shell from its interior: they criticized apartment houses for excessive height, low ceilings, narrow windows, and lack of air.[58] Early hygienists associated healthy sites with easy intercourse between interior and exterior, and their guidelines for healthy homes emphasized the importance of circulation: wide streets would help air to flow freely into and out of the apartment, and light must be allowed to enter it. For the original generation of hygienists, a healthy interior was not exclusively interior at all.[59]

As early as the 1840s, however, urban hygienists began to distinguish interior from exterior in ways that focused on the particular dangers that the apartment house posed to domestic order and health, using language that echoed the English discourse about lodging houses. Michel Lévy's *Traité d'hygiène publique et privé* (1844) argued that private, individual hygiene consisted in warding off external influences and appropriating external light and air for internal use; because the street was the home's waste outlet, the healthiest houses were those farthest from the street's "miasmic flow."[60] Lévy singled out the apartment house as a particularly unhygienic residence, since "cohabitation under the same roof" would lead to "miasmic commerce" and "particular endemics," due to "an exchange of wastes among the diverse parts of the population piled on top of one another from the ground level to the top floors."[61] Lévy explained his aversion to apartment houses in pragmatic terms, faulting their "strict parsimoniousness with space" and their "crampedness," but he also provided a social critique of the apartment building: "The house is the family's sanctuary: it should shelter only that natural group whose individuals are linked by community of origin, of instincts, and of physical and moral disposition."[62] By describing the family and the home as an isolated unit, Lévy argued that the physical space of the home should coincide with, rather than exceed, the dimensions of the family, an equation of architectural and social structures that corresponded to the equivalence he perceived between "physical and moral disposition."

Lévy's positions became major tenets of the public hygiene movement during the 1850s and after, when hygienists and other social reformers began to concentrate their energies on housing. An insistence on the equivalence between the physical state of residential interiors and their occupants' moral behavior became foundational for hygiene and housing reform from the 1850s on and had a series of consequences for hygienists' understanding of domestic space and social structures. The most obvious consequence, already visible in Lévy's work, was to assign enormous weight to "the home" and to define that home in terms of the isolation of its interior. Thus, in a report for the Société centrale des Architectes (1851) on methods for "purifying unhealthful residences,"

Adolphe Lance, an architect who worked for the government and wrote frequently for the architectural press, asserted the deterministic moral effects of dwellings: "there is a direct correlation between domestic residences and individual morals." Lance made the home's influence more visceral when he connected its temporal causality—the home as the origin, hence the cause, of human behavior—to a material causality that defined the home as metaphorically shaping its occupants: "our dwelling becomes as it were the mold of our private life." [63] The figure of the home as a container pressing on its occupants at every point implied that family life took shape exclusively and exhaustively within a residence, and that the exterior only functioned in domestic life as a negative and secondary site to which men could flee if their domestic interiors were lacking: "it is in order to flee . . . miseries that the father distances himself from the domestic hearth which he has begun to actively dislike, and contracts disorderly and immoral habits on the outside." The similarity in sound, in the original French, between *dehors* (outside) and *désordre* (disorder) underlined the equivalence between external space and chaos. [64]

For the hygienists, the apartment house failed to provide an adequate realization of the domestic interior because the common spaces that linked individual units compromised their integrity as isolated interiors. In a popular study of health and the home, J. B. Fonssagrives, a naval surgeon who became a professor of hygiene, argued for the coupling of *foyer* and *patrie,* home and nation, by stating that "the great social problem is to love one's house and to stay in it." Writing in 1871, Fonssagrives attributed France's "momentary debasement . . . and nervousness . . . in its moral life" to a general loss of "family spirit" and to the recent events of the Paris Commune. The Commune not only reiterated the long-standing association of Paris with revolution, it did so in terms of apartment houses and their potentially unruly inhabitants, who demanded rent waivers for the period of the Prussian siege and whose fighting tactics included gutting party walls to permit movement between buildings. [65] In arguing for the importance of staying at home, Fonssagrives specified that the home could not be an apartment house: "the caravanserai-like figure cut by modern houses in our big cities . . . establishes an epidemic solidarity among its diverse families," a "miasmic and unpleasant exchange." After pathologizing workers by qualifying the "solidarity" associated with labor unions as "epidemic," Fonssagrives praised the private house—using a word taken from England, the country that had successfully averted proletarian revolution and that

best signified the home: "The ideal home is a private family home," and
one could only "isolate one's self from others by means of an individual,
familial residence" in "this sanctuary of *home.*"[66]

To the structural problems posed by contiguous, internally divided
apartment houses, hygienists added the distinction between apartment
rental and home ownership, arguing (like the English legal reformers,
but with reference to a very different system of property ownership) that
what Lance called "the inviolability of private property" should be extended to working men.[67] Emile Cacheux, an engineer who presided
over the French Hygiene Society and spent much of his career improving workers' housing, asserted that domesticity and ownership had
equivalent effects: "Property and family life are in effect the two most
active instruments of moral improvement in the world."[68] In his tax-
onomy of *Les Ouvriers européens,* Frédéric Le Play wrote that "the
physical and moral condition of populations depends intimately on the
numerous schemes by which one manages to guarantee workers the possession of housing. . . . [T]his privilege of possession contributes more
than any other to developing the worker's taste for property and the
moral sentiments that attach him to it." The worker could attain property only by undergoing "a long series of trials."[69] Le Play, who sought
to reconcile industrialization with Catholicism, cast the worker who acquired property as an epic hero surmounting obstacles, a religious figure
enduring pain, and a self-made man overcoming adversity.

Proponents of ownership did not specify their economic objections to
rent but focused instead on an opposition between the purification and
progress offered by property, and the corruption and regression of apartment houses, "unhealthy barracks" whose "promiscuity . . . replaces,
as it were, the family with a communal clan or tribal life."[70] Hygienists
often criticized apartment buildings for their *promiscuité,* a word that
denoted crowding but also connoted sexual misconduct, just as the *propreté* (cleanliness) upon which they dwelt phonetically suggested *propriété* (property).[71] To the sexual disorder created by the apartment
house, hygienists counterposed women's moralizing presence in the domestic interior: "in Paris, woman is the angel of the domestic hearth,"
wrote Louis Lazare in *Les Quartiers pauvres de Paris.*[72] Reformers in
turn derived women's domestic influence from the form of the private
house. Charles Lucas, summarizing an 1879 lecture on the world history of housing, wrote that the ideal house originated in Rome as a two-
story building with the bedrooms on the top floor; its invention co-

incided with "the creation . . . of family life, the life that made woman the companion and not the slave or plaything of man, and which thus opened all the parts of the house to her, where her supreme influence will soon be felt, and for the better." Lucas's diachronic framework, which linked the Roman Republic's conjugal space to that of nineteenth-century France, was also a synchronic move to distinguish French domestic arrangements from colonial ones, since Lucas's allusions to woman as a sequestered "slave" referred not only to classical Greek households but also to nineteenth-century orientalist views of the harem. His insistence on the liberalism of Roman and French domestic arrangements occluded the extent to which that liberalism continued to limit women to the confines of the house, advocated legislative restrictions on women's work outside the home, and supported property ownership that benefited only men.[73]

The obvious impracticality of certain aspects of hygiene reform did not prevent its beliefs about apartment houses from becoming common currency across the political spectrum. Friedrich Engels, for example, ridiculed plans to make all workers into property owners in *The Housing Question* (1872), arguing that housing shortages and their resultant crowding and insalubriousness were epiphenomena of capitalist production and could not be resolved without abolishing that mode of production.[74] He ascribed hygienists' interest in workers' housing problems to a fear of epidemic and argued that they made housing problems into a moral issue because they could not advocate eliminating the existing social order that caused them. Engels even argued that workers benefited from *not* owning property: the propertyless worker was more mobile, hence more liberated.[75] *The Housing Question* thus refuted every tenet of housing reform—except its criticism of the apartment house. In the course of assessing proposals to turn renters into owners, Engels agreed that property could have value, however compromised, only if what was owned was a "cottage" and not an apartment.[76] Property in an apartment would produce only "scattered . . . part owners"; a system in which rent counted toward ownership made sense only in England, where "each married worker occupies a little house of his own."[77] That Engels's thorough critique of the housing reformers converged with their view of the apartment house as defectively fractional shows the extent to which an invidious distinction between the house and the apartment had become second nature, even to those dedicated to analyzing the blind spots of housing reform.

Architectural Discourse and the Problem of the Apartment House

After the 1840s the architectural profession began to move away from
the restrictions of a classical Beaux-Arts training and toward increased
integration with other professionals, particularly engineers versed in
new construction techniques and interior decorators purveying contemporary styles. Architectural journals and books began to supplement
and even replace formal architectural education, emphasizing eclecti-
cism and accessibility over specialized knowledge. Blending theory and
practice, "art" and "science," classical principles of composition with
modern industrial technique, those texts drew on philosophy, history,
and statistics to reach an audience of architects, engineers, decorators, archeologists, industrialists, property owners, and government officials.[78] Not surprisingly, then, the architects of the Second Empire and
Third Republic were closely allied with hygienists, often working alongside them on commissions and councils to improve housing, or as government inspectors assessing whether buildings met health standards.

Architectural writings expressed the same conviction as public health
reports that architecture exerted a moral influence on individuals, the
family, and the nation; like hygienic studies and domestic manuals, they
differentiated between men's responsibility to own property and women's
responsibility to attract men to the home.[79] An 1848 journal polemically
entitled *La Propriété: Journal des intérêts de tous*, "devoted openly . . .
to the defense of the sacred rights of property and family," set the tone
for the years to follow when it stated, "He who aspires to become a paterfamilias aspires to become a property owner [*propriétaire*]."[80] Several decades later, in an 1884 treatise on interior decoration, Emile Cardon assigned women the ability to protect the sacred space of the family
for men: "It is woman, the guardian angel of the home . . . who can
do the most to give us back the cult of the home and of the daily arts
that our fathers had."[81] Cardon's reference to the "fathers" of the past
made women into conduits, not owners, of domesticity: women would
return men to a more manly, authoritative precedent that was also more
homelike, but they themselves would be erased from this genealogy,
"giv[ing] . . . *back*" the home to men without benefiting from any corresponding return. Like the writers of domestic manuals, architects assumed the femininity of domesticity and ordered women to draw men
into an interior equated with property and a patriarchal heritage.

Architects arrived at many of the same positions as the other writers
we have examined who attempted to demarcate proper forms of domes-

ticity, but for different reasons and in terms of more concretely developed building plans. They shared the belief that dwellings should be as interiorized and private as possible, and that apartment houses compromised both of those standards. In a statement that architects cited approvingly for decades to follow, the second volume of Léonce Reynaud's *Traité d'architecture* (1858) asserted: "In bringing together under one roof families between whom no other link exists, one renders those residences less enclosed, less quiet, and one deprives private life of a portion of its self-sufficiency. The stairway is a sort of public way that opens right into the very interior of the house." [82] The architectural solution to this problem was to use decor and layout to create a clearer distinction between exterior and interior *within* the apartment. For example, in his influential *Grammaire des arts décoratifs: Décoration intérieure de la maison* (1882), the art historian Charles Blanc refined the standards for flooring by declaring that "perspective effects are absolutely forbidden in floor decoration." Blanc's orders stemmed partly from his understanding of the apartment as a sanctuary from the noise and activity of the street, as "an interior where things will form a spectacle without any jolts or noise." [83] Blanc aimed to remove action and accident from the home and dismissed interior perspective and *trompe l'oeil* effects in both floors and walls because they produced too much movement and presented too many dimensions. The more a flat surface suggested multiple dimensions, the more it resembled an open space through which one could pass, rather than a closed and solid barrier separating a room from what lay beyond it; therefore, Blanc wrote, wallpaper "must not simulate voids in architectural solids." [84]

Architects also began to create more separation between rooms newly defined as public (dining rooms, salons) and private (bedrooms, studies)—a solution that could work only in apartments designed for the wealthy, and one that departed from the July Monarchy practice of adjoining bedrooms to reception rooms. César Daly, the founding editor in 1840 of France's most important architectural journal, the *Revue générale de l'architecture et des travaux publics,* wrote in that journal's inaugural year that private architecture should take its models from public structures such as churches and clubs; he praised apartment houses for embodying the principle of "association" expounded by utopian socialists. [85] Twenty-four years later, when he began to publish a magisterial, lavishly illustrated nine-volume work on *L'Architecture privée au XIXe siècle sous Napoléon III* (1864–77), dedicated to Haussmann, Daly delineated a strict hierarchy of apartment house types in which the best buildings were those that differentiated most between public and private spaces. Daly's work echoed the principles articulated by English architects like Robert Kerr: he divided apartment buildings into three classes, with highest honors going to those that best drew "the boundary that must separate the salon—the setting for contact with the exterior—from the intimate rooms where the family lives" and exhibited "the most complete separation possible between contiguous apartments," between masters and servants, and when desired, between individual family members.[86] Nor was Daly's hierarchy idiosyncratic; Eugène Viollet-le-Duc, another premier architect of the Second Empire, who often disagreed theoretically with Daly, wrote in his *Entretiens sur l'architecture* (1863) that "we ask that each apartment be a sort of isolated sanctuary, independent, shielded from all eyes. . . . Today, more stringently than in the past, we ask that reception rooms be distinct from those reserved for living."[87] Viollet-le-Duc's opposition between receiving guests and the more genuine activity of simply "living" linked the spatial privacy created by isolation to an introverted domesticity claimed to be the only authentic existence.

Architects articulated the hygienists' prescriptions for physical isolation with urban observers' emphasis on interiorized subjectivity, and conversely criticized apartment houses for eroding individuality. Cardon, for example, dismissed apartments as "barracks," implying that their inhabitants became as indistinguishable as soldiers wearing the same uniform and sharing sleeping quarters.[88] Viollet-le-Duc associated apartment houses with a loss of both domesticity and architectural individuality that had corresponding effects on apartment occupants: "nothing can more thoroughly demoralize a population than those large apartment houses [*maisons à loyer*] which efface individual personalities and where love of family life [*le foyer*] is barely admissible."[89] Viollet-le-Duc's later work on *Habitations modernes* (1875) elaborated on this connection between home and the individualized self: "the wholesome whim of wanting a house of one's own requires first of all that one know one's self. . . . Only a personalized residence can develop the habit of being one's self [*être soi*], just as the habit of being at home [*chez soi*] imparts an individualized character to a residence; the one leads to the other." For Viollet-le-Duc, the self and the home merged into a single, circular space in which each influenced the other; with its repetition of reflexive grammatical forms, Viollet-le-Duc's language emphasized the reflexive character of that space and its iteration of the self.[90]

Professional concerns as well as an investment in individuality contributed to architects' preference for single-occupant houses over apartment buildings. Apartment houses were inferior sources of fees and prestige because their builders tended either to hire architects trained outside the elite Ecole des Beaux-Arts or to bypass architects altogether by copying designs from pattern books. Although both *hôtels* and apartment houses were private property, the separation of ownership and occupancy in the apartment (it was impossible to own a single apartment unit and a building's owner usually rented an apartment elsewhere) meant that the architect could not shape a building to an individual client's desires.[91] Daly deemed the apartment house a public form of architecture, "addressed . . . to the crowd"; it needed to satisfy "relatively general needs" and hence neither architect nor landlord could allow the apartment to express the unique, original, or even whimsical physiognomy that Daly considered to be truly good architecture.[92]

Daly drew both spatial and temporal conclusions from the fact that apartments were not designed for a specific individual. Apartment houses failed to create a permanent, organic unity between construction and decor, since in them,

> the tenant is nothing but a transitory guest, while the landlord of a private house is on the contrary presumed to be established in his dwelling forever . . . everything around him ought to take on a fixed and durable character. . . . Many objects that of necessity are mobile in an apartment house become favorably immobilized in a private house.

Daly assigned the purported transience and instability of the apartment dweller, that "transitory guest," to the apartment itself, with its "mobile . . . objects," suggesting both that the tenant did not merge with the space of the apartment, and that the space of the apartment was disrupted by furniture whose portability made it almost ambulatory. In the *hôtel*, by contrast, the fixity of both owner and objects made the furniture form an "ensemble" with the decorations and walls, which could themselves become "constitutive parts of the construction"; when the occupant became more permanent, so did the architect's handiwork.[93]

Architects' invocation of permanence often went hand in hand with calls to return to the ways of the past, a move we have already seen at work in other discourses. In architecture, the emphasis on temporality derived from a general tendency in architectural theory to historicize architectural explanations by telling the story of architecture as the story of its beginnings.[94] Enlightenment theories of architecture sought to establish its proper form in the present by determining what its original—and hence ideal—form had been in the past; during the Second Empire journals like Calliat's *Encyclopédie d'architecture* (published monthly from 1851 to 1862) continued to express that belief by regularly publishing articles on archeology as part of their mission to keep architects up to date. The demand for historically accurate building ornaments during the 1860s expanded the market for architectural pattern books, and architects began to study a more recent and specifically French past during the second half of the nineteenth century: books on topics such as *Les Hôtels historiques de Paris* (1852) suggested that Haussmann's demolition of old structures, as well as the physical destruction wrought by revolution and invasion in 1870 and 1871, inspired a heightened awareness of the age of the structures that remained, and of their contribution to the *patrimoine culturel* as material embodiments of both collective and individual history.[95] Historically unparalleled levels of razing and construction may have encouraged architects to evaluate building types in terms of temporal categories such as durability and ephemerality.

The banality of its form and the mobility of its inhabitants condemned the apartment house to a perpetual present tense in which it maintained insufficient ties to both the past and the future. And architectural writers, like the health reformers who promoted male property-ownership, identified the past and future of buildings as paternal and filial. Reynaud's *Traité d'architecture* equated physical solidity with patrilineal continuity when he wrote that "as a guarantee of durability, [solidity] . . . corresponds to . . . the desire to perpetuate our memory and our name."[96] It was a cliché of architectural discourse to state that apartment houses were incompatible with national ideas of masculinity. Charles Garnier, architect of the Paris opera house, wrote a history of domestic architecture that represented apartment houses as a degradation of original housing forms: because of their "subdivision," apartment houses led to a loss of "individual character"; they were "uniform" and banal; and most important, they disrupted the paternal transmission of familial space that Garnier nostalgically associated with an earlier age:

> Formerly . . . not only did a man die in the house where he was born, but sons lived where their fathers had lived. . . . The common room, which most often served as the parents' bedroom, which had seen the birth and death of several generations, and which for numerous years witnessed the celebrations, joys and sorrows of the family, as it were personified the family.

In the nineteenth century, the apartment house dismembered the paternal legacy, since as a consequence of population growth in Paris, "the high cost of land and the demands of family life condemned the solid and comfortable dwellings of the upper middle class, which used to be transmitted intact from father to son, to being split up; generally one had to divide houses into as many separate apartments as there were stories." [97] Cardon's *L'Art au foyer domestique* (1884) stated the connection between the paternal home of the past and the state of the nation in the present most clearly: "to refashion the domestic hearth according to how our fathers understood it, surely is to refashion our sorely bruised and tried nation [*patrie*]." [98]

In architectural discourse, the single-family house's persistence in time gave it a privileged relationship to history understood in masculine terms. César Daly interpreted permanence as masculine by arguing that because houses owned by their occupants were designed to last longer, they mediated better between national and individual taste, thus approaching the "grandeur and duration" of buildings designed for the collective nation; durability and generality would thus enable domestic architecture, normally the "feminine or minor branch" of architecture, to rise to the status of monumental, memorial architecture. [99] In his extremely popular *Histoire d'une maison* (1873), in which *histoire* meant both story and history, Viollet-le-Duc also used the house to mediate between the collective *patrie* and the individual family, to negotiate between the distaste for crowded living arrangements that resembled supposedly regressive group formations, such as the "clan" or the "tribe," and the conflicting demand for a patrifocal household in which sons would live in the same place as their fathers. [100] *Histoire d'une maison* is an architectural fable that begins in the summer of 1870 with a father deciding, against his wife's wishes, that his daughter and her new husband should not live in his house; he decides, that is, against an arrangement that would turn the paternal home into a quasi-apartment house and that would promote matriarchy (the husband living with his wife's relatives) rather than individualism. The father asks the son to design a house for his newly married sister; when the invasion of Paris prevents the family from leaving the village where they vacation, they decide to occupy their time by actually building the house, which becomes an antidote to the ravages of the Prussian invasion of Paris and the insurgencies of the Commune. The construction of a private home thus becomes the enabling condition of exogamous patriarchy, of the patrilineal transmission of knowledge, of the security of the fatherland, and of the narrative itself.

Convinced that enclosure and privacy were necessary to a domestic architecture that would buttress both a masculinized nation and a national masculinity, architects began to develop new criteria for apartment house facades, the site of greatest potential exposure to external, public view. The proliferation of window coverings during the Second Empire, which included a vogue for the simultaneous use of interior and exterior shutters, provided one means of rendering the facade opaque; theoretical reformulations of the facade provided another, as when Daly wrote that the facade exemplified the house's main purpose as "the family's clothing . . . destined to provide it with an envelope, to shelter and to lend itself to all its movements." [101]

Architects understood, however, that the facade could never completely shelter its occupants from view, and, as a result, they attempted to codify the facade's revelations as much as possible. At a time when many believed in "the influences that private events, enclosed within the limits of a private house, can exert on large political events that unfold in the exterior [au dehors]," it became imperative that whatever took place in the interior be above reproach, not only capable of being published to external view, but actively and deliberately expressed in the facade.[102] The facade came to be judged according to its "honesty," defined as its translation of what lay behind it. Using that criterion, the author of an article on "Edilité parisienne" in L'Opinion nationale condemned the apartments built on the newly completed rue de Rivoli for hiding "narrow apartments" behind their lavish facades and warned, "all too often, that is what the deceitful exteriors [dehors] that you admire from the street conceal." [103] Théodore Vacquer, in his introduction to Maisons les plus remarquables à Paris (1860–70), cited an architect who had proportioned all the windows in a building's facade to reflect the size and importance of the rooms behind them, and praised "that very rational method of translating on the exterior [au dehors] that which constitutes the interior." [104] Viollet-le-Duc argued that "[o]ne of the charms of good architecture consists in the intimate relation between interior and exterior decoration. Exterior decoration must prepare the spectator and present him with what he will discover upon entering the building"; the architect must seek "the correlation between the envelope and its contents, the sincere expression of the inside on the outside." [105]

Vacquer's, Daly's, and Viollet-le-Duc's notion of the facade as an expressive envelope differed radically from the July Monarchy conception of the facade as transparent, and that difference changed notions of what constituted a legible facade. For the architects of the Second Empire and early Third Republic, the facade achieved legibility and legitimacy when it translated the depths of the interior onto its surface *without* exposing the family's intimate secrets, and without revealing any discrepancy between external appearances and internal affairs—clearly a paradoxical imperative. Recall Daly's configuration of the facade as "the family's clothing . . . destined to provide it with an envelope, to shelter and to lend itself to all its movements": his metaphors exposed the contradictions inherent in the demand for the facade's opacity, since in his comment, the facade both conceals what it encloses by sheltering the family, and reveals what it envelops, by lending itself to all its movements. Architects, hygienists, and urban observers insisted that the house should serve as the family's protective clothing, but rarely developed fully the paradoxical consequences of their demand. In the following chapter, we will see how Zola's naturalist novel, *Pot-Bouille,* did not hesitate to show how the apartment house performed a *mis à nu* that undressed the bourgeois family and exposed its dirty laundry to view, while at the same time the novel developed fully a problem that other discourses of Paris glossed over—the impossibility of ever fully interiorizing the home.

5

Zola's Restless House

EMILE ZOLA'S *POT-BOUILLE*, WRITTEN IN 1882 and set in the early 1860s, is often read as an attack on Haussmannization. Zola's harsh novel about life in a middle-class apartment building, critics claim, demystified Haussmann's images of Parisian luxury and progress by exposing the literal and moral filth that lay behind the new apartment buildings' deceptively imposing facades.[1] Indeed, *Pot-Bouille* did engage with contemporaneous discourses about Paris but—as the previous chapter demonstrated—those discourses themselves did not simply celebrate a modernized, expanded city. Rather, they advocated "interiorization": the enclosure of the city itself, the reconception of the apartment house as an absolutely private space, and the sequestration of men, women, and children within the home.

The notion of interiorization is crucial to *Pot-Bouille*, which compresses the urban novel's multiple settings into a single middle-class apartment building viewed almost solely from within. Yet the novel's relationship to interiorization is complex, neither a simple replication of the discourses of public health and architecture, nor an outright rejection of them. As a naturalist novelist, Zola shared with many public health reformers a belief in environmental determinism, and the novel signals its investment in interiorization by enclosing the field of the urban bildungsroman and representing the family and the apartment building as coincident structures. However, where social hygienists considered secure interiors to be a solution, Zola's novel depicts interiorization itself as a problem. The novel relentlessly shows the impossibility of complete interiorization, focusing on the external limits that necessarily bound any interior; dramatizing the explosions and implosions that result precisely when interiorization approaches its purest state; and repeatedly demonstrating that even when contained within a single residence, families are riven by adultery, women's bodies fail to maintain their proper boundaries, and men's paternal authority becomes voided. Both the novel and reactions to it—which included lawsuits by people claiming to be recognizable models of the characters—reveal the tensions between an urban project intent on securing privacy by enclosing space and protecting it from view, and a naturalist concept of the book as both the record of a narrator's intervention in the scenes he had observed, and a conduit by which readers could enter those scenes.

The Interiorization of the Urban Novel

The opening passage of *Pot-Bouille* encapsulates both the entire novel to follow and the paradoxes of a modernized Paris constricted in its very expansion. "Rue Neuve-St-Augustin, a traffic jam halted the cab loaded with three trunks, which was bringing Octave from the Gare de Lyon."[2] The novel's first sentence emphatically places its hero in the middle of a new Paris. Octave is on a street with "new" attached to its name, in the precincts of the newly planned, still unbuilt opera house (19), near the site of the projected rue du Dix-décembre (later the rue du Quatre-septembre) (19, 212), and his ultimate destination, "a new house," is on another new street, the rue de Choiseul (11). These multiple signs of urban novelty place the narrative in a recently constructed present and simultaneously gesture toward Octave's future success as the inventor of the modern department store, Au Bonheur des Dames, also located in the renovated center of a rapidly changing, modernizing Paris.

Yet the opening paragraph suggests equally strongly that the new city's very traffic, commerce, and dynamism have the effect of stopping time and hindering progress through space, of depriving Octave of movement and comprehension. Circulation and traffic, taken to new extremes, produce paralysis. In the hiatus of a traffic jam, Octave's heightened appetite for urban stimulation threatens to become vertigo:

He remained surprised by the day's sudden end. . . . The oaths of the drivers thwacking the snorting horses, the endless shoulder-rubbing of the sidewalks, the hurried stream of shops overflowing with salespeople and customers dazed him [*l'étourdissaient*]; for, though he had dreamed of Paris as

cleaner, he hadn't dared to hope that its commerce would be so fierce, he felt
it publicly open to the appetites of robust men. (11)

The passage describes the city as an object to be consumed and Octave
as one of the "robust men" who will devour Paris and promote its consumption by others. The "publicly open" Paris and the commercially
hungry Octave share similar capacities for infinite expansion. Yet the
very volume of activity that makes the city so open also induces its aspiring consumer to shut down from a surfeit of stimuli and opportunity.
A "dazed" Octave experiences the double sensations implied by the verb
étourdir: the exhilaration and intoxication that signify a heightened sensitivity to stimuli, and the immobility, dizziness, and loss of consciousness that also accompany that state. And, just as the city's elasticity produces a corollary rigidity, its promise of endless outward expansion and
its availability for limitless consumption lead to its eventual enclosure
within the person who consumes it; by inciting appetite, Paris solicits its
own ingestion.

   Given the interplay of expansion and enclosure, movement and stillness that governs the novel's opening, it is not surprising that this novel
of new Paris rapidly contains its action within the domestic interior of a
bourgeois apartment building, the setting that will dominate the novel.
Critics often interpret that setting in terms of a thematics of interiorization.[3] Zola himself described the novel as depicting "the entire *interior*
life of one of our rich Parisian residences."[4] Brian Nelson, in *Zola and
the Bourgeoisie,* argues that the novel's "central character is . . . the
house itself" and describes the latter as an *"enveloping* symbol of the
corruption and decadence of the bourgeoisie," notable for its "hermetic
enclosure," its "closed doors and introverted apartments"; he also suggests that the apartment building's internal organization governs its
episodic structure, in which each chapter is "built around detachable,
self-enclosed scenes."[5] Janice Best points out that the novel's paradigmatic form is "a closed circle that turns back upon itself" and that the
novel's literal center, chapters nine and ten, corresponds to a narrative
apotheosis of interiorization when Octave enters the landlord's bedroom, "the house's true center."[6] Best's evocation of the closed circle
echoes the metaphor that Henri Céard used in an 1882 review of *Pot-
Bouille,* in which he called the building "a sort of large retort," com-
paring it to a closed laboratory vessel with a narrow outlet tube through
which substances escape only under the extreme pressure created by
heat, chemical reactions, and their own enclosure.[7] Céard's metaphor

translated the title phrase, *pot-bouille,* an idiom that used the image of a stewpot to signify everydayness, into the more hermetic realm of controlled experimentation, but whether as a bubbling meal or a laboratory retort, the title phrase evokes a strained, simmering containment, an eminently precarious interiorization.

The novel's insistence on interiorization in its plot, its structure, and its thematization of domestic space may account for critics' consistent unwillingness to read *Pot-Bouille* as one of Zola's *Parisian* novels.[8] (Indeed, critics rarely read *Pot-Bouille* at all, although the novel enjoyed great popularity during its serialization and upon initial publication; 30,000 copies were in print in 1883, compared to 27,500 copies of *Nana* in 1881.)[9] Unlike *Le Ventre de Paris* and *Au bonheur des dames, Pot-Bouille* does not focus on a commercial Parisian locale; unlike *Une Page d'amour* or *L'Oeuvre,* it lacks descriptive set pieces about the city; it provides neither *La Curée*'s fictional reenactment of Haussmannization nor *L'Assommoir*'s dramatic simulation of urban working-class life. The failure to read Zola's novel about an apartment house as a novel about Paris has stemmed in part from the critical tendency to oppose the city and the home, and hence to assume that a novel about domestic interiors cannot be a novel about the city; that assumption has led *Pot-Bouille*'s critics to neglect the apartment building's urban dimensions for its domestic ones, thus masking the extent to which the novel actively interiorizes both the apartment building and the city.[10]

At the very outset, the narrator interiorizes the apartment house by describing its apertures and corridors as oriented inward, and by suppressing any mention of the paths that lead outside the apartment. From Octave's first tour of the building to the novel's final passages, the narrator never describes windows, doors, or vestibules as leading to the street, although the views from a window onto a street or from a street into a window constitute two of the most important motifs of the *Rougon-Macquart* series as a whole.[11] No character in *Pot-Bouille* looks out or into a window, with one rule-proving exception: on first entering his fifth-floor room, Octave peers through his window into an internal courtyard, one of whose peculiarly decorated walls nullifies the window's function as a visual opening. Octave sees

> nothing but uniform windows, without a birdcage, without a flowerpot, displaying the monotony of their white curtains. To hide the large naked wall of the house on the left, which completed the square of the courtyard, someone had repeated the windows there, false, painted windows, with their shutters

eternally closed, behind which the cloistered lives of the neighboring apartments appeared to continue. (16)

This equation of true and false windows negates the window's potential
for transparency, as well as its ability to transport, visually, the inhabitant of an interior into a space external to it. From Octave's point of
view, the white curtains of the real windows replace a view with a void,
particularly since the French adjective attached to the curtains, *blanc,*
suggests blankness as well as whiteness (the absence of color). The windows' repetition, "uniformity," and "monotony" imply that even if the
interiors covered by the curtains were visible, there would be nothing to
see. The false windows signify claustration and block vision not only because they are opaque paintings rather than transparent openings, but
also because they simulate "eternally closed shutters." Even the clause
"without a birdcage, without a flowerpot" serves to negate an aspect of
the apartment house's potential continuity with exterior spaces, since in
the July Monarchy discourses discussed in chapter one, birdcages and
flowerpots were the decorations that typically marked the apartment
window as both a comical, miniaturized threshold between nature and
the city, and as a transparent, self-advertising conduit between the street's
sociability and the apartment's.

The narrator accentuates the apartment building's orientation inward
by commenting repeatedly on its enclosed, internal features: stairways
and landings, the closed doors of each apartment, and the interior courtyard. The narrator attaches epithets of silence to the hermetically sealed
staircase and associates the shiny surface of the doors with a closed system of mirror images: "Octave felt himself penetrated by the grave silence of the staircase. . . . It was the dead quiet of a bourgeois living
room, carefully enclosed, in which not a single breath entered from outside. Behind the beautiful doors of gleaming mahogany, there were, as it
were [*comme*], abysses of decency" (15). The public staircase becomes
a private room, and the luster of the doors deflects the possibility of seeing what lies behind them; their sheen reflects the inquisitive gaze back
upon itself. The presence of "as it were [*comme*]" between the assertive
"there were" and its predicate, "abysses of honesty," also safeguards the
doors from simply becoming revelatory mirrors, since *comme* indicates
that the doors can only resemble a likeness, not provide a view. That the
likeness the doors resemble is an "abyss" emphasizes the extent to
which the doors frustrate any direct or oblique vision of what lies thoroughly concealed behind them.[12]

In addition to describing the apartment house as a physically enclosed space with no external issues, *Pot-Bouille* interiorizes three overlapping plot lines that earlier nineteenth-century French fiction had given an outward-bound direction: the plot of urban conquest, in which a man makes his way in a city by dispersing his erotic and ambitious energies as widely as possible; the marriage plot, in which a woman or a man must travel outside her or his immediate domestic circle in search of a spouse; and the adultery plot, in which a wife or husband leaves home to meet a lover, or a lover intrudes on and at least temporarily sunders a closed marital unit. The interiorization of each of these plots in *Pot-Bouille* contributes to the representation of the apartment house as a perfectly self-enclosed space that internalizes urban activities and contains domestic relations.

In the manner of earlier nineteenth-century fictional provincials, such as Balzac's Eugène Rastignac and Lucien de Rubempré, Octave Mouret announces his ambition to conquer Paris early in the novel: "Conquering Paris is a must" (23).[13] Octave's topographical strategy for conquering the city, however, is counterintuitive: faced with the choice of sallying out into the urban fray or confining himself to home ground, he almost always chooses to stay at home. His exploration of the city thus takes the form of an investigation into the nooks and crannies of his apartment building, and true to the principle of the urban conquest narrative—that knowledge of the city translates into power within it—Octave's attachment to his domestic space does not go unrewarded.[14] When Octave has free time on his hands that he wants to "utilize," he pays "some visits in the house" (260). On one of his Sundays off he "persist[s] in absolutely not wanting to go out" and is treated as a result to the "unexpected spectacle" of a second-floor apartment whose open door reveals that it is used as a clandestine trysting place, not as the office the porter claims it to be (137). Immediately after, he visits the confines of Mme Juzeur's third-floor apartment, "which smelled a bit stuffy" with its "balmy, dead atmosphere of a casket" (139). Octave and Juzeur then begin to make love in the excessively enclosed rooms, as if to replicate within the third-floor apartment what he has just glimpsed inside the second-floor one.

Octave's many sexual liaisons with the women in his building simultaneously interiorize the plots of urban conquest (sexual and economic) and the adultery plot. When Campardon warns Octave, "if you bring a woman in here, it will cause a revolution" (16), Octave takes his advice literally by planning to seduce his neighbors: "it wasn't bringing women in, to take one in the house [*dans la maison*]" (79). Octave first gets involved with an immediate neighbor, Marie, who lives on his floor and whose propinquity constitutes her primary attraction: "Such a woman was very convenient; all he had to do was stretch out his arm, when he wanted her, and she didn't cost him a cent. . . . [I]n the end, this economy [*bon marché*] and convenience [*commodité*] moved him" (125). Octave's affair with Marie interiorizes the type of sexual exchange usually associated with the exterior activity of "streetwalking," since it blends the *commodité* of marriage with the *bon marché* of prostitution. While Marie's husband runs errands, Octave can quickly visit his "neighbor" (206); when her husband walks Marie's parents home, Octave can take her on his lap, "like a happy husband . . . finally returning home [*se retrouvant enfin chez lui*]" (143); but when Marie gets pregnant, Octave need not worry about supporting a child that she and her husband, we are told repeatedly, can ill afford.

Like Eugène Rastignac, who conflates sexual conquest with urban success when he cries "A nous deux" to a woman and to Paris at the end of *Le Père Goriot*, Octave plans to use women to gain a foothold in the city and asserts his "wish to make it by means of women. . . . [A]bove all he desired *la parisienne*" (286–287). Immediately after discounting Marie as a burden and counting up the women who have refused his sexual advances, he asks himself worriedly, "Was Paris going to refuse him?" (223). Octave asks himself this question when he is about to embark on a walk, and his silent question and unusual destination (out of the house) coincide with the centripetal action of a female voice drawing him back into the apartment building's circumference: "As he placed his foot on the sidewalk, a woman's voice called him, and he recognized Berthe" (223), another female neighbor who hires him to work for her and her husband in the building's ground-floor shop.

Octave quickly adds sexual intimacy to his amalgamation of residence and employment by seducing Berthe into an affair that remains singularly interior. The two meet throughout the apartment building—in the store, in her bedroom, in his room, and in a maid's room—but never in a hotel room, as he once suggests, nor during an outing. Octave and Berthe first have sex in the bedroom she shares with her husband, in a situation defined by its enclosure and isolation from external observation: "They were alone, free, sheltered from any surprise, the door bolted. This security, the room's enclosed balminess [*tiédeur enfermée*], penetrated them" (298). After seducing Berthe, Octave sustains that warmth by penetrating her household and business, both called *maison:* "Octave burrowed into the house [*faisait son trou dans la maison*] the way he burrowed into covers to get warm" (288). The French term for "burrow," *faire un trou,* anticipates the instabilities of interiorization that the novel fully dramatizes in other episodes: to establish himself deep within the house, Octave needs to penetrate it from outside in a way that literally "makes a hole," creates an opening that compromises the house's interiority.

Octave continues to combine several activities and functions into one compact space even after he has left the apartment on the rue de Choiseul. Toward the end of the novel, he realizes his professional and sexual ambitions by stepping outside the apartment building to marry the owner of Au Bonheur des Dames, Mme Hédouin; although it takes place outside the novel's central apartment building, that action still fulfills Octave's initial goal of translating a "commercial intimacy" (204) into a sexual one so that he will "find his bread and his bed" in the same place (214–215). His persistence produces a correspondingly circular temporal effect, reminiscent of the temporal contractions of Second Empire urban sketches: when he returns to the building as a married man in the novel's final chapter, Octave has "the singular sensation of beginning again. . . . [T]oday repeated yesterday" (461).

The novel subjects all the characters' sexual affairs to its interiorizing imperative. Berthe Josserand first appears returning from a party by foot, and we learn that she must walk out on the street rather than ride inside a carriage because she has once again failed to secure a husband (33). Success for Berthe, as for Octave, comes after she confines her sights to her domestic interior. Only after Berthe and her family have given up on searching all over Paris for a husband, and instead contract their horizons to their home, do they find one—Auguste Vabre, the landlord's son and the proprietor of the ground-floor boutique.[15] Berthe forces Auguste to propose by literally enclosing both of them: she "finally pushed Auguste into the window embrasure, where she confined him [*l'enfermait*] with her pretty gestures. . . . [T]he large red silk curtain . . . completely hid . . . Auguste and Berthe" (110, 117). This window, like other windows in *Pot-Bouille,* blocks vision in every direction. Berthe's and Auguste's momentary inability to see either the room or the street, their visual containment, foreshadows their permanent domestic containment within a single marital unit, formed after Berthe forces Auguste to propose by loudly drawing attention to the physical intimacy that has ensued from their spatial proximity. Interiorization governs even the narrator's description of the marriage negotiations. After Berthe screams, Auguste is secured as a husband, literally "wrapped up [*emballé*]" (119) and the priest must talk to Berthe in order to "cover up [*couvrir*] the scandal of the window with his consecrated character" (122).

Berthe's marriage is finalized in another interior when her father meets with Auguste's brother-in-law Duveyrier at the house of Duveyrier's mistress, "a house . . . where he can't refuse anything" (155). By calling the woman's apartment a *maison* in the most domestic sense of the word, the novel again subjects adultery to the same architectural enclosure as marriage. Marriage translates the union of two individuals into a corresponding spatial unity, but the domestication of adultery and prostitution situates activities external to and disruptive of marriage and the home at their very center. Indeed, the *Figaro*'s review of *Pot-Bouille* understood the novel's equation of adultery with prostitution to effect a substitution of one kind of "house" for another: "this is a house of assignation: the concierge should not be in her lodge, but on the doorstep, to inform the passersby, 'We have very pretty female tenants here.'" [16] In Zola's earlier novel, *Nana*, the imbrication of brothel [*maison close*] and home [*maison*] results when an aristocratic husband discovers that his wife has been unfaithful, as sexually unruly as the courtesan Nana, and figures that resemblance to himself as a resemblance between the furniture in the two women's houses. His knowledge of his wife's affair leads him to spend a night in the street, jealously watching her lover's house. *Nana* thus suggests that women's common sexuality dissolves distinctions between interiors and estranges men from their homes, driving them into the street.

In *Pot-Bouille*, however, men's alienation and women's interchangeability mean that any house can present itself as a self-enclosed and comforting interior. The novel thus multiplies interiors, makes no attempt to distinguish original and legitimate interiors from illicit copies, and represents no space as external to its series of uniform interiors. Duveyrier, exiled from his marital home by his wife, recovers domesticity with his mistress when he is driven to "make himself an amusing little interior elsewhere." Duveyrier is even more securely ensconced in his extramarital home than in his marital one, since his mistress "can't resort to kicking him out, as his wife does" (164). When Duveyrier's mistress finally does leave him, he interiorizes adultery even further by confining his sexual affairs to Adèle, a servant in his building. His son simultaneously beds the family cook, an act which his mother condones because she prefers "that the rascal [has] a mistress at home [*chez elle*]. . . . Outside [*au dehors*], who knew what a young man could catch" (425). Berthe's uncle Bachelard similarly keeps a mistress whose apartment radiates "a provincial, interior calm" (159). Its "dead air" replicates the atmosphere of Juzeur's rooms and contributes to the "happy good nature of this interior" (159, 161). That sepulchral interiority remains intact even after Bachelard's mistress has betrayed him by sleeping with another man, as if to assert that what takes place there leaves no mark and can never annul one interior's interchangeability with others.

Pot-Bouille even encloses its porters, who in earlier decades personified the traffic between street and home (see chapters one and two). The married couple who work in the building occupy an apartment whose only window opens onto the building's internal vestibule. The *portière,* Mme Gourd, is an invalid who rarely leaves the bedroom of her *loge* and who passes her time "lying in an armchair, her hands joined, doing nothing" (13), while her husband takes a more active, policing role within the building. The literature of the 1840s almost always portrayed the male porter as ineffectual and confined, the *portière* as active, shuttling between the apartment and the street. In this novel of the 1880s, however, the female porter has developed a body whose swellings "prevented her from going even as far as the sidewalk" (126).

Pot-Bouille's reconfiguration of the *portière* as immobile and cloistered suggests that interiorization has more crippling effects on women than it does on Octave (although we will see in the next sections that *failures* of interiorization particularly undermine paternal power in the novel). The novel shows female interiorization taken to such extremes that women who break the rule of female containment cannot simply walk out the door but must jump out of windows. During a party, a scandalous story circulates about a "girl who turned out badly," who despite being "perfectly brought up . . . [had] tried to throw herself into the street twice" (142); and when Berthe's husband reacts violently to her debts, "without crying out, choking with anger, she ran to open the window, as if to hurl herself onto the pavement" (296). If violent attempts to eject themselves from their apartment constitute the epitome of women's bad behavior, their good behavior entails becoming as perfectly self-contained as their apartment building appears to be. The novel describes female education, female conduct, and marriage in terms of internment, suffocation, and enclosure; even female servants are praised for rarely going out (29). Female education consists of shielding daughters from all external stimuli, "even from the slightest breezes of the street" (30), and forbidding them to "rest [their] . . . elbows on the windowsill" (87). This mode of education turns girls themselves into closed systems whose bodily surfaces yield no information about what lies within: the Campardon's daughter, Angèle, thus cultivates the "enigmatic air of a well brought-up girl, instructed to say nothing, and of whose true thoughts one knew nothing" (221). The ultimate goal of this education is marriage, which the novel's maternal characters frequently describe idiomatically as *cas[ant] sa fille*—literally, tucking their daughters away (72, 85, 109, 161). Yet the very extremes to which the novel takes the interiorization of women's lives and bodies leads not only to female stasis but to explosion, to the spectacular failures of interiorization that are the subject of the next section.

Interiorization's Failures

Interiorization in *Pot-Bouille* fails most obviously because of the servants who occupy the building. On the one hand, the novel advocates the right of all classes to enjoy domestic enclosure and criticizes the apartment's bourgeois tenants for depriving workers of the virtues of domestic privacy. In one episode, the apartment's porter and landlord threaten a male worker with eviction precisely because he wants to unite his family under one roof. When he brings his wife to his room for a conjugal visit with an explicitly reproductive aim—"to make a son" (146)—the porter and landlord respond that the presence of "this woman [*cette femme*]" is a "scandal." The worker then retorts that "this" is not just any *femme*— "c'est la mienne" (145). His shift from the demonstrative to the possessive modifies "woman" into "wife," but the landlord refuses to acknowledge the male worker's assertion of property in a woman and prevents him from translating marriage into a residential situation and a familial outcome.[17] In a similar episode, the landlord and magistrate Duveyrier condemns a pregnant woman worker for the infanticide she committed after he had evicted her from his building and yet he himself impregnates one of his servants, who also abandons her child. The bourgeois characters thus deny working-class tenants access to a familial interior, while granting themselves the privilege of interiorizing even adultery.

While the working-class characters who are exiled from their apartments represent the universality of the desire to create secure domestic interiors, the servants who work and live in the building pose a threat to the interiorization of even the bourgeois home. Servants import dangerous elements of urban life into the space of the apartment house and thus undermine the enclosure of domestic space. They work against its sanitization—a crucial result of successful interiorization, according to the hygienists discussed in the previous chapter. They are necessary evils, say the characters who employ them, and the narrator himself agrees. By frequently equating servants and their speech with sewage, the narrator emphasizes the danger to cleanliness posed by the very people hired to keep the house free from dirt. For example, Octave's and the reader's first clue that the building's bourgeois appearance is not all that it seems comes from his observation of the servants and their space, the interior courtyard onto which all the kitchens face:

> An awful noise escaped from it. . . . [T]he swarthy chambermaid and the fat cook, an exuberant old woman, were leaning into the narrow shaft of the interior courtyard in which, face to face, the kitchens of each floor were lit up. They shrieked together, their backs straining, while, from the bottom of this narrow passage, coarse shouts rose, mixed with laughter and curses. It was like the overflow of a sewer: all the servants of the house were there, relieving themselves. Octave recalled the bourgeois majesty of the grand staircase. (18)

The narrator exposes the building's bourgeois pretentions by juxtaposing Octave's memory of the ornate staircase with the dirt that he witnesses in the courtyard, yet the narrator also espouses the values underlying those pretentions when he anathematizes the servants as excremental and excessive: they are "swarthy"; they lean into a *boyau,* a word that means both a narrow passage and entrails and resembles the word for mud, *boue;* and the flow of their speech, equivalent to the flow of urine, transforms the courtyard into a sewer.

The servants' eruptions of and into filth, within the courtyard that is one of the apartment house's most enclosed spaces, both constitute the invasion of the building's interior by external forces and figure an implosion that contaminates and collapses the building's interior from within. The servants occupy a perfectly interiorized space, "the narrow shaft of the internal courtyard," whose windows do not open onto external vistas but mirror one another, "face to face"; the presence there of servants and sewers marks an interiorization so thorough that it incorporates and absorbs people and functions normally imagined as exterior to the home. Infrastructure becomes intrastructure, as Berthe discovers later in the novel when she hears the servants' conversation and confronts "a collapsed sewer that each morning spilled out there, *near her*" (327). That very interiorization, however, paradoxically makes the internal courtyard and its denizens equivalent to two urban elements, the street crowd and the sewer. The servants indulge in noisy swearing and act in unison, like a crowd; and because the courtyard forms a closed column, it becomes a sewer, which should not be visible above ground, within the home. Moving infrastructure inside undoes the apartment

house's interiorization, by making the center of the home reveal everything that it should hide, and by turning an internal courtyard into a
miniaturized city street scene. Actions and objects that normally belong
in the streets or lie invisible underground become visible and audible by
virtue of their installation within the building:

> the maids, from top to bottom, appeared at the windows, and violently ex-
> onerated themselves. The plug had been pulled, a flood of abominable words
> poured out of the cesspool. During the thaw, the walls of the courtyard
> dripped with humidity, a stench rose from the dark little courtyard, all the
> hidden decay of the stories seemed to melt and exhale itself through this
> sewer of the house. (464)

The riotous crowd that the bourgeois tenants later fear might invade their
house is already in place, in the form of their own servants, and the courtyard is a stagnant or overflowing sewer that does not lead waste out of
the house but keeps it circulating internally. The passage identifies that
waste as the product of the house's own internal collapse; what lay "hidden" within the apartments begins to "melt and exhale itself," not in a
purifying outward flow, but in a circular disintegration that folds the
building's decayed insides into its stagnant core.

Pot-Bouille also depicts the employers of these servants as subject to
failures of interiorization. Throughout the novel, the contradictions of
interiorization as a simultaneous movement outward and inward manifest themselves through the body's capacity to emit and absorb sounds
and breath. A host of characters oscillate between containment and explosion, strangulation and exclamation, deafness and hearing, or simultaneously engage in both. The novel features noises that move from one
interior to another, for example, in the characters' frequent whispers,
which transfer sound from one opening (the mouth) to another (the ear)
with as little exteriorization as possible. Indeed, the novel features an
obsessive whisperer, Trublot, who also thoroughly interiorizes sex by
sleeping only with servants who live in the apartment building. Interiorization of breath and air takes a more violent form when the narrative
refers to characters "strangled" by their emotions, to "the strangled
shape" of rooms, and to the "suffocating heat" of apartments (168, 197).

Those interiorizations in turn produce explosions, leading to cir-
cuitous relays in which neither movement outward nor inward ever becomes complete. Whispers and strangled noises alternate with shouts,
which represent the forceful expulsion of sound that cannot be contained.
The noise of music resonates throughout the novel in the form of the

standardized piano-playing that issues from each apartment at the same
time every day (24) and of Clotilde Duveyrier's musical performances;
in several scenes, music, blows, and conversation all vie to create an
overpowering noise that cannot be contained in any single room or apartment.[18] The Josserand household produces explosions of noise most
consistently: the mother yells, "letting everything out [*lâchant tout*]"
(35), and the son, Saturnin, "terrified the house with his blindingly violent crises" (52); his "muted knocks [*coups sourds*]" make themselves
heard over the sound of his sister's piano-playing (68). Explosion represents no easy escape from confinement, however, since Zola's language
makes Saturnin's explosive violence and externally oriented blows coincide with the introversion suggested by blindness and deafness (*sourd*,
though used in this sense to mean mute, literally means deaf).

These outpourings of sound constitute both explosions of noise and
demands to be heard—demands to be interiorized within a hearer's ears
that simultaneously reveal the auditor to be open to the exterior. Characters thus frequently protect their own interiority by temporarily cultivating deafness; for example, Mme Josserand's exhortations make her
daughters "deaf" to her pronouncements (35, 38). Clotilde's music,
which represents her attempt to incorporate guests into her social circle,
unwittingly both suffocates their voices and turns those voices into
breaches of her domestic interior: because of the noise created by her
playing, "the voices were smothered beneath the low ceiling, one caught
only a buzzing, like the sound of carts loaded with cobblestones, making the windowpanes tremble" (116). The "smothered" voices of her auditors seem to compress them back into the bodies that produce them,
but the same voices also undo the apartment's interiority by metaphorically enabling the street's sounds (carts) and even its substance (cobblestones) to invade the boundaries of the home. Though Jean Borie observes that in Zola's work "external pressure tends . . . to facilitate the
street's penetration into the home," in *Pot-Bouille*, internal pressure
paves the way for the entrance of the street.[19]

Several characters in particular come to emblematize the impossibility of perfect interiorization by combining containment and explosion in
one person, action, or scene. Although many are described as suffo-
cated, stifled, and strangled, the very same figures are just as frequently
associated with the verbs *déborder*, to overflow, to burst, and *lâcher*, to
release, to unleash. The guests at Mme Duveyrier's are packed so tightly
that they crush one another—*on s'écrasait*—yet that congestion immediately leads to an expansive brimming over—"two heavy streams of

black suits overflowed" (104; see also 115). Sometimes two characters are opposed, one representing containment, the other explosion: Hédouin's unflappable calm, her air of perfect self-sufficiency, produce the opposite effect on her employee Octave—he ends up "beside himself," literally "outside of himself [hors de lui]" (214). Mme Josserand's body constantly threatens to exceed the clothes and corsets that contain it, as when "her incensed bosom finally burst the bodice" of her dress (399). Saturnin, the Josserands' only son, is alternately sequestered and liberated, concealed within the apartment's most interior, invisible rooms or allowed free run of the building. Though he is often locked up, Saturnin also specializes in opening locks (143, 149) even breaking through such barriers as the windowpanes of a coach transporting him to an asylum. Saturnin himself understands people as bodily envelopes whose interior he wants to violate and open to view by "skewer[ing]" them (171); he repeatedly vows to slash people's skin—"I'm going to open the flesh of their belly" (61) or "bleed [them] like . . . pig[s]" (290)—but he knows that to do so, he must contain himself: when he tries to attack Auguste, he enters the sleeping alcove, the apartment's most interior space, "muffling [étouffant]" the sound of his steps (386). The novel thus suggests that interiorization cannot be sustained because the very activities and attributes associated with perfect interiorization—containment, enclosure, covering, wrapping, repression, silence, sequestration—produce diametrically opposite effects of explosion, discharge, excess, escape, and overflow.

The increasingly heightened expression of the interplay between bodily repression and outburst achieves its apotheosis in the novel's apparently incongruous final episode, a graphic and prolonged scene of birth, in which the Josserands' servant Adèle silently performs the "work of expulsion" (447) after a pregnancy so perfectly concealed—in that sense, so perfectly interiorized—that not one occupant of the apartment has noticed it. The containment of her hidden pregnancy gives way to the sunderings of labor: "it seemed to her that everything in her was breaking, she had the horrified feeling that her backside and her front were bursting, were no longer anything but a hole [trou] through which her life was streaming" (448). True to the novel's unresolvable oscillation between interiorization and exteriorization, Adèle ultimately conceals the infant that has exited her body by hiding it in a doorway located outside the apartment building but within the arcade contiguous to it (449).

When the novel enlists its central theme of adultery to represent the contradictions inherent in interiority, it posits a series of analogies and determining relations among the bodies of women, the bodies of fathers, and the facades and foundations of the apartment building. The characters' constant interiorization of adultery entails a paradoxical desire to create an interior so complete and secure that it would include even the extradomestic within the home. The Campardons, for example, expose the self-sufficiency of the domestic interior as inherently contradictory because they complete their couple by incorporating someone external to it. The Campardons become a "patriarchal" family (334) only after they have made their domestic arrangements polygamous and moved Gasparine, Mme Campardon's cousin and M. Campardon's mistress, into their apartment. Their family ties solidify as a result, in a process that combines expansion and contraction: "Octave understood that he hindered their expansion; he felt that he was one too many in such a united household" (208).[20]

Although adultery yields a more unified family interior, the novel also depicts interiorization leading to adulterous affairs that disrupt the family and the building; as critic Jean Borie puts it, "decent enclosure facilitates licentiousness."[21] Marie Pichon, Berthe Vabre, and Valérie Vabre are the exemplary results of the cloistered education that Zola condemned in articles written for the *Figaro* just before the publication of *Pot-Bouille*. In them he argued that the "suffocation" of girls within "narrow lodgings" led directly to hysterical "dizzy spells [*étourdissements*]" and that their enclosure and protection from the "outside [*dehors*]" encouraged them to commit adultery "out of stupidity," as a result of the mental "void [*vide*]" produced by claustration.[22]

Pot-Bouille represents adultery as both produced by and productive of a dangerous interiorization, but in a movement that repeats the novel's characteristic oscillation between internalization and externalization, it depicts the exteriorization that results from adulterous affairs as equally problematic. After Auguste breaks into Octave's room and catches him with his wife, Berthe flees but finds herself locked out of her apartment, forced to wander up and down the central stairway. Berthe remains trapped outside the internal space of domestic refuge and becomes a foreign element within her own house: "she collided with a closed door. Then, driven out from her own place, with no clothing, she lost her head, she rushed through all the floors, like a hunted beast who doesn't know where to crouch" (349). The narrative makes adultery pitiable by showing that it banishes a woman from her apartment into the building's public spaces, which it compares to the open space of the hunt; Berthe's motion as she moves from one space to another is relentlessly restless, but she also remains absolutely imprisoned as she runs up and down within the building.

Berthe's transformation into an alien, external presence within the house repeats itself at the level of the building when the narrator uncharacteristically presents the apartment house from an external point of view after news of Berthe's adultery becomes public. Her night in the staircase produces a scandal that exposes the building to external scrutiny and defines it in terms of its facade when, for the first time since the opening pages, the narrator describes the apartment on the rue de Choiseul from the vantage of the street and the point of view of noninhabitants: "the maids must have talked, because the women neighbors stopped, the shopkeepers came out by their doors, their eyes up in the air, searching and digging into [*fouillant*] the stories, in the wide-eyed way that people study houses where a crime has taken place" (358).

Fouillant, a word that literally means "digging," conveys the disruptive energy behind a gaze that probes the impenetrable unity of the facade. A few chapters later Duveyrier, the building's landlord (and Auguste's brother-in-law), shows the force that such a gaze has when he argues that the still-estranged spouses must reunite so that his house will no longer be exposed to public view: "he kept seeing . . . passersby looking at his house from top to bottom, this house that he and his father-in-law had enjoyed adorning with all the domestic virtues; this couldn't continue. . . . Therefore, in the name of public decency, he was pushing Auguste toward a reconciliation" (416). Adultery becomes inextricable with exteriorization for Duveyrier, who feels that his building is sullied simply because outsiders examine it. To be truly private, Duveyrier's worries imply, the building would have to be invisible from without, yet its "domestic virtues" become visible only if they are externally manifested as "public decency." Duveyrier wants the impossible: an externally apparent interiorization that displays its invisibility. His impossible wish captures the inherent contradictions of the facade, which both defines the interior by demarcating the difference between inside and outside, and makes complete interiorization impossible, since it endows the interior with an external surface.

Women's bodies and the apartment building's facade are particularly vulnerable to failures of interiorization in *Pot-Bouille*, perhaps because, as we have seen, they are also its primary sites; a failure in the integrity of the female body implies a failure of architectural integrity, and vice versa. That conflation of women's bodies with the building itself appears, for example, in the thoughts of two characters who live outside the apartment house but are privy to its secrets, the priest and the doctor, who focus their attention on the faulty interiority of the apartment's female inhabitants. "Both of them were in on the same secrets: while the priest received these women's confessions, the doctor, for thirty years, had been delivering the mothers' babies and caring for the daughters" (438). The doctor takes an analytical, almost dissecting stance toward his women patients when he imagines himself confronting the corruption that lies within them. He delivers "the exact observations of an old practitioner, with a profound knowledge of the underside of the neighborhood [*qui connaissait à fond les dessous de quartier*]. He let himself go, talking about the women . . . and, in his rage, sounded the . . . death-knell of a class, the decomposition and the crumbling of the bourgeoisie, whose decaying stays would crack of their own accord" (439). The doctor equates his medical knowledge with an archaeological capacity to dig beneath surfaces to "the underside"; when he equates "decomposition" with cracking "stays," he conflates the demise of a class with both architectural collapse and the disintegration of specifically female bodily supports.

Unlike the dissecting doctor, the priest covers up women's exposed interiors after they "open their hearts" to him. He attempts to bolster his parish's foundations and "tr[ies] above all to smother any scandal" (186), in order to recreate his parishioners as properly interiorized. The priest, however, suffers from architectural troubles of his own that also become distinctly feminine. The peculiar construction of his church, like that of the apartment house, fails to preserve the proper divisions among sacred, secular, and commercial spaces. Octave sees both that failure and the contradictions of the church's facade:

> He looked with curiosity at this church doorway, which one entered through a private residence, this porter's lodge where at night one would have to ring God's bell. . . . On the sidewalk, he lifted his eyes again: the house's naked facade stretched out, with its barred, curtainless windows; but the iron bars held back flower-boxes on the fifth-floor windows, and . . . narrow shops punctured the heavy walls, shops from which the clergy drew a profit. (217–218)

The church's unconventional entrance connects it to a private residence; the presence of flowerpots and the fissures in the walls created by the shops compromise the facade's "naked," ecclesiastic purity; and the church interior itself is under construction, hence "open to the great outdoors [*ouvert au grand air du dehors*]" (215).

The church's insufficient interiority comes to the fore during incidents of female adultery, when Valérie uses the church as a place of assignation, leaving her child with an attendant while she takes advantage of an internal passage in the church that allows her to exit, unseen, to the street (177). The flimsiness of the church is epitomized by a broken statue of the Virgin Mary, another indication that both the building and women fail to maintain their intactness by allowing their interiors either to be penetrated or to spill into view. The narrator draws our attention to images of the Virgin Mary, the symbol par excellence of inviolate female interiority, that depict even her insides as susceptible to exposure and to sexualization. In the novel's opening scene, Octave notices a picture of the Virgin as he visits Campardon's study, "a Virgin displaying, outside [hors] her open chest, an enormous flaming heart" (19). On a later visit to the church, Octave listens to the priest's plans to improve the arrangement of his theatrical sacred statues and in the process sees a statue of Mary handled in ways that highlight her corporeality and her liability to being split open:

> [The priest] turned to call out to a worker:
> "Lift the Virgin, you're going to end up breaking her thigh."
> The worker called to a fellow. Together, they grabbed the Virgin by the bottom [reins], then carried her aside, like a pale big girl who has fallen down stiff [raide] from a nervous attack.
> "Be careful!" repeated the priest who followed them amidst the rubble, "her dress is already cracked [fêlée]." (216)

The word fêlure recurs throughout Zola's oeuvre, where it signifies a simultaneously literal and figurative lesion linked to hereditary degeneration and the inherent flaws and deficiencies of female bodies.[23] Here, however, the robe . . . fêlée of the Virgin conflates the material cracking of an architectural and sculptural element, the statue, with the structural deficiences of the female body posited at other points in the narrative. Mme Campardon, who suffers from an unnamed gynecological ailment that dates "from her confinement," inspires her husband to remark, "women, they've always got something breaking" (20). When female characters do not crack open, they crack up, suffering from hysterical fits in which they alternate between petrified rigidity and uncontrollable trembling. Thus women in Pot-Bouille acquire the solidity of sound architectural elements only fitfully, when they lose conscious control of themselves and, as the Virgin appears to have done in the passage above, "fall down stiff . . . from . . . nervous attack[s]."

Octave's view of the church replaces its architectural and social function as a *foundation* with its appearance as a commercialized, cracked, and dissembling *facade*. *Pot-Bouille*'s alignment of faulty exteriors with a sexual *fêlure* in women's bodies aligns the novel with contemporary architectural diatribes against the apartment house's promiscuity, particularly with architectural writers' ambivalence about the exterior elements of residential buildings. *Pot-Bouille* accentuates the difficulties of interiorization by representing the facade that should cover and protect the interior as false and falsifying. Departing from Balzacian realism's dependence on physiognomy and the transparent legibility of external appearances, as well as from naturalism's usual investment in an environment whose significance is determining and hence determinate, *Pot-Bouille* depicts female and architectural facades that contradict what lies behind them, fail to signify at all, reveal too much, or suffer from structural deficiencies.[24]

Pot-Bouille portrays architectural facades as falsifying by underscoring the disjunction between the building's imposing facade and the unseemly actions that occur behind it. The narrative tends to place descriptions of the building's stately decor, often qualified as "honest," directly before or after episodes of illicit or improper behavior.[25] In descriptions of the building, feminized objects signify the architectural insufficiencies that make its surface both deceptive and cracked. The building whose interiority seems secure when the narrator describes its lustrous closed doors and silent staircases becomes associated instead with a facade both false and chipped when the narrator draws attention to the feminine objects that decorate the building's front, associates them with flimsiness and deception, and then has a character remark on the rents and fissures in the building's very walls. On the building's ornate first-floor facade, "women's heads supported a balcony with a finely worked cast-iron railing" while cupids unfurl the house number (12). In the vestibule, a female figure again appears in a supporting position: "a woman's figure, a sort of Neapolitan gilded all over, who carried on her head an amphora from which emerged three gas lamps" (13). Both the decapitated caryatids and the Neapolitan figure simulate supports, since they have no real weight-bearing functions. Indeed, both objects seem inherently shaky, turning the structural primacy of mechanical supports into the mere appearance of support, then into the superficiality of facade ornamentation. Furthermore, the narrator immediately associates the fragmented caryatids and the gilt Neapolitan lamp-bearer with his exposure of the building's architectural mendacity, its "false marble" panels, decorations that "imitated old silver" (13), and its "flaking" paint (17), which in turn prompt Campardon to comment that "these houses are built to make a big impression. . . . Only one mustn't dig [*fouiller*] too deeply into the walls. It's not even twelve years old and it's already coming apart [*ça part déjà*]" (18).

The narrative equates many of the female characters with the building's facade by endowing women with bodily surfaces that dissimulate their internal characters and conceal evidence of their secret actions.[26] Early in the novel, Octave exclaims on the difference between Valérie's face when veiled and when exposed, "how deceptive these veils are! I thought she seemed pretty" (65). The narrator subsequently transposes the veil's deceptiveness to Valérie's face itself, since when she confides in Octave about her bouts of hysteria and uncontrollable adultery, "[b]ehind the black stream of her loosened hair, which flowed down her shoulders, he thought he saw her husband's pitiful, beardless head" (95). Valérie's hair functions as a screen, a false facade behind which the cuckolded husband hides and through which he is viewed. Octave further conflates the deceptiveness of women's bodies and the building's facade when he simultaneously loses respect for both: "vexed at not having seen through [its walls] right away, behind the false marbles," he "slipped into an exaggerated contempt for what he believed he divined behind the tall mahogany doors. He didn't know anymore: these housewives, whose virtue initially froze him, now seemed as though they had to surrender on signal" (135, 141).

The novel's female characters become emblems of false representation, with bodies that act as falsifying facades even when naked.[27] The narrator makes several references to the contrast between the bourgeois women's attractive clothing and their dirty underwear, their "dubious undergarments [*dessous douteux*]." Because *dessous* can refer to both architectural foundations and women's undergarments, those comments assimilate the suspect unreliability of female genitalia to flimsy building constructions, both masked by attractive cladding. The similarly false nature of the building's facades and of women's bodies shifts nudity from a natural state in which things show what they truly are, to a complex, deceptive form of expression. Zola's initial plan for *Pot-Bouille* conceived of nudity as truth, since it set out to "show the bourgeoisie in the nude [*à nu*] . . . and show it . . . abominable, this class which proclaims itself to be order and honesty."[28] The apartment house's nudity fails to reveal abomination, however, because its surfaces never register what takes place within it: "nothing in the staircase retained a trace of the night's scandals, not the false marbles that had reflected the gallop of a wife in her nightgown, nor the carpeting from which the odor of her nudity had evaporated" (358).[29] Like the building's surfaces, women's bare faces also fail to reveal their actions and thoughts.[30] When women's bodies do expose their interior states, their truth-telling is involuntary or automatic and contradicts the women's conscious speech and manner. Valérie's hysteria leads her to expose her body but also results in a paralysis that makes her incapable of expressing herself, and Berthe's animated speech belies her automatized gestures of self-revelation when, in Octave's room, "she undressed herself with a mechanical hand, while, more and more animated, she raised her voice" (346).[31]

Even when facades remain intact and true, protecting the interiors they cover without dissimulating them, the novel's conflation of architectural facades and women's bodies depicts interiority as either expanding into emptiness or flattening out into pure superficiality. In descriptions of people and sites, the "bare [nu]" frequently slides into the "void [vide]." When Duveyrier visits the apartment that his mistress has deserted, the nudité of the empty rooms goes hand in hand with the vide des murs, stripped of decorations, wallpaper, even nails (239). Octave's first glimpse of Marie Pichon's "clear and empty eyes [yeux clairs et vides]" presages his access to her nudity and immediately precedes his view of the equally "clair et vide" uniformity of the "blank, white curtains [rideaux blancs]" opposite his window. The narrative propinquity of the windows' blankness to Marie's limpid vacuity underscores the similarity between the facade's architectural meaninglessness and Marie Pichon's affinity with emptiness [le vide] (98, 101). Even in the few instances when Marie does not signify too little, she signifies too much. The uncontrollable blushes that rise to the surface of her face (83, 84) make her skin transparent, and thus an insufficiently protective cover: "She could hide nothing, everything rose to her face [tout lui montait à la face], beneath her skin with its fine chlorotic transparency" (92). Marie is a woman with no interior to speak of, figured either as deeply empty or as pure facade, all face.

Women's bodies and actions not only relay the characteristics of perforated, falsifying, and blank facades but also destroy architectectural foundations and uprightness. Rather than hold the apartment house up, women seem built to bring it down. Even Mme Josserand's imposing, statuesque nudity, her "towering majesty [majesté de tour]" (175), has the obverse effect from a fortress or support, since she crushes and terrifies her husband: "His wife annihilated him when she displayed that giant's bosom, which he thought he felt collapsing [*dont il croyait sentir l'écroulement*] onto his nape" (36). The novel particularly links the adulterous female body to disintegration and to a spatial reversal of top and bottom. Women engaging in extramarital sex describe themselves as broken down—Valérie explains the confused state that precedes her affairs as *tout se cassait*—and when the apartment building's female occupants have sex, the narration consistently assigns them a posture that inverts foundations, *la tête en bas et les jambes en l'air*—"their heads upside down and their legs in the air" (134, 139).

Male characters in the novel, by contrast, rely on foundations. M. Duveyrier, a magistrate and the apartment building's eventual owner, conversationally warns an exclusively male group, "do not rattle society's foundations [*bases*], or everything will crumble [*tout croulera*]" (111); later the same men agree that "the Church would never disappear, because it was the foundation [*base*] of the family, just as it was the natural support [*soutien*] of governments" (121). The novel's conflation of women with cracked facades and collapsing foundations pits the men's patriarchal aspirations against the female bodies that consistently interfere with the transmission of paternal legacies. The novel thus repeatedly undermines the fundamental patriarchal fiction that men are the fathers of the children they call their own. Marie, while married to Jules and having an affair with Octave, has two children whose paternity is indeterminate; gossips repeat that Valérie's son has actually been fathered by a neighborhood butcher, not by her husband (81); and though neither Trublot nor Duveyrier lays claim to Adèle's child or even seems to be aware that she is pregnant, either could be the father.[32]

In the few cases where literal paternity is not at issue, patriarchal filiations dissolve in other ways. Octave, the agent of several adulteries and false paternities, is introduced to us in terms of his matriarchal connection to Madame Campardon, not Monsieur (12). Though the building's proprietor, Vabre, establishes a patriarchal clan of children, in-laws, and grandchildren under his roof, he extracts rent from them instead of granting them his largesse, and his death exposes him as an impoverished sham. Auguste, cuckolded almost immediately after marriage, lives in constant fear that his brother-in-law, Saturnin, will attack him. M. Josserand is a completely ineffectual father. Campardon, whose "two Mme Campardons" make him the novel's arch-patriarch, becomes an object of exposure and ridicule when we see his daughter, Angèle, and maid, Lisa, parodically reenact his affair with Gasparine with one another, perversely (in Zola's view) recasting patriarchal heterosexuality as female homosexuality (338).[33]

The novel's most intensive representation of patriarchal disintegration focuses on Vabre, who represents both the apartment building and paternal power as the landlord who is also the father or father-in-law of many of the building's tenants. The same phrase that the narrator applies to adulterous women—*la tête en bas et les jambes en l'air*—recurs during Vabre's funeral; as bearers carry his coffin out of the building, a servant shouts "you're putting him in upside down! [*vous le mettez la tête en bas!*]" (265). The placement of this exclamation suggests the upending of Vabre's body; although the next paragraph clarifies that only the "escutcheon bearing the deceased's monogram" has been inverted, the vividness of the initial image remains difficult to efface.[34]

The equation of the posture of female adultery with the implied upheaval of the building's landlord associates the failures of female and architectural uprightness with an undermining of paternal authority.[35] Vabre, for whom "the history of his house [and its] construction remained the saga [*roman*] of his existence" (108), has thoroughly identified his patriarchal authority with his architectural holdings. He pursues even his sole hobby—the obsessive classification of the names and works of every Salon artist—according to patriarchal principles, since he considers work by a woman unclassifiable once she has given up her father's name: "when a woman artist gets married and then exhibits under her husband's name, how could she be recognized?"(109). Yet even before the novel suggests that his dead body has assumed an adulterous woman's posture, Vabre shows signs of a shaky foundation. Though he imitates a successful paterfamilias by housing his two sons and daughter in his own building, he inverts paternal largesse: "he didn't much like to give . . . and pushed things to the point of demanding rent" (150). Instead of giving to his children, he takes from them and even fails to pay his children money he has promised them. The narrator suggests that this denatured economy precipitates Vabre's death, since he experiences a stroke soon after a violent argument with Valérie, who refuses to pay her rent until he supplies the money he had promised to his son upon marriage (230).

Vabre's attenuated paternal authority disintegrates completely during and after his death. He collapses while working on his catalog and ends up in a position that suggests he will no longer be able to execute his will through writing: "He had banged his face against the inkwell. A splash of ink covered his left eye, dripping in thin drops down to his lips"

(228–229). Speech and gesture equally fail him during his final moments. In the absence of a written will, his children gather eagerly around his deathbed to hear how he might decide to dispose of his property. In his last, "supreme effort . . . his hand mingled with his cards, he began to flounder, with the gesture of a happy baby. . . . [H]e wanted to speak, but he only stuttered one syllable, always the same . . . —Ga . . . ga . . . ga . . . ga" (257). After his death, the family opens the sealed chest that previously had represented Vabre's potential legacy, rendered all the more imposing because of its almost sacred inaccessibility. The chest is exposed, however, as empty of intelligence and value: "The family stood appalled in front of the notorious strongbox, which they had believed held the fortune under lock and key, and in which there was simply a world of singular objects, trash collected from the apartment . . . toys in fragments, stolen long ago from little Gustave" (270). The paterfamilias has stolen objects of no value from his grandson, and the *propriétaire* has robbed the house of its propriety by storing "debris." Vabre's facade is as false as that of his apartment, and even his ownership becomes a sham when his children discover he has gambled his money away and mortgaged the building three times to finance further "speculation" (270).

Another father dies in *Pot-Bouille,* but one who has been characterized as powerless and ineffectual from the start. "Crushed magisterially" by his wife (37), so self-effacing that "one would have taken him for a guest" in his own home (66), and engaged in the repetitive, mechanical work of filling in the blanks on a publisher's labels, Josserand begins where Vabre ends, as a remnant of paternal authority and ownership, unable to execute his own will in writing. Like Vabre, a trickle of liquid stains Josserand's face when he collapses, though in his case the blot consists of blood, not ink (410). Unlike Vabre, however, Josserand does stand for a proper paternal standard, albeit a financially impoverished one: he believes in keeping his promises and is tortured by his material inability to do so. Vabre never gets upset by his children's adulterous liaisons or potentially illegitimate offspring, but Josserand is "weighed down by personal shame" merely because Berthe accumulates debts (283). Vabre's death exposes a false idol of patriarchy, but Josserand's represents the destruction of a genuine, though ineffectual, ideal.

Like Vabre's, Josserand's death is linked to the deterioration of the building's worth and solidity. His fatal illness follows directly from his discovery of Berthe's adultery, which besmirches the building, particularly since the adulteress is "the landlord's sister-in-law" (359). The adultery that Duveyrier, the new proprietor, fears might stain his stair-case with the blood of a duel (379), instead stains Josserand's face with the blood of a shamed father. Berthe's infraction of the patriarchal in-junction against female adultery produces in her father a "rent [*un déchirement*], an open wound [*une plaie ouverte*], through which the rest of his life departed" (399). By literalizing this moral blow as a wound, the narrative equates Josserand's *déchirement* with the cracks and leaks that plague the apartment house.[36] The analogies between his collapse and the building's deepen when the doctor diagnoses him as suffering from *décomposition* (417), the same diagnosis he will make of the apartment house and its residents (439), and the same ill that the priest attempts to cure (462).

Paradoxes of Naturalism, Paradoxes of Interiorization

Pot-Bouille's depiction of decomposing paternal authority resonates in the novel with failures of writing: as we have seen, Vabre and Josserand both lose their ability to write or to represent their thoughts or will in any way, and that decline blends with the decline of the building that Vabre associates with writing when he calls the apartment his *roman,* literally his novel (108). The failures of paternal writing within the novel had an echo in an intriguing and well-publicized lawsuit brought against Zola during *Pot-Bouille*'s serial publication, a suit that challenged his claim to have authored his own work. The suit pitted two forms of prop-erty, both depicted as masculine, against each other: an individual's right to his patronymic versus an author's property in the names of his char-acters and, by extension, the author's right to recreate exterior reality in a fictional text.

During the course of *Pot-Bouille*'s publication in serial form, a lawyer for the Cour d'Appel named Duverdy brought a suit for slander against Zola, whose novel featured a character named Duverdy (later Duveyrier), also a magistrate at the Cour d'Appel. In a letter to his publisher, Zola resolved to take the case to court in order to defend the modern novel-ist's right to give his characters realistic names, names that would nec-essarily belong to real people, since Zola chose them from an address directory. Contrasting seventeenth-century novelists' practice of using mythological, abstract, or antiquated names to the modern novelist's procedure of taking names "from within the milieu in which . . . char-acters live, in order for the reality of the name to complete the reality of their physiognomy," Zola summed up the case by concluding that "M. Duverdy says that the patronymic is property; in that case, it is property that thousands of current novels violate daily." [37] Zola's word for "violate" was *violer,* which also meant "rape"; his choice of *violer,* rather than the equally appropriate word for theft, *voler,* feminized the possessor of the patronymic, virilized the writer, and thus prepared the way for Zola to appropriate to the writer any patronymic shared by a person and a character: "The name belongs to us, because we have made it ours through our talent." [38]

When Zola lost the case and was forced to change the name, he responded by renaming the character "Mr. Three Asterisks [*Monsieur Trois-Etoiles*]," a name that put into words the symbols normally used to designate an ostentatious anonymity. When he received other complaints, all from men, he initially responded by altering one other name, then balked and refused to change any more. The only two names that Zola changed belonged to the two successive owners of the apartment building in *Pot-Bouille:* Duverdy/Trois-Etoiles and Vabre, renamed Sans-Nom [No-Name] in the serial version. [39] Those new names represented Zola's loss of literary property rights in the courtroom outside his novel, but their reduction of male landlords' patronymics to signs of anonymity in fact continued the novel's project of destabilizing paternal property; dubbing Vabre "No-Name" echoed the narrative's mocking reduction of his name to the abbreviated "monogram" inverted on his coffin. [40]

A contemporary caricature from *La Chronique parisienne* (March 5, 1882) showed how the suit against Zola's naturalistic use of real names both compromised the patronymic's respectability and challenged the naturalist writer's authority. The caricature depicts a bourgeois in a top hat watching another man, possibly Zola with his back to us, cross out a line in an enormous book entitled *Pot-Bouille.* The caption reads: "I'm attached to keeping my proper name proper [*Je tiens à conserver mon nom propre*], hurry up M. Zola and take it out of your pot." The bourgeois citizen wants his name to be both clean, *propre,* and his own, proper to him. The "pot" refers to the large ink pot between the two men, to *Pot-Bouille* itself, and by extension to the apartment house. The cartoon raises a question: if the apartment house as Zola depicted it undermined both the *propreté* and *propriété* of bourgeois citizens, did it also undermine the writer's naturalist project of appropriating the external world for representation within a book?

Any answer to the question of whether the apartment house eroded Zola's naturalist methods must take into account the vagaries of the interiorization that structure Zola's representation of the apartment house. As we have seen, *Pot-Bouille* represents the apartment house as interiorized—secure from view, a solid container, closed to the exterior—yet simultaneously shows how that very interiority leads to collapses, fissures, and exposure. In his theoretical essays on the naturalist novel, however, Zola argued for the absolute separability of interiorization and exteriorization within the work of the novelist. "Le Roman expérimental," Zola's most important reflection on his methods, divided the novelist into two functions: "The novelist is made up of an observer and an experimenter." [41]

The "observer" remains the most familiar model of the naturalist writer, as someone who transcribes reality from a perfectly exterior position and thus guarantees the correspondingly perfect autonomy and interiority of a text/document unmarked by its author's subjectivity. Zola expressed the ideal of detached observation when he wrote that "[t]he novelist is nothing more than a clerk who does not permit himself to judge and to make conclusions. . . . He thus disappears . . . he simply displays what he has seen"; or, as Georg Lukács put it, the naturalist "is reduced to a mere spectator and chronicler of public life." [42]

The critical response to *Pot-Bouille*, however, underlined the paradoxes of interiority that we have already seen to operate within its narrative. Favorable and hostile critics alike identified *Pot-Bouille* as a limit-case of what Naomi Schor calls the "inclination of the naturalist novelist towards a position of complete exteriority." [43] For favorable critics, that exteriority conferred integrity on the novel's representations. Paul Alexis, in *Emile Zola: notes d'un ami* (1882) wrote approvingly that the narrator's invisibility in *Pot-Bouille* had finally "cleansed" Zola's naturalist style of the subjective involvement associated with "romanticism . . . the novel almost becomes a play. The writer effaces himself more and more, and no longer analyzes except through the facts." [44] In approximating a play, the novel approaches self-sufficiency, as though its characters had become independent of the writer's external interventions. Yet unfavorable critics argued that because the narrator was so exterior to his text and the reality to which it referred, *Pot-Bouille* lacked credibility as what it purported to be, an accurate record of Parisian life. Albert Wolff wrote in *Le Figaro* that "the man who has written several volumes on naturalism and on human documentation has composed *Pot-Bouille* like a fantasist. Neither an observer, nor a Parisian . . . has written this strange novel"; Henri Fouquier's review similarly contended that "M. Zola . . . is no longer an observer: he is a hallucinator." [45]

The paradoxical effects produced by the perfect exteriority of the "observer" also manifested themselves in Zola's definition of the novelist's other part, the "experimenter." Far from being the detached observer suggested by the scientific tenor of the term, the "experimenter" formed an intrinsic part of the text as its agent and catalyst: "the experimenter appears and initiates the experiment, by which I mean that he causes the characters to move [*fait mouvoir les personnages*] within a particular story." [46] The existence of an experimenter who had to merge with the work before any observation could take place clearly undermined the exteriority of the observer and the corresponding interiority of the text. [47] The notion of experiment also compromised the text's boundedness vis-à-vis the reader; as the critic Franc Schuerewegen notes in an essay on Balzac's and Zola's prefaces, "If the work constructs its own world, a *complete* world, must it not then also include the reading subject?" Schuerewegen extends the reader's inclusion in the text to the writer's when he recasts experimentation (as described by Zola in the preface to *Thérèse Raquin*) as a fantasy of "absorption of the creator by the creation. . . . By virtue of its mimetic project, the . . . naturalist . . . book . . . has *no exterior* [*est sans dehors*]." [48]

An 1882 caricature of *Pot-Bouille* referred the problem of the naturalist author's dual position—simultaneously external observer and interiorized experimenter—directly to the apartment house (fig. 24). Two Zolas appear in this cartoon, which depicts *Pot-Bouille* as an apartment building peeled of its facade: one Zola is inside the apartment house, dressed as a concierge seated in his *loge* (an equation of author and porter that echoes the *physiologies* of earlier decades), and another Zola is outside the house, fantastically doubled as an Asmodeus-like voyeur, perched on the roof and peering through a mansard window into a servant's room. Everything about that doubling works to destabilize the naturalist author's position: the Zola on the roof, unlike the diabolically powerful Asmodeus, literally has a precarious hold on the building he attempts to observe; Zola's social status as an author is debased by the sign that reads, "Speak to the concierge—Emile Zola—naturalist." Neither Zola can see all the characters as the cartoon's viewer can, and—undermining both the internal and the external authors' claims to represent the building—each Zola cancels the authenticity of the other, leaving us with no certifiable figure for the author.

The problem of the writer's position vis-à-vis what he represents recurs within the novel as the problem of the characters' relationship to the actions described by the narrative. Zola's novels often endow specific

FIGURE 24

"Pot-Bouille, ou tous détraqués mais tous vertueux." Caricature by A. Robida (1882). Zola appears at the top right, spying on the servants, and at the bottom right, as the building's
porter. In the cartoon's attempt to condense the novel's narrative sequences into a single space, Octave also appears on every
floor, enacting the novel's different episodes.

characters with the externality attributed to the novelist as observer, as critics have remarked. Sigmund Freud, for example, noted that in "certain novels, which might be called 'excentric' . . . the person introduced as the hero plays the least active part of anyone, and seems instead to let the actions and sufferings of other people pass him by like a spectator. Many of the later novels of Zola belong to this class."[49] Octave Mouret certainly belongs to the class of passive, external characters who "listen, look" (166), functioning more as a recording device than as the set of instinctual drives and hereditary destinies that define many naturalist characters. Although he integrates himself into the novel's action by internalizing and imitating what he observes, he also has what critics have called a "very passive . . . personality" for a protagonist and remains throughout the novel an "outsider . . . who does not really belong to the various spaces depicted."[50] Octave is frequently present as a witness during scenes that do not directly involve him and remains materially unaffected by scenes that do. Events define his character, and his presence defines events, but he remains liminal, never fully absorbed into the action. Far from eroding Zola's theoretical version of naturalism, the hero of his naturalist apartment-house novel appears to realize Zola's fantasy of a writer who combines the observer and the experimenter in a figure who is both part of the world he observes yet distinct from it.

Octave, however, is neither the only observer in *Pot-Bouille*, nor the only stand-in for the naturalist author; the apartment house also becomes the site of several crises of observation and narrative that undermine naturalist conventions. On the one hand, the novel features several male voyeurs—including the porter, Octave, and Trublot—whose actions are sanctioned as curiosity or professional responsibility and who thus authorize the transmission of information from characters to readers. On the other hand, the novel's several female voyeurs trouble that transmission, because their observation is compromised by being both incommunicable and punishable. Angèle, for example, loses no opportunity to look at naked women, doubly forbidden to her because of their nudity and their femininity; she stares "profoundly absorbed" by the sight of Valérie's exposed breasts (192) and is "immobilized" by the sight of the errant Berthe in her peignoir (351). So absorbed is she by what she sees that she becomes almost unconscious. Unlike Trublot and Octave, Angèle cannot transmit what she sees to the reader; instead, the narrator gives us the spectacle of Angèle looking. In other cases, female voyeurism becomes socially stigmatized: the servants become indignant when they discover that Juzeur's young maid has been spying on them

through keyholes, and the Campardons' cook, Julie, exclaims to the
other servants, "When you've seen what I've seen! . . . At old father
Campardon's house, there was a perfectly well brought-up niece who
used to go look at men through the keyhole" (133). In their avidity to
spy on others, these young women pay insufficient attention to their own
visibility and are caught in the act by other characters and by the narrator. In effect, they become cautionary figures for the hypervisibility and
punishable prurience of both the author and readers of naturalist novels.

In the figure of an unnamed writer on the second floor, by contrast,
the novel creates a thoroughly idealized figure of its own representational activity. In a moment of *mise-en-abîme* that clearly identifies the
novelist and the work he writes with Zola and the very novel we are
reading, a character reports that the police have pursued the novelist for
having written a book about the apartment house in which he lives—
"they even say that the landlord is in it"—a novel full of "filth about respectable people [*cochonneries sur les gens comme il faut*]." The other
tenants condemn the writer not only for besmirching them, but also for
"having sullied in his writings the house in which he sheltered his family," but the narrator defends the novelist as the apartment building's
only true paterfamilias, by giving us, for example, a brief glimpse of his
"two good-looking blond children, whose little hands quarreled over a
bouquet of roses" (436). The positive content of that glimpse (the children are attractive, playful, and exhibit none of the bad behavior that
characterizes the other children in the building) is less important than its
brevity, for ultimately, Zola can most credibly represent the writer's positive qualities by failing to represent him at all. The writer remains invisible throughout the novel: the narrator never describes his apartment;
no characters ever speak directly to him or to his family; our awareness
of his presence comes either from remarks upon his absence at weddings
and funerals (179, 267) or from fleeting glimpses of him outside the
building or on the street; and throughout the novel, he retains a "vague"
and irreproachable profile (138).

Only one other character remains as impenetrable to scrutiny:
Mme Hédouin, the one female character in the novel whose nudity is irreproachable because her perfectly unruffled interior admits no cracks on
its surface. Even when she appears in evening dress, her "shoulders and
arms bare [*nus*]," Hédouin retains her "calm beauty" (107) and "tranquil authority" (205). Unlike the other female characters, whose facades
collapse, who become surfaces with no depth, and who do not carry
themselves well but turn themselves upside down, Mme Hédouin has a

truly opaque and secure interior; yet that very quality, spatialized as a smooth surface and upright posture, temporalized as being "always the same" (453), posits a consistency that defies narrativization—"when one carries oneself so well, it's no longer interesting" (440).

The unnamed novelist and Mme Hédouin seem to represent a defense of interiorization as a moral ideal, just as other episodes in the novel trace failures of interiorization to moral turpitude. In that reading, both characters can maintain the integrity of their apartments, their families, and their bodies because they are impeccable. My reading has emphasized, however, that another, less explicit current of *Pot-Bouille* assigns failures of interiorization not to any individual's moral imperfections, but to logical impossibilities: every inside must have an outside that compromises pure interiority, by its very existence and by its susceptibility to fissure; total internalization collapses in on itself, producing either emptiness or the sheerness of the remaining membrane; and when interiority becomes the desired attribute of a text, the writer's and reader's presence constitute its necessary breaches. *Pot-Bouille* thematizes those impossibilities in its caving walls, deceptive facades, leaking women, and collapsing fathers. The novelist on the second floor and Mme Hédouin go beyond thematization, however, to embody the impossibility of maintaining interiorization within representation. Both approach the ideal of perfect interiorization because they are so hermetically enclosed that the reader has no access to them; only because the reader has no access to them can they remain hermetically enclosed.

Pot-Bouille thus clearly adopts many of the values of Zola's contemporaries, who sought to enclose the city, its apartments, and their inhabitants, but his commitment as a novelist to breaching interiority leads him to nudge those discourses into aporia. The characters who most fully realize the interiorization vaunted by the urban discourses of the Second Empire and early Third Republic are the vanishing point of the apartment-house narrative, since their interiority makes them tenants about whom there can be nothing to report. *Pot-Bouille* shows that if the apartment house's interior were ever rendered impervious to external observation—even and especially the author's and reader's—then the very foundations of the naturalist novel in observation and experiment would crumble, and the reader would be left holding a novel with no story to tell.

Notes

Introduction

1. *Le Journal intime de Caroline B.*, ed. Michelle Perrot and Georges Ribeill (Paris: Montalba, 1985), 14, 21, 25.

2. Jacques Raphael, "Le Portier de Paris," in *Paris, ou le livre des cent-et-un* (Paris: Ladvocat, 1832), 8:354.

3. "An Englishman's Castle," *Household Words*, December 27, 1851, 323, 322.

4. Robert Vaughan, *The Age of Great Cities: or, Modern Society Viewed in Its Relation to Intelligence, Morals, and Religion*; quoted in Mary Poovey, "Anatomical Realism and Social Investigation in Early Nineteenth-Century Manchester," *differences* 5, no. 3 (fall 1993): 1.

5. Of course, Paris was often decried for its dangers and London celebrated for its modernity; see, for example, Louis Chevalier, *Laboring Classes and Dangerous Classes in Paris during the First Half of the Nineteenth Century*, trans. Frank Jellinek (Princeton: Princeton University Press, 1973); and Judith Walkowitz, *City of Dreadful Delight: Narratives of Sexual Danger in Late-Victorian London* (Chicago: University of Chicago Press, 1992). Paris was, however, the chief locus of the notion of urban modernity, as Walkowitz's adoption of the French term "flaneur" to describe mid-Victorian urban observers suggests (see ch. 1, "Urban Spectatorship"). Paris and London were thus also opposed in terms of cosmopolitanism vs. domesticity, an opposition I take up in greater detail in chapters 3 and 4. François Bédarida and Anthony Sutcliffe have argued that for all classes, the street played a bigger role as a social space in Paris than in London ("The Street in the Structure and Life of the City: Reflections on

Nineteenth-Century London and Paris," in *Modern Industrial Cities: History, Policy, and Survival,* ed. Bruce M. Stave [Beverly Hills: Sage Publications, 1981], 36). For comparisons of British and French concepts of domesticity that emphasize the greater intensity and concreteness of the British discourse of home, see Pierre Reboul, "De l'intime à l'intimisme," in *Intime, intimité, intimisme* (Lille: Publications de l'université de Lille III, 1976), 7–12; and John Hollander, "It All Depends," in *Home: A Place in the World,* ed. Arien Mack (New York: New York University Press, 1993), 38 ("there is no word so loaded as 'home' in the Romance languages").

6. For critiques of theoretical attributions of passivity to space, see especially Gillian Rose, *Feminism and Geography: The Limits of Geographical Knowledge* (Minneapolis: University of Minnesota Press, 1993); Doreen Massey, *Space, Place, and Gender* (Minneapolis: University of Minnesota Press, 1994); Elizabeth Grosz, "Space, Time, and Bodies," in *Space, Time, and Perversion: Essays on the Politics of Bodies* (New York: Routledge, 1995), 83–101; Sue Best, "Sexualizing Space," in *Sexy Bodies: The Strange Carnalities of Feminism,* ed. Elizabeth Grosz and Elspeth Probyn (New York: Routledge, 1995), 181–194; and Patricia Yaeger, "Introduction: Narrating Space," in *The Geography of Identity,* ed. Patricia Yaeger (Ann Arbor: University of Michigan Press, 1996), 25.

In addition to the many works on French and British everyday life, urban history, and domestic history that I cite throughout, I have also drawn on scholars addressing those issues in a United States context, especially Elizabeth Blackmar, *Manhattan for Rent, 1785–1850* (Ithaca: Cornell University Press, 1989); Dolores Hayden, *The Grand Domestic Revolution: A History of Feminist Designs for American Homes, Neighborhoods, and Cities* (Cambridge, Mass.: MIT Press, 1981); Mary Ryan, *Women in Public: Between Banners and Ballots, 1825–1880* (Baltimore: Johns Hopkins University Press, 1990); and Gwendolyn Wright, *Building the Dream: A Social History of Housing in America* (New York: Pantheon, 1981).

7. T. J. Clark and Prendergast both mention instances of the imbrication of urban and domestic spaces, but neither integrates those observations into definitions of the urban. Clark discusses the effects that Haussmannization had on the cost of housing, but his reading focuses on charges that "the street was ending as a form of life" (T. J. Clark, *The Painting of Modern Life: Paris in the Art of Manet and His Followers* [Princeton: Princeton University Press, 1984], 57). A long list of sites that evinced the city's modernization notes "the new streets and apartment blocks" before dilating on "[e]xhibitions . . . *grands magasins* . . . restaurants . . . parks . . . cafés" (67). Clark's index includes cafés, parks, squares, streets, railways, and restaurants but no apartment buildings or any other kind of residential space. Prendergast writes that his book "takes in the following *topoi:* the view from the café, the panoramic vista, the underground city (the catacombs and the sewers), the market, the boulevard, the barricade, the park and the canal. I have generally ignored the world of interior and private space" (Christopher Prendergast, *Paris and the Nineteenth Century* [Oxford: Blackwell, 1992], 4). In his reading of the park as a feminine urban space, Prendergast steps back from the implications his interpretation has for the potentially urban qualities of the home by arguing that the park "is in any case effec-

tively folded back into the private, as coextensive with the domestic sphere to which women were held properly to belong" (175).

For examples of work that does include the residential within the purview of the urban, see Manuel Castells, *The City and the Grassroots: A Cross-Cultural Theory of Urban Social Movements* (Berkeley: University of California Press, 1983); Mark Girouard, *Cities and People: A Social and Architectural History* (New Haven: Yale University Press, 1985); and Donald Olsen, *The Growth of Victorian London* (New York: Penguin, 1976), and *The City as a Work of Art: London, Paris, Vienna* (New Haven: Yale University Press, 1986). See also Jane Jacobs, *The Death and Life of Great American Cities* (New York: Vintage, 1961); and Mary McLeod, "Everyday and 'Other' Spaces," in *Architecture and Feminism*, ed. Debra Coleman, Elizabeth Danze, and Carol Henderson (New York: Princeton Architectural Press, 1996), esp. her comments on Jacobs (24).

8. See Hannah Arendt, *The Human Condition* (New York: Doubleday, 1959); Jürgen Habermas, *The Structural Transformation of the Public Sphere: An Inquiry into a Category of Bourgeois Society*, trans. Thomas Burger (Cambridge, Mass.: MIT Press, 1991 [German original, 1962]); and Richard Sennett, *The Fall of Public Man: On the Social Psychology of Capitalism* (1974; reprint, New York: Vintage, 1978). In the vast notes for the *Passagenwerk*, Walter Benjamin indicates a much more complicated view of the home than he articulated in any published version of his essays. For the published essays, see Walter Benjamin, *Paris, capitale du XIXe siècle: le livre des passages*, ed. Rolf Tiedemann, trans. Jean Lacoste (Paris: Editions du cerf, 1989), and *Charles Baudelaire: A Lyric Poet in the Era of High Capitalism*, trans. Harry Zohn (London: Verso, 1989); for the notes, see *Paris, capitale du XIXe siècle*, 236, 239, 244.

9. See the work by Monique Eleb-Vidal and Anne Debarre-Blanchard cited in chapter one, note 7. A notable exception to the isolation of the home from its urban context is François Loyer, *Paris: Nineteenth-Century Architecture and Urbanism*, trans. Charles Lynn Clark (New York: Abbeville Press, 1988).

10. See, for example, Debora L. Silverman, *Art Nouveau in Fin-de-Siècle France: Politics, Psychology, and Style* (Berkeley: University of California Press, 1989); and Leora Auslander, *Taste and Power: Furnishing Modern France* (Berkeley: University of California Press, 1996).

11. For examples of points at which Auslander attributes a primary causality to large-scale shifts in political regimes, see *Taste and Power*, 21, 40; to shifts in the organization of production, 75; and to related shifts at both levels, 191.

12. See the works by Armstrong, Davidoff, Hall, Walkowitz, Poovey, Gallagher, B. Smith, Perrot, and Corbin cited throughout, as well as the works cited above by Massey, Rose, Ryan, Blackmar, Hayden, and Wright. See also Dolores Hayden, "What Would a Non-Sexist City Be Like?" in *The City Reader*, ed. Richard T. LeGates and Frederic Stout (New York: Routledge, 1996), 143–157.

13. See, for example, Elizabeth Wilson's critique of Wolff and Pollock in "The Invisible Flâneur," *New Left Review* 191 (January–February 1992): 90–110; and Rita Felski's discussion of women as exemplary figures of modernity in "The Gender of Modernity," in *Political Gender: Texts and Contexts*, ed. Sally Ledger, Josephine McDonagh, and Jane Spencer (New York: Harvester, 1994), 144–155. Daphne Spain questions whether the home is the site of greatest spatial

discrimination between men and women in *Gendered Spaces* (Chapel Hill: University of North Carolina Press, 1992), esp. 64. Lawrence Klein questions the respective associations of the public with men and the private with women in "Gender and the Public/Private Distinction in the Eighteenth Century: Some Questions about Evidence and Analytic Procedure," *Eighteenth-Century Studies* 29, no. 1 (1995): 97–109; as does Nancy Duncan, in "Renegotiating Gender and Sexuality in Public and Private Spaces," in her edited volume *Bodyspace: Destabilizing Geographies of Gender and Sexuality* (London: Routledge, 1996), 127–145. Bruce Robbins interrogates the coherence of our present versions of the public sphere in "The Public as Phantom," the introduction to his edited collection *The Phantom Public Sphere* (Minneapolis: University of Minnesota Press, 1993), esp. vii–ix, xiv, xv; see also the essays in Craig Calhoun, ed., *Habermas and the Public Sphere* (Cambridge, Mass.: MIT Press, 1992).

14. For examples, see Blackmar, *Manhattan for Rent,* 5, 11, 63–67, 112; Leonore Davidoff, "The Separation of Home and Work? Landladies and Lodgers in Nineteenth- and Twentieth-Century England," in *Fit Work for Women,* ed. Sandra Burman (New York: St. Martin's Press, 1979), 64–97; Michelle Perrot, "La ménagère dans l'espace parisien au XIXe siècle," *Annales de la recherche urbaine* 9 (1980): 3–22; Ellen Ross, *Love and Toil: Motherhood in Outcast London, 1870–1918* (New York: Oxford University Press, 1993); and Judith Walkowitz, *Prostitution and Victorian Society: Women, Class, and the State* (Cambridge: Cambridge University Press, 1980).

15. For a glaring recent example of a global, simplistic equation of femininity, interiors, and the private sphere, see Aaron Betsky, *Building Sex: Men, Women, Architecture, and the Construction of Sexuality* (New York: William Morrow, 1995). For an earlier version of this equation, see Philippe Ariès, "The Family and the City," *Daedalus* 106, no. 2 (spring 1977): 230–232. For a history of this equation in classical and early modern architectural treatises, see Mark Wigley, "Untitled: The Housing of Gender," in *Sexuality and Space,* ed. Beatriz Colomina (New York: Princeton Architectural Press, 1992), 327–389.

16. My definitions of cultural history and my assertion of the productive capacities of discourses are influenced by how cultural historians and literary critics working at the border between history and literary studies have deployed Foucault; in addition to the works I cite throughout by Nancy Armstrong, Leonore Davidoff and Catherine Hall, Catherine Gallagher, Nicholas Green, D. A. Miller, Mary Poovey, and Joan Scott, see Lynn Hunt, "History beyond Social Theory," in *The States of "Theory": History, Art, and Critical Discourse,* ed. David Carroll (New York: Columbia University Press, 1990), 95–111.

17. For geographers who argue that space is both a social product and a social force, and that material space is inseparable from discourses of space, see Henri Lefebvre, *The Production of Space,* trans. D. Nicholson-Smith (Oxford: Blackwell, 1991); Diana Agrest, "Toward a Theory of Production of Sense in the Built Environment," in *On Streets,* ed. Stanford Anderson (Cambridge, Mass.: MIT Press, 1978), 213–221, which focuses on how cultural codes produce space and place; Michel Foucault, "Space, Knowledge, and Power," in *The Foucault Reader,* ed. Paul Rabinow (New York: Pantheon, 1984), 253; Roger Friedland and Deirdre Boden, "NowHere: An Introduction to Space, Time, and

Modernity" in their edited collection *NowHere: Space, Time, and Modernity* (Berkeley: University of California Press, 1994), 1–60; Massey, *Space, Place, and Gender*, esp. 4, 177, 251, 254; Rose, *Feminism and Geography*, 89; and Edward Soja, *Postmodern Geographies: The Reassertion of Space in Critical Social Theory* (London: Verso, 1989), 7.

Writers who posit spaces (such as prisons, hospitals, workers' housing) as agents of social control often align themselves with Foucault; see, for example, Thomas A. Markus, *Buildings and Power: Freedom and Control in the Origin of Modern Building Types* (London: Routledge, 1993). Yet in an interview with Paul Rabinow, Foucault explictly argued against investing space with intentional agency, noting that "architects . . . are not the technicians or engineers of the three great variables—territory, communication, and speed"; that architects' intentions to control or to liberate are irrelevant to what actually transpires in buildings; and that when buildings are sites of freedom, that freedom derives not from architectural plans but from "the practice of liberty" ("Space, Knowledge, and Power," 244, 246; see also 247–248).

18. In addition to the interview with Foucault cited above, I have found the following critiques of architectural and environmental determinism very helpful: Agrest, "Toward a Theory of Production"; and Stanford Anderson, "People in the Physical Environment: The Urban Ecology of Streets," in *On Streets*, ed. Stanford Anderson, 1–11. For histories of nineteenth-century environmental determinism in Paris, see the works by Aisenberg and Shapiro cited in chapter 1, note 6, as well as Aisenberg's work cited in chapter 4, note 56.

19. I draw here particularly on Nancy Armstrong, *Desire and Domestic Fiction: A Political History of the Novel* (New York: Oxford University Press, 1987), 7–8; and D. A. Miller, *The Novel and the Police* (Berkeley: University of California Press, 1988), x–xiii, 21. I do not, however, adopt Armstrong's thesis that the private sphere was a ruse for veiling domestic desire's essentially public and political goals; nor do I view the novel in terms of its contribution to the normalizing power that Miller argues saturates modern regimes of the subject.

20. On the relationship between close reading and particularizing claims, see Margaret Cohen's introduction to *Compromising Positions: The Emergence of the Modern French Novel* (Princeton: Princeton University Press, forthcoming).

21. On the novel's articulation of the relations between public and private, see Mikhail Bakhtin, "Forms of Time and Chronotope in the Novel," in *The Dialogic Imagination: Four Essays*, ed. Michael Holquist, trans. Caryl Emerson and Michael Holquist (Austin: University of Texas Press, 1981), 122–127, 131–135, 256–257; D. A. Miller, *The Novel and the Police*, 162; Catherine Gallagher, *The Industrial Reformation of English Fiction, 1832–1867* (Chicago: University of Chicago Press, 1985), 113–184; Michael Warner, "The Mass Public and the Mass Subject," in *The Phantom Public Sphere*, ed. Bruce Robbins (Minneapolis: University of Minnesota Press, 1993), 236–238. For a study of how nineteenth-century discourses associated the novel with a threatening and threatened privacy that would erupt in and be contained by scandal, see William Cohen, *Sex Scandal: The Private Parts of Victorian Fiction* (Durham: Duke University Press, 1996). Michel Butor argues that all reading, but particularly the reading of realist novels, involves an exchange between the individual space of

the reader and the more general space of the text; see "The Space of the Novel," in *Inventory*, ed. Richard Howard (New York: Simon and Schuster, 1968), 33.

That novels bridge public and private can also be seen in the ease with which critics align the genre either with one or the other. For example, Roddy Reid (*Families in Jeopardy: Regulating the Social Body in France, 1750–1910* [Stanford: Stanford University Press, 1993], 144) defines the novel as public when he cites the conservative nineteenth-century critic Alfred Nettement's equation of the novel with the invasion of the home by the street. On the dangerous publicity of novels, see also Jann Matlock, *Scenes of Seduction: Prostitution, Hysteria, and Reading Difference in Nineteenth-Century France* (New York: Columbia University Press, 1994). Consider, however, the ease with which one of Eugène Sue's critics identified the novel as private: "a novel is not a square that one crosses but a place that one inhabits" (quoted in Benjamin, *Paris, capitale du XIXe siècle*, 240).

By focusing on elaborations of public and private as hallmarks of novelistic realism, I am displacing critics' traditional emphasis on realism's preoccupation with mimesis, representation, and truth-claims. For studies of realism and the urban novel that focus particularly on issues of mimesis and representation, see, in addition to the works by Auerbach, Barthes, Bernstein, Hamon, Prendergast, and Raymond Williams cited in subsequent chapters, Richard Maxwell, *The Mysteries of Paris and London* (Charlottesville: University Press of Virginia, 1992).

22. On the salon novel, see Bakhtin, "Forms of Time and Chronotope," 246–247; on the domestic novel, see Armstrong; on the urban novel, see Moretti and Williams; on the domestic novel as a defensive response to the crowd, see John Plotz, "Jealousy of the Crowd in British Literature, 1800–1850" (Ph.D. dissertation, Harvard University, 1997).

23. I cite the relevant works by Monnier and de Kock and discuss them in slightly more detail in footnotes to chapter 2. For Brough, see *Apartments, "Visitors to the Exhibition May Be Accommodated"* (London: Hailes Lacy, 1851); *A House out of Windows* (London: Hailes Lacy, 1852); *How to Make Home Happy* (London: Hailes Lacy, 1853); *Number One, Round the Corner* (London: Hailes Lacy, 1854); see also Frederic Hay, *Lodgers and Dodgers* (London: Hailes Lacy, 1871).

24. I am grateful to an anonymous reader for providing me with the example of Madame Defarge as *portière*.

25. See Janet Wolff ("The Invisible *Flâneuse:* Women and the Literature of Modernity," in *Feminine Sentences: Essays on Women and Culture* [Berkeley: University of California Press, 1990], 34–50); Griselda Pollock (*Vision and Difference: Femininity, Feminism, and Histories of Art* [London: Routledge, 1988]); and Prendergast, *Paris and the Nineteenth Century;* for examples of the continuing influence of the notion of the *flâneur,* see Keith Tester, ed., *The Flâneur* (New York: Routledge, 1994), and John Rignall, "Benjamin's *Flâneur* and the Problem of Realism," in *The Problems of Modernity: Adorno and Benjamin,* ed. Andrew Benjamin (London: Routledge, 1989), 112–121.

26. Letter of June 5, 1913, to Carla Seligson, in *The Correspondence of Walter Benjamin,* ed. Gershom Scholem and Theodor W. Adorno, trans. Manfred R. Jacobson and Evelyn M. Jacobson (Chicago: University of Chicago Press, 1994),

27. I have modified their translation of "sondern steinerne Coulissen zwischen man geht"; for the original German, see Walter Benjamin, *Gesammelte Briefe*, ed. Christoph Gödde and Henri Lonitz (Frankfurt: Suhrkamp, 1995), 1:105.

27. On the city as spectacle, see Nord, Green, and T. J. Clark, cited in subsequent chapters; see also Vanessa R. Schwartz, *Spectacular Realities: Early Mass Culture in Fin-de-Siècle Paris* (Berkeley: University of California Press, 1998).

28. In her gloss of this sentence, Hannah Arendt noted only the extent to which Benjamin described Paris as itself an interior or an apartment (*Men in Dark Times* [San Diego: Harcourt, Brace Jovanovich, 1968], 173–174).

1. Seeing through Paris

1. For a history of Paris during the July Monarchy, see Philippe Vigier, *Nouvelle histoire de Paris: Paris pendant la monarchie de juillet (1830–1848)* (Paris: Hachette, 1991). On the modernity of July Monarchy Paris, see Nicholas Green, *The Spectacle of Nature: Landscape and Bourgeois Culture in Nineteenth-Century France* (Manchester: Manchester University Press, 1990).

2. On the encoding and decoding of personal appearance during the earlier years of the Directory, see Margaret Waller, "Disembodiment as Masquerade: Fashion Journalists and Other 'Realist' Observers in Directory Paris," *L'Esprit créateur* (spring 1997): 44–54.

3. On transparency in Rousseau, see especially Jean-Jacques Rousseau, *Lettre à Monsieur d'Alembert sur les spectacles* (1758) and Jean Starobinski, *Rousseau: la transparence et l'obstacle* (Paris: Gallimard, 1971); on transparency in the French Revolution, see Lynn Hunt, *Politics, Culture, and Class in the French Revolution* (Berkeley: University of California Press, 1984); and Susan Maslan, "Representation and Theatricality in French Revolutionary Theater and Politics" (Ph.D. dissertation, Johns Hopkins University, 1997).

4. One of the most explicit articulations of this view is Erna Olafson Hellerstein, "Women, Social Order, and the City: Rules for French Ladies, 1830–1870" (Ph.D. dissertation, University of California, Berkeley, 1980). Hellerstein focuses on medical literature, which along with educational tracts and political writings was the most emphatic discourse of separate spheres in France. See also Janet Wolff, "The Invisible *Flâneuse*: Women and the Literature of Modernity," in *Feminine Sentences: Essays on Women and Culture* (Berkeley: University of California Press Press, 1990), 34–50. A selected list of historical studies that analyze nineteenth-century French bourgeois women's lives in terms of ideologies and practices sharply dividing public and private includes Joan Landes, *Women and the Public Sphere in the Age of the French Revolution* (Ithaca: Cornell University Press, 1988); Michelle Perrot, "La ménagère dans l'espace parisien au XIXe siècle," *Annales de la recherche urbaine* 9 (1980): 3–22; Michelle Perrot, ed., *A History of Private Life: From the Fires of Revolution to the Great War*, trans. Arthur Goldhammer (Cambridge, Mass.: Belknap Press of Harvard University Press, 1990); and Bonnie Smith, *Ladies of the Leisure Class: The Bourgeoises of Northern France in the Nineteenth Century* (Princeton: Princeton University Press, 1981), who dates the implantation of this ideology to the *second* half of the century.

My claim is not that a gendered distinction between public and private simply did not exist, but that it did not structure Parisian everyday life and its representations in the ways that previous scholarship would lead us to assume. However, pressure has also been applied to several other assumptions implicit in histories of everyday life that argue for the separation of public and private during the nineteenth century, in particular the assumption that an abstract public sphere can be mapped onto actual public spaces. For example, while many people defend the equation of a political public sphere with urban, collective spaces by citing Jürgen Habermas's discussion of the role of coffeehouses in the development of public opinion, Susan Maslan has shown that Habermas in fact separates a virtual public sphere, constituted by writing, from the materialized public spaces peopled by crowds ("Resisting Representation: Theater and Democracy in Revolutionary France," *Representations* 52 [fall 1995]: esp. 29–30). For an incisive analysis of the contradictions endemic to any attempt to separate public and private spheres, see Joan Wallach Scott, *Only Paradoxes to Offer: French Feminists and the Rights of Man* (Cambridge, Mass.: Harvard University Press, 1996).

Separating the abstract political realm from concrete public spaces also allows us to see that while women may have been excluded from political participation, they were actively present in many public spaces. Recent work on Paris cafés shows not only that women from all classes often frequented them, but also that cafés were both urban hubs open to a general public and places where patrons conducted domestic business (W. Scott Haine, *The World of the Paris Café: Sociability among the French Working Class, 1789–1914* [Baltimore: Johns Hopkins University Press, 1996], esp. 33–58).

5. On "sick Paris," and on Paris as a site where the bourgeoisie's anxiety about disease met its anxiety about the revolutions that had created but also threatened its power, see Catherine J. Kudlick, *Cholera in Post-Revolutionary Paris: A Cultural History* (Berkeley: University of California Press, 1996). Kudlick's social and political analysis of the anxiety, stigmatization, and unwitting self-fashioning at work in bourgeois views of the poor areas of Paris is astute and indisputable, but I argue that this view coexisted with the "optimistic, picturesque view" of Paris that Kudlick claims disappeared after the eighteenth century; indeed, "optimistic" and "picturesque" describe well nineteenth-century views of the city's *bourgeois* spaces (37). For an analysis that takes into account both bourgeois anxiety and bourgeois self-satisfaction, see Adeline Daumard, *La Bourgeoisie parisienne de 1815 à 1848* (Paris: S.E.V.P.E.N., 1963).

6. Louis Chevalier, *Laboring Classes and Dangerous Classes in Paris during the First Half of the Nineteenth Century,* trans. Frank Jellinek (Princeton: Princeton University Press, 1973), 28; see also 199. Chevalier's brand of environmentalism attributes social problems to biological causes, a simplification that Kudlick's work addresses and corrects. Other recent studies of the links between housing and disease in nineteenth-century France include Andrew Aisenberg, "Contagious Disease and the Government of Paris in the Age of Pasteur" (Ph.D. dissertation, Yale University, 1993); Ann-Louise Shapiro, *Housing the Poor of Paris, 1850–1902* (Madison: University of Wisconsin Press, 1985); and

David S. Barnes, *The Making of a Social Disease: Tuberculosis in Nineteenth-Century France* (Berkeley: University of California Press, 1995). For a critical analysis of July Monarchy statistical reports, see Joan Wallach Scott, "A Statistical Representation of Work: *La Statistique de l'industrie à Paris*, 1847–1848," in *Gender and the Politics of History* (New York: Columbia University Press, 1988), 113–138.

7. I draw here on the two major works on Parisian domestic architecture in the nineteenth century: Monique Eleb-Vidal and Anne Debarre-Blanchard, *Architectures de la vie privée: maisons et mentalités XVIIe–XIXe siècles* (Brussels: Archives d'Architecture moderne, 1989); and François Loyer, *Paris: Nineteenth-Century Architecture and Urbanism,* trans. Charles Lynn Clark (New York: Abbeville Press, 1988). On the evolution of the Parisian apartment building see Louis Hautecoeur, "Immeubles à loyer," in *Urbanisme et architecture: études écrites et publiées en l'honneur de Pierre Lavedan* (Paris: Laurens, 1954), 167–178; Patrick Céleste, "L'immeuble et son intérieur," *In Extenso* 9 (November 1985): 63–88; *Architectures parisiennes au XIXe siècle* (Exposition catalog, hôtel Sully, 1975); Paul Chemetov and Bernard Marrey, *Architectures: Paris, 1848–1914* (Paris: Dunod, 1980); Jean Castex, Jean-Charles Depaule, Philippe Panei, *Formes urbaines: de l'îlot à la barre* (Paris: Dunod, 1977); Adeline Daumard, *Maisons de Paris et propriétaires parisiens au XIXe siècle, 1809–1880* (Paris: Cujas, 1965); Jean-Louis Deaucourt, "Paris et ses concierges au XIXe siècle" (Thèse de doctorat, Université de Paris VII, 1989); Biagio Accolti Gil, *Paris: vestibules de l'éclectisme,* trans. Jean-Louis Proroyeur (Paris: Vilo, 1982); and *Le Parisien chez lui au XIXe siècle 1814–1914* (Paris: Archives nationales, 1976).

8. This arrangement seems less startling when we take into account that sixteenth- and seventeenth-century society barely distinguished between rooms in which one sat and rooms through which one passed. See Monique Eleb-Vidal, "Dispositifs et moeurs: du privé à l'intime," *In Extenso* 9 (November 1985): 217, 223. This vertical organization persisted well into the eighteenth century; see Annik Pardailhé-Galabrun, *The Birth of Intimacy: Privacy and Domestic Life in Early Modern France,* trans. Jocelyn Phelps (Cambridge: Polity Press, 1991), 52–53; and Jean-Pierre Babelon, *Demeures parisiennes sous Henri IV et Louis XIII* (Paris: Le Temps, 1965), 94.

9. The *hôtel privé* was also interchangeably called the *hôtel particulier*. On the *hôtel* as the origin of the bourgeois apartment building in Paris, see Céleste, "L'immeuble et son intérieur," 75–76; and Eleb-Vidal and Debarre-Blanchard, *Architectures de la vie privée,* 11, which argues that architects transposed the *hôtel*'s design onto the apartment, leading to an opposition between the two types when the *hôtel*'s several stories were compressed into the apartment unit's one. This argument is convincing, but incomplete. Because its authors isolate the development of building types from external phenomena such as urbanism (11), they produce a strictly architectural genealogy for the apartment building as the devolution of a classical, aristocratic housing type. A fuller account of the development of the apartment house would include (1) its partial origins in the *maison à allée,* a building type rarely erected by trained architects; (2) economic

factors that helped make rental property built to the maximum allowable height an increasingly attractive investment; and (3) the interaction of building type with urban form and culture, which I explore in detail here. On the economic history of apartment buildings, see Hautecoeur, "Immeubles à loyer"; Daumard, *Maisons de Paris;* and Jeanne Pronteau, "Construction et aménagement des nouveaux quartiers de Paris (1820–1826)," *Histoire des entreprises* 1, no. 2 (November 1958): 8–32.

10. See Eleb-Vidal and Debarre-Blanchard, *Architectures de la vie privée,* 78, 83, 238.

11. Roger Chartier, "Power, Space, and Investments in Paris," in *Edo and Paris: Urban Life and the State in the Early Modern Era,* ed. James L. McClain, John M. Merriman, and Ugawa Kaoru (Ithaca: Cornell University Press, 1994), 148.

12. See Loyer, *Paris,* 22–24. In buildings with several units per floor the cheapest, smallest apartments faced the courtyard. Loyer specifies that units close to the street were prized not only because their tenants had to climb fewer stairs, but because Parisians valued proximity to the density and exchanges of the street.

13. Building styles varied: sometimes window size was constant over the entire facade, sometimes only within sets of two or three stories, but in both cases the need for symmetry in the facade predominated over the varied proportions of the rooms behind the windows. In his introduction to *Les Etrangers à Paris* (Paris: Warée, 1844), x, Louis Desnoyers described a Parisian building in which a floor had been divided in half with no corresponding alteration to the structure and placement of the windows. As a result, "the windows of the current second floor go all the way down to the floor, and . . . those of the mezzanine start halfway up the wall and go all the way up to the ceiling." From an exterior vantage point, however, an observer would simply have seen one tall window and been unaware of the internal partition. (Translation mine; throughout, all translations not otherwise identified are my own.)

14. P.-H. Chombart de Lauwe et al., *Paris et l'agglomération parisienne* (Paris: Presses universitaires de France, 1952), 2:57. Chombart de Lauwe's emphasis on typology prevents him from making any historical distinctions, but the type of apartment that he uses as his model, the *îlot,* corresponds best to the *immeubles* built during the first half of the nineteenth century. See Castex et al., *Formes urbaines.*

15. William C. Ellis, "The Spatial Structure of Streets," in *On Streets,* ed. Stanford Anderson (Cambridge, Mass.: MIT Press, 1978), 115. Ellis also develops de Lauwe's point that contiguous apartments are oriented to the street: "we think of the facades as belonging to the street more than to the flanking buildings" (127).

16. See *Les Grands boulevards* (Paris: Musées de la ville de Paris, 1985), 209.

17. A 1607 edict of Henri IV had forbidden all *saillies* and *encorbellements* in order to create a city of flat facades; Louis XVIII's legislation allowed pilasters up to 10 cm deep and enabled people to apply for permission to build balconies that could not extend more than 80 cm and would be at least 6 m above street

level (see Paul Léon, "Maisons et rues de Paris," *Revue de Paris* [August 1910]: 848–849). The law specified that only nonpublic buildings were to be regulated by street size: "The height of the facades of houses in the city and suburbs of Paris, aside from those of public buildings, is fixed in proportion to the width of the streets" (quoted in M. Toussaint, *Nouveau manuel complet d'architecture ou traité de l'art de bâtir* [Paris: Roret, 1837], 42). The interpenetration of the spaces of the apartment building and the street is also evident in Balzac's suggestion, in "Histoire et physiologie des boulevards de Paris, de la Madeleine à la Bastille," that balconies serve as awnings for pedestrians in the rain (*Le Diable à Paris* [Paris: Hetzel, 1846], 2:94), and in the structure of arcades [*passages*], in which mezzanine apartments overlooked the enclosed commercial thoroughfares.

18. Police ordinance of June 9, 1824, quoted in Toussaint, *Nouveau manuel,* 42, 51. François Sergent, *Manuel alphabétique du propriétaire et du locataire et sous-locataire* (Paris: Mongie, 1826), 83, 87, 102, 119, and 217. On streetlights and street surveillance in the nineteenth century, see Wolfgang Schivelbusch, *Disenchanted Night: The Industrialization of Light in the Nineteenth Century,* trans. Angela Davies (Berkeley: University of California Press, 1988). On efforts to regulate the relations among buildings, streets, and the city, see Anne Thalamy, "Réflexions sur la notion d'habitat aux XVIIIe et XIXe siècles," in *Politiques de l'habitat,* ed. François Béguin et al. (Paris: Corda, 1977), 5–31. Like Ellis ("Spatial Structure"), Thalamy argues that "the street presents itself as the fundamental principle around which habitats are organized" (17) and that the city is in turn structured like a "habitat" (21), its public space subjected to spatial enclosure and to the putatively domestic criteria of comfort and viability (31).

19. See J. C. Maldan, *Les Embarras de Paris,* 2d ed. (Paris, 1839), 9.

20. On the construction of new neighborhoods on the Right Bank, see Pronteau, "Construction et aménagement."

21. On the technological developments that shaped architectural pattern books and their methods of representing buildings, see Antoine Picon, "Du traité à la revue: l'image d'architecture au siècle de l'industrie," in *Usages de l'image au XIXe siècle,* ed. Stéphane Michaud, Jean-Yves Mullier, and Nicole Savy (Paris: Créaphis, 1992), 153–164. On architectural training in the first half of the nineteenth century, see David Van Zanten, *Developing Paris: The Architecture of Duban, Labrouste, Duc, and Vaudoyer* (Cambridge, Mass.: MIT Press, 1987); and Annie Jacques, *La Carrière de l'architecte au XIXe siècle* (Paris: Editions de la réunion des musées nationaux, 1986).

22. Furthermore, the domestic manuals published in France during the first half of the nineteenth century, which I discuss in some detail in chapter 4, rarely specified whether or not they were directed at apartment-dwellers. Unlike English domestic manuals, which counseled readers to avoid living in lodgings, French domestic manuals did not recommend detached houses over apartments, nor did they suggest that apartment-house life posed obstacles to a proper domestic regime. Although they offered advice about room distribution, function and decoration, they did so in ways that could apply to either an apartment or house. Their failure to mark the difference between apartments and houses

allowed them to address the widest possible audience but also indicated the relative insignificance of the difference between apartments and houses during the first half of the nineteenth century.

23. Frédéric Soulié, in *Journal des débats*, October 1, 1841, quoted in *Le Parisien chez lui*, 94. See also Frances Trollope, *Paris and the Parisians in 1835* (London: Bentley, 1835), 1:349: "Another English innovation . . . has been attempted, and has failed. This was the endeavour to introduce *maisonnettes*, or small houses calculated for the occupation of one family." She attributed the failure of "maisonnettes" (a word and type that rarely appeared in French architectural pattern books) to their lack of porters. For an example of an architect who called apartment buildings *maisons*, see J. C. Krafft, *Plans, coupes, élévations des plus belles maisons et des hôtels construits à Paris et dans les environs* (Paris: published by the author, n.d.). A loose terminology that confounds apartment buildings and houses persists in France to this day: "The French language does not even have a word for home. There is the word, *maison*, which means house, but which can also refer to an apartment house, or simply a building"—as well as, quite often, a brothel (Norma Evenson, *Paris: A Century of Change, 1878–1978* [New Haven: Yale University Press, 1979], 199).

24. Victor Calliat, *Parallèle des maisons de Paris construites depuis 1830 jusqu'à nos jours* (Paris: Bance, 1850), 1. This characterization of apartment houses as modern, urban, current, and progressive was not exclusive to architects. Property owners who drafted a memo in 1829 to the government about the speculative apartment buildings they had constructed in the new districts of the Bourse, the Chaussée d'Antin, and St-Lazare similarly described their buildings as "more comfortable and more suitable to the tastes and needs of the present generation" (*Mémoire adressé par une réunion de propriétaires, architectes et constructeurs de la ville de Paris, à Messieurs les membres de la commission d'Enquête* [Paris: Librairie du commerce, 1829], 3).

25. J. C. Krafft, *Portes cochères et portes d'entrées des maisons et édifices publics de Paris*, 2d ed. (Paris: Bance, 1838), 2:3. Krafft also uses the word "modern" in conjunction with an apartment building later in his text when he identifies another apartment as "entirely modern" (9, referring to plate 73).

26. L. Roux, *Le Cabinet de lecture* (1838), quoted in *Le Parisien chez lui*, 42.

27. L[ouis]-A[mbroise] Dubut, *Architecture civile: maisons de ville et de campagne—ouvrage utile à tous constructeurs et entrepreneurs, et à toutes personnes qui, ayant quelques connaissances en construction, veulent elles-mêmes diriger leurs bâtiments* (Paris: Marie et Bernard, 1847; first published in 1803), 3. Dubut died in 1846, just after constructing the Blancs-Manteaux market in Paris.

28. Cited in Vigier, *Nouvelle histoire*, 210; emphasis added, original ellipses. The use of the word "formerly" here invokes a nostalgia for the image of the live-in landlord of earlier times, idealized in other 1840s texts. In his 1841 article "Le Propriétaire," Amédée Achard criticized a growing class of speculative landlords who "build houses the way other people manufacture fabric for sale" (in *Les Français peints par eux-mêmes* [Paris: Curmer, 1842], 5:341). On the apartment building as "at once wealth, capital, and dwelling place," see Hélène Lipstadt, "Housing the Bourgeoisie: César Daly and the Ideal Home," *Oppositions* 8 (spring 1977): 35. Loyer (*Paris*, 124) also discusses the transition from

single-family houses to apartments as a switch "from family property to investment property."

29. For a late July Monarchy take on the hostile relations between landlords and tenants, see the Daumier series *Locataires et propriétaires,* reprinted in Loys Delteil, *Le Peintre-graveur illustré (XIXe et XXe siècles): Honoré Daumier (V),* vol. 24 (Paris: Chez l'auteur, 1926), pls. 1594–1628. Daumard's work suggests that during the first half of the nineteenth century (as opposed to the second half), landlords were likely to come from the middle classes rather than from the wealthiest ranks, and that they usually concentrated their real-estate acquisitions in the neighborhood where they had acquired their wealth; only shopkeepers, who usually lived directly above their stores, tended to own the buildings in which they resided. The general perception that landlords were impersonal financiers may have been caused by the ever-increasing commodification of land once the French Revolution had made aristocratic and church estates available for sale. The specific view that in the 1840s landlords became more distant from their tenants may have been caused by the increasing attractiveness of stock market investments, which drew many middle-class investors away from real estate and concentrated more properties in the hands of fewer landlords (Lipstadt, "Housing the Bourgeoisie," 41).

30. M. [François] Thiollet, *Choix de maisons, édifices et monuments publics, de Paris et de ses environs,* 2d ed. (Paris: Bance, 1838), 3:6.

31. Krafft, foreword to *Portes cochères.*

32. [Louis-Marie] Normand fils, *Paris moderne, ou choix de maisons construites dans les nouveaux quartiers de la capitale et de ses environs* (Paris: Bance, 1837), 1, 5. The text noted that "luxury houses intended for habitation by a single family . . . have only a secondary place here" (5).

33. For discussions of the evolution of the modern city from the imperial city, see Van Zanten, *Developing Paris;* Richard Becherer, *Science Plus Sentiment: César Daly's Formula for Modern Architecture* (Ann Arbor, UMI Research Press, 1984); and Anthony Vidler, "The Scenes of the Street: Transformations in Ideal and Reality, 1750–1871," in *On Streets,* ed. Stanford Anderson (Cambridge, Mass.: MIT Press, 1978), 29–112.

34. Loyer, *Paris,* 99, 144.

35. When using monument in a strictly positive sense, architects often argued that only *hôtels* could be considered monumental. J. G. Legrand and C. P. Landon, in *Description de Paris et de ses édifices* (1808), 9, wrote that *hôtels* were close to "public monuments" but that apartment houses, especially those with stores on their ground floors, "cannot be categorized in the class of public monuments, nor that of *hôtels.* Pure speculation has given rise to them." Yet the scale and facade of the building in question, the Portiques du Temple, led them to qualify this criticism: "nevertheless there is a quality of simplicity and austerity not devoid of elegance that makes one remark it with interest" (26). In 1840 César Daly wrote an article entitled "De l'architecture domestique monumentale" (*Revue générale de l'architecture* 1, no. 4 [April 1840]: 197–205), in which he criticized apartments for taking on monumental scale without providing aesthetic appeal. In a slightly earlier article on domestic architecture in Paris ("De l'architecture domestique de Paris," *Revue générale de l'architecture* 1, no. 3

[March 1840]: 167), however, he praised modern apartment buildings as "true works of art" and argued that domestic architecture was more worthy of the public interest than monuments: "the public understands that it is still more important to be well housed every day, than to enjoy a view for several minutes while accidentally passing a public monument." On the monumental structure of apartments from the 1820s on, see Castex et al., *Formes urbaines*, 23–25. Finally, Michel Lévy, author of a *Traité d'hygiène publique et privée* (Paris: Baillière, 1844), acknowledged the apartment house's monumentality but criticized it for contributing to overcrowding: "The large buildings that exist in big cities and contribute to their monumental magnificence, can only contain such a large number of occupants by piling up numerous floors and through a strict spatial parsimony" (1:549).

36. Normand fils, *Paris moderne*, vol. 2, "Prospectus"; Krafft, *Plans, coupes, élévations*, 1; P[ierre] A[dolphe] Piorry, *Des habitations et de l'influence de leurs dispositions sur l'homme, en santé et en maladie* (Paris: Pourchet, 1838), 125. Monumentality was not always a positive term: some commentators criticized the apartment house's monumental display for expressing the self-exhibition of the urban middle classes, who, like the houses they lived in, emphasized appearance and decor over traditional forms of power such as land and lineage; divorced ownership from residence; and replaced stable familial legacies with an often labile speculative profit or dangerously high rent burden. Montigny's *Provincial à Paris* (1825) noted the current "building fever and the mania for construction" and connected this to the heightened ambitions of the new bourgeois: "People are no longer satisfied with their father's modest dwelling. Everyone in Paris wants a full set of chambers" (Montigny quoted in Chevalier, *Laboring Classes*, 187–188). A few July Monarchy texts articulated what would become a truism of the Second Empire discourse on apartment houses: that they destroyed the integrity of family life by bringing crowds of strangers into contact within the home, a realm defined by its exclusion of strangers (for example, *L'Edile de Paris*, March 1833, quoted in Chevalier, ibid., 463).

37. Loyer, *Paris*, 98.

38. *Les Grands boulevards*, 171.

39. M. Thiollet and H. Roux, *Nouveau recueil de menuiserie et de décorations intérieures et extérieures* (Paris: Bance, 1837), 12 (discussion of plate 72) and iii; the authors also praise both a private salon and a theater for their use of mirrors (2).

40. On the way that trompe-l'oeil in architecture transforms facades into three-dimensional objects with the apparent ability to penetrate or recede from a viewer's space, see Miriam Milman, *Le Trompe-l'oeil* (Geneva: Skira, 1982), 12, 72, 87; on the way that it promotes the interpenetration of the interior and exterior, see Miriam Milman, *Architectures peintes en trompe-l'oeil* (Geneva: Skira, 1986), 14.

41. On the primacy of drawing in French architecture, see Gil, *Paris*, 47, and Frances H. Steiner, *French Iron Architecture* (Ann Arbor: UMI Research Press, 1984), 12, who writes that the Ecole des Beaux-Arts emphasized drawing and "two-dimensional decoration and composition" rather than "three-dimensional constructional principles."

42. Margaret Cohen, "Panoramic Literature and the Invention of Everyday Genres," in *Cinema and the Invention of Modern Life,* ed. Leo Charney and Vanessa R. Schwartz (Berkeley: University of California Press, 1995), 227–252. Cohen places the *tableaux* and *physiologies* on a representational spectrum between the realist novel and the mass press, and links them to the "empirical practical realism" of Marx and early work in the social sciences because of their interest in description and classification, particularly of physical details and of a "referentially verifiable space" (228, 231). She also emphasizes the importance of illustration in these texts, contrasting their homogeneous visuals to the "heterogenericity" of their prose (232).

43. Richard Sieburth, "Une idéologie du lisible: le phénomène des 'Physiologies,'" *Romantisme* 47 (1985): 41. Sieburth is primarily interested in the ways that the *physiologies* and *tableaux,* as objects conspicuously designed to be consumed, transformed authors into producers and made the city an object to be displayed and purchased, thus neutralizing the political dangers of caricature and reducing the potential dangers of the anonymous crowd into miniature texts about recognizable stereotypes. Richard Terdiman comments on the *physiologies'* neutrality in the context of Daumier's political evolution in ch. 3 of *Discourse/Counter-Discourse: The Theory and Practice of Symbolic Resistance in Nineteenth-Century France* (Ithaca: Cornell University Press, 1985).

44. See Andrée Lhéritier, "*Les Physiologies:* catalogue des collections de la Bibliothèque nationale," *Etudes de Presse,* n.s., 9, no. 17 (1957): 13–58; and Claude Pichois, "Le succès des *Physiologies,*" ibid., 59–66.

45. Viollet-le-Duc was an exception to this rule of depopulated architecture: he included people in his architectural drawings, both to convey a sense of building scale and to insist on the imbrication of architectural and social structures (Picon, "Du traité à la revue," 162).

46. Paul de Kock et al., *La Grande ville: nouveau tableau de Paris* (Paris: Maulde et Renou, 1843–44), 1:139, and Frédéric Soulié, "La Maîtresse de maison de santé," in *Les Français peints par eux-mêmes* (Paris: Curmer, 1841), 4:350.

47. On the distinction between a "pictorial code" that depicted space as composed and a "spatial code" that represented space as something that a viewer might immerse herself in or move through, see Green, *Spectacle of Nature,* 2, 184. On the representation of facades as either frontal planes or three-dimensional spaces that one could enter, see Becherer, *Science Plus Sentiment,* 223. For a sustained analysis of these issues in the aesthetics of French painting from the eighteenth through the nineteenth centuries, see Michael Fried, *Absorption and Theatricality: Painting and Beholder in the Age of Diderot* (Berkeley: University of California Press, 1980); *Courbet's Realism* (Chicago: University of Chicago Press, 1990); and *Manet's Modernism, or, The Face of Painting in the 1860s* (Chicago: University of Chicago Press, 1996).

48. Walter Benjamin uses the term "store of information" in the context of a comparison of the *tableaux* and *physiologies* to the panoramas, popular visual amusements that projected illusionistic urban and natural scenes on interior walls and used lighting effects to simulate movement and change within the panoramic scene. He writes: "These books consist of individual sketches which,

as it were, reproduce the plastic foreground of those panoramas with their anecdotal form and the extensive background of the panoramas with their store of
information" (*Charles Baudelaire: A Lyric Poet in the Era of High Capitalism,*
trans. Harry Zohn [London: Verso, 1983], 35). Benjamin's point is both incisive
and suggestive, but I would argue for the apartment house as the crucial, missing term linking the *tableaux* to the panoramas. As Vidler ("Scenes of the Street,"
81) puts it, taking up two of Benjamin's key topics, "Both arcade and diorama
were interiors par excellence, but, of course, public interiors; and if the arcade
was seen as a city in miniature, then the Diorama extended this city to the entire world." Vidler describes the ways in which Parisian architectural types encapsulated reversible figure/ground, public/private, and exterior/interior relations. My argument here is that the apartment house was perceived as similarly
reversible, and that Benjamin's analogy between the *tableaux* and the panoramas works because of what both had in common with apartment houses.
Panoramas, like apartment buildings, could be divided into foreground and background; the apartment as a series of illuminated scenes resembled the panorama's
sequential displays; and the observer's position within a panorama, situated indoors but apparently looking "out" at an urban or natural landscape, bore a
deep relation to the position of an apartment-dweller looking out onto streets,
other windows, or rooftops.

49. For a text that molded its consumer simultaneously into a reader and
flâneur, see the *Panorama intérieur de Paris* (Paris: F. Sinmett, n.d.), whose pages
(contained between book covers) were not cut but continuous, so that they
folded out as a single sheet. That sheet consisted of a visual representation of a
boulevard sidewalk, viewed from a position that corresponds to the facing sidewalk on the other side of the boulevard. The image includes people, building facades, and side streets. The format allows us to read the street from left to right,
as though it were a page, but the visual perspective also gives the pages the depth
of a street (we understand the relation of the side streets to the facades as one of
background and foreground), and the directionality of the pages gives our reading of the book the continuous, horizontal linearity and mobility of walking in
a street (as opposed to the up and down motion of reading lines of text on facing pages in a printed book).

The mutual figuration of writing as architecture and architecture as writing
preceded the nineteenth century and can be traced through the graphic architectural notation discussed earlier in this chapter, as well as in etymology—for
example, the origin of the word "cornice" in "writing." For a detailed discussion of these interrelations, see Philippe Hamon, *Expositions: Literature and
Architecture in Nineteenth-Century France,* trans. Katia Sainson-Frank and Lisa
Maguire (Berkeley: University of California Press, 1992), esp. 15–50, 94–124.

50. The notion that a page could have more than one dimension and that
opaque white paper and black print could become transparent was literalized in
a type of drawing popular during the July Monarchy, in which the viewer pulled
on a flap (*volet*), usually an image of a door or window, to gain access to a hidden scene, usually of illicit sexual activity. For examples of these lithographs, see
Le Parisien chez lui, 46.

51. Frédéric Soulié, "Les Drames invisibles," in *Le Diable à Paris* (Paris: Hetzel, 1845), 1:118.

52. On the multiplicity of the *tableaux*, see Margaret Cohen, "Panoramic Literature," 232–239. Cohen discusses the ways in which this heterogeneity signifies a tension between the panoptic effect of a unified, objective overview and the more disruptive effects of an anarchic, phantasmatic experience of the everyday—like that of Lesage's Asmodée, the devilish voyeur of *Le Diable boiteux* (1707).

53. Van Zanten, *Developing Paris*, 225.

54. *Nouveau tableau de Paris, au XIXe siècle* (Paris: Mme Charles-Béchet, 1834), 1:3.

55. "Asmodée," in *Paris, ou le livre des cent-et-un* (Paris: Ladvocat, 1831), 1:5; emphasis added. Janin goes on to cite an article in the *Journal des débats* that identified the multiple authorship of the *Livre* as the hallmark of its modernity: "Here is a new book, if ever there was one; new by virtue of its content, new by virtue of its form, new by virtue of the procedure for its composition" (7). And later *tableaux* adhered to this multiply authored view of the city. The preface to the 1834 *Nouveau tableau de Paris,* 1:3, 5, stated that the book aimed to convey "this life of a thousand facets, this multiple aspect . . . circumscribed in our frame; we will reproduce the thousand traits of this large physiognomy. . . . [E]verything will be a contrast in this book; but how could the city, with its perpetual contrasts, be described otherwise?"

56. The ease with which Janin imagines a female transvestite belies the fact that women were legally barred from wearing men's clothes in public by Napoleon in 1800; see Marie-Jo Bonnet, *Un Choix sans équivoque: recherches historiques sur les relations amoureuses entre les femmes, XVIe–XXe siècles* (Paris: Denoël, 1981), 195–197. Nevertheless, women could obtain special permission to dress as men and the *tableaux* frequently described *lorettes* composing petitions to wear men's clothes. Visual representations of *bals masqués* frequently depicted women in men's clothes (and men in women's clothes), and Edouard de Beaumont's series of antifeminist cartoons, *Les Vésuviennes,* which appeared in *Le Charivari* from May to June 1848, depicted several scenes of women in men's shirts and pants (reprinted in Claire Goldberg Moses, *French Feminism in the Nineteenth Century* [Albany: State University of New York Press, 1984], 123–126).

57. "Coupe de maison," image by Karl Girardet, text by Dugald Stewart, *Magasin pittoresque* 15 (1847): 400. See also Paul de Kock's preface to *La Grande ville* (1843–44), which advocates abandoning the aerial position completely: "Let's walk aimlessly [*au hasard*] in Paris; we will not need to seek out subjects. . . . [W]e will visit all the neighborhoods; we will enter many houses, not by the roof, like the *Diable boiteux,* but by the door; it's less original, but more natural" (1:6).

58. On this feature of apartment houses, see Kent C. Bloomer and Charles W. Moore, *Body, Memory, and Architecture* (New Haven: Yale University Press, 1977), 47, who note that apartments resemble prisons in that they deny dwellers access to parts of the building that they occupy.

59. "Le Flâneur à Paris," anonymous [*par un flâneur*], in *Paris, ou le livre des cent-et-un* (Paris: Ladvocat, 1832), 6:100. The *flâneur* would be impossible in London, this text points out, "where all the houses are separated from passersby by wide ditches [*fossés*]"; the author was referring to the "areas" in front of London houses that led to their basements (98). Paul de Kock's popular novel *Mon Voisin Raymond* features a hero whose *flâneries* turn Parisian streets, theaters, magic shows, *and* apartments into spaces of chance encounter.

60. Wolff, "Invisible *Flâneuse.*"

61. Albéric Second, "Rue Notre-Dame-de-Lorette," in *Les Rues de Paris: Paris ancien et moderne,* ed. Louis Lurine (Paris: Kugelman, 1844), 1:139. For another example of a man who makes sense of Paris in terms of the female types ("milliners, extras . . . actresses") whom he observes from his apartment, "from story to story, balcony to balcony, street to street, from sidewalk to mezzanine," see Amédée Achard, "Le Nouveau Paris," in *Le Prisme: encyclopédie morale du dix-neuvième siècle* (Paris: Curmer, 1841), 148. The apartment house frequently appeared as a privileged site for the amalgamation of urban observation and a heterosexuality inflected by male voyeurism. See, for example, Paul de Kock, *Mon Voisin Raymond* (Paris: Gustave Barba, 1849): "She lives across from him . . . on a second floor, facing front. Grandmaison noticed her at her window: the street is wide, but he has a delicious spyglass [*lorgnette*]" (38). Note, however, that the word for spyglass, *lorgnette,* sounds almost identical to the word for a female type, the *lorette,* thus making a woman not only the object of a man's gaze but also almost an instrument that makes that gaze possible. Jann Matlock notes the identification of lorgnettes with women in July Monarchy iconography in "Censoring the Realist Gaze," in *Spectacles of Realism: Body, Gender, Genre,* ed. Margaret Cohen and Christopher Prendergast (Minneapolis: University of Minnesota Press, 1995), 28–65.

62. See, for example, Paul de Kock, *Les Bains à domicile* (Paris: Tresse, 1845), 3, in which a grisette complains that "[t]he landlord would like to establish a *droit de seigneur* over his tenants"; and the *Nouveaux tableaux de Paris* (Paris: Pillet, 1828), 141, which refer to a liaison between a tenant and a landlord satirically named Mr. Vulture. Similarly, in an essay on "Les Demoiselles à marier," Regnier Destourbet explained that fathers wish they could marry off their daughters by the same means as one might rent an apartment—"place a sign over the door: *To marry, a pretty young lady. . . . Address inquiries to the portier*" (in *Paris, ou le livre des cent-et-un* [Paris: Ladvocat, 1832], 6:112). And Emile Deschamps in "Les Appartements à louer" compared an apartment to a wife: "it is as difficult to lodge someone as to marry him. It is useless to know that one wants an apartment at a particular price or size; a wife with a particular dowry or shape; there is always some little thing that one doesn't know about"(ibid., 8:59). Maurice Alhoy, in *Physiologie de la lorette* (Paris: Aubert, n.d.), 32, attributed the conflation of female identity and real estate to women's own proclivity for names based on residences: "If she has been a tenant in a recently built house, she names herself *madame de Maisonneuve* [new house], or, in corrupted form, *madame de Maisonave.*"

63. Achard, "Le Propriétaire," 5:341; A. de Lacroix, "Les Appartements à louer," in *Le Prisme: encyclopédie morale du dix-neuvième siècle* (Paris: Curmer,

1841), 189; Achard, "Le Propriétaire," 5:341. See also "Le Jardin du Palais-Royal," which compared "une jolie ville" and "une jolie femme" (in *Paris au XIXe siècle* [Paris: Beauger, 1839], 5).

64. "Une Fenêtre du faubourg Saint-Jacques" identified the grisette as an *article de Paris*, a Parisian commodity, similar to a Bordeaux wine or the truffles of Périgueux (in *Paris au XIXe siècle* [Paris: Beauger, 1839], 35); while Alhoy (*Physiologie de la lorette*, 11) linked the grisette's disappearance to the effacement of the old Paris: "The grisette is a being who is tending to disappear, like the neighborhood in which she lives." *Les Embarras de Paris*, 5, used the feminine names of omnibus lines to compare them to sexualized women: "The White Ladies [*Dames Blanches*] grant you their sad favors; at another point, the Scotch-women [*les Ecossaises*] do the same along a different line."

65. See, for example, J. B. Ambs-Dalès, *Les Grisettes de Paris* (Paris: Roy-Terry, 1830), which organizes its chapters about different types of women workers according to the occupation associated with each neighborhood ("Quartier du Palais-Royal: modistes," "Quartier du Panthéon: blanchisseuses," etc.). Each chapter of this semipornographic text links the urban geography of women workers to prostitution. Similarly, in "La Femme sans nom" (*Les Français peints par eux-mêmes* [Paris: Curmer, 1840], 1:246–247, 253), Taxile Delord described one woman's life course in terms of her sexuality and her relationship to Parisian neighborhoods: the heroine, "curious to know what a destiny is," experiences a fall into sexual knowledge that teaches her that a "destiny . . . consists of a room on the fourth floor in the rue Tiquetonne"; as soon as she gets a younger lover, Mariette moves to a luxurious apartment on rue Notre-Dame-de-Lorette; when she becomes a thief's mistress, "in changing her status, she also changed her domicile," and moves into a *garni,* or lodging house. The story thus works to align women with a sexual fate legible only in terms of urban locations and architectural types. On the Parisian woman's bedroom, see Taxile Delord, *Physiologie de la parisienne* (Paris: Aubert, n.d.), 111: "In Paris, one forgets the name of one's first mistress, but one remembers her bedroom."

66. Gourdon, *Physiologie de l'omnibus* (1842), quoted in Roger-Henri Guerrand, *Moeurs citadines: histoire de la culture urbaine XIXe–XXe siècles* (Paris: Quai Voltaire, 1992), 124.

67. Laurent-Jan, "Où va une femme qui sort: énigme," in *Le Diable à Paris* (Paris: Hetzel, 1846), 2:156–157. Women who could profit from their own sexual exchange, however, were allowed less mobility: a series of prefectural circulars in 1829 and 1830 reduced prostitutes' freedom of movement, prohibiting them from walking together, standing in the streets, or appearing on the boulevards and in public gardens. See Jill Harsin, *Policing Prostitution in Nineteenth-Century Paris* (Princeton: Princeton University Press, 1985), 42–47.

68. On the sociability of the salons during the July Monarchy, see Anne Martin-Fugier, *La Vie élégante ou la formation du tout-Paris 1815–1848* (Paris: Fayard, 1990), esp. 92.

69. Louis Couailhac, *Physiologie du célibataire et de la vieille fille* (Paris: J. Laisné, 1841), 16, 123–124. The misogyny of this diatribe against a female cabal blends indistinguishably with its homophobia; an earlier section on unmarried men who have sex with other men starts out coyly ("Those [men] could

have been shut up for two thousand years . . . with our mother Eve, and Cain and Abel would still not have been born") then turns positively murderous when it differentiates between two types of men who have sex with other men (without ever explaining the difference) and states that "one set is to be pitied. . . . [T]he others . . . I regret heartily that we do not burn them in the public square, as we did in the time of our good ancestors!" (108). The evocation of burning at the stake links the "witches," whom Couailhac never describes as sexually active with one another, to male sexual transgressors.

70. M. J. Brisset, "La Ménagère parisienne," in *Les Français peints par eux-mêmes* (Paris: Curmer, 1841), 3:18; and Paul de Kock, *La Grande ville: nouveau tableau de Paris* (Paris: Au bureau central des publications nouvelles, 1842), 1:217.

71. The *Nouveaux tableaux de Paris* attributed women's presence in the street to their "need to make themselves seen" (2:100). See also Philibert Audebrand, "La Figurante," in *Les Français peints par eux-mêmes* (Paris: Curmer, 1840), 1:113.

72. Delord, *Physiologie de la parisienne*, 76–77.

73. Soulié also notes that he would not be surprised to see such an interaction among men of different classes, especially because men do not use sharp differences in dress to signify their differences in class (Frédéric Soulié, "La Bourse," in *Nouveau tableau de Paris, au XIXe siècle* [Paris: Mme Charles-Béchet, 1834], 3:41–42). Women were eventually banished from these galleries as well and forced to conduct their business outside the Stock Exchange building by means of male couriers. Frances Trollope also commented on Parisian women's affinity for stock market speculation: "The mania for gambling in the funds is vastly more extensive here than in London. The women are deeply engaged in it, and had established a parquet for themselves in one of the galleries at the Bourse, from whence they were lately expelled by an order of the Minister of Commerce, but they still continue their *agiotage* to the same extent in the outer passages. When Mr. Jauge was lately arrested . . . these irritated viragoes would have torn him in pieces, if the arrival of the gendarmes had not saved him from their fury" (*Paris and the Parisians in 1835*, 1:275).

74. Some writers associated female types other than the *portière* with a combination of urban and domestic knowledge; see, for example, L. Roux, "La Sage-femme," in *Les Français peints par eux-mêmes* (Paris: Curmer, 1840), 1:177–184; and Madame de Bawr, "La Garde," in ibid., 1:129–137.

75. For a social history of male and female porters in the nineteenth century, see Jean-Louis Deaucourt, *Premières loges: Paris et ses concierges au XIXe siècle* (Paris: Aubier, 1992); Deaucourt's thorough work is compromised by his insistence on reading descriptive and even literary texts as transparent sources of empirical data about the daily lives and duties of his subjects.

76. Deaucourt, "Paris et ses concierges," 488, 742.

77. In response to the upheaval of large-scale demolitions and increased class segregation by neighborhood effected by Haussmannization, Second Empire writers retrospectively perceived the July Monarchy as a time when buildings were more integrated by class, but this perception was more nostalgic than

accurate. On class restrictions in bourgeois buildings, see Daumard, *Maisons de Paris,* 90–92. She shows that in buildings aimed at the wealthy middle classes, the smaller apartments on the top floors were occupied by people of the same milieu such as unmarried lawyers or middle-level clerks. A March 1833 article for the property-owners' journal *L'Edile de Paris* argued against large buildings precisely because they "forced" landlords to "let to a crowd of persons unknown to one another and without proper references," which suggests little tolerance for working-class tenants in bourgeois buildings (quoted in Chevalier, *Laboring Classes,* 463).

78. Taxile Delord, *Paris-portière,* part of the series *Le Petit Paris* (Paris, n.d.), 3. This book probably appeared in the mid-1850s.

79. James Rousseau, *Physiologie de la portière* (Paris: Aubert, 1841), 6 and 61.

80. The *portière*'s daughter was stereotypically portrayed as a negative figure of class mobility. See, for example, Henry Monnier, "La Portière," in *Les Français peints par eux-mêmes* (Paris: Curmer, 1841), 3:41: "they dip into a world more elevated than that into which they were born. . . . From their first years, they travel perpetually from the *loge* to the apartments and from the apartments to the *loge.*"

Although the *tableaux* tended to contrast the female *portière* to the male *propriétaire,* in fact women owned property in relatively large numbers: in 1847, single women (who alone could hold legal title to property, aside from women *séparées de biens* from their husbands) constituted 29 percent of recently deceased landlords (Daumard, *Maisons de Paris,* 235). In an article on the development of the Right Bank during the 1820s, Pronteau cites several women among those who invested in and helped to construct these new neighborhoods. For a satirical typology of landladies, see Lacroix, "Appartements à louer," 189–194.

81. Physiologists took their inspiration from Lavater, whose work on physiognomy appeared in French translation in 1841. There Lavater wrote that "physiognomy is the science, the knowledge of the relationship that links the exterior to the interior, the visible surface to what it covers of the invisible" (*La Physiognomie ou l'art de connaître les hommes* [1841], quoted in Henri Gauthier, *L'Image de l'homme intérieur chez Balzac* [Geneva: Droz, 1984], 252).

82. If the physiologists read the *portière* as typical of the space she occupied, there also existed an architectural physiognomic tradition of reading space anthropomorphically: "the comparison of facades and faces was entrenched in the classical anthropomorphic tradition . . . [and] . . . gained currency from the mid-eighteenth century with the attempt to develop a coherent theory of character for different building types" (Anthony Vidler, *The Writing of the Walls: Architectural Theory in the Late Enlightenment* [Princeton: Princeton Architectural Press, 1987], 121).

83. Rousseau, *Physiologie,* 8 and 12.

84. Henry Monnier, *Le Roman chez la portière* (Paris: Au magasin central des pièces de Théâtre, 1855).

85. Rousseau, *Physiologie,* 63, 73. See also Henry Monnier, "Une Maison de Marais," in *Paris, ou le livre des cent-et-un* (Paris: Ladvocat, 1831), 1:342, in which he describes the porter's lodge as a courtroom: "There, every evening,

sits the tribunal presided over by the *portière*. There are judged all the actions of the tenants, questions of high politics, and literary productions."

86. Cited in Edith Melcher, *The Life and Times of Henry Monnier: 1799–1877* (Cambridge, Mass.: Harvard University Press, 1950), 92.

87. Jacques Raphael, "Le Portier de Paris," in *Paris, ou le livre des cent-et-un* (Paris: Ladvocat, 1833), 10:347. Among "Les Petites misères parisiennes" (in *Nouveau tableau de Paris, au XIXe siècle* [Paris: Mme Charles-Béchet, 1834], 6:286), which all focus on the difficulties of apartment living, Jules Janin includes the porter's all-seeing eyes: "living beneath the law of one's porter, and seeing always that pitiless Argus who knows what you do better than you do, who knows what you think better than you do, who reads the soul of the friend who visits you, and the sealed letter that he brings you."

88. "La Loge du portier," in *Paris au XIXe siècle* (Paris: Beauger, 1839), 17 and 18.

89. Edouard Monnais, in his article "Le Propriétaire," called the *portier* a "minister of the interior," "a minister of the police," and "a minister of war" (in *Nouveau tableau de Paris, au XIXe siècle* [Paris: Mme Charles-Béchet, 1834], 3:120); another article, by Achard ("Le Propriétaire," 5:341), described the *portier* as "a *chargé d'affaires* who knows all the secrets of this little state that we call an *hôtel*"; in "Appartements à louer," 193, Lacroix compared the *portier* to "a lawyer who pleads for bad causes, and often wins them"; and in *Mort aux locataires assez canailles pour ne pas payer leurs termes* (1854), Taxile Delord, Edmond Texier, and Arnould Frémy described the *portier* as a "subaltern autocrat," akin to a monarch in his ability to represent the landlord (Paris: Editions Seesam, 1990), 45–46. In his 1844 critique of Eugène Sue's *Les Mystères de Paris,* Karl Marx wrote: "The porter in Paris is the representative and spy of the landlord. . . . During the Terror, the Empire and the Restoration, the porter was one of the main agents of the secret police. . . . As a result, 'portier' and 'épicier' are considered insulting names and the porter prefers to be called 'concierge'" ("'Critical Criticism' as a Mystery-Monger," in *The Holy Family, or Critique of Critical Criticism,* trans. Richard Dixon and Clemens Dutt [Moscow: Progress, 1975], 92–93).

90. Monnier, "Une Maison de Marais," 333 and 342.

91. Another female type that male writers similarly characterized as trying to rule her household and dominate her husband was the female writer and intellectual, the *bas-bleu.* However, they also characterized this type as having explicitly feminist commitments; the bluestocking's *politics,* not her association with a particular type of space or labor, inspired her will to power within her household. See Frédéric Soulié, *Physiologie du bas-bleu* (Paris: Aubert, n.d.); Honoré Daumier's series "Bas-bleus" (1844) reprinted in *Intellectuelles et femmes socialistes,* ed. Jacqueline Armingeat (Paris: Editions Vilo, 1974); Eugène Guinot, "Les Veuves du Diable," in *Le Diable à Paris* (Paris: Hetzel, 1846), 2:269; and Jules Janin, "Le Bas-bleu," in *Les Français peints par eux-mêmes* (Paris: Curmer, 1842), 5:201–231. These writers consistently identified the female writer and thinker with a disorderly and eccentric home and portrayed her as the opposite of the housewife who actively produced order and aesthetic harmony.

92. See Rousseau, *Physiologie*, 17: the *portière* "maintains intimate relations . . . [with] the servants . . . above all with the female servants. With the latter . . . [s]he is always sure to find an echo in her interlocutrix [*interlocutrice*]."

93. Personal communication, Victoria Thompson, October 24, 1992.

94. Monnier, "Une Maison de Marais," 342; Rousseau, *Physiologie*, 23.

2. Balzac's Spatial Relations

1. On this descriptive procedure as characteristic of nineteenth-century realism, see Erich Auerbach, *Mimesis: The Representation of Reality in Western Literature*, trans. Willard R. Trask (Princeton: Princeton University Press, 1953), 454–492; Auerbach discusses *Le Père Goriot* on 468–473. For another analysis of descriptive movement in *Le Père Goriot*, see Philippe Hamon, *Expositions: Literature and Architecture in Nineteenth-Century France*, trans. Katia Sainson-Frank and Lisa Maguire (Berkeley: University of California Press, 1992), 103; see also Raymonde Debray-Genette, "Traversées de l'espace descriptif," *Poétique* 51 (September 1982): 329–344. For a discussion of the importance of the city to the type of realism exemplified by Balzac, see several works by Franco Moretti, including "Homo Palpitans: Balzac's Novels and Urban Personality," in *Signs Taken for Wonders: Essays in the Sociology of Literary Forms*, trans. Susan Fischer, David Forgacs, and David Miller (London: Verso, 1988), and *The Way of the World: The Bildungsroman in European Culture* (London: Verso, 1987); and essays on specific works by Balzac, including Henri Mitterand, "Le lieu et le sens: l'espace parisien dans *Ferragus*," in *Le Discours du roman* (Paris: Presses universitaires de France, 1980) 189–212; and Jeannine Guichardet, "Un Jeu de l'oie maléfique: l'espace parisien du *Père Goriot*," *Année balzacienne* 7 (1986): 169–189.

2. Critical approaches to Balzac's *La Comédie humaine* have suggested its affiliation with architecture mainly by privileging architecture as a topos within the texts or using architecture as a metaphor for the various texts' relationship to one another. Thus architectural structures are either described as central to Balzac's texts, located at their core as descriptive objects, personified agents, and indexes to character, or as external to those texts, overarching architectural metaphors that figure the *Comédie humaine* as a gallery of rooms, a cathedral, or a monument, with Balzac as their architect, archaeologist, or cartographer. The original source of these metaphors is Balzac himself, notably in the foreword to the *Comédie humaine* written in 1842 (*La Comédie humaine* [Paris: Gallimard, Editions de la Pléiade, 1976], 1:12–13). See also Allan H. Pasco, *Balzacian Montage: Configuring the "Comédie humaine"* (Toronto: University of Toronto Press, 1991), 12, 13, 18; and A. J. Mount, *The Physical Setting in Balzac's "Comédie Humaine"* (Hull: University of Hull Publications, 1966), which by cataloging most of Balzac's references to architecture, demonstrates that various theories of architectural determinism and expressionism pervade the *Comédie humaine*. Mount organizes his monograph along the lines of narrative functions such as characterization and historical interest and tends to equate description and architecture, which prevents him from analyzing the interactions between them. Because he does not distinguish different types of architectural objects, he

cannot assess whether certain types are associated with certain narrative functions. See also Juliette Frølich, *Pictogrammes: figures du descriptif dans le roman balzacien* (Oslo: Privat, 1985); and Jeannine Jallat, "Lieux balzaciens," *Poétique* 64 (November 1985): 473–481.

3. In "Censoring the Realist Gaze" (in *Spectacles of Realism: Body, Gender, Genre,* ed. Margaret Cohen and Christopher Prendergast [Minneapolis: University of Minnesota Press, 1995], 28–65), Jann Matlock shows just how strongly realism was identified with the exposure of what many thought should remain private and unseen. To make this point, she turns to the antirealist critics who advocated censoring the realist novel, particularly in the name of protecting women from seeing and being seen. Her valuable research does not, however, fully account for the dynamics of exposure within the novels themselves, which as we will see in this chapter depend both on maintaining privacy and transgressing it; nor does her interpretation cover the range of women's positions within realist observation, since at least one major Balzac novel depends on the figure of the *portière* for its own narration. Nor does Matlock's emphasis on a medical, anatomical model for the realist gaze fully exhaust the range of affiliations of realism to other discourses. As this chapter shows, a model for the omniscient narrator existed in the spaces of urban everyday life, including the apartment house.

4. For a discussion of the genealogy of Balzac's *Physiologie,* see my introduction to the English translation, in *The Physiology of Marriage* (Baltimore: Johns Hopkins University Press, 1997). See also Maurice Regard, preface to *Physiologie du mariage* (Paris: Garnier-Flammarion, 1968), 13–16. Further references to the *Physiologie* are to this French edition, and all translations are my own. For an analysis of the relation of Balzac's *Physiologie* to both the scientific physiologies that preceded it and the parodic 1840s physiologies that followed it, see Nathalie Basset, "La *Physiologie du mariage* est-elle une physiologie?" *Année balzacienne* 7 (1986): 101–114.

5. Balzac's emphasis on the importance of husbands' spatial control of wives was not without basis in France's Civil Code, which granted husbands the right to make their wives live under their roof. Furthermore, because a lease was considered an *acte privé* and married women under the code had no right to enter into such acts, which included contracts, a married woman was not legally able to lease an apartment in her own right. See François Sergent, *Manuel alphabétique du propriétaire et du locataire et sous-locataire* (Paris: Mongie, 1826), 1–2. On Balzac and the Civil Code, see Marie-Henriette Faillie, *La Femme et le code civil dans "la Comédie humaine" d'Honoré de Balzac* (Paris: Didier, 1968).

6. The narrator concludes by contradicting his initial assessment of the superlative dangers of the apartment: "Every man can apply to his apartment the precautions that we have recommended to the owner of an *hôtel,* and then the tenant will have the following advantage over the owner—an apartment that takes up less space is much more easy to inspect [*est beaucoup mieux surveillé*]" (166). The apartment ceases to be a danger, however, only if it is first converted into an *hôtel* by means of the *locataire*'s metamorphosis into someone who treats domestic space as a *propriétaire* would.

7. On architects' and hygienists' perceptions of walls as ducts, see Alain Corbin, *The Foul and the Fragrant: Odor and the French Social Imagination* (Cambridge, Mass.: Harvard University Press, 1986), 25: "Walls, intended to separate and support, also proved to be conduits, sites of complex upward movements, and like the soil, repositories of ancient filth. They combined deposits with the wafts of mephitisms and hence concealed a multiplicity of threats."

8. Honoré de Balzac, "Philosophie de la vie conjugale à Paris—Chaussée d'Antin," in *Le Diable à Paris* (Paris: Hetzel, 1845), 1:197–198. The passage ends this lament for a lost privacy with a metaphor that equates excessive female sexuality with such deficiencies of privacy: "Paris is a city that displays itself almost nude all the time, a city that is essentially courtesan and without chastity."

9. Honoré de Balzac, *Le Cousin Pons*, ed. Anne-Marie Meininger (Paris: Garnier, 1974), 4. Further references to this edition will appear within the text, followed by page number; all translations are my own.

10. Michel Butor, "Les Parents pauvres," in *Répertoire II: études et conférences 1959–1963* (Paris: Minuit, 1964), 193.

11. On the "antagonism" between the two texts, see André Lorant, *"Les Parents pauvres" d'Honoré de Balzac* (Geneva: Droz, 1967), 25.

12. Michael Lucey discusses the ways in which *Les Parents pauvres* also position Bette and Pons differently with respect to sexuality, defined as both affective relations and systems of alliance and inheritance ("Balzac's Queer Cousins and Their Friends," in *Novel Gazing: Queer Readings in Fiction,* ed. Eve Kosofsky Sedgwick [Durham: Duke University Press, 1997], 167–198). On Bette as a dangerous domestic agent, see for example, James R. McGuire, "The Feminine Conspiracy in Balzac's *La Cousine Bette,*" *Nineteenth-Century French Studies* 20, nos. 3–4 (spring–summer 1992): 295–304; and Peter Hulme, "Balzac's Parisian Mystery: *La Cousine Bette* and the Writing of Historical Criticism," *Literature and History* 11, no. 1 (spring 1985): 47–64, esp. 51, although Hulme misrepresents the aims of Bette's vengefulness by interpreting her character solely as a metaphor for the working class (52–53).

13. Honoré de Balzac, *La Cousine Bette* (Paris: Garnier, 1962), 62.

14. See Nicole Mozet, *"La Cousine Bette" d'Honoré de Balzac* (Paris: Editions pédagogie moderne, 1980), 68.

15. Christopher Prendergast aptly refers to the "vicissitudes" of the family in *La Cousine Bette* (*Balzac: Fiction and Melodrama* [London: Edward Arnold, 1978], 92). Yet even diversions from the familial sphere, such as adultery, stay within its bounds, as in the novel's opening scene, where M. Crevel attempts to seduce Mme Hulot, the mother of his daughter's husband and the wife of the friend who stole his mistress, all in the name of helping her marry off her daughter (who he suggests could marry him).

16. For apartment-house romances in the *tableaux,* in addition to the examples cited in the previous chapter, see Léon Gozlan, "Les Maîtresses à Paris," which describes how men become lovers with their women neighbors (in *Le Diable à Paris* [Paris: Hetzel, 1846], 2:105–122), as does Jean May, "Les Deux mansardes parisiennes" (in *Paris, ou le livre des cent-et-un* [Paris: Ladvocat, 1834], 14:39–76).

17. Paul de Kock's one-act vaudeville, *Les Bains à domicile* (Paris: Tresse, 1845), is set entirely in the bedroom of an apartment building's landlord. Throughout the play, the occupants of other floors pass through this bedroom, including a grisette who refuses to move from her fourth-floor apartment because her window faces the studio of her "cousin" (5)—a common designation for a lover, especially in farce. The play's various contretemps end when the grisette is allowed to keep her apartment and the landlord resolves his romance with the woman who rents an apartment on the first floor—a woman who has been parading under a false and inflated identity, but whom the grisette recognizes as a former grisette, thus illustrating the principle that there can be no strangers within the apartment-house plot: occupants are linked either by sexual relations (past and present) or some other knowledge of one another.

In Henry Monnier's play *Le Roman chez la portière* (Paris: Au magasin central des pièces de Théâtre, 1855), Hippolyte, the lover of the *portière*'s daughter, tries to rent an apartment incognito. The *portière* mistakes him for the landlady's nephew; when her mistake is corrected, the correction does not demonstrate that this urban stranger is, in fact, a stranger but instead reveals that this outsider is the long-lost child of Mme Floquet, one of the building's tenants.

18. See Paul de Kock, *Mon Voisin Raymond* (Paris: Gustave Barba, 1849), and *La Demoiselle du cinquième* (Brussels: Lebègue, 1857), for two exemplary instances of the apartment-house plot in fictional prose. De Kock's titles indicate a characteristic of the apartment-house novel—place-names that define protagonists by location and position—"on the fifth floor," or "next-door neighbor." For another example of the apartment-house plot, see "Les Jeunes Filles de Paris" (1831), which uses the apartment house as a device for the calibration of virtue and status; its fable of class and gender rewards the heroine's thrift and industry by having her move into a better apartment in her own building and then marry a neighbor from the building opposite. The two facing buildings form a circulatory system that adjusts class and character: after being ruined by the 1830 revolution, the haughty aristocrats and speculative financiers from the building across the street must pass through the crucible of Estelle's former attic apartment, while the bourgeois family never moves and Estelle herself travels first from the attic to a better apartment on the third floor and finally, through marriage, to the second-floor apartment in the facing building (M. Bouilly, "Les Jeunes Filles de Paris," in *Paris, ou le livre des cent-et-un* [Paris: Ladvocat, 1831], 3:29–62).

19. The narrator first mentions Pons's apartment in the context of a spatially diffuse character portrait; in the course of describing Pons's relationship with Schmucke, he mentions that the two men share an apartment "situated in a tranquil house in the tranquil rue de Normandie, in the Marais" (23). We hear no more about this building until twenty pages later, when the narrator describes Pons's building but stops short of describing his apartment, focusing instead on an elaborate description of the building's porters, the Cibots, and their *loge*. In chapter 34, the narrator provides a brief descriptive sentence about one room in Pons's apartment and fills this out slightly with another sentence in chapter 57. We learn that Pons and Schmucke have separate bedrooms because the narrator mentions that after Schmucke wakes up, he "went into Pons's bedroom [*cham-

bre]" (227); we can deduce that Pons's antechamber doubles as a dining room and communicates with Pons's bedroom because Cibot hears Pons fall on the dining-room tiles while she is standing on the staircase outside his apartment (163). The most schematic description of the layout of Pons's apartment, far from being a vehicle to describe his life, appears only after his death and coincides with Schmucke's eviction from the apartment.

20. On the representation of the museum in nineteenth-century French novels, see Luce Abélès, "Du *Cousin Pons* à *L'Aiguille creuse:* les musées privés romanesques au XIXe siècle," *Revue d'histoire littéraire de la France* 95, no. 1 (January–February 1995): 27–35; Philippe Hamon, "Le Musée et le texte," *Revue d'histoire littéraire de la France* 95, no. 1 (January–February 1995): 3–12; and Paul Pelckmans, *Concurrences au monde: propositions pour une poétique du collectionneur moderne* (Amsterdam: Rodopi, 1990).

21. For an excellent discussion of the museum episode in nineteenth-century British and U.S. literature, see Horst Kruse, "The Museum Motif in English and American Fiction of the Nineteenth Century," *Amerikastudien* 31, no. 1 (1986): 71–79. Kruse locates the main elements of the motif in Keats's poetry, but argues that the museum motif became a central element in the bildungsroman. The museum episode in Zola's *L'Assommoir* takes the observers' failure of understanding to its limit; Robert Lethbridge reads the episode as a *mise en abîme* of the novel's chief structural elements—the alternation between street and interior, and the move from unity to fragmentation ("A Visit to the Louvre: *L'Assommoir* Revisited," *Modern Language Review* 87, no. 1 [January 1992]: 41–55). Hamon ("Le Musée et le texte," 5–7) affiliates the museum episode with the bildungsroman by calling it the "museum stage" (*stade du musée*).

22. See Abélès, "Du *Cousin Pons,*" 33–34: other examples of the museum plot include Joris-Karl Huysman's *A rebours* and Jules Verne's *Vingt-mille lieus sous la mer;* Flaubert parodies the museum plot in *Bouvard et Pécuchet* by having his ridiculous heroes establish a home museum that solicits visitors.

23. See Abélès, "Du *Cousin Pons,*" 28.

24. Andrew McClellan, *Inventing the Louvre: Art, Politics, and the Origins of the Modern Museum in Eighteenth-Century Paris* (Cambridge: Cambridge University Press, 1994), 50. On the museum as a public institution, see also Georges Bataille, "Musée," in *Oeuvres complètes* (Paris: Gallimard, 1970), 1:239–240; Carol Duncan, "Art Museums and the Ritual of Citizenship," in *Exhibiting Cultures: The Poetics and Politics of Museum Display,* ed. Ivan Karp and Steven D. Lavine (Washington, D.C.: Smithsonian Institute Press, 1991), 94; Krzystof Pomian, *Collectors and Curiosities: Paris and Venice, 1500–1800,* trans. Elizabeth Wiles-Portier (London: Polity Press, 1990), 44, 264; Dominique Poulot, "Le Louvre imaginaire: essai sur le statut du musée en France, des lumières à la république," *Historical Reflections* 17, no. 2 (1991): 184–203; Vanessa R. Schwartz, "Museums and Mass Spectacle: The Musée Grévin as a Monument to Modern Life," *French Historical Studies* 19, no. 1 (spring 1995): 7–26; and Daniel J. Sherman, *Worthy Monuments: Art Museums and the Politics of Culture in Nineteenth-Century France* (Cambridge, Mass: Harvard University Press, 1989), 13, 94.

25. On the princely cabinet, which had its roots in the *Wunderkammer* of the Renaissance, see Colin Bailey, "Conventions of the Eighteenth-Century *Cabinet de tableaux*: Blondel d'Azincourt's *La Première idée de la curiosité*," *Art Bulletin 69*, no. 3 (September 1987): 431–447; Paula Findlen, "The Museum: Its Classical Etymology and Renaissance Genealogy," *Journal of the History of Collections 1*, no. 1 (1989): 59–78; and Pomian, *Collectors*. On the nineteenth-century collection, see Poulot, "Louvre imaginaire" and his article "L'Invention de la bonne volonté culturelle: l'image du musée au XIXe siècle," *Mouvement social 131* (April–June 1995): 35–64.

26. The Sebastiano painting in the Louvre to which the narrator refers has since been attributed to Bronzino.

27. Toward the end of the novel Pons imagines merging his collection with the public museum when he makes a false will bequeathing it to the Louvre, but he can do so (even speculatively) only after various characters have invaded the museum and destroyed the integrity of the collection.

28. Balzac noted that one of *Pons's* distinctive traits as a novel was that "it's a question of being interested in a man, an old man [*un vieillard*]" (viii). On the figure of the *célibataire* in Balzac, see Takao Kashiwagi, *La Trilogie des célibataires d'Honoré de Balzac* (Paris: Nizet, 1983). On the image of the bachelor in the *physiologies,* see the previous chapter. In those physiologies, the *célibataire* was either a libertine who seduced married women or a thrifty employer who made his female live-in servant into his mistress, in order to make one woman serve as many functions as possible without marrying her. On the bachelor in nineteenth-century British and American culture, see Katherine V. Snyder, *Bachelors, Manhood, and the Novel* (Cambridge: Cambridge University Press, forthcoming).

29. Even at the level of sexual detection, from which a critic might do well to abstain, it remains difficult to identify Pons and Schmucke as "gay." Certainly Pons and Schmucke offer a very different vision of queerness than the two best-known instances of male-male desire in Balzac's oeuvre, Zambinella in *Sarrasine* and Vautrin in *Le Père Goriot, Illusions perdues,* and *Splendeurs et misères d'une courtisane. Sarrasine* associates male-male desire with gender ambiguity and female impersonation, while Vautrin's homosexuality depends on his masculine charisma and appreciation of young men's beauty, his skill at profitably triangulating his desires for men through women who fuel his protégés' careers, and his exercise of conspiratorial power. For a discussion of Vautrin's character in relation to Balzac's literary project, see D. A. Miller's "Body Bildung and Textual Liberation," in *A New History of French Literature,* ed. Denis Hollier (Cambridge, Mass.: Harvard University Press, 1989), 681–687.

Pons's and Schmucke's relationship could be read as a variant of the nineteenth-century *female* romantic friendship, in which the asexuality ascribed to women and the spirituality of sublimated affections licensed passionate attachments between women and intense expressions of same-sex love. The narrator describes Pons's and Schmucke's experience of a spiritual connection: "Never perhaps had two souls so similar found one another in the human ocean. . . . These two musicians became in very little time necessary to one another. Reciprocally confiding each in the other, in a week they became like two brothers. . . . [Schmucke] found in Pons another version of himself [*un autre lui-même*]" (20–21). The two men meet in a girls' boarding-school, a site of intensive same-sex bonds, where Pons has been hired as much for his inability to arouse heterosexual desire in his students as for his musical abilities (10). Their relationship initially appears as a sign of their insufficiency and inability to attract women (a rarity in Balzac novels where even the most repulsive men are endowed with some sexual capital), like the "spinsters" understood by their contemporaries as unable to attract men: the narrator, after describing Pons's unattractive appearance, says that "bachelorhood was . . . for him less a taste than a necessity" and then adds, after telling the history of his friendship with Schmucke, that "he contracted the only marriage that society would allow him to make, he married a man"(19–20).

In his current work on *Les Parents pauvres* ("Balzac's Queer Cousins"), Lucey explores further the category of "friendship" and turns from interpreting the various answers that *Le Cousin Pons* provides to the riddle of Pons's sexuality to reading the various interests served by posing the question of sexuality at all, particularly as a question that could be answered univocally.

30. Walter Benjamin, *Paris, capitale du XIXe siècle: le livre des passages* (Paris: Editions du cerf, 1989), ed. Rolf Tiedemann, trans. Jean Lacoste, 224–228; English translation mine. Benjamin refers to *Le Cousin Pons* only once, in a brief note that suggests possible historical models for Balzac's fictional character, but his discussion of the collector is suffused with implicit references to Balzac.

Critics have often read *Le Cousin Pons* as a novel about collectors, collecting, and collections, interpreting the collection as a figure for the *Comédie*; for artistic creation; and for the production of fictive space. William Paulson ("Le Cousin parasite: Balzac, Serres, et le démon de Maxwell," *Stanford French Review* 9 [winter 1985]: 397–414) uses the novel to illustrate Michel Serres's theories of parasitical communication and exchange; Franc Schuerewegen ("*Muséum ou Crotéum:* Pons, Bouvard, Pécuchet et la collection," *Romantisme* 55 [1987]: 42–54) argues that the novel exemplifies Balzac's alignment with representational modernity (in contrast to Flaubert's postmodern collectors, Bouvard and Pécuchet).

31. Pons's relatives secure a husband for their daughter only by adding their country estate and Parisian townhouse to her dowry, thus alienating two entities that should be inalienable, landed property and a human being.

32. The narrator later draws another analogy between collectors and authors: "the pride of collectors . . . is certainly very strong, for it even rivals the pride of authors" (35).

33. Cibot's inability to appreciate what she steals links her to the novel's other female villain, Mme Camusot, who similarly cannot appreciate Pons's "treasures" and whom the narrator often refers to as "la Présidente," just as he refers to Cibot as "la Cibot." Mme Camusot, who also gets drawn into the plot against Pons, resembles the *portière* in her drive to gain visual or aural access to any space from which she is deprived access; both she and Cibot use mirrors to spy on rooms from which they have been barred.

34. Cibot's use of what Jean-Louis Deaucourt calls the "abusive possessive" form to describe her tenants was a characteristic aspect of the representation of

the *portière* ("Une Police des sentiments: les concierges et les portiers," *Romantisme* 68 [1990]: 50).

35. We have already learned that Cibot's nurturance is figuratively infanticidal: she has "invented" a sauce so delicious that "a mother could have eaten her child in it without noticing" (53–54).

36. This maxim initially seems to refer to a conversation between Cibot and Pons's doctor, but one page later we discover that it also refers to Brunner's earlier conversation with Pons, and that two conversations involving Pons have become public knowledge.

37. Rémonencq, who poses an equal threat to Pons, possesses the characteristics of a *portier* without actually being one: he sits daily at the door of his shop, gathering and disbursing information; his mercantile activity as a dealer in secondhand goods consists of gaining access to strangers' houses ("in this line of work, the difficulty consists in being able to introduce oneself into houses"), and his chief ambition is to marry a *portière,* Mme Cibot (115). Like the male porter of the *physiologies* and *tableaux,* however, the aspiring husband of a *portière* is nothing but an auxiliary, subsidiary power; within the novel, the motor of the plot against Pons is always either Mme Cibot or another *portière.* Cibot's role as a dispossessor is as overdetermined as Pons's dispossession, since even before joining the ranks of *portières,* commonly associated with invasions of privacy and appropriations of property, she has worked as an *écaillère,* an oyster-shucker at a restaurant. The narrator frames this information by telling us that Cibot's husband has reached "the porter's golden age; they are adapted to their lodge, the lodge has become for them what the shell is to the oyster" (48). Mme Cibot's skill as an *écaillère* thus must be read alongside of the description of M. Cibot's encrusted domesticity. He is molded to his *loge* like an "oyster" to its "shell," but his wife has been trained to dislodge oysters from their shells so that they can be purchased and consumed, just as she will remove and sell the "pearls" from Pons's collection and dislodge him as a source of descriptive knowledge.

38. In chapter 13, when he provides a treatise on the occult sciences, the narrator similarly leaves Cibot to embark on a digression that simultaneously surpasses Cibot's consciousness and yet remains anchored in her physical presence. Mme Cibot is about to consult a fortune-teller, and the narrator's discourse on the occult takes up, as its theme, precisely the ambivalence between material grounding in a place and immaterial extension in space that organizes the novel's narrative structure. Georges Poulet interprets Balzac's interest in the occult as an interest in dissolving the barriers of space and time to create a system in which "there is no longer any space as distance, any space as obstacle," in which the narrator or protagonist could be everywhere at once (*Etudes sur le temps humain: la distance intérieure* [Paris: Plon, 1952], 131).

39. Cibot is the only character who looks out a window, and all she sees is a wall; her outward gaze, however, is associated with the beginning of the plot to dispossess Schmucke and Pons. The apartment's windows appear only once to Schmucke, viewed from a position that has become irrevocably external to them: after being evicted from his former home, he looks at its windows, but not through them: "[Schmucke] looked, in the courtyard, one last time at the win-

dows of the apartment" (316). The only windows in the apartment that are mentioned are exceptions that prove the rule—the stained-glass windows in Pons's salon/museum. Stained-glass windows preclude the possibility of transparent vision from outside or from inside. On stained glass as translucent rather than transparent, and as a nineteenth-century symbol of distorted vision, see Hamon, *Expositions,* 39, 78.

40. Cibot also reworks in interesting ways a long tradition of representing servants, perhaps because the distribution of power in the *portière*-tenant relationship was much more even than it was in the relationship between an employer and domestic servant. On the history of the servant as speaker, narrator, and agent of plot in Western literature, and particularly in the British novel, see Bruce Robbins, *The Servant's Hand: English Fiction from Below* (New York: Columbia University Press, 1986).

41. D. A. Miller, *The Novel and the Police* (Berkeley: University of California Press, 1988), 14 and viii.

42. Ibid., 11, vii, and 11.

43. Ibid., 24. Miller calls this panoptic narration "a kind of providence . . . an ideal of the power of regulation" (24). Fredric Jameson also associates the omniscient narrator with a providential ideal or power and notes a tension in Balzac's narration between an illusion of invisibility and a striving for physical presence, between an omniscience that is "the aftereffect of the closure of the classical *récit,* in which the events are over and done with before their narrative begins . . . [that] projects something like an ideological mirage in the form of notions of fortune, destiny and providence or predestination," and "the gestures and signals of the storyteller . . . [that] symbolically attempt to restore the coordinates of a face-to-face storytelling institution" (*The Political Unconscious: Narrative as a Socially Symbolic Act* [Ithaca: Cornell University Press, 1981], 154–155).

44. Indeed, one critic has mistakenly argued that the concierge represents panoptic surveillance and constitutes "the final proof of the efficacity of panopticism in the quotidian exercise of power," a claim that effaces the extent to which the concierge remains firmly rooted in the very space that she observes, unlike the supervisor of the panopticon who himself becomes invisible (Lucienne Frappier-Mazur, "Le Discours du pouvoir dans *le Cousin Pons,*" in *Balzac et "les Parents pauvres,"* ed. Françoise van Rossum-Guyon and Michiel van Brederode [Paris: Société d'Enseignement supérieur, 1981], 29).

45. On the distinction between "place" and "space," see Robert David Sack, *Place, Modernity, and the Consumer's World: A Relational Framework for Geographical Analysis* (Baltimore: Johns Hopkins University Press, 1992), 37–42, 79–86; see also Eric Hirsch and Michael O'Hanlon, eds., *The Anthropology of Landscape: Perspectives on Place and Space* (Oxford: Clarendon Press, 1995); and Erwin Straus, who distinguishes "the conceptual homogeneous space of mathematics" from "perceptual space [what I am calling place], articulated in accordance with the specific corporeal organization of the experiencing person" ("The Upright Posture," in *Essays in Phenomenology,* ed. Maurice Natanson [The Hague: Marhuis Nijhoff, 1966], 180). Daniel Boisson's account of the representation of Paris in *Les Parents pauvres* intersects with the terms place and

space: he writes that Paris appears as either "visible and fragmentary (a juxta-position of neighborhoods, streets, houses)"—i.e., as a set of places—or as "impalpable and global"—an abstract space ("Paris dans *les Parents pauvres* d'Honoré de Balzac" [mémoire de maîtrise, sous la direction de J. Guichardet, Université de Paris III, 1970–71], i). Bette in *La Cousine Bette* exhibits the same ability to occupy space and place; see Françoise Gaillard, "La Stratégie de l'araignée (notes sur le réalisme balzacien)," in *Balzac et "les Parents pauvres,"* ed. Françoise van Rossum-Guyon and Michiel van Brederode (Paris: Société d'Enseignement supérieur, 1981), 185, 179.

46. A similar scene takes place earlier when Cibot visits Fraisier's apartment: "Mme Cibot went straight to the *loge,* she found there one of Cibot's colleagues, a cobbler, his wife, and two small children lodged in a space ten feet square, il-luminated by a small courtyard. A very cordial understanding was soon estab-lished between the two women, once Cibot had declared her profession, given her name, and spoken of the house on the rue de Normandie. After fifteen min-utes taken up by gossip [*commérages*] . . . Mme Cibot brought the conversation around to tenants and mentioned the man of law" (179).

47. The novel also genders Cibot's power over place and space as female by juxtaposing her mobility and activity with her husband's confinement and inac-tivity. Mme Cibot, not her husband, carries out domestic tasks for individual tenants, visibly represents the building, and carries out errands in the neighbor-hood and in the city. The novel makes a point of noting that Mme Cibot sweeps in front of the building and that M. Cibot rarely leaves his *loge.* The narrative takes M. Cibot's limited activity to the logical extreme of death, since when he becomes fatally ill, he is diagnosed as suffering from an occupational illness common to *portiers* who, unlike their more active wives, spend their days con-fined to a small space that receives little light or fresh air.

48. James W. Mileham, *The Conspiracy Novel: Structure and Metaphor in Balzac's "Comédie Humaine"* (Lexington, Ky.: French Forum, 1982), esp. 16, 26, 35, 38, 45, 48, 50, 52, 55, 60, 95, 96, 98, 100. In his essay on *Les Parents pauvres* (197), Michel Butor expresses this transformation in Pons somewhat differently; he writes that Pons "hides within himself a Bette on the verge of awakening." That Pons's metamorphosis into a *portière* is also a metamorpho-sis into Bette returns us to my earlier claim that Bette is a *portière* figure.

49. Héloïse's appearance occasions a series of apartment-house jokes, indi-cating that Pons has now gained control of the discourse of the apartment house: when a tenant, Mme Chapoulot, treats Héloïse as a source of potential sexual contagion, Héloïse indulges in apartment-house humor at her expense. Playing on the fact that apartments closer to the ground floor were more expensive, hence occupied by a supposedly more genteel class of tenant, Héloïse ridicules Mme Chapoulot's rudeness by saying, "Look—a second floor putting on the airs of a fourth!" (258).

50. Sauvage also turns Pons into a thing, into brute matter: Schmucke expe-riences an intense "pain" when he observes Mme Sauvage return Pons to a state of matter by means of "that type of packaging in which his friend was treated like a thing" (281). Later Schmucke adamantly refuses to have Pons embalmed:

"—Bons is a soul!" he insists. By contrast, Cibot "had just had her dear one embalmed" (291).

3. The Haunted London House

1. William H. White, "On Middle-Class Houses in Paris and Central London," in *Royal Institute of British Architects: Sessional Papers, 1877–78* (London, 1878), 28. In the forty-year period from 1840 to 1880 that this chapter addresses, very few other architects expressed a similar advocacy of the apartment building. Writing in *The Builder,* William Young ("'Model' Town Houses for the Middle Classes," *The Builder* 7, no. 356 [December 1849]: 566–569) proposed blocks of apartments with external galleries (that is, he proposed a prototype that blended the single-family house and the apartment building), and an anonymous author of a letter to the editor argued for the "convenience" of flats for some families ("Flats versus Lodgings," *The Builder* 26, no. 1309 [March 1868]: 182). Arthur Ashpitel and John Whichcord also advocated flats for England in *Town Dwellings: An Essay on the Erection of Fire-Proof Houses in Flats; A Codification of the Scottish and Continental Systems* (London: John Weale, 1855). Far more numerous were those architects who dismissed the Parisian apartment house; in addition to the many examples cited below, see W. H. Leeds, "An English Version of a French Plan," *Architectural Magazine* 3 (December 1836): 573–581, which particularly criticized the layout of the French flat for its multipurpose, communicating rooms; "French Flats," *Building News* 3, no. 8 (February 1857): 181–182; James Fergusson, *History of the Modern Styles of Architecture* (London: John Murray, 1862), 219; and "Houses in Flats," *The Architect* 10, no. 247 (September 1873): 141.

2. Throughout this chapter, I use the term "Victorian" (rather than the more cumbersome "mid-Victorian") to refer to the period from the late 1830s to 1880; the English conceptions of the metropolis, the home, and the relationship between the two changed so much after 1880 that the term "Victorian" could apply to those issues in that period only if qualified by an adjective such as "late."

3. White, "On Middle-Class Houses," 26.

4. Ibid., 29. White's reference to the air above the single-family house as the property of the house's proprietor was, despite its fanciful ring, a common allusion; Frederick Pollock (*The Land Laws,* 2d ed. [London: Macmillan, 1887], 16) noted that in England, "Even the air is not free, for the maxim is owner up to the height above and down to the depth beneath." See also the note to an 1885 edition of William Farr's works, glossing his definition of a house with a Shakespeare quotation found in Samuel Johnson's writings: "In the example which Johnson quotes, 'Sparrows must not build in his house eaves,' Shakespeare finely characterizes the house by its eaves: the man living under his own roof, not under another man's 'flat'" (*Vital Statistics: A Memorial Volume of Selections from the Reports and Writings of William Farr,* ed. Noel Humphreys [London: Offices of the Sanitary Institute, 1885], 10). The commentator thus places a definition of the English home within two foundational texts of the English language.

5. White, "On Middle-Class Houses," 29.

6. Ibid., 30, 31.

7. Thomas Webster and Mrs. William Parkes, *An Encyclopaedia of Domestic Economy* (London: Longman, Brown, Green and Longman, 1844). Joseph Gwilt's *Encyclopaedia of Architecture, Historical, Theoretical, and Practical* (London: Longman, Brown, Green and Longman, 1842), 811, similarly noted that "[i]n London, and indeed throughout the towns of England, the habits of the people lead them to prefer separate houses for each family." Gwilt idiosyncratically dismissed the "rows of mean-looking buildings" that resulted from the decision to build horizontally rather than vertically, but his criticism did not indicate support for building upward in flats instead; it simply chastised urban residential architecture for falling short of the ideal of free-standing houses.

8. Cited in E. Royston Pike, *Human Documents of the Victorian Golden Age* (London: Allen and Unwin, 1967), 235. Registrar General George Graham made this remark in agreement with a lengthy citation from a "German naturalist, Dr [*sic*] Carus," who had commented on "English dwelling-houses, which stand in close connection with that long-cherished principle of separation and retirement, lying as the very foundation of the national character. . . . [I]t is that that gives the Englishmen that proud feeling of personal independence, which is stereotyped in the phrase, 'Every man's house is his castle'. . . . In England, every man is master of his hall, stairs, and chambers." Note the unintended irony of Carus's formulation that English houses "stand in close connection" with a "principle of separation," in which the paradox of a national body formed by the separateness of its members recurs. Graham pointed out that the practice of building separate single-family houses was based on a feeling that "as it is natural, is universal," but "stronger in England than it is on the Continent" and abandoned in Scotland and in northern cities where people lived in flats (234–235).

9. Indeed, that census had defined a house as "all the space within the external and party walls of the building." A subsequent registrar general, William Farr, noted that the earlier definition did not correspond to the realities of internal subdivision: "Thus it became impossible to count either each room or each storey as a separate house, although it might be separately occupied or owned" (quoted in *Vital Statistics*, 9–10).

10. "Houses in Flats for London," *The Builder* 34, no. 1718 (January 1876): 25.

11. "Professor Cockerell's Lectures, no. IV," *The Builder* 1, no. 7 (March 1843): 80.

12. "To the Architectural Student," *The Builder* 1, no. 10 (April 1843): 119; "English Domestic Architecture," *The Builder* 1, no. 36 (October 1843): 431 (reprint of an 1831 article in the *Quarterly Review*).

13. For an example of the association of France with revolution in the context of a discussion of housing, see the bishop of Oxford's 1848 speech to the Society for Improving the Condition of the Labouring Classes (a society that focused on building housing for workers) in which he noted that "[t]he great social movements in a neighbouring country have been, for some new and fancied general fraternity . . . for superseding family life. Now, here is the very principle

of poison most actively at work. God has formed family life to be in every separate family" (*The Labourer's Friend* no. 49 [June 1848]: 101).

For two exceptional articles in the popular press that suggested, like White's, that French flats more closely approximated the English domestic ideal than actual English houses in London, see "An Englishman's Castle," *Household Words,* December 27, 1851, 322; and "Our House," *Household Words,* March 20, 1852, 41.

14. Hector Gavin, *The Habitations of the Industrial Classes: Their Influence on the Physical and on the Social and Moral Condition of These Classes* (London: Society for Improving the Condition of the Labouring Classes, 1850), vii, 16.

15. "The Grosvenor-Place and Pimlico Improvements of the Marquis of Westminster," *The Builder* 25, no. 1255 (February 1867): 122. T. H. S. Escott, *England: Its People, Polity and Pursuits* (London: Cassell, Petter, Galpin, 1879), 2:4. See also "Houses in Flats," 25; and "Living in Flats," *Saturday Review,* October 23, 1875, 515. At the turn of the century, the German architectural historian Hermann Muthesius predicted that were flats to become widespread, they would "spell the demise of one of the best aspects of the English heritage" (*The English House,* ed. Dennis Sharp, trans. Janet Seligman [1904–5; Oxford: BSP Professional Books, 1979], 9).

16. Anthony S. Wohl, *The Eternal Slum: Housing and Social Policy in Victorian London* (London: Edward Arnold, 1977), 15; James Hole, paper given at the 1884 International Health Exhibition, quoted in ibid., 166; Nicholas Taylor, "The Awful Sublimity of the Victorian City" (in *The Victorian City: Images and Realities,* ed. H. J. Dyos and Michael Wolff [London: Routledge and Kegan Paul, 1976], 2:435). Historians of London continue to describe flats as terrifying anomalies; in the preface to an edited volume on *Multi-Storey Living: The British Working Class Experience* (London: Croom Helm, 1974), ix, Anthony Sutcliffe writes that "[t]his book is about an oddity . . . the potentially horrific concept of the vertical stacking of families."

17. Quoted in "Metropolitan Building Act," *The Builder* 1, no. 21 (July 1843): 253.

18. Octavia Hill, "The Influence of Model Dwellings upon Character" [1892], in *House Property and Its Management* (New York: Macmillan, 1921), 44–45.

19. Chambers were small rooms or sets of rooms whose tenants contracted to use the servants employed by the building's managers—a cross between hotels, which provided food and cleaning services, and dormitories, which offered long-term stays in institutional or professional settings. Because the best-known sets of chambers in London were those provided for the exclusively male entrants into the legal profession at Temple and Lincoln's Inns, they were also associated largely with unmarried men. See, for example, "Our House," 42, whose narrator distinguishes his building of middle-class flats from chambers primarily in terms of the marital status of its occupants: "It is an odd humour, but our landlord has a horror of 'Chambers'. . . . [H]e lets to none but families. Bachelors have applied in vain: vainly have spinsters exerted their powers of persuasion." For more on the relationship between bachelors and apartment living,

in a U.S. context, see Katherine V. Snyder, "A Paradise of Bachelors: Remodeling Domesticity and Masculinity in the Turn-of-the-Century New York Bachelor Apartment," *Prospects* (forthcoming).

Model dwellings for the working classes were the offshoot of private enterprises established in the 1840s to link reforms in the living conditions of the working poor to investment opportunities. In the 1840s the Society for Improving the Condition of the Labouring Classes hired Henry Roberts to design working-class apartments in Clerkenwell (1845) and Streatham Street (1849–50) and promised investors rates of return ranging from 5 percent to 17 percent (the annual reports of the associations suggest that in most cases 5 percent was the actual rate delivered). The Streatham Street buildings, located near New Oxford Street, were intended to rehouse some of the tenants who had been dislocated from their homes in the "Rookery," a poor neighborhood that the government had partially razed. See " 'Fourth Report' of the Society for the Improvement of the Condition of the Labouring Classes," *The Labourer's Friend* no. 49 (June 1848): 83–89. An 1851 Labouring Classes Lodging Houses Act provided a limited incentive to build working-class housing by permitting vestries, the unit of metropolitan government in London, to purchase land and build working-class houses with money borrowed on anticipated tax revenues. H. A. Darbishire designed worker's housing for the Metropolitan Association for the Improvement of the Dwellings of the Industrial Classes, formed in 1853, as well as flats in Bethnal Green for Angela Burdett-Coutts, a wealthy philanthropist who sponsored many other architectural projects in London. The 1855 Labourers' Dwelling Act made housing for workers an attractive investment by "providing for the registration of joint-stock companies" incorporated to build "dwelling-houses for the labouring classes." See Henry Roberts, *The Improvement of the Dwellings of the Labouring Classes,* reprinted from the *Transactions of the National Association for the Promotion of Social Science,* Liverpool meeting, October 1858 (London: Ridgeway, 1859), 10. A United States philanthropist provided the funds for a set of "Peabody Buildings," launched in 1862, constructed around closed central courtyards and separated from the rest of the neighborhood by a gate, an architectural feature that often earned them "the epithet 'barracky' " (Wohl, *Eternal Slum,* 164). For an exhaustive list of model lodgings built by 1860, see John Hollingshead, "London Model Lodging-Houses," *Good Words* 2 (1861): 170–174. J. T. Emmet reported that by 1875, private model residences housed about 26,000 people ("The Ethics of Urban Leaseholds," *British Quarterly Review* 69 [April 1879]: 328).

Only the most stable and high-earning workers could afford to live in model dwellings, and by even the most sympathetic accounts, such housing was inhabited by a tiny percentage of the London population: in 1861, the Metropolitan Association buildings housed about 2,200 people; the society had built nine buildings for a total of 1,900 people; and various other organizations provided apartments for about 2,000 people (Hollingshead, ibid.).

The flats whose construction was documented in the architectural press include Henry Ashton's Victoria Street apartments (1853); Belgrave Mansions (1867); the less ambitious Albert Mansions (1870); the Queen Anne's Gate buildings erected near St. James' Park (1874), an unusually tall ten-story block that offered a choice between private or communal dining services; several blocks of flats built on New Kent Road in 1876, designed for different classes of tenant; twenty-four flats in six blocks designed for middle-class occupancy built in Stoke Newington in 1876; a new set of flats on Victoria Street designed by F. Butler in 1877; and middle-class flats consisting of four rooms each erected in Kennington in 1878. For a detailed description of Ashton's Victoria Street apartments, see *The Builder*, 11, no. 565 (December 1853): 721–722.

20. When Henry Ashton designed a group of flats for wealthy tenants in Victoria Street in 1853, his plans exhibited French influence to the extent that each block had a porter, a service stair, and six shops located on the ground floor. However, the blocks were relatively short (four stories), contained only two apartments per floor, and had individual entrances rather than one grand porte cochère and vestibule (*The Builder* 11, no. 565 [December 1853]: 1). The citations refer to discussions of model dwellings for the poor; the first comes from a description of the Streatham Street buildings in *The Pictorial Handbook to London* (London: Henry G. Bohn, 1854), 266; the second from Henry Roberts, one of the chief architects of model flats (*Improvement,* 35). See also the designs in Banister Fletcher, *Model Houses for the Industrial Classes* (London: Longmans, Green, 1871), 8, which eliminated all the external features typical of the apartment house in designs for houses that were internally subdivided into flats but externally "call[ed] no attention to the fact that the same building is occupied in common by more than one family."

21. See Leonore Davidoff and Catherine Hall, *Family Fortunes: Men and Women of the English Middle Class, 1780–1850* (Chicago: University of Chicago Press, 1987); Judith Walkowitz, *City of Dreadful Delight: Narratives of Sexual Danger in Late-Victorian London* (Chicago: University of Chicago Press, 1992); Deborah Epstein Nord, *Walking the Victorian Streets: Women, Representation, and the City* (Ithaca: Cornell University Press, 1995); Nancy Armstrong, *Desire and Domestic Fiction: A Political History of the Novel* (New York: Oxford University Press, 1987); Catherine Gallagher, *The Industrial Reformation of English Fiction, 1832–1867* (Chicago: University of Chicago Press, 1985); and Mary Poovey, *Uneven Developments: The Ideological Work of Gender in Mid-Victorian England* (Chicago: University of Chicago Press, 1988). In addition see Elizabeth Langland, *Nobody's Angels: Middle-Class Women and Domestic Ideology in Victorian Culture* (Ithaca: Cornell University Press, 1995), which develops Armstrong's thesis that "the house and its mistress served as a significant adjunct to a man's commercial endeavors" (8) and that middle-class women's domestic work served to maintain class barriers (18, 21); and *The Best Circles: Society Etiquette and the Season* (1973; reprint, London: Cresset Library, 1986), in which Leonore Davidoff shows that throughout the Victorian period, middle- and upper-class homes were sites both of female sequestration and of female sociability, domestic centers in which women handled the business of making and breaking alliances; far from being separate from a public realm, the domestic sphere mediated between the family and political and economic institutions.

Although the domestic ideal originated with the middle classes, it also influenced the working classes and the aristocracy, a point Gallagher makes about the "Condition of England" debates into which she folds her discussion of domestic discourse (*Industrial Reformation*, xiv). See Mark Girouard, *Life in the English Country House: A Social and Architectural History* (Harmondsworth: Penguin, 1980), 270; Anna Clark, *The Struggle for the Breeches: Gender and the Making of the British Working Class* (Berkeley: University of California Press, 1995), 248–263; and Joseph W. Childers, "Feminine Hygiene: Women in Edwin Chadwick's Sanitation Report," *Prose Studies* 17, no. 2 (August 1994): 23–37. Clark emphasizes that domestic ideology worked to reduce working-class women's power, while Childers emphasizes the material barriers that prevented working-class families from achieving the domestic ideal in practice after they had embraced it in theory. While I agree that the middle-class domestic ideal became hegemonic, in this chapter I emphasize that not only the poor, but also many middle-class families in London failed to achieve the domestic ideal they embraced.

22. On the rural nature of the Victorian domestic ideal, see Lori Loeb, *Consuming Angels: Advertising and Victorian Women* (New York: Oxford University Press, 1994), 23, and further discussion below. While Davidoff and Hall have an extensive and valuable section on "the creation of a middle-class home," *Family Fortunes* focuses on the industrial town of Birmingham and on rural areas before 1850; many of their claims need to be modified for the capital: by 1851, 2,500,000 people lived in greater London alone.

23. In John Bartlett, *Familiar Quotations* (Boston: Little, Brown, 1980), 172 the quotations are "For a man's house is his castle, *et domus sua cuique tutissimum refugium* [and one's home is the safest refuge to everyone]" (*Third Institute* [1644]), and "The house of everyone is to him as his castle and fortress, as well as for his defense against injury and violence as for his repose" (*Semayne's Case. 5 Report* 91); in Bergen Evans, *Dictionary of Quotations* (New York: Delacorte Press, 1968), 327 the citation reads "A man's house is his castle" (*Institutes III* [1628–1644]).

24. G. K. Chesterton pointed to that shift when he glossed what the aphorism meant to a Victorian reading public: "The Englishman's house is most sacred, not merely when the King cannot enter it, but when the Englishman cannot get out of it." Chesterton cited the aphorism in the by-then conventional form of "an Englishman's home is his castle" (*Charles Dickens: A Critical Study* [New York: Dodd Mead, 1911], 166–167). Henry Mayhew wrote in 1852, "The maxim that an 'Englishman's home is his castle' . . . still shows that the dwelling of the family has ever been considered in this country as a kind of social sanctuary"; Mayhew's gloss on the phrase explicitly transformed its original political reference into a social one, and generated the paradox of a sociability based not on interaction but on isolation ("Home Is Home, Be It Never So Homely," in *Meliora, or Better Times to Come*, ed. Viscount Ingestre [Charles Shrewsbury] [1852; reprint, London: Frank Cass, 1971], 1:262–263).

The shifting interpretations of "an Englishman's home is his castle" matched a more general displacement, at midcentury, of political conflicts over how extensive to make participation in a common nation to agreement about the constitution of that nation as a series of social cells whose shared characteristic was domestic privacy, that is, a lack of commonality. On the displacement of political "contests between . . . classes" by "the struggles of men of all classes for the opportunity to achieve . . . domestic life," see Mary Poovey, "Domesticity and Class Formation: Chadwick's 1842 *Sanitary Report,*" in *Subject to History: Ideology, Class, Gender,* ed. David Simpson (Ithaca: Cornell University Press, 1991), 65–83. For a broader discussion of the displacement of political conflict by domestic reconciliation in mid-nineteenth-century England, see Gallagher, *Industrial Reformation,* 113–184.

In *London's Teeming Streets, 1830–1914* (London: Routledge, 1993), xi, 9–10, 79, James Winter contends that freedom in the street continued to define nineteenth-century Englishness, particularly for working-class men, but he also notes that the English emphasis on domestic privacy made the very word "street" a pejorative one (8), led many urban reformers to view streets as impervious to reform (153), and encouraged the middle classes to define privacy as "control by individuals over who and what entered their personal space" (78). Indeed, to support the last claim, he cites a diarist who in 1863 invoked the metaphor of the house as castle to protest his home's invasion by street noises (78).

Twentieth-century studies of British domesticity continue to invoke Coke's phrase: H. J. Dyos (*Victorian Suburb: A Study of the Growth of Camberwell* [Leicester: Leicester University Press, 1961], 22) argues that the combined values of "respectability" and "romanticism . . . created in suburbia the apotheosis of the Englishman's castle," while John Gloag simply titles his history of the English house *The Englishman's Castle* (London: Eyre and Spottiswoode, 1944).

25. Many developments throughout the nineteenth century anchored the masculinity of the home. Davidoff and Hall, *Family Fortunes,* demonstrate in detail the extent to which the realms of family and home became central to middle-class male identity, especially in the Evangelical circles on which they focus. Carol T. Christ points out that Coventry Patmore's idealization of women as angels of the house corresponded to a masculine desire for domestic retreat ("Victorian Masculinity and the Angel in the House," in *A Widening Sphere: Changing Roles of Victorian Women,* ed. Martha Vicinus [Bloomington: Indiana University Press, 1977], 146–162). Mark Girouard shows that the English country house became an increasingly male preserve over the course of the century, with more rooms devoted to male leisure and sociability and more houses built in the Gothic style commonly described as masculine (*The Victorian Country House,* rev. ed. [New Haven: Yale University Press, 1979], 34, 55). In "The Woman's World of British Aestheticism, 1870–1910" (Ph.D. dissertation, Cornell University, 1996), Talia Schaffer shows that from 1870 on, men such as John Ruskin, William Morris, Charles Eastlake, and Oscar Wilde sought to appropriate the home from women by defining it as a sphere for the exercise of masculine connoisseurship. On the attention devoted to and the tensions generated by the exclusively masculine domesticity of the nineteenth-century bachelor, see Snyder, "Paradise of Bachelors."

26. Charles Dickens, *Great Expectations* (Oxford: Oxford University Press, 1993), 203–206, 288. Wemmick's "castle" also represents the absolute split between his private sentiments (revealed only at home) and his public concealment of those sentiments, which begins as soon as he leaves his house and becomes absolute by the time he reaches work. Note that Dickens privileges the private

pole when he describes the public realm as negated by domestic instruments: "Wemmick got dryer and harder as we went along. . . . At last, when we got to his place of business . . . he looked as unconscious of his Walworth property as if the Castle and the drawbridge and the arbour and the lake and the fountain and the Aged, had all been blown into space together by the last discharge of the Stinger [the gun that guards his house]" (207–208).

27. W. R. Greg, quoted in Wohl, *Eternal Slum*, 65. In *The Evolution of the English House* (1933; reprint, New York: British Book Centre, 1975), 211, Sidney Oldall Addy aligns Englishness with English houses by citing medieval methods of calculating money that made "[t]he house . . . the basis of the English coinage" and "a measure of rights and liabilities."

28. Francis Cross, *Hints to All about to Rent, Buy, or Build House Property*, 4th ed. (London: Nelson, 1854), 22. On the home as a site of associations, see also Francis Cross, "A Word to the Wise: Dwelling Houses," *The Builder* 7, no. 343 (September 1849): 411; the anonymous "London as It Was in 1800, and Is in 1844," *The Builder* 2, no. 77 (July 1844): 371; and J. Dowson, "Essay on the Metaphysics of Architecture," *Architectural Magazine* 3 (June 1836): 245–246.

29. John Ruskin, *The Seven Lamps of Architecture* (1880; reprint, New York: Dover Publications, 1989), 178–179; emphasis added. Walter Pater also described the house as the repository of memories, even as an embodiment of a past self, in "The Child in the House" (1878): in Pater's aestheticist discourse, the childhood house appears first as the narrator's memory of it, then as his image of it, and his purpose in visualizing "that half-spiritualised house" is to watch "the gradual expansion of the soul which had come to be there." The home is spiritualized and the self materialized, "inward and outward being woven through and through each other into one inextricable texture." The essay culminates with the narrator's evocation of ghosts of past residents whom he imagined continued to live in the house, just as the house, which when he left it "touched him like the face of one dead," continues to live in his mind (Walter Pater, *Selected Works*, ed. Richard Aldington [London: Heinemann, 1948], 33, 45).

30. Ruskin, *Seven Lamps*, 186, 42 n.16, 3, 28, 54. See also David Laing, *Plans of Buildings Public and Private* (London: Taylor, 1818), i; John Billington, *The Architectural Director* (London: Richardson and Taylor, n.d.), 36; and Cross, *Hints*, 98. A. Welby Pugin's famous plea for a return to the styles of the past, *Contrasts* (London: printed for the author, and published by him, 1836), 31, summed up his criticism of modern architecture by stating that it had produced nothing "which could be handed down as an honourable specimen of the architectural talent of the time." For a discussion of how Ruskin, Pugin, and Charles Eastlake described architecture as the embodiment of history, see Christina Crosby, "Reading the Gothic Revival: 'History' and *Hints on Household Taste*," in *Rewriting the Victorians: Theory, History, and the Politics of Gender*, ed. Linda M. Shires (New York: Routledge, 1992), 101–115.

Ruskin cemented the relationship between architectural permanence and the freehold ownership of property in a final, aphoristic note to a revised edition of *Seven Lamps*, 210: "Build nothing that you can possibly help,—and let no land on building leases." Ruskin took the notion that property, like memories, linked generations to its logical conclusion when he warned that property never belonged to anyone in the present but was merely held on sufferance from the past and in trust for the future: "We have no right to touch [old buildings] . . . they are not ours. They belong partly to those who built them, and partly to all the generations of mankind who are to follow us. The dead have still their right in them. . . . [T]heir right over [them] does not pass away with their death: still less is the right to the use of what they have left vested in us only. It belongs to all their successors"(197).

31. Mrs. William Parkes, *Domestic Duties, or, Instructions to Young Married Ladies, on the Management of Their Households* (London: Longmans, 1825), 35.

32. John Loudon, "Cottage Economy," in *Library of Useful Knowledge* (London: Baldwin and Craddock, 1840), 3:3.

33. On property ownership's role in defining an emergent middle class in early nineteenth-century England, see Davidoff and Hall, *Family Fortunes*, 19–20, 24; the authors note that most middle-class homes were rented (357–358), thus raising the question of how the middle class resolved the contradiction between the practice of renting and the ideal of property ownership (I address this question in the subsequent sections of this chapter). Historian F. M. L. Thompson sketches an answer to this question by claiming that because so many middle-class families rented their homes, property-ownership had little relevance to the English middle classes. This argument mistakenly equates the absence of any stigma on renting with the absence of an ideal of property ownership. That equation is a mistake because the practice of renting never challenged the hegemony of the property-owning ideal per se; no middle-class discourse ever cautioned against ownership or argued that it was better to rent than to own, while many deplored the problems of renting and praised ownership of one's own home. Thus, when Thompson slips from pointing out that one could be respectable and a renter to arguing that "ownership-occupancy denoted no particular social position," he contradicts his own point by showing that working-class artisans promoted building societies precisely because home-ownership embodied respectability and thrift (*The Rise of Respectable Society: A Social History of Victorian Britain 1830–1900* [Cambridge, Mass.: Harvard University Press, 1988], 168).

Furthermore, the existence of an extensive literature agitating for the democratization of freehold property, discussed in detail below, also indicates that owning one's house was the ideal—albeit an "ideal" ideal, since most Englishmen were barred from realizing it. George Brodrick, for example, referred to "the peculiar privileges" of the "proprietor" of land, "never, perhaps . . . more eagerly coveted than at present" (*English Land and English Landlords: An Enquiry into the Origin and Character of the English Land System, with Proposals for Its Reform* [London: Cassell, 1881], 268). His comment reiterated a similar one made by Robert Williams over forty years earlier; inveighing against the monopoly in freeholds, Williams praised "the POSSESSION OF SEPARATE HOUSES! May the time soon come when every man taking to himself a wife, may be able to take her to his own free and independent home, and that, by the exercise of a common right, due to his manhood and willingness to work" (*London Rookeries*

and Colliers' Slums [1839; reprint, New York: Garland Publishing, 1985], 79).
The protest against the actual barriers to owning one's home was based on expectations that such ownership should be possible.

On the importance of landed property to English concepts of political rights, see Asa Briggs, *The Making of Modern England, 1783–1867: The Age of Improvement* (New York: Harper and Row, 1965), 239, who points out that in the debates over what became the 1832 Reform Bill, "Whigs and Tories were agreed . . . that landed property had a special part to play in guaranteeing the stability of the social order and the authority of the Constitution." The vote was eventually extended both to freeholders and to householders whose leases most closely approximated ownership—tenants of only one landlord, tenants paying rates, tenants who had lived in their house for at least a year, tenants whose house was worth at least 10 pounds annually. The Reform Bill thus shifted the electorate's basis from pure property ownership to a combination of income and residential conditions that mitigated the perceived ills of tenancy. In both political and social terms, status increased with proximity to ownership; while this meant that renters as well as owners could be accommodated within the electorate, it also maintained ownership proper as the ultimate ideal.

34. Francis Cross, *Landed Property: Its Sale, Purchase, Improvement, and General Management* (London: Simpkin, Marshall, 1857), 9. See also F. M. L. Thompson, *English Landed Society in the Nineteenth Century* (London: Routledge and Kegan Paul, 1963), 4, 6.

35. Architects interested in professionalization (through societies such as the Institute of British Architects) sought to regulate fees and training; they defined themselves as artists concerned with the aesthetics of building, and as managers in charge of craftsmen and engineers specializing in construction. Nevertheless, many builders absorbed the functions of the architect and many architects worked as surveyors or contractors. On architects and builders in the nineteenth century, see the articles in Jane Fawcett, ed., *Seven Victorian Architects* (University Park: Pennsylvania State University Press, 1977); Hermione Hobhouse, *Thomas Cubitt: Master Builder* (New York: Universe, 1971); John Wilton-Ely, "The Rise of the Professional Architect in England," in *The Architect: Chapters in the History of a Profession*, ed. Spiro Kostof (New York: Oxford University Press, 1977), 180–208; and Andrew Saint, *The Image of the Architect* (New Haven: Yale University Press, 1983) and "The Building Art of the First Industrial Metropolis," in *London—World City: 1800–1840*, ed. Celina Fox (New Haven: Yale University Press, 1992), 60.

36. Richard Brown, *Domestic Architecture* (London: George Virtue, 1841), emphasis added; William Young, *Town and Country Mansions and Suburban Houses* (London: Spon, 1879), 1.

37. Architectural journals such as John Loudon's *Architectural Magazine* (established in 1834 as a monthly supplement to his *Encyclopaedia of Architecture* [1832–33]) and George Godwin's *Builder* (established 1842) addressed a general audience that explicitly included men and women, architects and builders, specialists and amateurs alike. Their publications resisted the emerging specialization of fields such as architecture and engineering by addressing all as-

pects of buildings—aesthetic, scientific, mechanical, and legal. On the architectural press, see John Gloag, *Mr Loudon's England: The Life and Work of John Claudius Loudon* (Newcastle upon Tyne: Oriel Press, 1970), 80; Melanie Louise Simo, *Loudon and the Landscape: From Country Seat to Metropolis, 1783–1843* (New Haven: Yale University Press, 1988); Ruth Richardson, "George Godwin of *The Builder:* Indefatigable Journalist and Instigator of a Fine Victorian Visual Resource," *Visual Resources* 6 (1989): 121–140; and Robert Thorne, "George Godwin and Architectural Journalism," *History Today* 37 (August 1987): 11–17.

38. The following figures give a sense of the scope of the building boom in London during the first six decades of the nineteenth century: London's housing stock increased by 20 percent in the first three decades of the nineteenth century alone, and the building trades constituted the largest group of workers in London (over 60,000 in 1851). London's many building booms after the Napoleonic Wars led to the development of most of the areas west, north, and south of Westminster, as well as some of those to the east. Peak building periods included 1823–25; the 1830s (the development of Hyde Park Gardens and of the Kensington area from Bayswater to Notting Hill Gate); the 1840s (when Cubitt developed the Grosvenor estate in Belgravia and Pimlico, the northern suburbs of Highbury Park and Stoke Newington, and southern suburbs including Clapham); 1853; and 1867–68. (Depressions in building and real estate corresponded to larger economic slumps in 1847–48, 1857, and 1871–72.) The development of cheap railway transport within London in the 1860s led to more building in the northern and southern neighborhoods of Islington, Camberwell, Somers and Camden Towns, and Pentonville. In all these cases, the dominant building type was the suburban terraced house or the semidetached villa; the London building boom also led to much construction of churches and a smaller, strictly controlled increase in public houses.

39. On zoning in London's newly built neighborhoods, see Hobhouse, *Thomas Cubitt;* and Michael Hunter, *The Victorian Villas of Hackney* (London: Hackney Society Publication, 1981), 52. Cubitt worked with ground landlords to implement restrictive covenants that prevented anyone from leasing to lodging houses, butchers, tallowers, or hatters; he placed the few commercial buildings he deemed acceptable on the outer rim of neighborhoods whose centers contained only houses; and his leases forbade any industrial or trade activity within individual houses.

40. H. Muthesius, *English House,* 79. Victorian domestic architecture and decor remained fairly impervious to the warnings of sanitary reformers, who emphasized that air needed to circulate in order to eliminate the stagnant "miasmas" that they believed caused infections. See Mary Poovey, *Making a Social Body: British Cultural Formation, 1830–1864* (Chicago: University of Chicago Press, 1995), 83; and "Domesticity and Class Formation."

41. J. J. Stevenson, *House Architecture* (London: Macmillan, 1880), 2:47. For examples of main rooms turned away from front entrances, see the plans in J. G. Jackson, *Designs for Villas* (London: James Carpenter, 1829). For examples of corridor plans, see J. Hedgeland, *First Part of a Series of Designs for Private*

Dwellings (London: Printed for G. and W. B. Whittaker, 1821); H. Muthesius, *English House*, 79; Stefan Muthesius, *The English Terraced House* (New Haven: Yale University Press, 1982), 99. Leeds's 1835 article ("English Version," 575) criticized the "amphibious" rooms of French apartments and noted that the French "nation has not been able to get beyond such imperfections as dining-rooms and bed-rooms which are common thoroughfares." In "Figures, portes et passages" (*Urbi: arts, histoire et ethnologie des villes* 5 [April 1982]: 32, 34, 40), Robin Evans associates the primacy of the corridor plan with a modern psychology in which the individual is disfigured by the presence of others; Evans also points out that paradoxically, the corridor plan assigns an equal weight to the pathway defined by the corridor although the plan's ostensible purpose is to privilege the space defined by the room.

42. Robert Kerr, *The Gentleman's House, or, How to Plan English Residences, from the Parsonage to the Palace* (London: John Murray, 1864) 35, 74–5. On the importance of keeping cooking smells out of the dining room, see Young, *Town and Country*, 11.

43. R. Furneaux Jordan, *A Picture History of the English House* (New York: Macmillan, 1959), 92 and caption to plate 239.

44. On the differences between Georgian and Victorian terraces, see J. J. Stevenson, "Street Architecture," in *Transactions of the National Association for the Promotion of Social Science*, ed. Charles Wager Ryalls (London: Longmans, Green, 1877), 754–755. On the ways that London middle-class society emphasized a new privacy in the 1830s and 1840s, see Davidoff, *The Best Circles*, 22–24. She cites the distance placed between employers and servants; the closure of public places such as Vauxhall and the masquerade balls, where different classes had mingled since the late eighteenth century; and the growth of semiprivate social institutions such as clubs. On the practice of setting houses back from the street, see Hunter, *Victorian Villas*, 52, and David A. Reeder, "Suburbanity and the Victorian City" (Second H. J. Dyos Memorial Lecture, delivered May 20, 1980 at the University of Leicester Victorian Studies Centre), 3. On the enclosure of square gardens, see Davidoff, *The Best Circles*, 32; and Geoffrey Tyack, *James Pennethorne and the Making of Victorian London* (Cambridge: Cambridge University Press, 1992), 87. In London's wealthiest districts, such as Belgravia, the streets leading to particular squares or neighborhoods were also often closed to public traffic.

45. Kerr, *Gentleman's House*, 484. On the distinction between Georgian and Victorian building styles, see also S. Muthesius, *English Terraced*, 172–174. For an example of recessed doors that helped to distinguish the entrances of adjoining terraced houses, see Elizabeth Burton, *The Early Victorians at Home, 1837–1861* (London: Longman, 1972), 67. In her *London Journal*, Flora Tristan remarked on "the iron railings of sober design which seem to isolate each home from the crowd" (*Flora Tristan's London Journal: A Survey of London Life in the 1830s*, trans. Dennis Palmer and Giselle Pincet [London: George Prior, 1980], 2; originally published as *Promenades dans Londres* in 1840).

46. Alfred Cox, *The Landlord's and Tenant's Guide* (London: published by the author, 1853), 13; the word "daguerreotype" is emphasized in the original.

See also Henry-Russell Hitchcock, *Early Victorian Architecture in Britain* (London: Architectural Press, 1954), 1:4.

47. On the relaxation of symmetry in nineteenth-century architecture, see H. S. Goodhart-Rendel, *English Architecture Since the Regency: An Interpretation* (London: Constable, 1953), 32.

48. Loudon, "Cottage Economy," 3:3; and John C. Loudon, *The Suburban Gardener and Villa Companion* (London: Longman, Orme, Brown, Green and Longmans, 1838), 1.

49. On the expression of the rural ideal in the Victorian middle-class house, see J. Mordaunt Crook, "Metropolitan Improvements: John Nash and the Picturesque," in *London—World City: 1800–1840*, ed. Celina Fox (New Haven: Yale University Press, 1992), 83; H. Muthesius, *English House*, 135; and T. R. Slater, "Family, Society, and the Ornamental Villa on the Fringes of English Country Towns," *Journal of Historical Geography* 4, no. 2 (1978): 143. In *Family Fortunes*, 361, Davidoff and Hall write that "[t]he inherent anti-urbanism of middle-class culture was reflected in the quintessential image of early nineteenth-century desirable housing, the *white cottage* with thatched roof and porch embowered with honeysuckle and roses."

For a discussion of the various meanings of the garden in Victorian literature (as a retreat from the city, as the enclosure of nature, and as a turn inward to pursue self-cultivation), see Andrew Griffin, "The Interior Garden and John Stuart Mill," in *Nature and the Victorian Imagination*, ed. U. C. Knoepflmacher and G. B. Tennyson (Berkeley: University of California Press, 1977), 171–186. On the suburban expression of the rural ideal, see Walter L. Creese, "Imagination in the Suburb," in ibid., 49–67; and for a valuable demystification of the rural ideal, see George H. Ford, "Felicitous Space: The Cottage Controversy," in ibid., 29–48.

50. "Cottage Economy," *The Builder* 1, no. 24 (July 1843): 293; "Houses to Let," *Household Words*, March 20, 1852, 6.

51. On English antiurbanism, see Jean-Paul Hulin, "'Rus in Urbe': A Key to Victorian Anti-Urbanism?" in *Victorian Writers and the City*, ed. Jean-Paul Hulin and Pierre Coustillas (Lille: Publications de l'université de Lille III, 1979), 11–40. On the rural house and country village as the model units of the English social body, see Leonore Davidoff, Jean L'Esperance and Howard Newly, "Landscape with Figures: Home and Community in English Society," in *The Rights and Wrongs of Women*, ed. Juliet Mitchell and Ann Oakley (Harmondsworth: Penguin, 1976), esp. 140–143. In *The Best Circles*, 13, Davidoff also refers to the "middle-class adulation of the country gentleman ideal and the absence of a truly urban, bourgeois life-style." See also Simo, *Loudon*, 99. In *The Early Victorians at Home*, Burton cites Felicia Hemans's *Homes of England*, and Mary Russell Mitford's *Our Village* as examples of idealizations of English country life. In *The Victorian Country House*, 154–155, Girouard makes the valuable point that such idealizations of the rural invented a tradition of rural comfort and grandeur that had never really existed.

52. See Michael Booth, "The Metropolis on Stage," in *The Victorian City: Images and Realities*, ed. H. J. Dyos and Michael Wolff (London: Routledge and Kegan Paul, 1976), 1:213. To compound the paradox, Booth points out that

most melodramas adopted an antiurban viewpoint (the city as corrupting influence), although at the same time their use of detailed sets representing London attracted theater audiences.

53. Tyack, *Pennethorne*, 310, 24.

54. While Friedrich Engels's *Condition of the Working Class in England* and other texts that focused on housing in the new industrial towns adopted attitudes and discursive procedures similar to those of the texts I discuss here, this chapter addresses texts about London alone; any attempt to generalize the claims made here to the discourse of the industrial city should take into account the significant differences between London and cities like Manchester or Liverpool (e.g., in the latter, landlords were often employers, and housing was designed specifically for workers, generating housing types, such as back-to-back houses, which did not exist in London). Raymond Williams characterizes the difference between London and the industrial cities as one between a city whose "apparent randomness" concealed the presence in it of a "determining system," versus cities whose determining system was fully legible (*The Country and the City* [New York: Oxford University Press, 1973], 154).

55. In *London Illustrated 1604–1851: A Survey and Index of Topographical Books and Their Plates* (Phoenix: Onyx Press, 1983), Bernard Adams summarizes the technical innovations (such as the use of aquatint and the introduction of steel engraving) and the changes in the reading public (such as a growing interest in architectural aesthetics) that created a market for illustrated works on London. He divides those works into several categories: pictorial guidebooks; accounts by "perambulators"; street views (including trade directories); historical surveys of London; and texts focusing on antiquarian London. He notes that the chief innovations of popular texts such as Rudolph Ackermann's *Microcosm of London* (1810, with illustrations by Rowlandson) and Thomas Shepherd's *London in the Nineteenth Century* was their inclusion of human figures to create animated street scenes and architectural settings. Adams also notes that collectors often clipped prints to place in albums or on the walls of houses, suggesting that during this period, English tastes were not structured around an opposition between interior decor and the architecture of metropolitan exteriors. However, few of those works equated London with its homes; with the exception of antiquarian works that depicted houses from earlier historical periods and the occasional depiction of a town mansion, the illustrated works Adams catalogs rarely included residential buildings in their representations of London, thus implicitly defining the city in terms of commercial, civic, and monumental spaces.

56. First published in monthly parts in 1820, issued in volume form in 1821, and reissued in 1823, 1830, 1841, 1870, and 1904, *Life in London* gave "serial publishing its greatest impetus," well before Dickens's *Pickwick Papers*. See J. C. Reid, *Bucks and Bruisers: Pierce Egan and Regency England* (London: Routledge and Kegan Paul, 1971), 52, 76. In 1821 Fanny Burney reissued *Evelina* as *Female Life in London*; that she retitled her novel to echo Egan's title indicates both the immense popularity of Egan's text and the essential continuity between Regency and late eighteenth-century discourses of the metropolis.

57. Deborah Epstein Nord, "The City as Theater: From Georgian to Early Victorian London," *Victorian Studies* 31 (winter 1988): 159. Nord aligns Egan's work with Book 7 of Wordsworth's *Prelude*, the essays of Lamb, de Quincey, and Hazlitt, the metropolitan improvements of Regency London, and urban visual spectacles to produce an impressive synthesis of the urban discourse of the 1820s but, in my view, mistakenly describes the urban spectators of the 1820s as "precursors of more engaged Victorian urban investigators." According to Nord, the Victorians differed from Egan only by turning his objects of distanced spectatorship into subjects of systemic social misery (160, 186). Nord's vision of continuity stems from her argument that writers like Egan used the theatrical viewpoint to "keep . . . at bay an awareness of the new social realities that would ultimately dominate urban consciousness" (159); where Nord assumes that later Victorian writers were better observers of the same social realities, I assume that those writers were instrumental in creating a *new* perception of urban reality, one that defined urban reality in terms of the homes of the poor.

In " 'Terra Incognita'—An Image of the City in English Literature, 1820–1855," *Prose Studies* 5 (1982): 61–84, F. S. Schwarzbach argues for the continuity between Regency and Victorian discourses of the city on the basis of a shared image of the city as labyrinth, maze, and uncharted territory to be explored. However, Schwarzbach cites only one text from the 1820s and does not address *Life in London* at all, which would considerably complicate his claims for continuity and for a predominant "terra incognita" image in the 1820s.

58. Carol Bernstein, *The Celebration of Scandal: Toward the Sublime in Victorian Urban Fiction* (University Park: Pennsylvania State University Press, 1991), 86. While Bernstein's analysis of *Life in London* generates insightful descriptions of its textual procedures and draws interesting parallels between Egan's text and the fashionable novel, her interpretations are far less lucid. For example, she quickly moves from asserting that in *Life in London*, "the attempt to represent the city by means of narrative only distances whatever it is that we take to be urban reality" (thus assuming an opposition between "narrative" and "reality" that she develops in her first chapter) to noting that "[w]e need construe this as a deficiency, however, only if we insist that the text be a transparent record of potentially real experience" (87). Whether—and why—we should insist one way or the other remains unclear.

59. Charles Dickens, *Sketches by Boz,* ed. Dennis Walder (London: Penguin, 1995); see especially the "Seven Sketches from Our Parish," 17–66, and "The Streets—Night," 74–80.

60. The interplay of urban discourses of London and Paris had already been initiated by Egan himself, who incorporated material from French sources into *Life in London,* which in turn was quickly translated into French in 1823; pirated versions of Egan's text also included a work on Paris. See Reid, *Bucks and Bruisers,* 52, 74.

61. For a discussion of Smith's life, see Raymund Fitzimons, *The Baron of Piccadilly: The Travels and Entertainments of Albert Smith 1816–1860* (London: Geoffrey Bles, 1967). For an example of how Smith incorporated domestic interiors into his urban sketches, see *The Natural History of 'Stuck-Up' People* (London: Bogue, 1847), 10–19, which integrates a detailed description of a

family's house into a larger urban scene; see also the easy juxtaposition in *Gavarni in London: Sketches of Life and Character,* ed. Albert Smith (London: Bogue, 1849), of chapters on "Music in the Drawing-Room" and "Music in the Streets"; the latter chapter, by Albert Smith, is unusual for its neutral, even appreciative evocation of middle-class lodgings (21–27).

62. Smith's works sold well, but as a publishing phenomenon they were comparable neither to the contemporary flood of works exposing the evils of London nor to the much larger-scale production of Parisian *physiologies* and *tableaux* in 1830s and 1840s France. Indeed, from the late 1840s through the 1870s the French models that Smith had imported were themselves inflected by the antiurban premises of the English discourse on London (see chapter four).

63. For typologies of Victorian urban discourse, see Bernstein, *Celebration,* who discusses the tropes of unspeakability and hyperbole in ch. 1, and Anne Humpherys, "The Geometry of the Modern City: G. W. M. Reynolds and *The Mysteries of London,*" *Browning Institute Studies* (1983): 69–80, which explicates the illegibility and legibility simultaneously figured by the image of the city as maze. Peter Keating's pioneering collection *Into Unknown England 1866–1913: Selections from the Social Explorers* (Manchester: Manchester University Press, 1976) outlines the chief characteristics of mid- and late-Victorian urban observers, while Deborah Epstein Nord focuses on the imperial implications of their project in "The Social Explorer as Anthropologist: Victorian Travellers among the Urban Poor," in *Visions of the Modern City,* ed. William Sharpe and Leonard Wallock (Baltimore: Johns Hopkins University Press, 1987), 122–134. In ch. 1 of *City of Dreadful Delight* ("Urban Spectatorship"), Walkowitz emphasizes the contrast between mobile, male urban observers and their construction of the prostitute, the public streetwalker, as an "equivocal" figure in their urban landscape.

Some scholars have been particularly anxious to distinguish the unique qualities of Henry Mayhew's *London Labour and the London Poor* by pointing to his use of personal interviews and his proto-sociological interest in classification, as well as his focus on the systemic problems posed by employment conditions, rather than on the morality of individual workers. See, for example, Eileen Yeo, "Mayhew as Social Investigator," in *The Unknown Mayhew,* ed. Eileen Yeo and E. P. Thompson (New York: Pantheon, 1975), 51–95. However, even an advocate of uniqueness such as Asa Briggs (introduction to *The Illustrated Mayhew's London,* ed. John Canning [London: Weidenfeld and Nicolson, 1986], 9) contradicts his own claim by calling Mayhew's work "the first unofficial inquiry into the state of the people by a private individual" and citing a description of it as the "first 'blue book' ever published in penny numbers"; both phrases admit the continuity of Mayhew's work with earlier state-sponsored surveys such as Chadwick's (see Childers, "Feminine Hygiene"; Poovey, "Domesticity and Class Formation"; and R. A. Lewis, *Edwin Chadwick and the Public Health Movement, 1832–1854* [London: Longmans, Green, 1952]). While the specificities of the texts that comprised the discourse of urban observation merit attention, so do their remarkable commonalities, and my focus here is their convergence on the lodging house as an urban evil.

64. As I show in detail in chapter four, the discussion of *maisons garnies* in

particular and the relationship between public health and housing in general underwent notable changes between the first and second halves of the century, in part because the French discourse began to model itself on the English one. As early as the 1830s, however, the French produced a discourse of urban poverty that may have provided models for English urban observers; a key instance was the work of Parent-Duchatelet, who in the 1830s published influential reports on prostitution in Paris and on the city's sewage system. For a discussion of the discourse of urban observation in France before 1850, see Louis Chevalier's landmark work, *Laboring Classes and Dangerous Classes in Paris During the First Half of the Nineteenth Century,* trans. Frank Jellinek (Princeton: Princeton University Press, 1973); and Catherine Kudlick's more nuanced reassessment of many of Chevalier's sources (*Cholera in Post-Revolutionary Paris: A Cultural History* [Berkeley: University of California Press, 1996]), which contribute to an analysis of the bourgeois discourse about the urban poor.

It is important to note, however, the significant difference between the urban discourses of Paris and London: as I showed in chapter one, the Parisian bourgeoisie produced a popular and long-standing discourse that idealized its urban experience; London's bourgeoisie did not.

65. *Sinks of London Laid Open* (London: J. Duncombe, 1848), 5, 7.

66. Captain Hay, a police commissioner, *Parliamentary Papers* (1852), quoted in Leonore Davidoff, "The Separation of Home and Work? Landladies and Lodgers in Nineteenth- and Twentieth-Century England," in *Fit Work for Women,* ed. Sandra Burman (New York: St. Martin's Press, 1979), 72. Similar accounts of lodging houses appear throughout Henry Mayhew's writings on the London poor; see *The Morning Chronicle Survey of Labour and the Poor* (Sussex: Caliban, 1980), 3:75, 77, 93.

67. Françoise Barret-Ducrocq usefully explains that people who moved to lodging houses were too poor to pay a weekly rent but not so destitute as to enter a workhouse (*Love in the Time of Victoria: Sexuality, Class and Gender in Nineteenth-Century London* [London: Verso, 1991], 22).

68. T. Haraven and J. Modell, "Urbanisation and the Malleable Household: An Examination of Boarding and Lodging in American Families," quoted in Davidoff, "Separation of Home and Work," 65; [Antony D. Cooper], unsigned review of the *Reports of the Society for Improving the Condition of the Labouring Classes* (1845–1846): *First Report of the Constabulary Force Commissioners,* 1839, *Quarterly Review* 82 (December 1847): 142; Mary Bayly, *Ragged Homes and How to Mend Them* (London: Nisbet, 1860), 15; Mayhew, *Morning Chronicle Survey,* 3:77, 4:4, 56; John Garwood, *The Million-Peopled City; or, One-Half of the People of London Made Known to the Other Half* (London: Wertheim and Macintosh, 1853), 47; Henry Mayhew, "The Low Lodging-houses of London," in *Mayhew's London,* ed. Peter Quenell (London: Pilot Press, 1949), 146.

69. "Buildings—Mansions—Flats—Residences—Dwellings," *The Builder* 36, no. 1823 (January 1878): 31.

70. John Ruskin, *Lectures on Architecture and Painting* (New York: Wiley and Halsted, 1856), 78. See also Letter 29, "La Douce Amie," in *Fors Clavigera* (1873; London: George Allen, 1896), 2:101–102.

71. Thomas Beames, *The Rookeries of London* (1852; reprint, London: Frank Cass, 1970), 3, 2.

72. An exposé of lodging houses entitled *Sinks of London Laid Open,* illustrated by George Cruikshank, called the lodging house it investigated "a brothel" and a "modern Sodom"; its unusual example of the corrosive effect of lodging houses on established hierarchies was a "man-woman," a woman who dissolves the usual segmentations of gender and sexuality by dressing as a man and marrying another woman (18, 19, 66). On incest in lodgings, see Anthony S. Wohl, "Sex and the Single Room: Incest among the Victorian Working Classes," in *The Victorian Family: Structure and Stresses,* ed. Anthony S. Wohl (London: Croom Helm, 1978), 197–216.

73. Peter Gaskell, *The Manufacturing Population of England* (London: Baldwin and Craddock, 1833), 93, 137. Decades later, the housing reformer Octavia Hill outlined a similar relationship between domestic space and social form, with an emphasis on reform rather than degeneration: "Even a third rate house with a backyard of its own is better than . . . modern flats . . . because when the tenant can command his own front door and staircase, he can preserve the unity of his family" (quoted in W. T. Hill, *Octavia Hill* [London: Hutchinson, 1956], 14).

74. Charles Kingsley, "Great Cities, and Their Influence for Good and Evil," in *Miscellanies,* 2d ed. (London: Parker, 1860), 2:327.

75. Thomas Archer, *The Pauper, the Thief, and the Convict: Sketches of Some of Their Homes, Haunts and Habits* (London: Groombridge, 1865), 98. For two other examples of the lodging house as a source of corruption, see Mayhew, *Morning Chronicle Survey,* 3:106; and [Cooper], *Reports,* 143.

76. "Modern House-Building," *Building News* 13, no. 619 (November 1866): 756; "The Dwellings of the Working Classes Inferior to Those of the Pauper and the Prisoner," excerpt from *Bentley's Magazine* in *The Builder* 2, no. 98 (December 1844): 631.

77. John Hollingshead, *Ragged London in 1861* (London: Smith, Elder, 1861), 54–55; emphasis added.

78. [Cooper], *Reports,* 143.

79. *Knight's London,* ed. Charles Knight (London: J. S. Virtue, n.d. [1850s]), 3:267. Hector Gavin similarly wrote of lodging houses that "it is scarcely possible to convey to a mixed audience anything like a just and true idea of the filthy abomination and degrading scenes which meet the eyes of those who inspect them" (*Unhealthiness of London,* lecture delivered at the Western and Eastern Literary and Scientific Institutions, Leicester Square, sponsored by the Health of Towns, and of London Associations [London: Churchill, 1847], 27–28).

80. Archer, *Pauper, Thief,* 15.

81. Urban observers consistently emphasized the need to make lodging houses visible to a middle-class gaze. The proposals of a society for improving workers' housing even identified invisibility as a disadvantage for poor people, who would then be "without the range of the observation, and the wholesome control of their more prosperous neighbours" ("The Working Classes," *The Builder* 1, no. 22 [July 1843]: 263). Such warnings about the dire consequences

of invisibility authorized a self-righteous voyeurism that was primarily directed at the tenants of lodging houses, rarely at the aristocratic and middle-class landlords who owned and rented unsafe and unhealthy buildings. Texts like George Godwin's *London Shadows: A Glance at "Homes of the Thousands"* (1854), cited in Mary Poovey, "Anatomical Realism and Social Investigation in Early Nineteenth-Century Manchester," *differences* 5, no. 3 (fall 1993): 11; and Hector Gavin's *Sanitary Ramblings* (London: Churchill, 1848) featured illustrations of lodging houses with their facades peeled off to reveal dirty and dark interiors. And in *Picturesque Sketches of London, Past and Present* (London: Office of the National Illustrated Library, 1852), 230–234, Thomas Miller began his discussion of the poor central London district of St. Giles by inviting his readers to "enter these streets and peep into those dark, close, unhealthy, and forbidding-looking rooms. . . . Behold! the curtain is at last uplifted, and those are living and breathing forms that sit or stand before us. . . . Let us lift up the flap of this cellar, and see what is going on below." See also Hollingshead, *Ragged London,* 221, 232. The association of working-class housing with a public rather than a private realm was adumbrated by the urban explorers' recourse to anthropological and/or statistical methods, which described slums quantitatively, in terms of categories and aggregates. See Poovey, "Anatomical Realism," esp. 10–12. See also John Fisher Murray's introduction to *The World of London* (Edinburgh: Blackwood, 1843), 1:5, 4, 7, which argued both for an individualized, anthropological understanding of London and for a statistical understanding of the city that proceeds through "generalization."

82. Garwood, *Million-Peopled City,* 2, 37. See also *Knight's London,* 3:269; Wohl, *Eternal Slum,* 5; and Hollingshead, *Ragged London,* 7, on hidden poverty: "It burrows in holes and corners, at the back of busy thoroughfares."

83. An 1873 survey found that "four-fifths of the land of the United Kingdom was owned by less than 7,000 persons," and, as late as 1904, 150 landlords owned one half of all the land in England. See Lord Derby's Return of Owners of Land ("the new Domesday survey"), paraphrased in F. M. L. Thompson, *English Landed Society,* 27. Land was the source of many aristocrats' wealth: according to W. D. Rubinstein (*Men of Property: The Very Wealthy in Britain Since the Industrial Revolution* [London: Croom Helm, 1981]), the duke of Westminster's income in 1883 was around £325,000, with £225,000 derived from the houses leased on his London estates.

84. Emmet, "Ethics of Urban Leaseholds," 321.

85. See Slater, "Family, Society," 134.

86. See H. J. Dyos, *Victorian Suburb,* 87–89; Neil Jackson, "The Speculative House in London c. 1832–1914" (Ph.D. dissertation, the Polytechnic of the South Bank, London, 1982); H. Muthesius, *English House,* 72–73; S. Muthesius, *English Terraced,* 21.

87. Emmet, "Ethics of Urban Leaseholds," 321–322.

88. Hitchcock, *Early Victorian,* 409.

89. Dyos, *Victorian Suburb,* 90; A. Cox, *Landlord's and Tenant's,* 103. Cox wrote that "Freehold houses in London are very seldom to be secured" (69). Even Octavia Hill, one of the Victorian era's most famous philanthropic "land-

lords," did not own the houses she managed but paid £750 for leaseholds with fifty-six years left to run (Octavia Hill, "Cottage Property in London," in *Homes of the London Poor,* 2d ed. [London: Macmillan, 1883]; the chapter first appeared in the *Fortnightly Review,* November 1866).

90. Frank Banfield, *The Great Landlords of London* (London: Spencer Blackett, n.d. [1888]), 9, specified that those "shackles" were particular to Londoners; Emmet, "Ethics of Urban Leaseholds," 301.

91. Joseph Kay, *Free Trade in Land,* 9th ed. (London: Kegan Paul, 1885), 18. For other legal reformers who cited the French model approvingly, see also Brodrick, *English Land,* 303, and Banfield, *Great Landlords,* 13. Writers attributed the generalization of property ownership in France to the breakup and sale of aristocratic and church lands during and after the French Revolution, and to the Napoleonic Code's abolition of primogeniture.

92. Banfield, *Great Landlords,* 23. Banfield also compared English ground landlords to despotic "Oriental monarchs": "And this is to be deplored—that the terrible anxiety of the many, and their attachment to home, should minister to the triumph of an autocratic whim. Pharaoh and his prerogatives are an anachronism in modern London" (72).

93. For a detailed analysis of the relationship between political freedom—and unfreedom—and the "mobilization of property" (25) earlier in the century, which emphasizes the extent to which all property became subject to capital, see Celeste Langan, *Romantic Vagrancy: Wordsworth and the Simulation of Freedom* (Cambridge: Cambridge University Press, 1995).

94. In *Semi-Serious Observations of an Italian Exile during his Residence in England* (1833), Count Pecchio observed an "advantage" to the ninety-nine-year leasehold house: "by this method, posterity is not hampered or tyrannised over. Every generation can choose and build its own houses, according to its own caprices, and its own necessities" (quoted in Saint, "Building Art," 69). No *English* writer, however, ever praised the ephemerality of the ninety-nine-year house. On the status of leases in inheritance law, see Brodrick, *English Land,* 97–98; William Cruise, *A Digest of the Laws of England Respecting Real Property,* 4th ed. (London: Saunders and Benning, 1835), 227; K. E. Digby, *An Introduction to the History of the Law of Real Property* (Oxford: Clarendon Press, 1875), 125, 169–170 (who notes that although leaseholds are classed with personal property, they technically represent rights over something immoveable, and thus have "received the mongrel name of 'chattels real'"); F. Pollock, *Land Laws,* 139–140; and A. W. B. Simpson, *A History of the Land Law* (Oxford: Clarendon Press, 1986), 250. Pollock noted that leaseholds, unlike freeholds, represent not rights but contracts, and that in cities such as London where a few ground landlords owned almost all the land, the strength of those contracts was vitiated: "It is evidently absurd to speak of freedom of contract in relation to such a system [where town lands] . . . are a monopoly in the hands of the landowner" (155).

95. Emmet, "Ethics of Urban Leaseholds," 305–306. Pollock's commentary on the land laws reached a similar conclusion (all freehold is really leasehold) on a different basis when he showed that "No absolute ownership of land is recog-

nised by our law-books except in the Crown" (*Land Laws,* 12). William Blackstone similarly explained that land held in "fee simple," one of the common terms for freehold, technically meant land "held of a superior," i.e,. the king; see *Commentaries on the Laws of England Applicable to Real Property,* 2d ed. (Toronto: Rowsell and Hutchison, 1880), 115–116. Before them, Karl Marx had also argued for the irreducibly alienated nature of all property in his *Economic and Philosophic Manuscripts of 1844,* ed. and intro. by Dirk J. Struik, trans. Martin Milligan (New York: International, 1964), 101, 102, 100. Marx wrote that once land has become commodified within a capitalist economy, "all personal relationship between the proprietor and his property cease[s]" and the maxim "l'argent n'a pas de maître" expresses "the complete domination of dead matter over mankind," so that the putative owner and ruler is in fact owned and ruled by money. Yet even in a more organic and direct feudal ownership, described by the maxim "nulle terre sans seigneur," ownership is often not absolute but instead dispossesses (or is only the appearance of ownership): "The domination of the land as an alien power over men is already inherent in feudal landed property. The serf is the adjunct of the land. Likewise, the lord of an entailed estate . . . belongs to the land. It inherits him." While being owned by a landed estate remains more substantial than being owned by the dead hand of capital, in both cases property is in no sense absolute. As part of a very different political program, Brodrick made a similar argument against primogeniture and settlements, as well as leaseholds, because the former "convert the nominal owner of land into a tenant-for-life" (*English Land,* 89).

For a reading of the impossibility of absolute ownership in an American literary context, see Walter Benn Michaels, "Romance and Real Estate," in *The Gold Standard and the Logic of Naturalism: American Literature at the Turn of the Century* (Berkeley: University of California Press, 1987), 85–112.

96. Emmet ("Ethics of Urban Leaseholds," 308–309) calculated the average length of residence for a Londoner in any one house as three years. Historians suggest that even people who could afford 8- to 10-bedroom establishments usually took out 5- to 7-year leases; see, for example, F. M. L. Thompson, *Hampstead: Building a Borough, 1650–1964* (London: Routledge and Kegan Paul, 1974), 277.

97. L. L. Y., "The Middle-Class Dwellings of London," *Building News* 3, no. 20 (May 1857): 477; Charles Eastlake, *Hints on Household Taste,* 2d rev. ed. (London: Longmans, Green, 1869), 22. Cross (*Hints,* 20, 39) made similar remarks on the flimsiness of many leasehold houses, citing numerous puns on leases and houses falling in (expiring and collapsing) at the same time.

98. "Falling of Houses," *The Builder* 1, no. 17 (June 1843): 205, and *The Builder* 2, no. 94 (November 1844): 577–578. See also "To Let or to Sell," *Building News* 12, no. 545 (June 1865): 432; and Cross, "Word to the Wise," 36. Commenting on rising rents in London, Cross cited a poem whose final couplet ran: "For they fancy the rents must fall / With the houses themselves bye and bye" (39).

99. *The Builder* 3, no. 116 (April 1845): 193. See also "Crack Houses," *The Builder* 2, no. 83 (September 1844): 462.

100. "Apartments, Furnished," *Household Words,* July 16, 1853, 457–463.

101. "How to Build a House and Live in It," *Blackwood's Edinburgh Magazine* 59 (June 1846): 761, 763.

102. "Scamping," *Chambers's Journal* 56, no. 787 (January 1879): 49.

103. Ruskin, "La Douce Amie," 100. On the semidetached house, see Hunter, *Victorian Villas,* 31.

104. William H. White, "Houses in Flats," *The Builder* 34, no. 1729 (March 1876): 291. For contemporary mentions that single-family houses were occupied as multiple-occupancy apartments even by lower- to upper-middle class individuals and families, see George Augustus Sala, "Houses to Let," in *Gaslight and Daylight with Some London Scenes They Shine Upon* (London: Tinsley, 1872), esp. 217–222; William J. Short, "Remarks on Street Architecture," *Architectural Magazine* 2 (August 1835): 391; James Grant, *The Great Metropolis,* first series (London: Saunders and Otley, 1836), 2:201; Cross, *Landed Property,* 69; Percival Gordon Smith and Keith Downes Young, "Architecture," in *Our Homes, and How to Make Them Healthy,* ed. Shirley Foster Murphy (London: Cassell, 1883), 179. See also [Peter Cunningham], *Murray's Handbook for Modern London* (London: John Murray, 1851), xxxiii.

105. Ashpitel and Whichcord, *Town Dwellings,* 14. The advertisements in Alfred Cox's monthly *Illustrated Property Advertiser* show that the discourse of domestic complaint, however heightened its rhetoric, did not misrepresent actual dwelling practices; its London listings were divided into "Unfurnished Houses" and "Furnished Houses," included ample sections on "Parts of Houses" under both categories, and solicited a clientele that was middle-class, but not wealthy, since the majority of the advertisements sought "genteel" tenants to rent various portions of a house. Advertisers offered a drawing room and bedroom suitable for "a small family without children," specified that "an elderly gentleman—say a member of one of the clubs, or some elderly lady, or other desirable party would be preferred," and emphasized that "quiet and perfect respectability are imperatively looked for" in the tenant of a set of second-floor rooms near New Bond Street (*Illustrated Property Advertiser,* May 1855, 41; July 1855, 106; May 1855, 46).

106. William Young equated middle-class houses with lodging-houses in "'Model' Town Houses for the Middle Classes," 566: "'[O]nly one-fourth of the dwelling-houses in the metropolis are occupied by one family each.' The remainder, though constructed to be similarly tenanted, are ('common' or uncommon, as the case may be), mere lodging-houses—sham *private dwellings,* which they are not,—ill arranged, uncomfortable *lodgings,* which they were never built to be."

107. *Illustrated Property Advertiser,* May 1855, 43.

108. Smith and Young, "Architecture," 180; Emmet, "Ethics of Urban Leaseholds," 309; "Modern House-Building," 756.

109. Emmet, "Ethics of Urban Leaseholds," 323, 333.

110. On the realist novel's affinity for the urban and its opposition to it in the name of domesticity, see, for example, Peter Conrad (*The Victorian Treasure House* [London: Collins, 1973], 10, 65, 67), who argues both that the city has an intimate connection to the realist novel on the basis of their shared prolifer-

ation of detail, and that Dickens's novels effect a "transformation of London" that is part of a larger "recoil into the private life" and turns the city into a series of disaggregated domestic interiors. The most developed version of this argument is in Alexander Welsh, *The City of Dickens* (Oxford: Clarendon Press, 1971), vi, 142, which argues that in Dickens's work, London represents the earthly city of sin and suffering, opposed to a heavenly one "of hearth and home," and concludes that the novels celebrate the home "as the antithesis of the city." Other critics have complicated the claim that the British novel opposed the street and the home. Keating, for example (*Unknown England*, 16), notes that in Dickens "[e]ven the respectable middle-class characters are continually drawn to the streets; their homes are merely temporary stopping places or final havens of rest in which no one can really believe." Anne Humpherys ("Generic Strands and Urban Twists: The Victorian Mysteries Novel," *Victorian Studies* 34 [1991]: 455–472) contends that *Bleak House* poses secret urban connections (the strands of a "rope" plot) as a corrective against the failures and fragmentation of urban institutions. In "'A Surprising Transformation': Dickens and the Hearth" (in *Nature and the Victorian Imagination*, ed. U. C. Knoepflmacher and G. B. Tennyson [Berkeley: University of California Press, 1977], 153–170), Robert Patten shows that in Dickens's works, the city as well as the country can take on the renewing qualities of the hearth. And in "Street Figures: Victorian Urban Iconography" (in *Victorian Literature and the Victorian Visual Imagination*, ed. Carol T. Christ and John O. Jordan [Berkeley: University of California Press, 1995], 237, 235), Richard Stein asserts that in *Oliver Twist, Nicholas Nickleby*, and *Great Expectations*, "the jumble and confusion of the streets threaten to reclaim from us the hard-won security of domestic shelter," while at the same time showing that the urban cannot be kept separate from the domestic interior.

111. Reeder ("Suburbanity," 14) demonstrates that in the 1850s and 1860s, the suburbs became more crowded; had a more heterogeneous class composition; experienced an influx of the commerce and industry that had initially been excluded; and attained a spatial density associated with the urban.

112. "A House to Let," coauthored by Charles Dickens, Wilkie Collins, and Elizabeth Gaskell, appeared in the extra Christmas number of *Household Words*, December 7, 1858, 1–36; "The Ghost at Laburnum Villa," in *Belgravia* 2 (August 1870): 213–222; Sheridan Le Fanu, "The Haunted House in Westminster," *Belgravia* 6 (January 1872): 261–285; "The Haunted Lodging House," in *Sharpe's London Magazine* 28 (1858): 127–134. An exhaustive list of the haunted-house stories published between 1850 and 1870 would take up too much space; I cite and discuss many, but not all, of those stories in the following pages.

113. Vernon Lee [Violet Paget], preface [1889] to *Hauntings: Fantastic Stories* (Freeport: Books for Libraries Press, 1971), viii, ix, x.

114. Terry Castle argues that the Enlightenment worked to produce a new version of the irrational in *The Female Thermometer: Eighteenth-Century Culture and the Invention of the Uncanny* (New York: Oxford University Press, 1995); see especially the introduction and "Phantasmagoria and the Metaphorics of Modern Reverie."

115. John H. Ingram, *The Haunted Homes and Family Traditions of Great Britain*, 3d ed. (London: W. H. Allen, 1886), 150.

116. Compton Mackenzie, *Our Street* (New York: Doubleday, 1932), 33. A correspondent reporting a haunted house similarly wrote that it was "modern— fifty years old at the most . . . the least likely place . . . to harbour a ghost" (Elliott O'Donnell, *Haunted Houses of London* [London: Eveleigh Nash, 1909], 52). And compare the comments of a lawyer in Charlotte Riddell's 1875 work "The Uninhabited House" (in *Five Victorian Ghost Novels*, ed. E. F. Bleiler [New York: Dover Publications, 1971], 20), who "would not believe that where gas was, any house could be ghost-ridden."

117. See, for example, George Augustus Sala, "City Spectres," in *Gaslight and Daylight*, 136–143; and Mrs. Haweis's observation in *The Art of Decoration* (London: Chatto and Windus, 1881), 381: "[e]very narrow and muddy old road has its associations, its haunting figures of the past which we should be sorry to lose."

118. E. J. Clery, *The Rise of Supernatural Fiction, 1762–1800* (Cambridge: Cambridge University Press, 1995), 17, 16. Clery interprets the Cock Lane ghost "apparition" in 1762 as a metropolitan spectacle that helped to define a market for supernatural fiction. Clery notes the "happy marriage of supernaturalism and modernity" in which "supernatural fiction figures as the ultimate luxury commodity, produced by an 'unreal need' for unreal representations" (5, 7). Clery's analysis of the late eighteenth century is persuasive but fails to distinguish between supernatural fiction and other equally commodified literary forms; furthermore, Clery's account cannot hold for the later haunted-house stories, which were not perceived as simply "unreal."

119. "The Latest Thing in Ghosts," *Once a Week* 6 (January 1862): 100.

120. Ruskin, *Seven Lamps*, 8, 72, 151, 160. Ruskin emphasized the connection between the house as a repository of memories and its development into a personified, sympathetic entity in its own right: "good men . . . would be grieved, at the close of [their lives], to think that the place of their earthly abode, which had seen, and *seemed almost to sympathise in,* all their honor, their gladness or their suffering . . . was to be swept away . . . that . . . there was no warm monument in the hearth and house to them." The hesitation to personify buildings expressed by "seemed almost" disappears as the section develops: a few pages later, we read that "the greatest glory of a building . . . is in its Age, and in that deep sense of voicefulness, of stern watching, of mysterious sympathy, nay, even of approval or condemnation, which we feel in walls that have long been washed by the passing waves of humanity." Ruskin depicts houses as not only embodying the nebulous "associations" of quotidian domestic comfort but also materializing the spirits of vigilant ancestors (179, 187).

121. *The Builder* 1, no. 2 (February 1843): 18, and George Godwin, "Architecture for the Poor," *The Builder* 3, no. 105 (February 1845): 62. See also "Remarks on London Street Houses and Shop Fronts" (by "R.") in Loudon's *Architectural Magazine* 1 (May 1834): 115; Loudon, "Cottage Economy," 3:3. See also Gavin, *Habitations*, 12, 53, 67, 70; S. H. Brooks, *Treatise on the Erection of Dwelling Houses* (London: John Weale, 1860), vi; Thomas Harris, *Victorian Architecture* (London: Bell and Daldy, 1860), 4; Haweis, *Art of Decora-*

tion, 31. Ruskin summed up this tradition in the aphorism, "All practical laws are the exponents of moral ones" (*Seven Lamps,* 4). Similarly, as we have seen, bad house and street architecture were commonly considered "one leading cause of the demoralization of the lower classes of the population" (*The Builder* 4, no. 154 [January 1846]: 25). Occasionally, writers reversed the rhetoric of personification to imply that morality was susceptible to merely physical amelioration, as when Cooper wrote of the need "to drain and ventilate the morals of the people" (*Reports,* 148); see also Kingsley, "Great Cities," 321.

122. R. C. Finucane, *Appearances of the Dead: A Cultural History of Ghosts* (London: Junction Books, 1982), 190. Julia Briggs makes a similar point in *Night Visitors: The Rise and Fall of the English Ghost Story* (London: Faber, 1977), 14.

123. On spiritualism, see Finucane, *Appearances.* Janet Oppenheim (*The Other World: Spiritualism and Psychical Research in England, 1850–1914* [Cambridge: Cambridge University Press, 1985], 8; see also 141, 150, 219) writes that the home medium was the most influential: "private mediums, in small domestic circles, brought spiritualism more intimately into the lives of countless believers than could the public settings of professional mediums. It is, after all, far more compelling to see one's own dining table in motion than to read about the antics of someone else's furniture." See also Logie Barrow, *Independent Spirits: Spiritualism and English Plebeians, 1850–1910* (London: Routledge and Kegan Paul, 1986), 9.

124. F. J. Theobald, *Homes and Work in the Future Life* (London: Psychological Press Association, 1885), 6, 11. See also Charles Maurice Davies, *Unorthodox London: Or, Phases of Religious Life in the Metropolis,* 2d ed. (London: Tinsley, 1874), 302–303 (originally published as columns in the *Daily Telegraph*); and Oppenheim, *The Other World,* 61. George Eliot took the spatial framework of spiritualism for granted when, in an 1872 letter discussing spiritualism with Harriet Beecher Stowe, she wrote that "the division between within and without in this sense seems to become every year a more subtle and bewildering problem" (quoted in Alex Owen, *The Darkened Room: Women, Power and Spiritualism in Late Nineteenth-Century England* [London: Virago, 1980], 20).

125. See, for example, the cases cited in Peter G. Beidler, *Ghosts, Demons, and Henry James: "The Turn of the Screw" at the Turn of the Century* (Columbia: University of Missouri Press, 1989), 47, 48, 56, 66. Beidler is citing, respectively, *Proceedings of the Society for Psychical Research* [PSPR] 3 (1885): 126–132; Frederick G. Lee, *More Glimpses of the World Unseen* (1878); and *PSPR* 6 (1889): 255–259.

126. Charles Maurice Davies, "Spiritualism," in *Unorthodox London,* 302. See also Dinah Mulock's "Last House in C– Street" (1856), set in London lodgings, whose narrator frames her story by explaining that "it was in the early days of table-moving, when young folk ridiculed and elder folk were shocked at the notion of calling up one's departed ancestors into one's dinner-table, and learning the wonders of the angelic world by the bobbings of a hat or the twirlings of a plate" (in *Victorian Ghost Stories: An Oxford Anthology,* ed. Michael Cox and R. A. Gilbert [Oxford: Oxford University Press, 1991], 44 [hereafter Cox

and Gilbert, *Victorian Ghost*]). For examples of the imbrication of ghosts and domestic architecture, including reprints of floor plans, see Ernest Bennett, *Apparitions and Haunted Houses: A Survey of Evidence* (London: Faber and Faber, 1939), which collects a range of testimony, much from the 1880s; Ingram, *Haunted Homes;* O'Donnell, *Haunted Houses;* Robert Dale Owen, *Footfalls on the Boundary of Another World* (Philadelphia: Lippincott, 1872).

127. For detailed accounts of the rise of the periodical press in England, see Patricia Anderson, *The Printed Image and the Transformation of Popular Culture 1790–1860* (Oxford: Clarendon Press, 1991); Margaret Beetham, *A Magazine of Her Own? Domesticity and Desire in the Woman's Magazine, 1800–1914* (London: Routledge, 1996); and Joanne Shattock and Michael Wolff, eds., *The Victorian Periodical Press: Samplings and Soundings* (Leicester: Leicester University Press, 1982).

128. Montague Summers underscores that almost all Victorian supernatural tales appeared in these periodicals and also adds *Blackwood's,* the *Family Herald Supplement,* and the *Young Ladies' Journal* as important venues for ghost stories. See Montague Summers, introduction to *The Supernatural Omnibus* (London: Gollancz, 1931), 28–31. For a brief discussion of the Victorian ghost story's connection to the periodical press, see Stewart Marsh Ellis, "The Ghost Story and Its Exponents," in *Mainly Victorian* (1925; reprint, Freeport: Books for Libraries Press, 1969), 322–331.

129. On the French supernatural tale, see Joan C. Kessler's introduction to *Demons of the Night: Tales of the Fantastic, Madness, and the Supernatural from Nineteenth-Century France* (Chicago: University of Chicago Press, 1995), xi–li, and the representative stories in that anthology. Kessler notes that in Guy de Maupassant's "Qui Sait?," one of the few tales that apparently focuses on a house, the house functions mainly as a psychological symbol: "the protagonist's house reflects the reclusive inner sanctum of his own mind" (xlvi). On spiritualism in France, see Lynn Louise Sharp, "Rational Religion, Irrational Science: Men, Women, and Belief in French Spiritism, 1853–1914" (Ph.D. dissertation, University of California, Irvine, 1996).

130. Charles Maurice Davies, "A Night in a Ghost-Chamber," *Belgravia* 9 (November–February 1872): 381. On the difference in architectural setting between Gothic and Victorian supernatural fiction, see, for example, Bleiler (*Five Victorian,* vi), who defines typical Victorian ghost fiction as focusing on "everyday middle-class life, with realistic detail predominant, usually domestic"; and the introduction by Michael Cox and R. A. Gilbert to *Victorian Ghost,* ix–x: "it is in the 1850s that the distinct, anti-Gothic character of the Victorian ghost story begins to emerge. . . . [T]he Victorian ghost story was typically domestic in tone and inclined to blur the boundaries between fact and fiction." See also Manuel Aguirre (*The Closed Space: Horror Literature and Western Symbolism* [Manchester: Manchester University Press, 1990], 115, 121), who writes that "Victorian horror . . . shows a trend toward adapting the fantastic to the bourgeois and replacing the castle by mansions, houses, apartments." Aguirre fails to develop this comment, however, and instead defines the Victorian horror story in terms of the theme of "the haunted individual"; the inaccuracy of that

claim is reflected in his examples, almost none of which are Victorian or English (he cites texts by Hogg, Maturin, Hoffman, and James).

131. A vast literature exists on the Gothic; for overviews that discuss the identifying features of Gothic novels, see Chris Baldick, introduction to *Oxford Book of Gothic Tales* (Oxford: Oxford University Press, 1992), xi–xxiii; Elizabeth MacAndrew, *The Gothic Tradition in Fiction* (New York: Columbia University Press, 1979); Ronald Paulson, "Gothic Fiction and the French Revolution," *ELH* 48 (1981): 532–554; Eino Railo, *The Haunted Castle: A Study of the Elements of English Romanticism* (London: Routledge, 1927); and Eve Kosofsky Sedgwick, *The Coherence of Gothic Conventions* (New York: Arno Press, 1980).

132. For an example of a male narrator marked as rational, see Le Fanu's "Haunted House in Westminster," 261, in which the narrator hears a ghost story from "an elderly man . . . dry, sad, quiet . . . who had known better days, and had always maintained an unexceptional character. No better authority could be imagined for a ghost-story."

133. In *Victorian Ghost,* 115. Compare this to the opening of Edgar Allan Poe's "Black Cat," cited by Rosemary Jackson as an example of the fantastic's opposition to realism: "I neither expect nor solicit belief," a formulation Jackson links to the "impossibility of verification of events" in the fantastic mode (*Fantasy: The Literature of Subversion* [London: Methuen, 1981], 37).

134. See Roland Barthes, *S/Z* (Paris: Editions du Seuil, 1970).

135. See, for example, "The Haunted Grange," *Dublin University Magazine* 2 (July–December 1833): 693, which begins, "It was in the autumn of 1830" and locates its action in the "little village of Boreham." When dates or proper names of streets are suppressed, it is in the name of referential discretion; see, for example, "An Authentic Narrative of a Haunted House," *Eclectic Magazine* 58 (January 1863): 54: "Within the last eight years—the precise date I purposely omit."

136. The narrator of "The Story of Clifford House" (in Cox and Gilbert, *Victorian Ghost,* 218), for example, describes the London house she rents and its "Wide, lofty apartments, staircases, and landings; a handsome dining-room panelled in velvety dark-green 'flock' and gold; a handsome drawing-room panelled in pale cream-colour and gold; airy bed-chambers and dressing-rooms."

On the realism of Victorian supernatural fiction, see Harvey Sucksmith (*The Narrative Art of Charles Dickens: The Rhetoric of Sympathy and Irony in His Novels* [Oxford: Clarendon Press, 1970], 77–78), who distinguishes the Gothic novel from nineteenth-century tales of terror in general on the basis of the latter's commitment to meticulous, thorough description; and Edith Birkhead (*The Tale of Terror: A Study of the Gothic Romance* [London: Constable, 1921], 182), who analyzes the realism of Bulwer-Lytton's "Haunted and the Haunters." In "Purity and Danger: *Dracula,* the Urban Gothic, and the Late Victorian Degeneracy Crisis," *ELH* 59 (1992): 197–225, Kathleen Spencer defines a nineteenth-century genre she calls "urban gothic" and "fantastic" (using a different definition than Todorov) as a mode that stages violations of reality within a realistic narrative; she notes that the nineteenth-century fantastic emphasized

"the modernity of the setting," and that a "modern setting means an urban setting." Spencer's emphasis on realism and on a particularly urban genre of the supernatural, which she elaborates in a reading of *Dracula*, is compelling, but the
term "urban gothic" suggests a misleading continuity between the Gothic and
nineteenth-century supernatural fiction.

The realistic form of Victorian ghost stories shows that they did not belong
to the category that Tzvetan Todorov has dubbed the "fantastic," which he
defines in terms of the uncertainty of both the protagonist and the reader as to
whether the events described are really taking place; see *The Fantastic: A Structural Approach to a Literary Genre,* trans. Richard Howard (Cleveland: Case
Western Reserve University Press, 1973). See also Christine Brooke-Rose, *A
Rhetoric of the Unreal: Studies in Narrative and Structure, Especially of the
Fantastic* (Cambridge: Cambridge University Press, 1981); and R. Jackson (*Fantasy,* 14, 21, 26, 123), who emphatically opposes the fantastic to realism in both
formal and ideological terms.

137. In a discussion of late eighteenth-century drama criticism about representations of the supernatural, Clery (*Rise of Supernatural,* 38) shows that as
people began to believe less in ghosts, they came to believe more in their response to them, thus creating a specifically aestheticized supernatural that was
neither patently false, nor assertively real: "The naturalness of response would
recuperate the improbability of the object." In the case of the Victorian ghost
story, not only the naturalness of fearful responses but also the naturalization
effected by realistic technique helped to recuperate the improbability of the
supernatural.

138. On spectrality as an intermediate state between the absolute immateriality of "spirit" and the full materiality of the physical, see Jacques Derrida,
*Specters of Marx: The State of the Debt, the Work of Mourning, and the New
International,* trans. Peggy Kamuf (New York: Routledge, 1994), 6. Derrida
also remarks on the temporal intermediacy of the ghost throughout; see, for example, 25, 73, 103.

139. The reading I present here focuses on the ghosts as representations of
a troubling difference within the middle class; it is not meant to exclude other
interpretations of ghosts. For example, they might be servants, whose working-class presence both defined and disrupted the middle-class household, as
suggested by Peter Stallybrass's and Allon White's chapters on the city and
middle-class domesticity in *The Politics and Poetics of Transgression* (Ithaca:
Cornell University Press, 1986). In some stories, such as "The Story of Clifford
House" or Rhoda Broughton's "Man with the Nose," the ghosts clearly represent repressed aspects of female agency and sexuality; in Broughton's story, the
female sexuality that can be expressed only with a ghostly "man with a nose"
emerges in the metropolitan sites of a continental city's hotels, museums, and
streets.

For an interpretation of architectural haunting that focuses on the uncanny
as a metaphor for alienation in the modern metropolis, see Anthony Vidler, *The
Architectural Uncanny: Essays in the Modern Unhomely* (Cambridge, Mass.:
MIT Press, 1992), especially the first section on "Houses." For a work that considers how haunting recurs in representations of Paris (in Walter Benjamin, the

surrealists, and nineteenth-century texts), see Margaret Cohen, *Profane Illumination: Walter Benjamin and the Paris of Surrealist Revolution* (Berkeley: University of California Press, 1993). In ch. 4, "The Ghosts of Paris," Cohen argues that the eruption of ghosts in André Breton's *Nadja* needs to be read in terms of the narrator's historical and subjective stance toward the capital's revolutionary past. It is symptomatic of the differences in French and British history that in Cohen's reading of haunted Paris, the repressed referent (to simplify her argument enormously) is revolution, while in my reading of haunted London, the repressed referent is the distance between dwelling practices and bourgeois ideals.

140. The conditions of London housing also pervaded residences outside the metropolis, since even haunted-house stories set in the country revolved more often around renting houses than owning them. See, for example, two works by Charlotte Riddell: "The Uninhabited House" and "The Open Door" (1882), in Cox and Gilbert, *Victorian Ghost*, 256–282.

Stories set, at least in part, in flats and lodgings, include Dickens, "The Story of the Bagman's Uncle" (in *Classic Ghost Stories* [New York: Dover Publications, 1975]), opening amidst Edinburgh's streets of flats; Wilkie Collins's "The Dream Woman" (in *Classic Ghost Stories*), whose frame and central narrative concentrate on episodes in an inn; Collins's "Miss Jéromette and the Clergyman" (1875; in Cox and Gilbert, *Victorian Ghost*, 201, 215), in which the ghost of a woman who had "lodged" in a "shabby little house in a by-street" in London appears in the vicinity of a country house; Thomas Street Millington, "No Living Voice" (1872; in Cox and Gilbert, *Victorian Ghost*, 190–197); and F. Anstey, "The Wraith of Barnjum" (1879; in *Nightcaps and Nightmares: Ghosts with a Touch of Humour*, ed. Peter Haining [London: William Kimber, 1983], 45–59).

In Sheridan Le Fanu's "Green Tea" (1869; in *Ghost Stories*, ed. Susan Hill [London: Hamish Hamilton, 1983], 180), the haunted Reverend Jennings "beats a retreat from the vicarage, and returns to London—where, in a dark street off Piccadilly, he inhabits a very narrow house," whenever he feels a ghostly visitation impending. "Green Tea" is significant because even though it is a ghost story that focuses on the hero's torment by an evil monkey spirit, it still marshals the paraphernalia of the haunted-house story. Chapter X is entitled "Home" and takes place after Reverend Jennings has confessed his troubles to the narrator; the exorcism that accompanies confession is associated with a new domestication of the environment, since this chapter begins with the narrator recounting "I made him have candles lighted, and saw the room looking cheery and inhabited before I left him" (202). Despite this, the reverend cuts his throat in that room (located this time in a suburban house that he actually owns, in Richmond), indicating to the reader that the evil spirit ultimately pervaded domestic Richmond as easily as it did haunted Piccadilly.

141. "The Uninhabited House," 3.

142. "The Haunted and the Haunters," in *Classic Ghost Stories* (New York: Dover Publications, 1975), 293, 294, 297, 320, 309.

143. Rhoda Broughton, "The Truth, the Whole Truth, and Nothing but the Truth," in Cox and Gilbert, *Victorian Ghost*, 75.

144. "The Story of Clifford House," 218, 219, 231.

145. For a discussion of how a Gothic novel like Horace Walpole's *Castle of Otranto* used ghosts to stage the vagaries of property transmission, see Clery, *Rise of Supernatural*, 72–77. Some Victorian ghost stories—though not ones set in London—continued to focus on disruptions of property transmission, both for the aristocracy and the middle class. See, for example, Sheridan Le Fanu, "Sir Dominick Sarsfield" in *Classic Ghost Stories* (New York: Dover Publications, 1975), 1–15; Bram Stoker, "The Judge's House," in ibid., 211; Thomas Ingoldsby, "The Spectre of Tappington," in *Nightcaps and Nightmares: Ghosts with a Touch of Humour,* ed. Peter Haining (London: William Kimber, 1983), 14; Sheridan Le Fanu, "Squire Toby's Will," in *Oxford Book of English Ghost Stories,* ed. Michael Cox and R. A. Gilbert (Oxford: Oxford University Press, 1986), 25–50; and M. E. Braddon, "The Shadow in the Corner," in ibid., 51–68.

146. Charles Dickens, "The Lawyer and the Ghost" (1836), in *Nightcaps and Nightmares: Ghosts with a Touch of Humour,* ed. Peter Haining (London: William Kimber, 1983), 42–43.

147. "The Story of Clifford House," 218, 220; the reference to "thin walls" comes from Broughton, "The Truth, the Whole Truth," 79.

148. "The Latest Thing in Ghosts," 103.

149. Charles Dickens, "To Be Taken with a Grain of Salt" (1865), in Cox and Gilbert, *Oxford Victorian,* 56–57.

150. "The Haunted and the Haunters," 296.

151. Sheridan Le Fanu, "An Account of Some Strange Disturbances in Aungier Street," in Cox and Gilbert, *Victorian Ghost,* 23. A story called "The Haunted Garden," while not technically a ghost story, confirms the conjunction between haunting, contagion, and a failure to maintain the insularity of the middle-class house; in describing how his "garden was haunted by a plant," the narrator explains how the "little strip of garden behind the house . . . divided from that of my neighbour on each side by a well-kept privet edge," is overtaken by a planting of horseradish that, growing uncontrollably, invades his neighbor's garden. The plant is "noxious," emits a "horrid effluvium," and a "curious smell." As in most haunted-house stories, the ghostly entity makes the house uninhabitable and unrentable (*Temple Bar* 24 [November 1868]: 257, 258, 263, 264).

152. "The Haunted and the Haunters," 316–317.

153. Anstey, "The Wraith of Barnjum," 50, 54.

154. "The Haunted and the Haunters," 308; "To Be Taken with a Grain of Salt," 57, 61.

155. "The Shadow in the Corner," 51, 57.

156. "Strange Disturbances," 25, 29.

157. Sheridan Le Fanu, "The Ghost of a Hand," in *Roald Dahl's Book of Ghost Stories* (New York: Farrar, Straus and Giroux, 1983), 156–158.

158. Ibid., 159.

159. "The Lawyer and the Ghost," 43; this is one of the tales interpolated in *The Pickwick Papers* (1836–37) but, according to Peter Haining, may have been written earlier (*Nightcaps and Nightmares,* 41).

160. Dr. John Hogg's discussion of health statistics in *London As It Is: Being a Series of Observations on the Health, Habits, and Amusements of the People*

(London: Macrone, 1837), 82, 99, for example, attributed greater annual mortality to London relative to the entire population and explained that "a large town is but an extensive camp, and is liable to be infested with the same diseases . . . endemic in camps"; London thus replicated, on an aggregated scale, the "close and filthy . . . haunts" of the poor.

161. *Knight's London*, 3:254, 255, 270. Only in 1891 did a *Journal of the Royal Statistical Society* article assert that there was no cause and effect relationship between high density in residences and high mortality rates (cited in Wohl, *Eternal Slum*, 174).

162. Gavin, *Unhealthiness of London*, 37, 39; [Cooper], *Reports*, 146.

163. Dr. Letheby, *Report on the Sanatory* [sic] *Condition of the City of London*, quoted in John Knox, *The Masses Without!* (London: Judd and Glass, 1857), 15.

164. Chris Brooks, *Mortal Remains: The History and Present State of the Victorian and Edwardian Cemetery* (Exeter: Wheaton, 1989), 35.

165. "Modern House-Building," 756.

166. "Crack Houses," 462.

167. Chadwick quoted in C. Brooks, *Mortal Remains*, 34. See also George Walker's lurid and influential *Gatherings from Graveyards* (1839; New York: Arno Press, 1977), 2, 3, 5, which explained that dead bodies were a "cause of disease and death" and compared them to the poor, who were linked to corpses by their unhealthful "physical condition," which made them "living spectres . . . crawling about our streets"; James Ewing Ritchie, *About London* (London: William Tinsley, 1860), 193–194, described the contamination of London's water by burial grounds.

168. James Stevens Curl, *The Victorian Celebration of Death* (Detroit: Partridge Press, 1972), 26; C. Brooks, *Mortal Remains*, 2. Curl discusses the crowding of graveyards on 42. James Ewing Ritchie, in *The Night Side of London* (London: Tweedie, 1857), 9, offered representative statistics about overcrowding in London: London covered 122 square miles, contained 327,391 houses, 2,362,236 people, and "the number of families living in one room is estimated as high as 150,000." In 1853 Garwood (*Million-Peopled City*, 37) remarked on the Westminster district as "one of the most populous in London, almost every house being crowded with numerous families and multitudes of lodgers."

169. *Payne's Illustrated London* (London: E. T. Bram, 1847), 335; T. Miller, *Picturesque Sketches*, 269. George Augustus Sala drew similar connections between London and its churchyards in *Twice 'Round the Clock; or the Hours of the Day and Night in London* (London: Houlston and Wright, 1859), 318. For other descriptions of crowding in the graveyards of central London, see David W. Bartlett, *London by Day and Night; or, Men and Things in the Great Metropolis* (New York: Hurst, n.d [ca. 1850]), 94–97; and Beames, *Rookeries*, 14.

170. Sala, *Twice 'Round*, 351.

171. Both housing and burial reform became implicated in the conflict between London's local vestries and Parliament's attempts at centralized planning, although the same local boards regulated lodging houses and the disposal of the dead (C. Brooks, *Mortal Remains*, 43).

172. On the Parisian cemetery, see Richard Allan Etlin, "The Cemetery and the City: Paris, 1744–1804" (Ph.D. dissertation, Princeton University, 1978), 153–154, 209. Etlin shows that from the eighteenth century forward, both the city and its cemeteries were built to be more legible, constructed on the basis of rational, classificatory grid systems, and secularized; cemeteries could be part of the city because they were like the city. On the suburban character of London's cemeteries, see Michel Ragon, *The Space of Death: A Study of Funerary Architecture, Decoration, and Urbanism,* trans. Alan Sheridan (Charlottesville: University Press of Virginia, 1983), who discusses the "suburban ideology" at work in cemeteries that sold freehold plots, and David Cannadine, "War and Death, Grief and Mourning in Modern Britain" (in *Mirrors of Mortality: Studies in the Social History of Death,* ed. Joachim Whaley [London: Europa Publications, 1981], 192), who states that cemeteries built to be "romantic, rural retreats were essentially an analogue of romantic, rural suburbia."

173. *Payne's Illustrated London,* 337.

174. On the founders of the London Cemetery Company, see Felix Barker, *Highgate Cemetery: Victorian Valhalla* (Salem, N.H.: Salem House, 1984), 11; the chairman's speech is also quoted on 15. On the architecture and landscaping of Victorian cemeteries, see C. Brooks, *Mortal Remains,* and Curl, *Celebration.* Burial companies had to install the same kinds of infrastructure and obey the same restrictive covenants as the developers of suburban housing estates (C. Brooks, *Mortal Remains,* 41).

175. T. Miller, *Picturesque Sketches,* 275. See also John C. Loudon, *On the laying out, planting and managing of cemeteries* (1843), quoted in Curl, *Celebration,* 83.

176. T. Miller, *Picturesque Sketches,* 275. For another text that contrasted "the city Churchyard" to the "suburban Cemetery" and advocated the positive haunting possible in the latter, see Laman Blanchard, "A Visit to the General Cemetery at Kensal Green," *Ainsworth's Magazine* 2 (1842): 177–188.

177. C. Brooks, *Mortal Remains,* 11. Curl (*Celebration,* 17) also notes that the "middle classes purchased freeholds wherever possible, for 'family graves.'" However, Curl mistakenly draws a simple analogy between owning house property and owning burial property when he writes that "Property became within the reach of all enterprising men, and the family grave, like the family house, became a mark of substance. The family, united in life, was to remain even so in death" (25). Rather, the family was unable to remain united in life in a house that it could own, and as a result the grave became overinvested as a site of spatial and familial unity.

An appendix to the American edition of Edwin Chadwick's *Report on the Results of a Special Inquiry into the Practice. of Interment in Towns* (Philadelphia: C. Sherman, 1845) underscored the impossibility of having freehold property in a church graveyard, citing the judgement of the Right Hon. Lord Stowell (44–48) that burial grounds in churchyards constituted common property, not property that could be alienated to any individual in perpetuity; Stowell pointed out that especially in crowded cities, "the indulgence of an exclusive possession is unavoidably limited," since otherwise the spaces devoted to dead people would crowd out the living. The latter point was made more literally in Margaret Oliphant's ghost tale "A Beleaguered City" (1880), in *A Beleaguered City and Other Stories* (Oxford: Oxford University Press, 1988), 3–114.

178. C. Brooks, *Mortal Remains*, 7; Brooks is discussing the Père Lachaise cemetery in Paris, which pioneered the sale of freehold plots.

179. Article in *The Gentleman's Magazine* (1832), quoted in C. Brooks, *Mortal Remains*, 62.

180. Octavia Hill, "Our Common Land," in *Our Common Land (and Other Short Essays)* (London: Macmillan, 1877), 7, 14.

181. Octavia Hill, "The Future of Our Commons," in ibid., 205–206.

182. Octavia Hill, "Open Spaces," in ibid., 105, 108, 111.

4. Enclosing Paris

1. Ferdinand Silas, "Les propriétaires vengés," *Le Bourgeois de Paris*, May 12, 1855, 4.

2. On Haussmannization, see Jean Castex et al., *Formes urbaines: de l'îlot à la barre* (Paris: Dunod, 1977), 16–19; Jeanne Gaillard, *Paris: la ville, 1852–1870* (Paris: Champion, 1977); David Harvey, "Paris, 1850–1870," in *Consciousness and the Urban Experience* (Baltimore: Johns Hopkins University Press, 1985), 63–220; David Pinkney, *Napoleon III and the Rebuilding of Paris* (Princeton: Princeton University Press, 1958); David Van Zanten, *Building Paris: Architectural Institutions and the Transformation of the French Capital, 1830–1870* (Cambridge: Cambridge University Press, 1994), 214. Literary critics and art historians also often correlate Haussmann's modernization of Paris with the rise of a representational modernism that emphasized vision itself, particularly fleeting or incomplete views, and generated a culture of the crowd, of spectatorship, and of conspicuous consumption. See, for example, Christopher Prendergast, *Paris and the Nineteenth Century* (Oxford: Blackwell, 1992), 6, 8, 69; T. J. Clark, *The Painting of Modern Life: Paris in the Art of Manet and His Followers* (Princeton: Princeton University Press, 1984); and Priscilla Parkhurst Ferguson, *Paris as Revolution: Writing the Nineteenth-Century City* (Berkeley: University of California Press, 1994). Feminist accounts of modernism by Janet Wolff and Griselda Pollock demonstrate that the designated agents of modernity and modernism, the *flâneur* and the artist, have been defined as necessarily masculine, and that female artists during the Second Empire inscribed urban strictures on female mobility and spectatorship in their paintings; see *Vision and Difference: Femininity, Feminism, and Histories of Art* (London: Routledge, 1988), 66. Pollock bases her argument in part on Janet Wolff's "Invisible *Flâneuse*" (first published in 1985).

3. Napoleon III had, of course, spent many of his years of exile in London and even had a house in the northern London suburb of St. John's Wood. See Alan Montgomery Eyre, *St. John's Wood: Its History, Its Houses, Its Haunts and Its Celebrities* (London: Chapman and Hall, 1913), vi.

4. Leonardo Benevolo mentions Napoleon III's commission of the Henry Roberts translation in *The Origins of Modern Town Planning*, trans. Judith Landry (Cambridge, Mass: MIT Press, 1967), 119.

5. For good summaries of the street improvements in London, which included the installation of gas streetlights; the paving of streets; improved sewage systems; the razing of docks to embank the Thames; the innovation of an underground subway; the renovation and construction of many new monuments; and the spread of many new building types, including hotels, train stations, and office blocks, see Thomas Burke, *The Streets of London through the Centuries*, 4th ed. (London: Batsford, 1949); Percy J. Edwards, *History of London Street Improvements, 1855–1897* (London: London County Council, 1898); Philippa Glanville, *London in Maps* (London: The Connoisseur, 1992), 41–45; Christopher Hibbert, *London: The Biography of a City* (New York: William Morrow, 1969); and Geoffrey Tyack, *Sir James Pennethorne and the Making of Victorian London* (Cambridge: Cambridge University Press, 1992). Edwards, writing for the London County Council, whose creation in the 1880s finally endowed London with a centralized planning committee, emphasized that the mid-Victorian Metropolitan Board of Works had been able to carry out only local, piecemeal changes because it lacked the central powers of finance or expropriation that Haussmann exercised; James Winter (*London's Teeming Streets* [London: Routledge, 1993], 17, 45) also emphasizes the difference between the modernization of London and Paris.

6. Charles Lucas, *Exposition universelle internationale de 1878, à Paris: compte rendu—conférence sur l'habitation à toutes les époques* (Paris: Imprimerie nationale, 1879), 32. In an article on "The Parks" (in *Gavarni in London: Sketches of Life and Character,* ed. Albert Smith [London: Bogue, 1849], 113), Albert Smith remarked on the difficulty of translating English notions of home into French: "It is fortunate that our English words *home* and *comfort* have no synonyms in their language. If they had, the Parisians would be painfully worried to understand the meaning of them." After 1850, however, Parisian urban discourse claimed to understand the meaning of those concepts very well and, as we will see, suggested various means of making Parisian housing conform more closely to the British concept of home.

7. François Sergent, *Nouveau manuel complet du propriétaire et du locataire,* rev. Charles Vasserot (Paris: Roret, 1865), v.

8. For statistics on rent increases, see Adeline Daumard, *Maisons de Paris et propriétaires parisiens au XIXe siècle, 1809–1880* (Paris: Cujas, 1965). For discussions of Haussmannization's effects on Parisians from a range of political perspectives, see Victor Calland and Albert Lenoir, *Institution des palais de famille: solution de ce grand problème—le confortable et la vie à bon marché pour tous,* 2d ed. (Paris, 1855), which advocated combining property ownership with collective living in a utopian domestic program; for similar critiques of Haussmannization, see Taxile Delord, Edmond Texier, and Arnould Frémy, *Mort aux locataires assez canailles pour ne pas payer leurs termes* (1854; Paris: Editions Seesam, 1990); M. Delamarre, "Question des loyers," series in *La Patrie,* 1861; Alexandre Weill, *Paris inhabitable: ce que tout le monde pense des loyers de Paris et personne ne dit,* 3d ed. (Paris: Dentu, 1860). For a conservative view supporting tenants, see M. de Bussy [pseudonym of Charles Marchal], *Question actuelle: propriétaires et locataires—de la cherté des loyers dans Paris-Lyon-Bordeaux-Lille-Rouen-Marseille, etc. et des moyens sûrs et immédiats d'y remé-*

dier (Paris: Eugène Pick, 1857), 10, 11; for a liberal one, see Louis Bellet, "Les Loyers dans Paris," *La Patrie,* April 3, 1861.

9. On landlords in Paris, see Daumard, *Maisons de Paris,* who notes that during the Second Empire, property ownership did become more concentrated in the hands of the wealthier members of the middle class whose main occupation consisted of investing in real estate, in contrast to the earlier part of the nineteenth century, when many people even in the lower middle-class were likely to own one or two buildings (235, 242). Throughout the century, however, few landlords lived in a building that they owned (253–254).

10. Victor Bellet, *Les Propriétaires et les loyers à Paris* (Paris: Dentu, 1857), 29, 40.

11. Ibid., 38; and Weill, *Paris inhabitable,* 9.

12. Alexandre Weill, *Qu'est-ce que le propriétaire d'une maison à Paris: suite de Paris inhabitable* (Paris: Dentu, 1860), 2.

13. Eugène Pelletan, *La Nouvelle Babylone* (1862), quoted in Judith F. Stone, "The Republican Brotherhood: Gender and Ideology," in *Gender and the Politics of Social Reform in France, 1870–1914,* ed. Elinor Accampo, Rachel Fuchs, and Mary Lynn Stewart (Baltimore: Johns Hopkins University Press, 1995), 42.

14. J. Gaillard, *Paris: la ville,* 525–531; the Goncourts quoted in T. J. Clark, *Painting of Modern Life,* 34, and 274 n.17; their comments, emended for publication in 1891, were originally made in 1861.

Gaillard's evidence (in what is otherwise a prodigiously researched work) for the introverted nature of Paris during the Restoration and July Monarchy is scanty and bases its interpretations of physical structures on presentist assumptions that have little to do with the social meanings assigned to those structures in the mid-nineteenth century; compare, for example, her discussion of the *passages* (526), to Nicholas Green, *The Spectacle of Nature: Landscape and Bourgeois Culture in Nineteenth-Century France* (Manchester: Manchester University Press, 1990).

For a departure from a simple view of Second Empire Paris as "extroverted," see Clark, *Painting of Modern Life.* Clark shows that Haussmann's Paris was associated as much with an ability to confound legible imagery as with the provision of ordered spectacle (47–50); ultimately, Clark understands Parisian imagery as a homogenizing substitute for real urban relations, Parisian spectacle as antithetical to "collective life" and "complex negotiation in the public realm," and as contemporary with "[t]he essential separation of public life from private, and the thorough invasion of both by capital" (64). In the art of Manet and other avant-garde painters who concentrated on Parisian subjects, Clark finds not only a dialectic between representations of the effacement of class relations and of their "resilience," but also a way of painting that undermined spectacle by presenting vision as fundamentally lacking (64, 72–76). For Clark, the separation of public life from private life and the intensification of public life through its commodification caused a more positive earlier version of the public to disappear.

In *Art Nouveau in Fin-de-Siècle France: Politics, Psychology, and Style* (Berkeley: University of California Press, 1989), Debora L. Silverman offers an interpretation of the Goncourt brothers' house in which she contends that the "impetus to create . . . [a] home as aristocratic fortress was the new invasive metropolis. . . . To struggle against this menace of invasive public life, the Goncourts enclosed themselves in a world of private interiors" (20). Though like Silverman I identify a Second Empire turn to the interior as "fortress," I disagree with her claims that such interiorization was idiosyncratic, that it depended on eighteenth-century aristocratic models, that it necessarily entailed feminization (34, 36), and that it represented a retreat from the city; rather, interiorization was given both a more recent and a much more ancient historical date; it required that the home be defined as masculine; and it acted on urban space in its entirety, making the notion of a retreat from the urban more complex than Silverman suggests.

For a sense of how the arguments I make in this chapter could be extended to the realm of visual culture, see Michael Fried's recent comments that interiority, not extroversion, defined the modernity of nineteenth-century French painting (*Manet's Modernism, or, The Face of Painting in the 1860s* [Chicago: University of Chicago Press, 1996]). In his reading of the painters he identifies as "The Generation of 1863" and of Edmond Duranty's 1876 critical essay on *La Nouvelle Peinture,* Fried displaces the usual association of modernity in painting with representations of exterior spaces coded as public. Fried notes that "for Duranty and other art critics of the 1860s and 1870s the effect of modernity was closely linked with representations of types [linked to the revival of the *physiologies* in the 1860s], and that in turn was faciliated, if indeed it was not made possible, by the evocation of the particular closed milieux—the absorptive worlds or cloisters—in which those types had their habitual . . . place" (259). After citing Duranty's description of modern drawing as depending on "the observation of the intimacy of man with his apartment" (260), Fried notes that Duranty's essay elaborates "a theory of the cloister into a theory of the *apartment,* or rather of the relation between the modern urban individual and the particular social spaces—interiors and streets—in which he or she was not just to be found but to be found imprinted, habituated, distracted, absorbed" (260); Duranty offers a vision of "a network of spaces which, for all their seeming openness and accessibility, were fundamentally *closed*" (261).

15. Michelle Perrot, "La ménagère dans l'espace parisien au XIXe siècle," *Annales de la recherche urbaine* 9 (1980): 7, 12, 16, 20; Siegfried Kracauer, *Orpheus in Paris: Offenbach and the Paris of His Time,* trans. Gwenda David and Eric Mosbacher (New York: Knopf, 1938), 25; Clark, *Painting of Modern Life,* 50–52, discusses the removal of work from the streets; see also Haine, *Paris Café,* 156; and J. Gaillard, *Paris: la ville,* 329–330.

16. Van Zanten, *Building Paris,* 217.

17. On the perspectival arrangement of streets under Haussmann, see Anthony Sutcliffe, *Paris: An Architectural History* (New Haven: Yale University Press, 1993), 86. Stylistic differences between apartment buildings and monuments became more marked during the Second Empire; see Sutcliffe (*Paris,* 88) and François Loyer (*Paris: Nineteenth-Century Architecture and Urbanism,* trans. Charles Lynn Clark [New York: Abbeville Press, 1988], 237–238), who argues that even though apartment buildings became larger under Haussmann (about one story taller) and hence more monumental in scale, the structural dif-

ferences between apartments and monuments increased: apartment buildings were attached in rows of uniform height (strictly enforced according to Haussmann's new building regulations), while monuments were free-standing, volumetric rather than planar, and architecturally unique.

18. As contemporary architectural critics have pointed out, when streets get wider and their function as bearers of traffic overrides all other uses, they both reduce the importance of the buildings that flank them and become spatially and phenomenologically independent of them. See William C. Ellis, "The Spatial Structure of Streets," in On Streets, ed. Stanford Anderson (Cambridge, Mass.: MIT Press, 1978), 115–118; and Joseph Rykwert, "The Street: The Use of Its History," in On Streets, ed. Stanford Anderson (Cambridge, Mass.: MIT Press, 1978), 14–16.

19. See Castex et al., Formes urbaines, 154, who write that as family life began to inscribe itself in distinct sites, in specialized neighborhoods within Paris and specialized rooms within the apartment, "housing itself [began to] function . . . in opposition to the exterior"; see also J. Gaillard, Paris: la ville, 531.

20. Charles Gourlier, "Des voies publiques et des maisons d'habitation à Paris," Encyclopédie d'architecture: journal mensuel, supplement to 2, no. 9 (1852): 73–96. Gourlier represented a solidly mainstream voice in both architecture and urbanism: trained at the Ecole des Beaux-Arts, he worked as an inspector general and belonged to the Société centrale des Architectes.

21. For examples of continuities between July Monarchy and Second Empire urban literature, see texts such as Maxime du Camp's six-volume Paris: ses organes, ses fonctions et sa vie dans la seconde moitié du XIXe siècle (1869–75), which anatomized Parisian history, geography, style, and social mores; several important collectively authored anthologies, such as Paris chez soi (1854), Paris et les parisiens au XIXe siècle (1856), and Paris-guide (1867); and the physiologies that enjoyed a brief period of renewal from 1866–69.

22. This transformation occurred gradually over the course of the 1850s. The points of view and techniques of July Monarchy writings on the city persisted in some cases into the 1850s. In 1854, for example, a tableau called Paris chez soi ("Par l'élite de la littérature contemporaine" [Paris: Boizard, 1854], 3) appeared; its title suggested the nascent interiorization of the city but its introductory chapter, entitled "A travers les rues," suggested the continued ease with which writers could speak interchangeably of homes and streets. Significantly, this volume also maintained the generic tradition of emblazoning the "example of the Diable boiteux . . . the immortal Asmodeus" across its opening pages.

23. Léo Lespès [pseud. Timothée Trimm], Spectacles vus de ma fenêtre (Paris: Faure, 1866).

24. Attesting to the sale value of words connoting domesticity, two collections of stories by Emile Souvestre that had little or nothing to do with home life carried the titles Les Anges du foyer (Paris: Michel Lévy, 1858) and Les Anges du logis (Pont-à-Mousson: Haugenthal, 1859).

25. On the transition from July Monarchy to Second Empire views of the city in Balzac and Baudelaire, see Ferguson, who writes (Paris as Revolution, 94), "Balzac's controlling narrator gives way to Baudelaire's anguished poet, for whom exploration of the city is a pretext for exploration of the self."

26. Emile Souvestre, *Un Philosophe sous les toits: journal d'un homme heureux* (Paris: Michel Lévy, 1850), 1, 6.

27. Ibid., 31.

28. Ibid., 29–34. The narrator's assimilation of every episode and character that he observes into a reflection, a *miroir* of his own personal dilemma (whether to choose an ambitious new job or remain content with his old one) also contributes to his interiorization of the city's heterogeneity into the homogeneity of his own consciousness. Baudelaire took up the observation of others through a window as a version of self-observation and self-creation in the prose poem "Les Fenêtres" (in *Le Spleen de Paris: petits poèmes en prose* [1869; Paris: Livres de Poche, 1972], 139–140). "Intérieur," a poem by Emile Villars (in *Le Roman de la parisienne [Mélange]* [Paris: Librairie centrale, 1866], 61, 64), similarly incorporated spaces that earlier writers had conceived of as exterior into a single, encapsulating unit. Villars takes up the familiar theme of a man observing a woman in a building that faces his own. The device of repeating every stanza's first line in its last enforces each stanza's unity by enclosing the varied intervening lines between identical phrases. The first stanza immediately asserts the virtual nonexistence of any visual barrier between the two apartments, which become united by the ubiquity of the observing "I": "Je la vois sans qu'elle s'en doute, / Le soir, derrière la redoute / D'un store presque aérien, / Haut rempart qui ne défend rien. / Je la vois sans qu'elle s'en doute." Though the poem thus begins like a July Monarchy seduction story, it departs from those conventions by concluding with the narrator's sensory incorporation of his neighbor's apartment rather than with any actual movement into it: the narrator does not finally see into his neighbor's apartment, nor enter it; instead, he hears what takes place in it. The poem's final stanza begins and ends with the line, "Plus rien. J'entends le lit craquer [Nothing more. I hear her bed creak]," suggesting that though the woman still occupies a physically separate interior, the poet has incorporated it into his own perceptual apparatus without having physically entered it.

29. Louis Jacquier, *L'Amour à Paris* (Paris: Chez tous les libraires, 1862), 147–148, 155–156. Narrower streets would have been associated with Paris before Haussmann.

30. Villars, "Intérieur."

31. Léo Lespès, "La Guerre des fenêtres: journal du siège d'une jolie femme," in *Paris dans un fauteuil: types, histoires et physionomies* (Paris: Lasalle, 1855), 21–35.

32. Edmond Texier, *Le Tableau de Paris* (Paris: Paulin et Le Chevalier, 1852–53), 56, 276.

33. Victor Fournel (*Ce qu'on voit dans les rues de Paris* [Paris: Delahays, 1858], 263, 261) writes that the *badaud* is a "mobile daguerrotype . . . who retains the slightest traces and in whom the city reproduces its movement and the public spirit reproduces its multiple physiognomy."

34. Jean François Eugène Robinet, *"Finissons Paris!" Observations sur l'édilité moderne* (Paris: Ritti, 1879), 12.

35. Théophile Gautier, "Mosaïque de ruines," in *Paris et les parisiens au XIXe siècle* (Paris: Morizot, 1856), 40. The journalist Fournel, author of several works on Paris, combined the economic and the ecological narratives when he

wrote in 1865 that "what the administration, in enlarging the streets, has given the city in terms of air, landlords have taken away in even larger measure by shrinking apartments. . . . [T]he vastness and multiplicity of the new roads has whittled away at space everywhere" (Victor Fournel, *Paris nouveau et Paris futur* [Paris: Lecoffre, 1865], 61).

36. The complete quote is "Never, in any era, has there been less interior and familial virtue than today. Everything that one used to give to intimate affections, to domestic duties, now is transferred to insane and completely exterior ambitions" (Nestor Roqueplan, *Regain: la vie parisienne* [Paris: Librairie nouvelle, 1853], 44).

37. Gustave Claudin, *Paris* (Paris: Dentu, 1862), 80.

38. Alfred Delvau, *Histoire anecdotique des cafés et cabarets de Paris* (Paris: Dentu, 1862), v.

39. Although cafés began to put tables out on the street during this period, the majority of seats were still located inside the building and writers continued to refer to even the largest café as a *maison*. See, for example, Gustave Claudin, *Entre minuit et une heure: étude parisienne* (Paris: Dentu, 1868), 29.

40. Alfred Delvau, *Les Dessous de Paris* (Paris: Poulet-Malassis, 1860), 3–5, 8, 133–135.

41. Fournel, *Paris nouveau*, 61, 71.

42. Pariset's advice (Mme Pariset, *Encyclopédie des dames: manuel de la maîtresse de maison, ou lettres sur l'économie domestique* [Paris: Audot, 1821], 4, 8) on economizing, on choosing and furnishing an apartment, on supervising servants, and on cooking and dressing, emphasized qualities also considered essential to governing or running a business: spatial and temporal regulation, "order" and "regularity." Pariset's use of an administrative metaphor to describe the housewife's financial duties also rendered women's work equivalent to bourgeois men's: "Consider yourself," a friend tells a prospective bride, "a true minister of the interior, and never neglect the direction of your administration." The tendency to equate the home with a political office appeared in other domestic manuals written during the 1820s. Marie-Armande Gacon-Dufour's *Manuel complète de la maîtresse de maison . . . ou guide pratique pour la gestion d'une maison à ville et à la campagne* (Paris: Roret, 1826) indicated by its very title that the work of the home differed little from work in an administrative or commercial concern—all required skilled *gestion,* a noun meaning management or administration with legal, political, and financial connotations. The 1828 reedition of that work emphasized the financial rewards of the housewife's expertise; its subtitle was *Guide pratique pour la gestion d'une maison et de la parfaite ménagère, ou guide pratique pour la gestion d'une maison à la ville et à la campagne, contenant les moyens d'y maintenir le bon ordre et d'y établir l'abondance,* 2d ed., rev. and expanded by Mme Celnart (Paris: Roret, 1828). Gacon-Dufour's 1826 text opened with an aphorism: "Every mistress of a house probably has her *régime d'administration*" (1). The use of a term as redolent of bureaucratic politics as *régime d'administration* suggested that the housewife performed work equivalent to her husband's; the use of the generalizing adjective *toute* suffused the statement with an imperative, universalizing force that identified all housewives as a class of worker.

43. Pariset wrote of "the imperious sentiment which a woman must feel for her home [*son chez-elle*]" but argued that women experienced a "need to stay in or return to" their homes only because they had made them into private paradises for themselves, not for their families: "she must feel [*se trouver*] better there than anywhere else; she must stay there as much as possible." The use of the imperative word "must [*doit*]" lends authority to this prescription for self-indulgence, while the reflexive form "*se* trouver" emphasizes the self-pleasuring, self-sufficient character of this location (ibid., 23).

44. Mme Pariset, *Nouveau manuel complet de la maîtresse de maison, suivi d'un appendice par Mesdames Gacon-Dufour, Celnart* (Paris: Roret, 1852), 288.

45. Ibid., 315. For a discussion of how domestic manuals targeted women for the inculcation of new standards of cleanliness, see Geneviève Heller, "*Propre en ordre*": *habitation et vie domestique 1850–1930 —l'exemple vaudois* (Lausanne: Editions d'en bas, 1979). On changes in bourgeois attitudes toward dirt, see Alain Corbin, *The Foul and the Fragrant: Odor and the French Social Imagination* (Cambridge, Mass.: Harvard University Press, 1986).

46. La comtesse de Bassanville, *Le Trésor de la maison: guide des femmes économes* (Paris: Brumet, 1867), 35.

47. Louise d'Alq, *La Vie intime*, 2d ed. (Paris: Bureaux des *Causeries familières*, 1881), ix; *La Science de la vie: conseils et réflexions à l'usage de tous* (Paris: Bureaux des *Causeries familières*, n.d.), 206–207.

48. La comtesse de Bassanville, *L'Art de bien tenir une maison* (Paris: Librairie H. Aniéré, 1878).

49. Julie Fertiault, *Le Ménagier français* (Paris: Bureaux du Conseiller des Dames et des Demoiselles, 1863), 7.

50. De Bassanville, *Trésor de la maison*, 6; and *Art de bien tenir*, 2.

51. M. G. Belèze, *Le Livre des ménages: nouveau manuel d'économie domestique* (Paris: Hachette, 1860), 365; Adolphe Puissant, *De l'économie domestique et de l'éducation dans les classes ouvrières* (Paris: Baillière, 1872), 7.

52. D'Alq, *Le Maître et la maîtresse de la maison* (Paris: Bureaux des *Causeries familières*, n.d), 14.

53. On the importance of statistics to nineteenth-century French government, see Joan Wallach Scott, "A Statistical Representation of Work: *La Statistique de l'industrie à Paris, 1847–1848*," in *Gender and the Politics of History* (New York: Columbia University Press, 1988), 113–138; Scott emphasizes that statistics are representations of social order, and as such help to create it. My account of the public health movement in this paragraph and the following one is drawn from Catherine Kudlick, *Cholera in Post-Revolutionary Paris: A Cultural History* (Berkeley: University of California Press, 1996), 65–103; Ann-Louise Shapiro, *Housing the Poor of Paris, 1850–1902* (Madison: University of Wisconsin Press, 1985), 2–22; and Andrew Aisenberg, "Contagious Disease and the Government of Paris in the Age of Pasteur" (Ph.D. dissertation, Yale University, 1993).

54. The Conseil de Salubrité was founded in 1802; the Commission des Logements insalubres was founded in 1851. The prefect of the Seine was in charge of infrastructural improvements, including embellishments, water sup-

ply, sewage, and roads, while the prefect of the police enforced public health legislation and also gathered much statistical information.

55. On the connection between private property and citizenship, see, for example, Roger-Henri Guerrand, *Les Origines du logement social en France* (Paris: Éditions ouvrières, 1967), 17–19. J. Gaillard (*Paris: la ville,* 27–28) discusses the ways that landlords, heavily represented in the magistrature, resisted governmental initiatives that clashed with strict interpretations of the rights of private property.

56. Andrew Aisenberg, "Contagious Poverty" (manuscript, 1995), 28. For the ways in which the private sphere was a creation of the state, see also Elinor Accampo, "Gender, Social Policy, and the Formation of the Third Republic: An Introduction," in *Gender and the Politics of Social Reform in France, 1870–1914,* ed. Elinor Accampo, Rachel Fuchs, and Mary Lynn Stewart (Baltimore: Johns Hopkins University Press, 1995), 1–27.

57. See Henri Bayard, *Mémoire sur la topographie médicale des Xe, XIe et XIIe arrondissements de la ville de Paris* (Paris: Baillière, 1844), 17–18; and Claude Lachaise, *Topographie médicale de Paris* (Paris: Baillière, 1822), 133. Lachaise wrote that he would not discuss interiors because "the authorities cannot extend their surveillance that far," although he also argued that overcrowding caused illness, thus anticipating later interventions by doctors into the homes of workers and the poor.

58. Lachaise, *Topographie,* 120, 129.

59. "[A] house has few drawbacks when its openings are spacious, there is good ventilation inside, and it is exposed to the sun"(P[ierre] A[dolphe] Piorry, *Des habitations et de l'influence de leurs dispositions sur l'homme, en santé et en maladie* [Paris: Pourchet, 1838], 42–43, 53). See also the annual reports of the Conseil de Salubrité, which from 1840–45 exhibited a steadily increasing concern with interiors as distinct objects of investigation but included dwellings under the rubric of "public hygiene" and discussed them in terms of infrastructural elements such as chimneys and heating systems without citing evidence gathered from direct observation of individual apartments (*Rapports généraux des travaux du conseil de Salubrité pendant les années 1840 à 1845 inclusivement,* published by order of M. le pair de France, préfet de Police [Paris: Bouquin, 1847]). Like Piorry, the authors of these reports emphasized the importance of constructing apartments so that air and light could easily pass in and out of them (310).

60. Michel Lévy, *Traité d'hygiène publique et privée* (Paris: Baillière, 1844), 1:544.

61. Ibid., 549.

62. Ibid.

63. Adolphe Lance, *Rapport sur la proposition de M. Harvu-Romain, relative à l'assainissement des habitations insalubres,* 2d ed. (Amiens: Caron, 1851), 1, 5.

64. Ibid., 10. Lance acknowledged the importance of the street as a source of air but couched that acknowledgment in terms of an analogy that interiorized the street: "streets are to cities what lungs are to the human body" (12). The

anthropomorphism of the city-as-human-body reduced even the most external elements of that organism to internalized ones.

65. See Kristin Ross (*The Emergence of Social Space: Rimbaud and the Paris Commune* [Minneapolis: University of Minnesota Press, 1988], 4; see also 38), who includes among the Commune's revolutionary effects on spatial organization "the relationship of Paris to the provinces, the Commune as immense 'rent strike,' the post-Haussmann social division of the city and the question of who, among its citizens, has a 'right to the city' . . . or the military and tactical use of city space during the street fighting," and a commitment to horizontality, which symbolized a contestation of social hierarchies. For a discussion of how the Commune and its aftermath sharpened the antagonism between landlords and tenants, especially working-class tenants, see Guerrand, *Origines du logement,* 183–184, 234.

66. J.-B. Fonssagrives, *La Maison: étude d'hygiène et de bien-être domestiques* (Montpellier: Gras, 1871), vi–viii, 68, 67, 61. On the bourgeois equation of revolution, disease, and Paris, see Kudlick, *Cholera.*

67. Lance, *Rapport,* 2.

68. Emile Muller and Emile Cacheux, introduction to *Les Habitations ouvrières en tous pays: situation en 1878—avenir* (Paris: Rejey, 1879), iv.

69. Frédéric Le Play, *Les Ouvriers européens: études sur les travaux, la vie domestique et la condition morale des populations ouvrières de l'Europe* (Paris: Imprimerie impériale, 1855), 36.

70. Ibid.

71. For the conjunction of *promiscuité* and *malpropreté,* see Octave du Mesnil, *Les Garnis insalubres de la ville de Paris, rapport fait à la commission des logements insalubres* (Paris: Baillière, 1878), 2.

72. Louis Lazare, *Les Quartiers pauvres de Paris* (Paris: Bibliothèque municipale, 1869), 65.

73. Lucas, *Compte rendu,* 27. On liberalism and the hygienists' insistence that women confine themselves to the interior, see Aisenberg, "Contagious Poverty." On French Republican legislation that limited women's right to work, see Accampo, "Gender, Social Policy," 9.

74. Friedrich Engels, *The Housing Question,* ed. C. P. Dutt (New York: International, n.d.), 22. Engels refuted the analogy that "petty-bourgeois socialism" made between wage workers and tenants, arguing that housing shortages did not affect workers as a *class,* but as people with less money to spend on housing: when workers had adequate money, housing shortages posed no problem for them, but the surplus value created by their labor was always appropriated, no matter how high their wages.

75. "In order to create the modern revolutionary class of the proletariat, it was absolutely necessary to cut the umbilical cord which still bound the worker of the past to the land"; the proletarian who is "completely propertyless . . . [is] liberated from all traditional fetters and *free as a bird*"(ibid., 28; see also 17).

76. Ibid., 54.

77. Ibid., 34, 33.

78. On the architectural press during the second half of the nineteenth cen-

tury, particularly César Daly's *Revue générale de l'architecture* (1840–90), see Marc Saboya, *Presse et architecture au XIXe siècle: César Daly et "la Revue générale de l'architecture et des travaux publics"* (Paris: Picard, 1991), esp. 69–85.

79. See, for example, an article by the architect and archeologist Albert Lenoir in *Les Hôtels historiques de Paris,* ed. Georges Bonnefons (Paris: Lecou, 1852), xi, in which he used the image of the mirror to figure the perfect unity between architecture and social customs that would in turn guarantee continuity from one generation to the next: "No art is more subject than architecture to moral influences; it is a mirror in which morals are reflected and thus transmitted to future generations."

80. *La Propriété: journal des intérêts de tous,* April 16, 1848, 1.

81. Emile Cardon, *L'Art au foyer domestique (la décoration de l'appartement)* (Paris: Renouard, 1884), 95.

82. Léonce Reynaud, *Traité d'architecture* (Paris: Librairie pour l'architecture, 1858), 2:522.

83. Charles Blanc, *Grammaire des arts décoratifs; décoration intérieure de la maison* (Paris: Renouard, 1882), 137.

84. Ibid., 69. Blanc also banned decorative inscriptions on floors, an interdiction that may have been related to the presence of writing as an index of the difference between public and private buildings; monuments had always been defined in part by the words inscribed upon them, and by the early 1890s writing, particularly signatures, had become the criterion for differentiating between signed *édifices publiques* and unsigned *édifices privés*.

85. César Daly, "De l'architecture domestique monumentale," *Revue générale de l'architecture* 1, no. 4 (April 1840): 203.

86. Ibid., 17, 19. Daly thus praised the *hôtel* for allowing rooms devoted to *l'intimité* to be separated by floor from rooms that were "blended with the exterior world by virtue of our relationships, either of business or of pleasure . . . that is to say, public"(15). In his hierarchy of apartment buildings, first-class buildings were built on block-size lots and had only one apartment per floor; their facades abounded with framing elements that differentiated separate apartments from one another; and Daly's floor plans for them accentuated their aura of privacy by eliminating any sign of the servant's quarters that were actually present. Second-class buildings had shops on the ground floor, more than one apartment per floor, and facades that expressed the demarcations among floors less clearly. Third-class apartments had more apartments both per building and per floor than the other two classes and brought bedrooms into closer contact with dining rooms and salons.

87. Eugène Emmanuel Viollet-le-Duc, *Entretiens sur l'architecture* (Paris: Morel, 1863), 272, 281.

88. Cardon also wrote that "Parisian dwellings . . . put the tenant in the greatest possible contact with the public way" (Cardon, *L'Art au foyer domestique,* 9).

89. Viollet-le-Duc, *Entretiens,* 305.

90. Eugène Emmanuel Viollet-le-Duc, *Habitations modernes* (1875; Brussels: Mardaga, 1979), 2.

91. For a sociological study of Parisian landlords that charts patterns of property-ownership throughout the nineteenth century, see Daumard, *Maisons de Paris*.

92. César Daly, *L'Architecture privée au XIXe siècle sous Napoléon III* (Paris: Ducher, 1864), 1:17.

93. Ibid., 14–15.

94. On the recourse of architectural historians to explanations in terms of origins, see Joseph Rykwert, *On Adam's House in Paradise: The Idea of the Primitive Hut in Architectural History*, 2d ed. (Cambridge, Mass.: MIT Press, 1989).

95. Bonnefons, ed., *Hôtels historiques*. On the expanded demand for architecture books, see Malcolm Daniel, *The Photographs of Edouard Baldus* (New York: Metropolitan Museum of Art, 1994), 117.

96. Reynaud, *Traité*, 13.

97. Charles Garnier and A. Ammann, *L'Habitation humaine* (Paris: Hachette, 1892), 779–780, 798.

98. Cardon, *Art au foyer*, 37. Cardon reiterates this sentiment again on 117. See also Oscar Riz-Paquot, who opened his *Art de bâtir, meubler et entretenir sa maison, ou manière de surveiller et d'être soi-même architecte-entrepreneur-ouvrier* (Paris: Laurens, n.d [ca.1890]), v, by citing a paternal adage about the importance of the single-family house: "To each his own house, was a saying of our fathers, and they were perfectly correct: man does not truly feel happy until he has a home of his own, a house where he reigns as lord and master."

99. Daly, *Architecture privée*, 1:13.

100. Eugène Emmanuel Viollet-le-Duc, *Histoire d'une maison* (Paris: Hetzel, n.d. [1873]).

101. Daly, *Architecture privée*, 10. Viollet-le-Duc also employed the metaphorical series house-clothing-shelter in *Histoire d'une maison*, 28: "the habitat should be, for man or for his family, a garment made to his measure, and . . . when a lodging is in perfect accord with the manners and habits of those whom it shelters underneath its roof, it is excellent."

102. Bonnefons, ed., *Hôtels historiques*, xii.

103. Ferdinand de Lasteyrie, "Edilité parisienne," *L'opinion nationale*, April 11, 1861.

104. Théodore Vacquer, *Maisons les plus remarquables à Paris construites pendant les trois dernières années* (Paris: Caudrilier, 1860–1870), 26.

105. Viollet-le-Duc, *Entretiens*, 2:210, 212. Note that those criteria also differentiated the apartment house from the individual family home, since only the latter promoted the long-term occupancy that enabled the facade and the interior walls to "always carry the stamp of its owner's habits" (ibid., 305).

5. Zola's Restless House

1. See, for example, André Fermigier, preface to *Pot-Bouille* (Paris: Gallimard, 1982), 7–19.

2. Emile Zola, *Pot-Bouille*, preface by François Nourissier, notes by Pierre Marotte (Paris: Livres de Poche, 1984), 11. All further references to this edition will appear in the text followed by page number, and all translations are my own.

Pot-Bouille was first published in serial form in *Le Gaulois;* several passages appeared in the first published edition (Paris: Charpentier, 1882) that had been expurgated from the newspaper edition.

3. Indeed, some critics have suggested that all of Zola's novels are essentially claustrophobic and interiorizing. Lewis Kamm, for example ("The Structural and Functional Manifestation of Space in Zola's *Rougon-Macquart," Nineteenth-Century French Studies* 3, nos. 33–34 [spring–summer 1975]: 224), takes as fundamental "Zola's propensity to portray closed spatial worlds in which characters and events often seem imprisoned within rigidly defined limits."

4. Quoted in Henri Mitterand, *"Notice"* to *Pot-Bouille* (Paris: Gallimard, 1982), 464.

5. Brian Nelson, *Zola and the Bourgeoisie: A Study of Themes and Techniques in "Les Rougon-Macquart"* (Totowa, N.J.: Barnes and Noble, 1983), 131, 132, 140, 145; emphasis added.

6. Janice Best, *Expérimentation et adaptation: essai sur la méthode naturaliste d'Emile Zola* (Paris: Corti, 1986), 114.

7. Henri Céard, review of *Pot-Bouille,* in *La Vie moderne,* July 1, 1882, quoted in Colette Becker's preface to *Pot-Bouille* in *Les Rougon-Macquart: histoire naturelle et sociale d'une famille sous le Second Empire,* ed. Colette Becker (Paris: Robert Laffont, 1992), 3:360.

8. Kenneth Cornell's suggestion ("Zola's City," *Yale French Studies* 32 [1964]: 108) that "Zola's most memorable achievement in the presentation of Paris comes from his use of the multiple-family dwelling" has been disregarded by most subsequent critics.

9. Information on *Pot-Bouille's* print run comes from Elisabeth Parinet, "La librairie Flammarion, 1875–1914," quoted in Jean-Yves Mollier, "Emile Zola et le système éditorial français," *Les Cahiers naturalistes* 67 (1993): 260.

10. Jean Borie (*Zola et les mythes, ou de la nausée au salut* [Paris: Editions du Seuil, 1971], 129) comments generally that "the *Rougon-Macquart's* house may shelter a secret: that the opposition of public and private is after all merely the 'interiorization' of a more general opposition that isolates the entire edifice and separates the inside from the outside." Philip Solomon argues ("The Space of Bourgeois Hypocrisy in Zola's *Pot-Bouille," Kentucky Romance Quarterly* 32, no. 3 [1985]: 256) that the novel's opening establishes the apartment house as a "refuge" from the street, a space of secure interiority. He remarks that the distinction between apartment and street quickly breaks down, a point I develop further on.

11. On windows in *Les Rougon-Macquart* and Zola's other fiction, see Borie, *Zola,* 203; John C. Lapp, "The Watcher Betrayed and the Fatal Woman: Some Recurring Patterns in Zola," *PMLA* 74, no. 3 (June 1959): 276–284; Jacques Noiray, "La Symbolique de l'espace dans *La Curée," L'Information littéraire* 39, no. 1 (1987): 17; Naomi Schor, "Zola: From Window to Window," *Yale French Studies* 42 (1969): 39, 47; and Philip Walker, "The Mirror, the Window, and the Eye in Zola's Fiction," *Yale French Studies* 42 (1969): 52–67.

12. Nelson (*Zola,* 140) and Solomon ("Bourgeois Hypocrisy," 257) thus oversimplify when they state, respectively, that the doors "mirror" and the stairway "reflects" the hidden lives of the building's occupants.

13. François Nourissier (introduction to *Pot-Bouille* in *Oeuvres complètes d'Emile Zola,* ed. Henri Mitterand [Paris: Cercle du livre précieux, 1966], 4:369) views *Pot-Bouille* as essentially a novel about Octave's urban ambitions, summarizing its plot quite simply as "a young man conquers Paris." The summary of *Pot-Bouille* in *Le Docteur Pascal* (ed. Jean Borie [Paris: Garnier-Flammarion, 1975], 153) puts it similarly: "Octave Mouret . . . the audacious conqueror, sharp-witted, determined to wrest from women the kingship of Paris." For a discussion of Balzac's conquering Parisian hero, see Franco Moretti, *The Way of the World: The Bildungsroman in European Culture* (London: Verso, 1987), 133, 165, which argues that a character like Rastignac becomes fully identified with the city's "boundlessness and speed" and with the "dynamism, change, novelty" that capitalism equates with desire.

14. As we saw earlier, Janice Best (*Expérimentation,* 114) argues that the high point of Octave's urban conquest coincides with his accession to the innermost spaces of the apartment: "The novel's center (chapters 9 and 10) coincides . . . with the moment when Octave gains access to the actual center of the house and prepares to discover its secrets."

15. Although the presence of a store on the ground floor of the apartment building sets it apart referentially from the Haussmann-era apartments described in the previous chapter, as a plot device the store allows the narrative to keep more characters inside the building, since they do not have to leave it to go to work. The novel thus reverses the meaning ascribed to domestic self-containment by the discourses described in the preceding chapter.

16. Albert Wolff, review of *Pot-Bouille* in *Le Figaro,* April 22, 1882, quoted in *Oeuvres complètes d'Emile Zola,* ed. Eugène Fasquelle, notes by Maurice Le Blond (Paris: François Bernouard, 1927), 11:453. On the centrality of the "opposition between home and house" for bourgeois fiction, see Naomi Schor, *Zola's Crowds* (Baltimore: Johns Hopkins University Press, 1978), 99.

17. The porter and landlord even extend their horror of strange women invading their residence to a single woman worker who does live in the building, but whose presence strikes them as scandalous, particularly when her pregnancy begins to show. M. Gourd insists on removing this "stain" on the building and has her evicted in her eighth month of pregnancy.

18. At a social event where Saturnin's kicks overpower Berthe's music, the narrator comments that Mme Josserand's brother, M. Bachelard, "had scandalously disturbed *les bords de l'Oise* by making remarks aloud" (69); on another occasion, we read that "in the back of the neighboring room, one heard Saturnin's snores" (104). Mme Josserand also functions as a figure for an overly acute hearing that transcends the physical and social barriers that should make certain sounds inaccessible: on one occasion "she bent her ear toward the ceiling, as if she wanted to hear, through the mezzanine, what was happening on the first floor" (250–251); on another the narrator remarks upon her entrance into a room that "probably, she had been listening at the door" (282).

19. Borie, *Zola,* 138.

20. Solomon ("Bourgeois Hypocrisy," 260) describes this episode as "domesticating" adultery.

21. Borie, *Zola,* 150.

22. Emile Zola, "L'Adultère dans la bourgeoisie," in *L'Encre et le sang*, ed. Henri Mitterand (Paris: Editions complexe, 1989), 220, 221, 222, 228, 230.

23. On the *fêlure* in general, see Borie, *Zola*; on female sexuality in Zola as *fêlure*, see Janet Beizer, "The Body in Question: Anatomy, Textuality, and Fetishism in Zola," *L'Esprit créateur* 29, no. 1 (1989): 50–60. Beizer suggests that *Pot-Bouille* connects the feminine *fêlure* to metaphors of dirt and "transubstantiat[es]" it into a "juxtaposed stream of gossip and dirty dish water" (51).

24. On physiognomy in Balzac and Zola, see Christopher Rivers, *Face Value: Physiognomical Thought and The Legible Body in Marivaux, Lavater, Balzac, Gautier, and Zola* (Madison: University of Wisconsin Press, 1994). Rivers notes that "[t]he relation between Zola and physiognomy is neither explicit nor obvious, as was the case . . . with Balzac"; he then analyzes the relationship between Zola's naturalist aesthetics and physiognomic reading; and finally, shows that *Nana* is about the "impossibility (or at least limitation)" of physiognomic readings of the body, and hence "is in direct contradiction to Zola's positivistic theory of the experimental novel" (175, 191). Rivers's claim that the female body becomes particularly illegible in *Nana* resonates with my reading of female bodies in *Pot-Bouille*, but in the latter novel women's bodies are not utterly unreadable; rather, they are legible as false.

25. As Borie notes (*Zola*, 143), "[t]he 'severe' facade, the 'decent' staircase, the 'chaste' door, far from securing their functions as guards and judges, far from preserving and forbidding, or worse, remaining neutral, become what they are, inert things, wood and plaster."

26. Several male characters in the novel have notably grotesque bodies, particularly M. Duveyrier, whose skin eruptions become compounded by a deviated jawbone resulting from a botched suicide attempt. Though the novel thus does not confine its attributions of decaying bodies to women, this example confirms that the novel specifically associates the *deceptive* body with women, since Duveyrier's ugliness does correspond precisely to his inner moral state.

27. As Fermigier remarks (preface to *Pot-Bouille*, 12), the apartment house in the novel follows the stylistic laws laid down during the Second Empire for new domestic architecture in that it is "above all an architecture of facades." He argues that the building's need to "appear" corresponds to that of its female inhabitants (16). Nelson (*Zola*, 140) suggests a similar correspondence between female bodies and domestic architecture when he writes that "the closed doors and introverted apartments of *Pot-Bouille* mirror the inviolable bodies of the bourgeois ladies within them." My reading differs from Nelson's on the question of whether these doors are closed or open; I argue that the novel establishes the importance of interiority only in order to highlight the ways in which bourgeois women's bodies and the apartment building *fail* to be closed structures. Symptomatic of the particular way in which Nelson misreads this aspect of the text is his account, in this context, of Mme Campardon as suffering from a "vaginal constriction" (140). Nothing in the text, however, specifies the precise nature of her gynecological problems, which could consist just as easily of excessive discharges as of excessive closure.

28. N.A. fr. 10321, fol. 1, quoted in Elliott M. Grant, "The Political Scene in Zola's *Pot-Bouille*," *French Studies* 8, no. 3 (July 1954): 346.

29. *Pot-Bouille* thus contradicts Borie's generalization (*Zola*, 162) that in the *Rougon-Macquart*, "sin marks" and "leaves an ineffable trace."

30. Susan Yates points out that Lisa teaches Angèle how to control her *regard* in this way and that the two women develop a language of secret gestures that does not correspond to the words they speak in the presence of other people (*Maid and Mistress: Feminine Solidarity and Class Difference in Five Nineteenth-Century French Novels* [New York: Peter Lang, 1991], 115).

31. Though never a hysteric, Mme Duveyrier similarly divides the "regular and continuous movement" of her hands from her focused "intelligence," since she reads while playing piano scales, "without causing the mechanism of her fingers to sustain the least slackening" (363).

32. Valérie's affair with the butcher also provides another instance of the outside invading the bourgeois interior. In an article on Bataille and Zola ("Bloody Sundays," *Representations* 28 [fall 1989]: 77–89), Denis Hollier argues that urban modernization requires moving the death and violence of the slaughterhouse to the outskirts of the city. He explains that Zola opposed Haussmannization because it made the city a place of leisure rather than a pure space of productive work. Extrapolating from Hollier's analysis, I note that Valérie's adulterous *flânerie* and her reproductive liaison with a butcher, both of which take place within central Paris, become in Zola's novel signs of a bourgeois and feminine mode of urban degeneration.

33. Zola had expressed his disapproval of lesbianism in his preface to Adolphe Belot, *Mademoiselle Giraud ma femme* (Paris: Dentu, 1879), in which he described sex between women as a "vice," "monstrous," and a "crime" (iii, iv, viii). In his outline for *Pot-Bouille*, Zola speculated that he would either have Lisa put Angèle in sexual contact with Gustave "or pervert her as a lesbian." He originally intended this action to take place on the servants' floor, which contains single rooms; his decision to locate it in Angèle's room places it centrally in the bourgeois, familial interior (N.A. fr. 10319, fol. 253, quoted in Lapp, "Watcher Betrayed," 282).

This imitation of heterosexual relations by two women repeats an earlier instance where Mme Josserand imitates a prospective husband in order to teach her daughter, Berthe, how to flirt with men (51). While Berthe proves an inept pupil and that scene ends with her mother angrily slapping her (52), Lisa and Angèle are mutually enthusiastic mimics who share a "rabid intimacy"—a *rage d'intimité* (30). Both cases undermine the dignity of the husband-cum-patriarch.

34. The ease with which this passage can be misread was indicated by a reviewer who cited the undignified inversion of Vabre's body in a long list of *Pot-Bouille*'s challenges to the reader's disbelief; in a response, Zola corrected the misreading. This exchange, which took place in the pages of *Gil Blas*, April 27, 1882, is reprinted in the Becker edition of Zola's *Rougon-Macquart*, 3:1482–1488.

35. It is also important to note that the entire novel is written under the sign of paternal collapse, since Octave Mouret bears the legacy of his father, who, as Schor (*Zola's Crowds*, 38) puts it in her commentary on *La Conquête du Plassans*, "is supplanted as master of the family, dispossessed as owner of the house."

36. The narrator describes his death in terms of the negative interiorization that, as we have seen, characterizes apartment-house life—his honesty "suffo-

cated him" and he departs "strangled." As his final utterance, "he stammered Saturnin's name," singling out the character who most exemplifies oscillation between imprisonment and explosion (427).

37. Emile Zola, letter of January 29, 1882, in *Correspondance,* ed. B. H. Bakker (Montreal: Presses de l'Université de Montréal, 1978), 4:261–262.

38. Ibid., 262. Zola adds that had the novel appeared first in book form, the name of a character would belong also to the publisher who possessed clear property rights in the thousands of copies of books she or he printed. Pitting the bearer of the name against the producer of the book, he wrote: "In the face of his name, which is his property, there would be the books, which would be the property of the publisher" (264). Duverdy's lawyer won the case by arguing that while in general novelists must be allowed to use real names, a novelist as obscene as Zola could not. Zola responded by affirming the force of future generations, which he made his own with the collective possessive pronoun; though he could not seek reparations for the lawyer's slander in any contemporary court, there was, he asserted, "a court . . . [of] last resort: I mean our children" (276).

39. Zola, *Oeuvres complètes,* ed. Fasquelle, 11:434.

40. In an article on "La Propriété littéraire" (in ibid., 41:81–82), Zola worked out the similarities and differences between literary property and other kinds of property in terms of paternal legacies. Though the literary work, he wrote, had finally become "real property," it was still only a limited property because copyright lasted no longer than fifty years after the author's death, "so that the direct heirs, if there are any, find themselves despoiled . . . legally dispossessed." Zola likened this dispossession to being "expropriated" for the sake of "public utility," invoking the expropriations of private property (often residential) during Haussmann's prefecture to juxtapose the dilution of literary property and the compromised property available to owners of apartment houses.

41. Emile Zola, "Le Roman expérimental" (1879), in *Le Roman expérimental* (Paris: Garnier-Flammarion, 1971), 63.

42. Zola, "Le Naturalisme au théâtre" (1881), in ibid., 150; Georg Lukács, "The Zola Centenary," in *Critical Essays on Emile Zola,* ed. David Baguley (Boston: G.K. Hall, 1986), 84. This version of naturalism was expressed most forcefully in attacks on it. For example, Ferdinand Brunetière's review of *Pot-Bouille* ("A propos de *Pot-Bouille,*" in *Le Roman naturaliste,* 7th ed. [Paris: Calmann-Lévy, 1896], 295) took naturalism to task for reducing observation to a completely external view of human relations and cautioned that "observation does not consist solely of knowing how to open one's eyes to the exterior world, as they think at Medan . . . it is the interior that must be reached." Edmond Goncourt's comments on *Pot-Bouille* in his journal (entries of February 2, 1882, and February 17, 1882, quoted in Henri Guillemin, *Présentation des "Rougon-Macquart"* [Paris: NRF Gallimard, 1964], 197–198) criticized it for taking external observation so far that it became secondhand and the novelist himself disappeared completely from the scene observed, even as an invisible voyeur or eavesdropper; he called *Pot-Bouille* a novel "manufactured 'not out of observations, but out of hearsay [*racontars*]'" and referred to it as "this *Pot-Bouille,* with tales made up by disciples, without a scene observed from nature, without a word heard or understood [*sans une parole entendue*]."

43. Schor, *Zola's Crowds,* 132.

44. Quoted in Emile Zola, *Les Rougon-Macquart,* ed. Henri Mitterand (Paris: Gallimard, Bibliothèque de la Pléiade, 1964), 3:1624.

45. Albert Wolff, "Courrier de Paris," *Le Figaro,* April 22, 1882, quoted in *Les Rougon-Macquart,* ed. Becker, 3:1477; Henri Fouquier [Nestor], review of *Pot-Bouille, Gil Blas,* April 27, 1882, in ibid., 1482.

46. Zola, "Roman expérimental," 63.

47. Zola attempted to resolve the problem that the experimenter's involvement with the text posed to the observer's separation from the text by positing that, once the experiment had been provoked, "[t]he experimenter must then disappear or rather transform himself instantaneously into an observer" (ibid.). Obviously even disappearance and instantaneous transformation cannot efface the experimenter's crucial initial involvement.

48. Franc Schuerewegen, "De la nécessité préfacielle (Balzac, Zola)," *French Forum* 16, no. 2 (May 1991): 177, 184.

49. Sigmund Freud, "The Poet and Day-dreaming," quoted in Borie, *Zola,* 126.

50. Borie, *Zola,* 167; Kamm, "Structural and Functional Manifestation," 236. See also Colette Becker, who explains that Octave is the "main thread of the narrative" because he "is the hero *or* the spectator of . . . several parallel plots" (preface to *Pot-Bouille,* 3:355; emphasis added).

Bibliography

Primary Sources

About, Edmond. "Dans les ruines." In *Paris: guide par les principaux écrivains et artistes de la France*. Paris: Librairie internationale, 1867.

Achard, Amédée. "Le Nouveau Paris." In *Le Prisme: encyclopédie morale du dix-neuvième siècle*, 146–149. Paris: Curmer, 1841.

———. "Le Propriétaire." In *Les Français peints par eux-mêmes*, 5:337–344. Paris: Curmer, 1842.

"Address." *The Builder* 1, no. 1 (December 1842): 1.

Alhoy, Maurice. *Physiologie de la lorette*. Paris: Aubert, n.d.

d'Alq, Louise. *Le Maître et la maîtresse de la maison*. Paris: Bureaux des *Causeries familières*, n.d.

———. *La Science de la vie: conseils et réflexions à l'usage de tous*. Paris: Bureaux des *Causeries familières*, n.d.

———. *La Vie intime*. 2d ed. Paris: Bureaux des *Causeries familières*, 1881.

Ambs-Dalès, J. B. *Les Grisettes de Paris*. Paris: Roy-Terry, 1830.

Anstey, F. "The Wraith of Barnjum." In *Nightcaps and Nightmares: Ghosts with a Touch of Humour*, ed. Peter Haining, 45–59. London: William Kimber, 1983.

"Apartments, Furnished." *Household Words*, July 16, 1853, 457–463.

Archer, Thomas. *The Pauper, the Thief, and the Convict; Sketches of Some of Their Homes, Haunts and Habits*. London: Groombridge, 1865.

Ashpitel, Arthur, and John Whichcord. *Town Dwellings: An Essay on the Erection of Fire-Proof Houses in Flats; A Codification of the Scottish and Continental Systems*. London: John Weale, 1855.

Audebrand, Philibert. "La Figurante." In *Les Français peints par eux-mêmes,* 1:113–120. Paris: Curmer, 1840.

"An Authentic Narrative of a Haunted House." *Eclectic Magazine* 58 (January 1863): 54–61.

Balzac, Honoré de. *La Comédie humaine.* 12 vols. Paris: Gallimard, Editions de la Pléiade, 1976.

———. *La Cousine Bette.* Paris: Garnier, 1962.

———. *Le Cousin Pons.* Ed. Anne-Marie Meininger. Paris: Garnier, 1974.

———. "Histoire et physiologie des boulevards de Paris, de la Madeleine à la Bastille." In *Le Diable à Paris,* 2:89–104. Paris: Hetzel, 1846.

———. "Philosophie de la vie conjugale à Paris—Chaussée d'Antin." In *Le Diable à Paris,* 1:165–211. Paris: Hetzel, 1845.

———. *Physiologie du mariage.* Paris: Garnier-Flammarion, 1968.

Banfield, Frank. *The Great Landlords of London.* London: Spencer Blackett, n.d. [1888].

Bartlett, David W. *London by Day and Night: or, Men and Things in the Great Metropolis.* New York: Hurst, n.d. [ca. 1850].

Bassanville, la comtesse de. *L'Art de bien tenir une maison.* Paris: Librairie H. Aniéré, 1878.

———. *Le Trésor de la maison: guide des femmes économes.* Paris: Brumet, 1867.

Baudelaire, Charles. "Les Fenêtres." In *Le Spleen de Paris: petits poèmes en prose,* 139–140. 1869. Paris: Livres de Poche, 1972.

Bawr, Madame de. "La Garde." In *Les Français peints par eux-mêmes,* 1:129–137. Paris: Curmer, 1840.

Bayard, Henri. *Mémoire sur la topographie médicale des Xe, XIe et XIIe arrondissements de la ville de Paris.* Paris: Baillière, 1844.

Bayly, Mary. *Ragged Homes and How to Mend Them.* London: Nisbet, 1860.

Beames, Thomas. *The Rookeries of London.* 1852. Reprint, London: Frank Cass, 1970.

Belèze, M. G. *Le Livre des ménages: nouveau manuel d'économie domestique.* Paris: Hachette, 1860.

Bellet, Louis. "Les Loyers dans Paris." *La Patrie,* April 3, 1861.

Bellet, Victor. *Les Propriétaires et les loyers à Paris.* Paris: Dentu, 1857.

Billington, John. *The Architectural Director.* London: Richardson and Taylor, n.d.

Blackstone, William. *Commentaries on the Laws of England Applicable to Real Property.* 2d ed. Toronto: Rowsell and Hutchison, 1880.

Blanc, Charles. *Grammaire des arts décoratifs; décoration intérieure de la maison.* Paris: Renouard, 1882.

Blanchard, Laman. "A Visit to the General Cemetery at Kensal Green." *Ainsworth's Magazine* 2 (1842): 177–188.

Bleiler, E. F, ed. *Five Victorian Ghost Novels.* New York: Dover Publications, 1971.

Bonnefons, Georges, ed. *Les Hôtels historiques de Paris.* Paris: Lecou, 1852.

Bouilly, M. "Les Jeunes Filles de Paris." In *Paris, ou le livre des cent-et-un,* 3:29–62. Paris: Ladvocat, 1831.

Braddon, M. E. "The Shadow in the Corner." In *Oxford Book of English Ghost Stories*, ed. Michael Cox and R. A. Gilbert, 51–68. Oxford: Oxford University Press, 1986.

Brierre de Boismont, A. *De la menstruation, considérée dans ses rapports physiologiques et pathologiques*. Paris: Baillière, 1842.

Brisset, M. J. "La Ménagère parisienne." In *Les Français peints par eux-mêmes*, 3:17–24. Paris: Curmer, 1841.

Brodrick, George. *English Land and English Landlords: An Enquiry into the Origin and Character of the English Land System, with Proposals for Its Reform*. London: Cassell, 1881.

Brooks, S. H. *Designs for Cottage and Villa Architecture*. London: Thomas Kelly, n.d. [1839].

———. *Treatise on the Erection of Dwelling Houses*. London: John Weale, 1860.

Brough, William. *Apartments, "Visitors to the Exhibition May Be Accommodated."* London: Hailes Lacy, 1851.

———. *A House out of Windows*. London: Hailes Lacy, 1852.

———. *How to Make Home Happy*. London: Hailes Lacy, 1853.

———. *Number One, Round the Corner*. London: Hailes Lacy, 1854.

Broughton, Rhoda. "The Man with the Nose." In *Ghost Stories*, ed. Susan Hill, 38–53. London: Hamish Hamilton, 1983.

———. "The Truth, the Whole Truth, and Nothing But the Truth." In *Victorian Ghost Stories: An Oxford Anthology*, ed. Michael Cox and R. A. Gilbert, 74–82. Oxford: Oxford University Press, 1991.

Brown, Richard. *Domestic Architecture*. London: George Virtue, 1841.

"Buildings—Mansions—Flats—Residences—Dwellings." *The Builder* 36, no. 1823 (January 1878): 31–32.

Bulwer-Lytton, Edward. "The Haunted and the Haunters." In *Classic Ghost Stories*, 293–330. New York: Dover Publications, 1975.

Bussy, M. de [pseudonym of Charles Marchal]. *Question actuelle: propriétaires et locataires—de la cherté des loyers dans Paris-Lyon-Bordeaux-Lille-Rouen-Marseille, etc. et des moyens sûrs et immédiats d'y remédier*. Paris: Eugène Pick, 1857.

Calland, Victor, and Albert Lenoir. *Institution des palais de famille: solution de ce grand problème—le confortable et la vie à bon marché pour tous*. 2d ed. Paris, 1855.

Calliat, Victor. *Parallèle des maisons de Paris construites depuis 1830 jusqu'à nos jours*. Paris: Bance, 1850.

Camp, Maxime du. *Paris: ses organes, ses fonctions et sa vie dans la seconde moitié du XIXe siècle*. 6 vols. 2d ed. Paris: Hachette, 1873.

Cardon, Emile. *L'Art au foyer domestique (la décoration de l'appartement)*. Paris: Renouard, 1884.

Chadwick, Edwin. *A Report on the Results of a Special Inquiry into the Practice of Interment in Towns*. Philadelphia: C. Sherman, 1845.

Classic Ghost Stories. New York: Dover Publications, 1975.

Claudin, Gustave. *Entre minuit et une heure: étude parisienne*. Paris: Dentu, 1868.

———. *Paris*. Paris: Dentu, 1862.

Collins, Wilkie. "The Dream Woman." In *Classic Ghost Stories,* 183–206. New York: Dover Publications, 1975.

———. "Miss Jéromette and the Clergyman." In *Victorian Ghost Stories: An Oxford Anthology,* ed. Michael Cox and R. A. Gilbert, 198–217. Oxford: Oxford University Press, 1991.

Cooper, Antony D. "Art. VI.—1. *Reports of the Society for Improving the Condition of the Labouring Classes.* 1845–1846. 2. *First Report of the Constabulary Force Commissioners.* 1839." *Quarterly Review* 82 (December 1847): 142–152.

"Cottage Economy." *The Builder* 1, no. 24 (July 1843): 293.

Couailhac, Louis. *Physiologie du célibataire et de la vieille fille.* Paris: J. Laisné, 1841.

Cox, Alfred. *The Illustrated Property Advertiser.* 1855.

———. *The Landlord's and Tenant's Guide.* London: Published by the author, 1853.

Cox, Michael, and R. A. Gilbert, ed. *Oxford Book of English Ghost Stories.* Oxford: Oxford University Press, 1986.

———. *Victorian Ghost Stories: An Oxford Anthology.* Oxford: Oxford University Press, 1991.

"Crack Houses." *The Builder* 2, no. 83 (September 1844): 462.

Cross, Francis. *Hints to All about to Rent, Buy, or Build House Property.* 4th ed. London: Nelson, 1854.

———. *Landed Property: Its Sale, Purchase, Improvement, and General Management.* London: Simpkin, Marshall, 1857.

———. "A Word to the Wise: Dwelling Houses." *The Builder* 7, no. 343 (September 1849): 411.

Cruise, William. *A Digest of the Laws of England Respecting Real Property.* 4th ed. London: Saunders and Benning, 1835.

[Cunningham, Peter]. *Murray's Handbook for Modern London.* London: John Murray, 1851.

Dahl, Roald, ed. *Roald Dahl's Book of Ghost Stories.* New York: Farrar Straus and Giroux, 1983.

Daly, César. *L'Architecture privée au XIXe siècle sous Napoléon III.* 9 vols. Paris: Ducher, 1864–77.

———. "De l'architecture domestique de Paris." *Revue générale de l'architecture* 1, no. 3 (March 1840): 165–169.

———. "De l'architecture domestique monumentale." *Revue générale de l'architecture* 1, no. 4 (April 1840): 197–205.

Davies, Charles Maurice. *Mystic London: Or, Phases of Occult Life in the Metropolis.* London: Tinsley, 1875.

———. "A Night in a Ghost-Chamber." *Belgravia* 9 (November–February 1872): 377–385.

———. *Unorthodox London: Or, Phases of Religious Life in the Metropolis.* 2d ed. London: Tinsley, 1874.

Delamarre, M. "Question des loyers." *La Patrie,* 1861.

Delord, Taxile. "La Femme sans nom." In *Les Français peints par eux-mêmes,* 1:245–256. Paris: Curmer, 1840.

———. *Paris-portière*. Paris, n.d.

———. *Physiologie de la parisienne*. Paris: Aubert, n.d.

Delord, Taxile, Edmond Texier, and Arnould Frémy. *Mort aux locataires assez canailles pour ne pas payer leurs termes*. 1854. Paris: Editions Seesam, 1990.

Delvau, Alfred. *Les Dessous de Paris*. Paris: Poulet-Mallassis, 1860.

———. *Histoire anecdotique des cafés et cabarets de Paris*. Paris: Dentu, 1862.

Deschamps, Emile. "Les Appartements à louer." In *Paris, ou le livre des cent-et-un*, 8:55–90. Paris: Ladvocat, 1832.

Desnoyers, Louis. Introduction to *Les Etrangers à Paris*. Paris: Warée, 1844.

Destourbet, Regnier. "Les Demoiselles à marier." In *Paris, ou le livre des cent-et-un*, 6:111–132. Paris: Ladvocat, 1832.

Le Diable à Paris. Paris: Hetzel, 1845–46. 2 vols.

Dickens, Charles. *Great Expectations*. Oxford: Oxford University Press, 1993.

———. "The Lawyer and the Ghost." In *Nightcaps and Nightmares: Ghosts with a Touch of Humour*, ed. Peter Haining, 41–44. London: William Kimber, 1983.

———. *Sketches by Boz*. Ed. Dennis Walder. London: Penguin, 1995.

———. "The Story of the Bagman's Uncle." In *Classic Ghost Stories*, 16–33. New York: Dover Publications, 1975.

———. "To Be Taken with a Grain of Salt." In *Victorian Ghost Stories: An Oxford Anthology*, ed. Michael Cox and R. A. Gilbert, 55–64. Oxford: Oxford University Press, 1991.

Dickens, Charles, Wilkie Collins, and Elizabeth Gaskell. "A House to Let." *Household Words*, December 7, 1858, 1–36.

Digby, K. E. *An Introduction to the History of the Law of Real Property*. Oxford: Clarendon Press, 1875.

Dowson, J. "Essay on the Metaphysics of Architecture." *Architectural Magazine* 3 (June 1836): 245–249.

Dubut, L[ouis]-A[mbroise]. *Architecture civile: maisons de ville et de campagne—ouvrage utile à tous constructeurs et entrepreneurs, et à toutes personnes qui, ayant quelques connaissances en construction, veulent elles-mêmes diriger leurs bâtiments*. 1803. Paris: Marie et Bernard, 1847.

Dwellings Committee of the Charity Organisation Society. *Dwellings of the Poor: Report of the Dwellings Committee of the Charity Organisation Society*. London: Longmans, Green, 1873.

"The Dwellings of the Working Classes Inferior to Those of the Pauper and the Prisoner." *The Builder* 2, no. 98 (December 1844): 631.

Eastlake, Charles. *Hints on Household Taste*. 2d rev. ed. London: Longmans, Green, 1869.

Emmet, J. T. "The Ethics of Urban Leaseholds." *British Quarterly Review* 69 (April 1879): 301–333.

Engels, Frederick. *The Housing Question*. Ed. C. P. Dutt. The Marxist Library, no. 23. New York: International, n.d.

"English Domestic Architecture." *The Builder* 1, no. 36 (October 1843): 431–432.

"An Englishman's Castle." *Household Words*, December 27, 1851, 321–324.

Escott, T. H. S. *England: Its People, Polity and Pursuits.* Vol. 2. London: Cassell, Petter, Galpin, 1879.

"Falling of Houses." *The Builder* 1, no. 17 (June 1843): 205.

"Une Fenêtre du faubourg Saint-Jacques." In *Paris au XIXe siècle,* 35–36. Paris: Beauger, 1839.

Fergusson, James. *History of the Modern Styles of Architecture.* London: John Murray, 1862.

Fertiault, Julie. *Le Ménagier français.* Paris: Bureaux du *Conseiller des Dames et des Demoiselles,* 1863.

"Le Flâneur à Paris." In *Paris, ou le livre des cent-et-un,* 6:95–110. Paris: Ladvocat, 1832.

"Flats for the Middle Classes." *Building News* 15, no. 697 (May 1868): 323.

"Flats versus Lodgings." *The Builder* 26, no. 1309 (March 1868): 182.

Fletcher, Banister. *Model Houses for the Industrial Classes.* London: Longmans, Green, 1871.

Fonssagrives, J.-B. *La Maison: étude d'hygiène et de bien-être domestiques.* Montpellier: Gras, 1871.

Fournel, Victor. *Ce qu'on voit dans les rues de Paris.* Paris: Delahays, 1858.

———. *Paris nouveau et Paris futur.* Paris: Lecoffre, 1865.

"'Fourth Report' of the Society for Improving the Condition of the Labouring Classes." *The Labourer's Friend* 49 (June 1848): 83–109.

Les Français peints par eux-mêmes. 8 vols. Paris: Curmer, 1840–42.

Frémy, Arnould. *Les Moeurs de notre temps.* Paris: Librairie nouvelle, 1861.

"French Flats." *Building News* 3, no. 8 (February 1857): 181–182.

Gacon-Dufour, Marie-Armande Jeanne. *Manuel complète de la maîtresse de maison et de la parfaite ménagère, ou guide pratique pour la gestion d'une maison à la ville et à la campagne.* Paris: Roret, 1826.

———. *Manuel complète de la maîtresse de maison et de la parfaite ménagère, ou guide pratique pour la gestion d'une maison à la ville et à la campagne, contenant les moyens d'y maintenir le bon ordre et d'y établir l'abondance,* rev. Mme Celnart. 2d ed. Paris: Roret, 1828.

Garnier, Charles, and A. Ammann. *L'Habitation humaine.* Paris: Hachette, 1892.

Garwood, John. *The Million-Peopled City; or, One-Half of the People of London Made Known to the Other Half.* London: Wertheim and Macintosh, 1853.

Gaskell, Peter. *The Manufacturing Population of England.* London: Baldwin and Craddock, 1833.

Gautier, Théophile. "Mosaïque de ruines." In *Paris et les parisiens au XIXe siècle,* 38–43. Paris: Morizot, 1856.

Gavin, Hector. *The Habitations of the Industrial Classes: Their Influence on the Physical and on the Social and Moral Condition of These Classes.* London: Society for Improving the Condition of the Labouring Classes, 1850.

———. *Sanitary Ramblings.* London: Churchill, 1848.

———. *Unhealthiness of London, and the Necessity of Remedial Measures.* London: Churchill, 1847.

"The Ghost at Laburnum Villa." *Belgravia* 2 (August 1870): 213–222.

Godwin, George. "Architecture for the Poor." *The Builder* 3, no. 105 (February 1845): 61–62.

Gourlier, Charles. "Des voies publiques et des maisons d'habitation à Paris." *Encyclopédie d'architecture: journal mensuel* 2, no. 9 (supplement) (1852): 73–96.

Gozlan, Léon. "Les Maîtresses à Paris." In *Le Diable à Paris*, 2:105–122. Paris: Hetzel, 1846.

Grant, James. *The Great Metropolis.* Vol. 2. First series. London: Saunders and Otley, 1836.

Greenwood, James. *The Wilds of London.* London: Chatto and Windus, 1874.

"The Grosvenor-Place and Pimlico Improvements of the Marquis of Westminster." *The Builder* 25, no. 1255 (February 1867): 121–123.

Guinot, Eugène. "Les Veuves du Diable." In *Le Diable à Paris*, 2:260–279. Paris: Hetzel, 1846.

Gwilt, Joseph. *An Encyclopaedia of Architecture, Historical, Theoretical, and Practical.* London: Longman, Brown, Green and Longman, 1842.

Haining, Peter, ed. *Nightcaps and Nightmares: Ghosts with a Touch of Humour.* London: William Kimber, 1983.

Harris, Thomas. *Victorian Architecture.* London: Bell and Daldy, 1860.

"The Haunted Garden." *Temple Bar* 24 (November 1868): 257–266.

"The Haunted Grange." *Dublin University Magazine* 2 (July–December 1833): 693–702.

"The Haunted Lodging House." *Sharpe's London Magazine* 28 (1858): 127–134.

Haweis, H. R. *The Art of Decoration.* London: Chatto and Windus, 1881.

Hay, Frederic. *Lodgers and Dodgers.* London: Hailes Lacy, 1871.

Hedgeland, J. *First Part of a Series of Designs for Private Dwellings.* London: Printed for G. and W. B. Whittaker, 1821.

Hill, Octavia. *Homes of the London Poor.* 2d ed. London: Macmillan, 1883.

———. *House Property and Its Management.* New York: Macmillan, 1921.

———. *Our Common Land (and Other Short Essays).* London: Macmillan, 1877.

Hill, Susan, ed. *Ghost Stories.* London: Hamish Hamilton, 1983.

Hogg, Dr. John. *London As It Is: Being a Series of Observations on the Health, Habits, and Amusements of the People.* London: Macrone, 1837.

Hollingshead, John. "London Model Lodging-Houses." *Good Words* 2 (1861): 170–174.

———. *Ragged London in 1861.* London: Smith, Elder, 1861.

"Houses in Flats." *The Architect* 10, no. 247 (September 1873): 141.

"Houses in Flats for London." *The Builder* 34, no. 1718 (January 1876): 25–27.

"Houses to Let." *Household Words*, March 20, 1852, 5–11.

"How to Build a House and Live in It." *Blackwood's Edinburgh Magazine* 59 (June 1846): 758–765.

Hume, Reverend A. *Condition of Liverpool, Religious and Social; Including Notices of the State of Education, Morals, Pauperism, and Crime.* Liverpool: Printed by T. Brakell, 1858.

Humphreys, Noel, ed. *Vital Statistics: A Memorial Volume of Selections from the Reports and Writings of William Farr.* London: Offices of the Sanitary Institute, 1885.

Ingoldsby, Thomas [Richard Barham]. "The Spectre of Tappington." In *Nightcaps and Nightmares: Ghosts with a Touch of Humour,* ed. Peter Haining, 14–40. London: William Kimber, 1983.

Ingram, John H. *The Haunted Homes and Family Traditions of Great Britain.* 3d ed. London: W. H. Allen, 1886.

Jackson, J. G. *Designs for Villas.* London: James Carpenter, 1829.

Jacquier, Louis. *L'Amour à Paris.* Paris: Chez tous les libraires, 1862.

Janin, Jules. "Asmodée." In *Paris, ou le livre des cent-et-un,* 1:1–16. Paris: Ladvocat, 1831.

———. "Le Bas-bleu." In *Les Français peints par eux-mêmes,* 5:201–231. Paris: Curmer, 1842.

———. "Les Petites misères parisiennes." In *Nouveau tableau de Paris, au XIXe siècle,* 6:273–289. Paris: Mme Charles-Béchet, 1834.

"Le Jardin du Palais-Royal." In *Paris au XIXe siècle,* 5–6. Paris: Beauger, 1839.

Kay, Joseph. *Free Trade in Land.* Preface by John Bright. 9th ed. London: Kegan Paul, 1885.

Keating, Peter, ed. *Into Unknown England, 1866–1913: Selections from the Social Explorers.* Manchester: Manchester University Press, 1976.

Kerr, Robert. *The Gentleman's House, or, How to Plan English Residences, from the Parsonage to the Palace.* London: John Murray, 1864.

Kessler, Joan C. *Demons of the Night: Tales of the Fantastic, Madness, and the Supernatural from Nineteenth-Century France.* Chicago: University of Chicago Press, 1995.

Kingsley, Charles. "Great Cities, and Their Influence for Good and Evil." In *Miscellanies,* 2:318–345. 2d ed. London: John W. Parker and Son, 1860.

Kock, Paul de. *Les Bains à domicile.* Paris: Tresse, 1845.

———. *La Demoiselle du cinquième.* Brussels: Lebègue, 1857.

———. *La Grande ville: nouveau tableau de Paris.* Vol. 1. Paris: Au bureau central des publications nouvelles, 1842.

———. *Mon Voisin Raymond.* Paris: Gustave Barba, 1849.

Kock, Paul de, et al. *La Grande ville: nouveau tableau de Paris.* Vol. 1. Paris: Maulde et Reneau, 1843–44.

Knight, Charles. *Knight's London.* London: J. S. Virtue, n.d. [1850s].

Knox, John. *The Masses Without!* London: Judd and Glass, 1857.

Krafft, J. C. *Plans, coupes, élévations des plus belles maisons et des hôtels construits à Paris et dans les environs.* Paris: published by the author, n.d.

———. *Portes cochères et portes d'entrées des maisons et édifices publics de Paris.* 2d ed. Paris: Bance, 1838.

Lachaise, Claude. *Topographie médicale de Paris.* Paris: Baillière, 1822.

Lacroix, A. de. "Les Appartements à louer." In *Le Prisme: encyclopédie morale du dix-neuvième siècle,* 189–194. Paris: Curmer, 1841.

Laing, David. *Plans of Buildings Public and Private.* London: J. Taylor, 1818.

Lance, Adolphe. *Rapport sur la proposition de M. Harvu-Romain, relative à l'assainissement des habitations insalubres.* 2d ed. Amiens: Caron, 1851.

Lasteyrie, Ferdinand de. "Edilité parisienne." *L'Opinion nationale,* April 11, 1861.

"The Latest Thing in Ghosts." *Once a Week,* January 18, 1862, 99–103.

Laurent-Jan. "Où va une femme qui sort: énigme." In *Le Diable à Paris,* 2:151–160. Paris: Hetzel, 1846.

Lazare, Louis. *Les Quartiers pauvres de Paris.* Paris: Bibliothèque municipale, 1869.

Lecocq de Montborne, Mme. *De la société contemporaine: religion, noblesse, bourgeoisie.* Paris: Dentu, 1855.

Lee, Vernon [Violet Paget]. *Hauntings: Fantastic Stories.* Freeport: Books for Libraries Press, 1971.

Leeds, W. H. "An English Version of a French Plan." *Architectural Magazine* 3 (December 1836): 573–581.

Le Fanu, Sheridan. "An Account of Some Strange Disturbances in Aungier Street." In *Victorian Ghost Stories: An Oxford Anthology,* ed. Michael Cox and R. A. Gilbert, 19–36. Oxford: Oxford University Press, 1991.

———. "The Ghost of a Hand." In *Roald Dahl's Book of Ghost Stories,* ed. Roald Dahl, 154–161. New York: Farrar Straus and Giroux, 1983.

———. "Green Tea." In *Ghost Stories,* ed. Susan Hill. London: Hamish Hamilton, 1983.

———. "The Haunted House in Westminster." *Belgravia* 6 (January 1872): 261–285.

———. "Sir Dominick Sarsfield." In *Classic Ghost Stories,* 1–15. New York: Dover Publications, 1975.

———. "Squire Toby's Will." In *Oxford Book of English Ghost Stories,* ed. Michael Cox and R. A. Gilbert, 25–50. Oxford: Oxford University Press, 1986.

Legrand, J. G., and C. P. Landon. *Description de Paris et ses édifices.* 2 vols. Paris: Treuttel and Wurtz, 1808.

Lenoir, Albert. "De l'architecture des anciens hôtels." In *Les Hôtels historiques de Paris,* ed. Georges Bonnefons, xi–xvi. Paris: Lecou, 1852.

Le Play, Frédéric. *Les Ouvriers européens: études sur les travaux, la vie domestique et la condition morale des populations ouvrières de l'Europe.* Paris: Imprimerie impériale, 1855.

Lespès, Léo. "La Guerre des fenêtres: journal du siège d'une jolie femme." In *Paris dans un fauteuil: types, histoires et physionomies,* 21–35. Paris: Lasalle, 1855.

——— [pseudonym of Timothée Trimm]. *Spectacles vus de ma fenêtre.* Paris: Achille Fauré, 1866.

Lévy, Michel. *Traité d'hygiène publique et privée.* Vol. 1. Paris: Baillière, 1844.

"Living in Flats." *Saturday Review,* October 23, 1875, 515–516.

L. L. Y. "The Middle-Class Dwellings of London." *Building News* 3, no. 20 (May 1857): 477–478.

"La Loge du portier." *Paris au XIXe siècle,* 17–18. Paris: Beauger, 1839.

"London as It Was in 1800, and Is in 1844." *The Builder* 2, no. 77 (July 1844): 370–371.

Loudon, John C. "Cottage Economy." In *Library of Useful Knowledge,* 3:3. London: Baldwin and Craddock, 1840.

———. *The Suburban Gardener and Villa Companion.* London: Longman, Orme, Brown, Green and Longmans, 1838.

Lucas, Charles. *Exposition universelle internationale de 1878, à Paris: compte rendu—conférence sur l'habitation à toutes les époques.* Paris: Imprimerie nationale, 1879.

Maldan, J. C. *Les Embarras de Paris.* 2d ed. Paris, 1839.

Marx, Karl. *The Holy Family, or Critique of Critical Criticism.* Trans. Richard Dixon and Clemens Dutt. Moscow: Progress, 1975.

———. *Economic and Philosophic Manuscripts of 1844.* Ed. and intro. by Dirk J. Struik. Trans. Martin Milligan. New York: International, 1964.

May, Jean. "Les Deux mansardes parisiennes." In *Paris, ou le livre des cent-et-un,* 14:39–76. Paris: Ladvocat, 1834.

Mayhew, Henry. "Home Is Home, Be It Never So Homely." In *Meliora, or Better Times to Come,* ed. Viscount Ingestre [Charles Shrewsbury], 1:258–280. 1852. Reprint, London: Frank Cass, 1971.

———. *Mayhew's London.* Ed. Peter Quennell. London: Pilot Press, 1949.

———. *The Morning Chronicle Survey of Labour and the Poor: The Metropolitan Districts.* Vols. 3 and 4. Sussex: Caliban, 1980.

Mazerolle, Pierre. *La Misère à Paris: les mauvais gîtes.* Paris: Sartorius, 1875.

Mémoire adressé par une réunion de propriétaires, architectes et constructeurs de la ville de Paris, à Messieurs les membres de la commission d'Enquête. Paris: Librairie du commerce, 1829.

"Metropolitan Building Act." *The Builder* 1, no. 21 (July 1843): 253.

Mesnil, Octave du. *Les Garnis insalubres de la ville de Paris, rapport fait à la commission des logements insalubres.* Paris: Baillière, 1878.

Meynadier, Hippolyte. *Paris sous le point de vue pittoresque, ou éléments d'un plan général d'ensemble de ses travaux d'art et d'utilité publique.* Paris: Dauvin et Fontaine, 1843.

Miller, Thomas. *Picturesque Sketches of London, Past and Present.* London: Office of the National Illustrated Library, 1852.

Millington, Thomas Street. "No Living Voice." In *Victorian Ghost Stories: An Oxford Anthology,* ed. Michael Cox and R. A. Gilbert, 190–197. Oxford: Oxford University Press, 1991.

"Modern House-Building." *Building News* 13, no. 619 (November 1866): 755–756.

Monnais, Edouard. "Le Propriétaire." In *Nouveau tableau de Paris, au XIXe siècle,* 3:111–131. Paris: Mme Charles-Béchet, 1834.

Monnier, Henry. "La Portière." In *Les Français peints par eux-mêmes,* 3:33–42. Paris: Curmer, 1841.

———. *Le Roman chez la portière.* Paris: Au magasin central des pièces de Théâtre, 1855.

———. "Une Maison de Marais." In *Paris, ou le livre des cent-et-un,* 1:333–344. Paris: Ladvocat, 1831.

Muller, Emile, and Emile Cacheux. Introduction to *Les Habitations ouvrières en tous pays: situation en 1878—avenir.* Paris: Rejey, 1879.

Muller, Emile, and Octave du Mesnil. *Des habitations à bon marché au point de vue de la construction et de la salubrité: rapport présenté au congrès international des habitations à bon marché.* Paris: Baillière, 1889.

Mulock, Dinah. "The Last House in C– Street." In *Victorian Ghost Stories: An Oxford Anthology,* ed. Michael Cox and R. A. Gilbert, 44–54. Oxford: Oxford University Press, 1991.

Murray, John Fisher. *The World of London.* Edinburgh: Blackwood, 1843.

Musset, Paul de. "Parisiens et parisiennes." In *Paris et les parisiens au XIXe siècle,* 403–457. Paris: Morizot, 1856.

Nicholson, Peter. *The Builder's and Workman's New Director.* Rev. ed. London: J. Taylor, 1834.

Normand, [Louis-Marie], fils. *Paris moderne, ou choix de maisons construites dans les nouveaux quartiers de la capitale et de ses environs.* Paris: Bance, 1837.

Nouveau tableau de Paris, au XIXe siècle. Paris: Mme Charles-Béchet, 1834. 7 vols.

Nouveaux tableaux de Paris. Paris: Pillet, 1828.

O'Donnell, Elliott. *Haunted Houses of London.* London: Eveleigh Nash, 1909.

Oliphant, Margaret. "A Beleaguered City." In *A Beleaguered City and Other Stories,* 3–114. Oxford: Oxford University Press, 1988.

"Our House." *Household Words,* March 20, 1852, 41–42.

Owen, Robert Dale. *Footfalls on the Boundary of Another World.* Philadelphia: Lippincott, 1872.

Panorama intérieur de Paris. Paris: F. Sinmett, n.d.

Paris chez soi. Paris: Boizard, 1854.

Paris et les parisiens au XIXe siècle. Paris: Morizot, 1856.

Paris-guide par les principaux écrivains et artistes de la France. Paris: Librairie internationale, 1867.

Paris, ou le livre des cent-et-un. 15 vols. Paris: Ladvocat, 1831–34.

Pariset, Mme. *Encyclopédie des dames: manuel de la maîtresse de maison, ou lettres sur l'économie domestique.* Paris: Audot, 1821.

———. *Nouveau manuel complet de la maîtresse de maison, suivi d'un appendice par Mesdames Gacon-Dufour, Celnart.* Paris: Roret, 1852.

Parkes, Mrs. William [Frances Byerley]. *Domestic Duties, or, Instructions to Young Married Ladies, on the Management of Their Households.* London: Longmans, 1825.

Pater, Walter. *Selected Works.* Ed. Richard Aldington. London: Heinemann, 1948.

Payne's Illustrated London. London: E. T. Bram, 1847.

Perks, Sidney. *Residential Flats of All Classes.* London: B. T. Batsford, 1905.

Perrot, Michelle, and Georges Ribeill, eds. *Le Journal intime de Caroline B.* Paris: Montalba, 1985.

The Pictorial Handbook to London. London: Henry G. Bohn, 1854.

Pike, E. Royston. *Human Documents of the Victorian Golden Age.* London: Allen and Unwin, 1967.

Piorry, P[ierre] A[dolphe]. *Des habitations et de l'influence de leurs dispositions sur l'homme, en santé et en maladie.* Paris: Pourchet, 1838.

Pollock, Frederick. *The Land Laws.* 2d ed. London: Macmillan, 1887.

"Professor Cockerell's Lectures, no. IV." *The Builder* 1, no. 7 (March 1843): 80–81.

La Propriété: journal des intérêts de tous, April 16, 1848.

Pugin, A. Welby. *Contrasts.* London: Printed for the author, and published by him, 1836.

Puissant, Adolphe. *De l'économie domestique et de l'éducation dans les classes ouvrières.* Paris: Baillière, 1872.

R. "Remarks on London Street Houses and Shop Fronts." *Architectural Magazine* 1 (May 1834): 113–117.

Ranyard, Ellen. *The Missing Link.* New York: Carter, 1860.

Raphael, Jacques. "Le Portier de Paris." In *Paris, ou le livre des cent-et-un,* 8: 345–367. Paris: Ladvocat, 1832.

Rapports généraux des travaux du conseil de Salubrité pendant les années 1840 à 1845 inclusivement. Paris: Boucquin, 1847.

Raymond, Emmeline. *Le Secret des parisiennes.* Paris: Firmin Didot, 1866.

Reynaud, Léonce. *Traité d'architecture.* Vol. 2. Paris: Librairie pour l'architecture, 1858.

Riddell, Charlotte. "The Open Door." In *Victorian Ghost Stories: An Oxford Anthology,* ed. Michael Cox and R. A. Gilbert, 256–282. Oxford: Oxford University Press, 1991.

———. "The Uninhabited House." In *Five Victorian Ghost Novels,* ed. E. F. Bleiler, 1–112. New York: Dover Publications, 1971.

Ritchie, James Ewing. *About London.* London: William Tinsley, 1860.

———. *The Night Side of London.* London: Tweedie, 1857.

Riz-Pacquot. *L'Art de bâtir, meubler et entretenir sa maison, ou manière de surveiller et d'être soi-même architecte-entrepreneur-ouvrier.* Paris: Laurens, n.d. [ca. 1890].

Roberts, Henry. *The Improvement of the Dwellings of the Labouring Classes.* London: Ridgeway, 1859.

Robinet, Jean François Eugène. *"Finissons Paris!" Observations sur l'édilité moderne.* Paris: Ritti, 1879.

Roqueplan, Nestor. *Regain: la vie parisienne.* Paris: Librairie nouvelle, 1853.

Rousseau, James. *Physiologie de la portière.* Paris: Aubert, 1841.

Roux, L. "Le Commissionnaire." In *Les Francais peints par eux-memes,* 3:241–248. Paris: Curmer, 1841.

———. "La Sage-femme." In *Les Français peints par eux-mêmes,* 1:177–184. Paris: Curmer, 1840.

Ruskin, John. "La Douce Amie." In *Fors Clavigera,* 2:97–124. 1873. London: George Allen, 1896.

———. *Lectures on Architecture and Painting.* New York: Wiley and Halsted, 1856.

———. *The Seven Lamps of Architecture.* 1880. Reprint, New York: Dover Publications, 1989.

Sala, George Augustus. *Gaslight and Daylight with Some London Scenes They Shine Upon.* London: Tinsley, 1872.

———. *Twice 'Round the Clock; or the Hours of the Day and Night in London.* London: Houlston and Wright, 1859.

"Scamping." *Chambers's Journal* 56, no. 787 (January 1879): 49–51.

Schlesinger, Max. *Saunterings in and about London.* London: Nathaniel Cooke, 1853.

Second, Albéric. "Rue Notre-Dame-de-Lorette." In *Les Rues de Paris: Paris ancien et moderne,* ed. Louis Lurine, 1:131–140. Paris: Kugelman, 1844.

Sergent, François. *Manuel alphabétique du propriétaire et du locataire et sous-locataire.* Paris: Mongie, 1826.

———. *Nouveau manuel complet du propriétaire et du locataire.* Rev. Charles Vasserot. Paris: Roret, 1865.

Short, William J. "Remarks on Street Architecture." *Architectural Magazine* 2 (September 1835): 389–393.

Silas, Ferdinand. "Les propriétaires vengés." *Le Bourgeois de Paris,* May 12, 1855, 3–4.

Sinks of London Laid Open. London: J. Duncombe, 1848.

Smith, Albert. *The Natural History of 'Stuck-Up' People.* London: Bogue, 1847.

———, ed. *Gavarni in London: Sketches of Life and Character.* London: Bogue, 1849.

Smith, Charles Manby. *The Little World of London, or, Pictures in Little of London Life.* London: Arthur Hall, Virtue, 1857.

Smith, Percival Gordon, and Keith Downes Young. "Architecture: Composite Middle-Class Houses." In *Our Homes, and How to Make Them Healthy,* ed. Shirley Foster Murphy, 179–187. London: Cassell, 1883.

Soulié, Frédéric. "La Bourse." In *Nouveau tableau de Paris, au XIXe siècle,* 3:27–54. Paris: Mme Charles-Béchet, 1834.

———. "Les Drames invisibles." In *Le Diable à Paris,* 1:85–120. Paris: Hetzel, 1845.

———. "La Maîtresse de maison de santé." In *Les Français peints par eux-mêmes,* 4:345–352. Paris: Curmer, 1841.

———. *Physiologie du bas-bleu.* Paris: Aubert, n.d.

Souvestre, Emile. *Les Anges du foyer.* Paris: Michel Lévy, 1858.

———. *Les Anges du logis.* Pont-à-Mousson: Haugenthal, 1859.

———. *Un Philosophe sous les toits: journal d'un homme heureux.* Paris: Michel Lévy, 1850.

Stevenson, J. J. *House Architecture.* 2 vols. London: Macmillan, 1880.

———. "Street Architecture." In *Transactions of the National Association for the Promotion of Social Science,* ed. Charles Wager Ryalls, 751–769. London: Longmans, Green, 1877.

Stewart, Dugald. "Coupe de maison." *Magasin pittoresque* (1847): 400–402.

Stoker, Bram. "The Judge's House." In *Classic Ghost Stories,* 211–228. New York: Dover Publications, 1975.

"The Story of Clifford House." In *Victorian Ghost Stories: An Oxford Anthology,* ed. Michael Cox and R. A. Gilbert, 218–238. Oxford: Oxford University Press, 1991.

Texier, Edmond. *Le Tableau de Paris*. Paris: Paulin et Le Chevalier, 1852–53.

Theobald, F. J. *Homes and Work in the Future Life*. London: Psychological Press Association, 1885.

Thiollet, M. [François]. *Choix de maisons, édifices et monuments publics, de Paris et de ses environs*. Vol. 3. 2d ed. Paris: Bance, 1838.

Thiollet, M., and H. Roux. *Nouveau recueil de menuiserie et de décorations intérieures et extérieures*. Paris: Bance, 1837.

Tissot, Amédée de. *Paris et Londres comparés*. Paris: A. J. Ducollet, 1830.

"To Let or to Sell." *Building News* 12, no. 545 (June 1865): 432.

"To the Architectural Student." *The Builder* 1, no. 10 (April 1843): 119.

Toussaint, M. *Nouveau manuel complet d'architecture ou traité de l'art de bâtir*. Paris: Roret, 1837.

Tristan, Flora. *Flora Tristan's London Journal: A Survey of London Life in the 1830s*. Trans. Dennis Palmer and Giselle Pincet. London: George Prior, 1980. Originally published as *Promenades dans Londres* (1840).

Trollope, Frances. *Paris and the Parisians in 1835*. Vol. 1. London: Bentley, 1835.

Vacquer, Théodore. *Maisons les plus remarquables à Paris construites pendant les trois dernières années*. Paris: Caudrilier, 1860–70.

Villars, Emile. *Le Roman de la parisienne (Mélange)*. Paris: Librairie centrale, 1866.

Viollet-le-Duc, Eugène Emmanuel. *Entretiens sur l'architecture*. Paris: Morel, 1863.

———. *Habitations modernes*. 1875. Reprint, Brussels: Mardaga, 1979.

———. *Histoire d'une maison*. Paris: Hetzel, 1873.

Walker, George. *Gatherings from Graveyards*. 1839. Reprint, New York: Arno Press, 1977.

Walsh, J. H. *A Manual of Domestic Economy*. London: G. Routledge, 1857.

Webster, Thomas, and Mrs. William Parkes [Frances Byerley]. *An Encyclopaedia of Domestic Economy*. London: Longman, Brown, Green and Longman, 1844.

Weill, Alexandre. *Paris inhabitable: ce que tout le monde pense des loyers de Paris et personne ne dit*. 3d ed. Paris: Dentu, 1860.

———. *Qu'est-ce que le propriétaire d'une maison à Paris: suite de Paris inhabitable*. Paris: Dentu, 1860.

White, William H. "Houses in Flats." *The Builder* 34, no. 1729 (March 1876): 291.

———. "On Middle-Class Houses in Paris and Central London." *Royal Institute of British Architects: Sessional Papers, 1877–78*, 21–34. London, 1878.

Williams, Robert. *London Rookeries and Colliers' Slums*. 1839. Reprint, New York: Garland Publishing, 1985.

Wood, Mrs. Henry. "Reality or Delusion?" In *Victorian Ghost Stories: An Oxford Anthology*, ed. Michael Cox and R. A. Gilbert, 115–129. Oxford: Oxford University Press, 1991.

"The Working Classes." *The Builder* 1, no. 22 (July 1843): 263–264.

Young, William. "'Model' Town Houses for the Middle Classes." *The Builder* 7, no. 356 (December 1849): 566–569.

————. *Town and Country Mansions and Suburban Houses*. London: Spon, 1879.

Zola, Emile. "L'Adultère dans la bourgeoisie." In *L'Encre et le sang*, ed. Henri Mitterand, 220–231. Paris: Editions complexe, 1989.

————. *Correspondance*. Ed. B. H. Bakker. Vol. 4. Montreal: Presses de l'Université de Montréal, 1978.

————. *Le Docteur Pascal*. Ed. Jean Borie. Paris: Garnier-Flammarion, 1975.

————. *Oeuvres complètes d'Emile Zola*. Ed. Eugène Fasquelle, notes Maurice Le Blond. Paris: Bernouard, 1927.

————. Ed. Henri Mitterand. Paris: Cercle du livre précieux, 1966.

————. *Pot-Bouille*. Paris: Livres de Poche, 1984.

————. Preface to *Mademoiselle Giraud ma femme*, by Adolphe Belot. Paris: Dentu, 1879.

————. "La Propriété littéraire." In *Oeuvres complètes*, ed. Eugène Fasquelle, notes Maurice Le Blond, 41:81–89. Paris: Bernouard, 1927.

————. *Le Roman expérimental*. Paris: Garnier-Flammarion, 1971.

————. *Les Rougon-Macquart: histoire naturelle et sociale d'une famille sous le Second Empire*. Ed. Colette Becker. Paris: Robert Laffont, 1992.

————. Ed. Henri Mitterand. Vol. 3. Paris: Gallimard, Bibliothèque de la Pléiade, 1964.

Secondary Sources

Abélès, Luce. "Du *Cousin Pons* à *L'Aiguille creuse:* les musées privés romanesques au XIXe siècle." *Revue d'histoire littéraire de la France* 95, no. 1 (January–February 1995): 27–35.

Accampo, Elinor. "Gender, Social Policy, and the Formation of the Third Republic: An Introduction." In *Gender and the Politics of Social Reform in France, 1870-1914*, ed. Elinor Accampo, Rachel Fuchs, and Mary Lynn Stewart, 1–27. Baltimore: Johns Hopkins University Press, 1995.

Accampo, Elinor, Rachel Fuchs, and Mary Lynn Stewart, eds. *Gender and the Politics of Social Reform in France, 1870-1914*. Baltimore: Johns Hopkins University Press, 1995.

Adams, Bernard. *London Illustrated 1604-1851: A Survey and Index of Topographical Books and Their Plates*. Phoenix: Onyx Press, 1983.

Addy, Sidney Oldall. *The Evolution of the English House*. 1933. Reprint, New York: British Book Centre, 1975.

Agrest, Diana. "Toward a Theory of Production of Sense in the Built Environment." In *On Streets*, ed. Stanford Anderson, 213–221. Cambridge, Mass.: MIT Press, 1978.

Aguirre, Manuel. *The Closed Space: Horror Literature and Western Symbolism*. Manchester: Manchester University Press, 1990.

Aisenberg, Andrew. *Contagion: Disease, Government, and the "Social Question" in Nineteenth-Century France*. Stanford: Stanford University Press, 1998.

————. "Contagious Disease and the Government of Paris in the Age of Pasteur." Ph.D. dissertation, Yale University, 1993.

———. "Contagious Poverty." Manuscript, 1995.

Anderson, Patricia. *The Printed Image and the Transformation of Popular Culture 1790–1860.* Oxford: Clarendon Press, 1991.

Anderson, Stanford. "People in the Physical Environment: The Urban Ecology of Streets." In *On Streets,* ed. Stanford Anderson, 1–11. Cambridge, Mass.: MIT Press, 1978.

———, ed. *On Streets.* Cambridge, Mass.: MIT Press, 1978.

Arendt, Hannah. *The Human Condition.* New York: Doubleday, 1959.

———. *Men in Dark Times.* San Diego: Harcourt, Brace, Jovanovich, 1968.

Architectures parisiennes au XIXe siècle. Exhibition catalog from the hôtel Sully, 1975.

Ariès, Philippe. "The Family and the City." *Daedalus* 106, no. 2 (spring 1977): 227–235.

Armingeat, Jacqueline, ed. *Intellectuelles et femmes socialistes.* Paris: Editions Vilo, 1974.

Armstrong, Nancy. *Desire and Domestic Fiction: A Political History of the Novel.* New York: Oxford University Press, 1987.

Auerbach, Erich. *Mimesis: The Representation of Reality in Western Literature.* Trans. Willard R. Trask. Princeton: Princeton University Press, 1953.

Auslander, Leora. *Taste and Power: Furnishing Modern France.* Berkeley: University of California Press, 1996.

Babelon, Jean-Pierre. *Demeures parisiennes sous Henri IV et Louis XIII.* Paris: Le Temps, 1965.

Bailey, Colin. "Conventions of the Eighteenth-Century *Cabinet de tableaux:* Blondel d'Azincourt's *La première idée de la curiosité.*" *Art Bulletin* 69, no. 3 (September 1987): 431–447.

Bakhtin, Mikhail. "Forms of Time and Chronotope in the Novel." In *The Dialogic Imagination: Four Essays.* Ed. Michael Holquist. Trans. Caryl Emerson and Michael Holquist, 84–258. Austin: University of Texas Press, 1981.

Baldick, Chris. Introduction to *Oxford Book of Gothic Tales.* Oxford: Oxford University Press, 1992.

Barker, Felix. *Highgate Cemetery: Victorian Valhalla.* Salem, N.H.: Salem House, 1984.

Barnes, David S. *The Making of a Social Disease: Tuberculosis in Nineteenth-Century France.* Berkeley: University of California Press, 1995.

Barret-Ducrocq, Françoise. *Love in the Time of Victoria: Sexuality, Class and Gender in Nineteenth-Century London.* London: Verso, 1991.

Barrow, Logie. *Independent Spirits: Spiritualism and English Plebeians, 1850–1910.* London: Routledge and Kegan Paul, 1986.

Barthes, Roland. *S/Z.* Paris: Editions du Seuil, 1970.

Bartlett, John. *Familiar Quotations.* Boston: Little, Brown, 1980.

Basset, Nathalie. "La *Physiologie du mariage* est-elle une physiologie?" *Année balzacienne* 7 (1986): 101–114.

Bataille, Georges. "Musée." In *Oeuvres complètes,* 1:239–240. Paris: Gallimard, 1970.

Becherer, Richard. *Science Plus Sentiment: César Daly's Formula for Modern Architecture.* Ann Arbor: UMI Research Press, 1984.

Becker, Colette. Preface to *Pot-Bouille*. In *Les Rougon-Macquart: histoire naturelle et sociale d'une famille sous le Second Empire*, ed. Colette Becker, 3:341–361. Paris: Robert Laffont, 1992.

——— *Zola en toutes lettres*. Paris: Bordas, 1990.

Bédarida, François, and Anthony Sutcliffe. "The Street in the Structure and Life of the City: Reflections on Nineteenth-Century London and Paris." In *Modern Industrial Cities: History, Policy, and Survival*, ed. Bruce M. Stave, 21–38. Beverly Hills: Sage Publications, 1981.

Beetham, Margaret. *A Magazine of Her Own? Domesticity and Desire in the Woman's Magazine, 1800–1914*. London: Routledge, 1996.

Beidler, Peter G. *Ghosts, Demons, and Henry James: "The Turn of the Screw" at the Turn of the Century*. Columbia: University of Missouri Press, 1989.

Beizer, Janet. "The Body in Question: Anatomy, Textuality, and Fetishism in Zola." *L'Esprit créateur* 29, no. 1 (1989): 50–60.

Benevolo, Leonardo. *The Origins of Modern Town Planning*. Trans. Judith Landry. Cambridge, Mass.: MIT Press, 1967.

Benjamin, Walter. *Charles Baudelaire: A Lyric Poet in the Era of High Capitalism*. Trans. Harry Zohn. London: Verso, 1983.

———. *The Correspondence of Walter Benjamin*. Ed. Gershom Scholem and Theodor W. Adorno. Trans. Manfred R. Jacobson and Evelyn M. Jacobson. Chicago: University of Chicago Press, 1994.

———. *Gesammelte Briefe*. Ed. Christoph Gödde and Henri Lonitz. Vol. 1. Frankfurt: Suhrkamp, 1995.

———. *Paris, capitale du XIXe siècle: le livre des passages*. Ed. Rolf Tiedemann. Trans. Jean Lacoste. Paris: Editions du cerf, 1989.

Bennett, Ernest. *Apparitions and Haunted Houses: A Survey of Evidence*. London: Faber and Faber, 1939.

Bernstein, Carol. *The Celebration of Scandal: Toward the Sublime in Victorian Urban Fiction*. University Park: Pennsylvania State University Press, 1991.

Best, Janice. *Expérimentation et adaptation: essai sur la méthode naturaliste d'Emile Zola*. Paris: Corti, 1986.

Best, Sue. "Sexualizing Space." In *Sexy Bodies: The Strange Carnalities of Feminism*, ed. Elizabeth Grosz and Elspeth Probyn, 181–194. New York: Routledge, 1995.

Betsky, Aaron. *Building Sex: Men, Women, Architecture, and the Construction of Sexuality*. New York: William Morrow, 1995.

Birkhead, Edith. *The Tale of Terror: A Study of the Gothic Romance*. London: Constable, 1921.

Blackmar, Elizabeth. *Manhattan for Rent, 1785–1850*. Ithaca: Cornell University Press, 1989.

Bloomer, Kent C., and Charles W. Moore. *Body, Memory, and Architecture*. New Haven: Yale University Press, 1977.

Boisson, Daniel. "Paris dans *les Parents pauvres* d'Honoré de Balzac." Mémoire de maîtrise. Université de Paris III, 1970–71.

Bonnet, Marie-Jo. *Un Choix sans équivoque: recherches historiques sur les relations amoureuses entre les femmes, XVIe–XXe siècles*. Paris: Denoël, 1981.

Booth, Michael. "The Metropolis on Stage." In *The Victorian City: Images and Realities,* ed. H. J. Dyos and Michael Wolff, 1:211–224. London: Routledge and Kegan Paul, 1976.

Borie, Jean. *Zola et les mythes, ou de la nausée au salut.* Paris: Editions du Seuil, 1971.

Briggs, Asa. Introduction to *The Illustrated Mayhew's London,* ed. John Canning. London: Weidenfeld and Nicolson, 1986.

———. *The Making of Modern England, 1783–1867: The Age of Improvement.* New York: Harper and Row, 1965.

Briggs, Julia. *Night Visitors: The Rise and Fall of the English Ghost Story.* London: Faber, 1977.

Brooke-Rose, Christine. *A Rhetoric of the Unreal: Studies in Narrative and Structure, Especially of the Fantastic.* Cambridge: Cambridge University Press, 1981.

Brooks, Chris. *Mortal Remains: The History and Present State of the Victorian and Edwardian Cemetery.* Exeter: Wheaton, 1989.

Brunetière, Ferdinand. "A propos de *Pot-Bouille.*" In *Le Roman naturaliste,* 277–299. 7th ed. Paris: Calmann-Lévy, 1896.

Burke, Thomas. *The Streets of London through the Centuries.* 4th ed. London: Batsford, 1949.

Burton, Elizabeth. *The Early Victorians at Home, 1837–1861.* London: Longman, 1972.

Butor, Michel. "Les Parents pauvres." In *Répertoire II: études et conférences 1959–1963,* 193–198. Paris: Minuit, 1964.

———. "The Space of the Novel." In *Inventory,* ed. Richard Howard, 31–38. New York: Simon and Schuster, 1968.

Calhoun, Craig, ed. *Habermas and the Public Sphere.* Cambridge, Mass.: MIT Press, 1992.

Cannadine, David. "War and Death, Grief and Mourning in Modern Britain." In *Mirrors of Mortality: Studies in the Social History of Death,* ed. Joachim Whaley, 187–242. London: Europa Publications, 1981.

Castells, Manuel. *The City and the Grassroots: A Cross-Cultural Theory of Urban Social Movements.* Berkeley: University of California Press, 1983.

Castex, Jean, Jean-Charles Depaule, and Philippe Panei. *Formes urbaines: de l'îlot à la barre.* Paris: Dunod, 1977.

Castle, Terry. *The Female Thermometer: Eighteenth-Century Culture and the Invention of the Uncanny.* New York: Oxford University Press, 1995.

Céleste, Patrick. "L'immeuble et son intérieur." *In Extenso* 9 (November 1985): 63–88.

Chartier, Roger. "Power, Space, and Investments in Paris." In *Edo and Paris: Urban Life and the State in the Early Modern Era,* ed. James L. McClain, John M. Merriman, and Ugawa Kaoru, 132–152. Ithaca: Cornell University Press, 1994.

Chemetov, Paul, and Bernard Marrey. *Architecture: Paris, 1848–1914.* Paris: Dunod, 1980.

Chesterton, G. K. *Charles Dickens: A Critical Study.* New York: Dodd Mead, 1911.

Chevalier, Louis. *Laboring Classes and Dangerous Classes in Paris during the First Half of the Nineteenth Century*. Trans. Frank Jellinek. Princeton: Princeton University Press, 1973.

Childers, Joseph W. "Feminine Hygiene: Women in Edwin Chadwick's Sanitation Report." *Prose Studies* 17, no. 2 (August 1994): 23–37.

Chombart de Lauwe, P.-H., et al. *Paris et l'agglomération parisienne*. Vol. 2. Paris: Presses universitaires de France, 1952.

Christ, Carol T. "Victorian Masculinity and the Angel in the House." In *A Widening Sphere: Changing Roles of Victorian Women*, ed. Martha Vicinus, 146–162. Bloomington: Indiana University Press, 1977.

Clark, Anna. *The Struggle for the Breeches: Gender and the Making of the British Working Class*. Berkeley: University of California Press, 1995.

Clark, T. J. *The Painting of Modern Life: Paris in the Art of Manet and His Followers*. Princeton: Princeton University Press, 1984.

Clery, E. J. *The Rise of Supernatural Fiction, 1762–1800*. Cambridge: Cambridge University Press, 1995.

Cohen, Margaret. *Compromising Positions: The Emergence of the Modern French Novel*. Princeton: Princeton University Press, forthcoming.

———. "Panoramic Literature and the Invention of Everyday Genres." In *Cinema and the Invention of Modern Life*, ed. Leo Charney and Vanessa R. Schwartz, 227–252. Berkeley: University of California Press, 1995.

———. *Profane Illumination: Walter Benjamin and the Paris of Surrealist Revolution*. Berkeley: University of California Press, 1993.

Cohen, William. *Sex Scandal: The Private Parts of Victorian Fiction*. Durham: Duke University Press, 1996.

Conrad, Peter. *The Victorian Treasure House*. London: Collins, 1973.

Corbin, Alain. *The Foul and the Fragrant: Odor and the French Social Imagination*. Cambridge, Mass.: Harvard University Press, 1986.

Cornell, Kenneth. "Zola's City." *Yale French Studies* 32 (1964): 106–111.

Cox, Michael, and R. A. Gilbert. Introduction to *Victorian Ghost Stories: An Oxford Anthology*, ed. Michael Cox and R. A. Gilbert. Oxford: Oxford University Press, 1991.

Creese, Walter L. "Imagination in the Suburb." In *Nature and the Victorian Imagination*, ed. U. C. Knoepflmacher and G. B. Tennyson, 49–67. Berkeley: University of California Press, 1977.

Crook, J. Mordaunt. "Metropolitan Improvements: John Nash and the Picturesque." In *London—World City: 1800–1840*, ed. Celina Fox, 77–96. New Haven: Yale University Press, 1992.

Crosby, Christina. *The Ends of History: Victorians and "the Woman Question."* New York: Routledge, 1991.

———. "Reading the Gothic Revival: 'History' and *Hints on Household Taste*." In *Rewriting the Victorians: Theory, History, and the Politics of Gender*, ed. Linda M. Shires, 101–115. New York: Routledge, 1992.

Curl, James Stevens. *The Victorian Celebration of Death*. Detroit: Partridge Press, 1872.

Dällenbach, Lucien. "Le pas-tout de la *Comédie*." *Modern Language Notes* 98 (1983): 702–11.

Daniel, Malcolm. *The Photographs of Edouard Baldus.* New York: Metropolitan Museum of Art, 1994.

Daumard, Adeline. *La Bourgeoisie parisienne de 1815 à 1848.* Paris: S.E.V.P.E.N., 1963.

———. "Conditions de logement et position sociale." In *Le Parisien chez lui au XIXe siècle 1814–1914.* Paris: Archives nationales, 1976.

———. *Maisons de Paris et propriétaires parisiens au XIXe siècle, 1809–1880.* Paris: Cujas, 1965.

Daunton, M. J., ed. *Housing the Workers 1850–1914: A Comparative Perspective.* Leicester: Leicester University Press, 1990.

Davidoff, Leonore. *The Best Circles: Society Etiquette and the Season.* 1973. Reprint, London: Cresset Library, 1986.

———. "The Separation of Home and Work? Landladies and Lodgers in Nineteenth- and Twentieth-Century England." In *Fit Work for Women,* ed. Sandra Burman, 64–97. New York: St. Martin's Press, 1979.

Davidoff, Leonore, and Catherine Hall. *Family Fortunes: Men and Women of the English Middle Class, 1780–1850.* Chicago: University of Chicago Press, 1987.

Davidoff, Leonore, Jean L'Esperance, and Howard Newly. "Landscape with Figures: Home and Community in English Society." In *The Rights and Wrongs of Women,* ed. Juliet Mitchell and Ann Oakley, 139–175. Harmondsworth: Penguin, 1976.

Deaucourt, Jean-Louis. "Paris et ses concierges au 19e siècle." Thèse de doctorat, Université de Paris VII, 1989.

———. "Une Police des sentiments: les concierges et les portiers." *Romantisme* 68 (1990): 49–60.

———. *Premières loges: Paris et ses concierges au XIXe siècle.* Paris: Aubier, 1992.

Debray-Genette, Raymonde. "Traversées de l'espace descriptif." *Poétique* 51 (1982): 329–44.

Delteil, Loys. *Le Peintre-graveur illustré (XIXe et XXe siècles): Honoré Daumier (V).* Vol. 24. Paris: Chez l'auteur, 1926.

Derrida, Jacques. *Specters of Marx: The State of the Debt, the Work of Mourning, and the New International.* Trans. Peggy Kamuf. New York: Routledge, 1994.

Duncan, Carol. "Art Museums and the Ritual of Citizenship." In *Exhibiting Cultures: The Poetics and Politics of Museum Display,* ed. Ivan Karp and Steven D. Lavine, 88–103. Washington, D.C.: Smithsonian Institute Press, 1991.

Duncan, Nancy. "Renegotiating Gender and Sexuality in Public and Private Spaces." In *Bodyspace: Destabilizing Geographies of Gender and Sexuality,* ed. Nancy Duncan, 127–145. London: Routledge, 1996.

Dyos, H. J. *Victorian Suburb: A Study of the Growth of Camberwell.* Leicester: Leicester University Press, 1961.

Edwards, Percy J. *History of London Street Improvements, 1855–1897.* London: London County Council, 1898.

Eleb-Vidal, Monique. "Dispositifs et moeurs: du privé à l'intime." *In Extenso* 9 (November 1985): 213–236.

Eleb-Vidal, Monique, and Anne Debarre-Blanchard. *Architectures de la vie privée: maisons et mentalités XVIIe–XIXe siècles.* Brussels: Archives d'Architecture moderne, 1989.

Ellis, Stewart Marsh. "The Ghost Story and Its Exponents." In *Mainly Victorian,* 322–331. 1925. Reprint, Freeport: Books for Libraries Press, 1969.

Ellis, William C. "The Spatial Structure of Streets." In *On Streets,* ed. Stanford Anderson, 112–131. Cambridge, Mass.: MIT Press, 1978.

Etlin, Richard Allan. "The Cemetery and the City: Paris, 1744–1804." Ph.D. dissertation, Princeton University, 1978.

Evans, Bergen. *Dictionary of Quotations.* New York: Delacorte Press, 1968.

Evans, Robin. "Figures, portes et passages." *Urbi: arts, histoire et ethnologie des villes* 5 (April 1982): 23–41.

Evenson, Norma. *Paris: A Century of Change, 1878–1978.* New Haven: Yale University Press, 1979.

Eyre, Alan Mongtomery. *St. John's Wood: Its History, Its Houses, Its Haunts and Its Celebrities.* London: Chapman and Hall, 1913.

Faillie, Marie-Henriette. *La Femme et le code civil dans "la Comédie humaine" d'Honoré de Balzac.* Paris: Didier, 1968.

Fawcett, Jane, ed. *Seven Victorian Architects.* University Park: Pennsylvania State University Press, 1977.

Felski, Rita. "The Gender of Modernity." In *Political Gender: Texts and Contexts,* ed. Sally Ledger, Josephine McDonagh, and Jane Spencer, 144–155. New York: Harvester, 1994.

Ferguson, Priscilla Parkhurst. *Paris as Revolution: Writing the Nineteenth-Century City.* Berkeley: University of California Press, 1994.

Fermigier, André. Preface to *Pot-Bouille.* Paris: Gallimard, 1982.

Findlen, Paula. "The Museum: Its Classical Etymology and Renaissance Genealogy." *Journal of the History of Collections* 1, no. 1 (1989): 59–78.

Finucane, R. C. *Appearances of the Dead: A Cultural History of Ghosts.* London: Junction Books, 1982.

Fitzimons, Raymund. *The Baron of Piccadilly: The Travels and Entertainments of Albert Smith 1816–1860.* London: Geoffrey Bles, 1967.

Ford, George H. "Felicitous Space: The Cottage Controversy." In *Nature and the Victorian Imagination,* ed. U. C. Knoepflmacher and G. B. Tennyson, 29–48. Berkeley: University of California Press, 1977.

Foucault, Michel. "Space, Knowledge, and Power." In *The Foucault Reader,* ed. Paul Rabinow, 239–256. New York: Pantheon, 1984.

Fox, Celina, ed. *London—World City: 1800–1840.* New Haven: Yale University Press, 1992.

Frappier-Mazur, Lucienne. "Le Discours du pouvoir dans *le Cousin Pons.*" In *Balzac et "les Parents pauvres,"* ed. Françoise van Rossum-Guyon and Michiel van Brederode, 21–32. Paris: Société d'Enseignement supérieur, 1981.

Fried, Michael. *Absorption and Theatricality: Painting and Beholder in the Age of Diderot.* Berkeley: University of California Press, 1980.

———. *Courbet's Realism.* Chicago: University of Chicago Press, 1990.

———. *Manet's Modernism, or, The Face of Painting in the 1860s.* Chicago: University of Chicago Press, 1996.

Friedland, Roger, and Deirdre Boden. "NowHere: An Introduction to Space, Time, and Modernity." In *NowHere: Space, Time, and Modernity,* ed. Roger Friedland and Deirdre Boden, 1–60. Berkeley: University of California Press, 1994.

Frølich, Juliette. *Pictogrammes: figures du descriptif dans le roman balzacien.* Oslo: Privat, 1985.

Gaillard, Françoise. "La Stratégie de l'araignée (notes sur le réalisme balzacien)." In *Balzac et "les Parents pauvres,"* ed. Françoise van Rossum-Guyon and Michiel van Brederode, 179–187. Paris: Société d'Enseignement supérieur, 1981.

Gaillard, Jeanne. *Paris: la ville, 1852–1870.* Paris: Champion, 1977.

Gallagher, Catherine. *The Industrial Reformation of English Fiction: Social Discourse and Narrative Form, 1832–1867.* Chicago: University of Chicago Press, 1985.

Gauthier, Henri. *L'Image de l'homme intérieur chez Balzac.* Geneva: Droz, 1984.

Georgel, Chantal. *La Rue.* Paris: Hazan, 1986.

Gil, Biagio Accolti. *Paris: vestibules de l'éclectisme.* Trans. Jean Louis Proroyeur. Paris: Vilo, 1982.

Girouard, Mark. *Cities and People: A Social and Architectural History.* New Haven: Yale University Press, 1985.

———. *Life in the English Country House: A Social and Architectural History.* Harmondsworth: Penguin, 1980.

———. *The Victorian Country House.* Rev. ed. New Haven: Yale University Press, 1979.

Glanville, Philippa. *London in Maps.* London: Connoisseur, 1992.

Gloag, John. *The Englishman's Castle.* London: Eyre and Spottiswoode, 1944.

———. *Mr Loudon's England: The Life and Work of John Claudius Loudon.* Newcastle upon Tyne: Oriel Press, 1970.

Goodhart-Rendel, H. S. *English Architecture Since the Regency: An Interpretation.* London: Constable, 1953.

Les Grands boulevards. Paris: Musées de la ville de Paris, 1985.

Grant, Elliott M. "The Political Scene in Zola's *Pot-Bouille.*" *French Studies* 8, no. 3 (1954).

Green, Nicholas. *The Spectacle of Nature: Landscape and Bourgeois Culture in Nineteenth-Century France.* Manchester: Manchester University Press, 1990.

Griffin, Andrew. "The Interior Garden and John Stuart Mill." In *Nature and the Victorian Imagination,* ed. U. C. Knoepflmacher and G. B. Tennyson, 171–186. Berkeley: University of California Press, 1977.

Grosz, Elizabeth. "Space, Time, and Bodies." In *Space, Time, and Perversion: Essays on the Politics of Bodies,* 83–101. New York: Routledge, 1995.

Guerrand, Roger-Henri. *Moeurs citadines: histoire de la culture urbaine XIXe–XXe siècles.* Paris: Quai Voltaire, 1992.

———. *Les Origines du logement social en France.* Paris: Editions ouvrières, 1967.

Guichardet, Jeannine. "Un Jeu de l'oie maléfique: l'espace parisien du *Père Goriot.*" *Année balzacienne* 7 (1986): 169–189.

Guillemin, Henri. *Présentation des "Rougon-Macquart."* Paris: NRF Gallimard, 1964.

Habermas, Jürgen. *The Structural Transformation of the Public Sphere: An Inquiry into a Category of Bourgeois Society.* Trans. Thomas Burger. Cambridge, Mass.: MIT Press, 1991.

Haine, W. Scott. *The World of the Paris Café: Sociability among the French Working Class, 1789–1914.* Baltimore: Johns Hopkins University Press, 1996.

Hamon, Philippe. *Expositions: Literature and Architecture in Nineteenth-Century France.* Trans. Katia Sainson-Frank and Lisa Maguire. Berkeley: University of California Press, 1992.

———. "Le Musée et le texte." *Revue d'histoire littéraire de la France* 95, no. 1 (January–February 1995): 3–12.

Harsin, Jill. *Policing Prostitution in Nineteenth-Century Paris.* Princeton: Princeton University Press, 1985.

Harvey, David. "Paris, 1850–1870." In *Consciousness and the Urban Experience,* 63–220. Baltimore: Johns Hopkins University Press, 1985.

Hautecoeur, Louis. "Immeubles à loyer." In *Urbanisme et architecture: études écrites et publiées en l'honneur de Pierre Lavedan,* 167–178. Paris: Laurens, 1954.

Hayden, Dolores. *The Grand Domestic Revolution: A History of Feminist Designs for American Homes, Neighborhoods, and Cities.* Cambridge, Mass.: MIT Press, 1981.

———. "What Would a Non-Sexist City Be Like? Speculations on Housing, Urban Design, and Human Work." In *The City Reader,* ed. Richard T. LeGates and Frederic Stout, 143–157. New York: Routledge, 1996.

Heller, Geneviève. *"Propre en ordre": habitation et vie domestique 1850–1930 —l'exemple vaudois.* Lausanne: Editions d'en bas, 1979.

Hellerstein, Erna Olafson. "Women, Social Order, and the City: Rules for French Ladies, 1830–1870." Ph.D. dissertation, University of California, Berkeley, 1980.

Hibbert, Christopher. *London: The Biography of a City.* New York: William Morrow, 1969.

Hill, W. T. *Octavia Hill.* London: Hutchinson, 1956.

Hirsch, Eric, and Michael O'Hanlon, eds. *The Anthropology of Landscape: Perspectives on Place and Space.* Oxford: Clarendon Press, 1995.

Hitchcock, Henry-Russell. *Early Victorian Architecture in Britain.* 2 vols. London: Architectural Press, 1954.

Hobhouse, Hermione. *Thomas Cubitt, Master Builder.* New York: Universe, 1971.

Hollander, John. "It All Depends." In *Home: A Place in the World,* ed. Arien Mack, 27–45. New York: New York University Press, 1993.

Hollier, Denis. "Bloody Sundays." *Representations* 28 (fall 1989): 77–89.

Hulin, Jean-Paul. "'Rus in Urbe': A Key to Victorian Anti-Urbanism?" In *Victorian Writers and the City,* ed. Jean-Paul Hulin and Pierre Coustillas, 11–40. Lille: Publications de l'université de Lille III, 1979.

Hulme, Peter. "Balzac's Parisian Mystery: *La Cousine Bette* and the Writing of Historical Criticism." *Literature and History* 11, no. 1 (spring 1985): 47–64.

Humpherys, Anne. "Generic Strands and Urban Twists: The Victorian Mysteries Novel." *Victorian Studies* 34 (1991): 455–472.

———. "The Geometry of the Modern City: G. W. M. Reynolds and *The Mysteries of London.*" *Browning Institute Studies* (1983): 69–80.

Hunt, H. J. *Balzac's "Comédie Humaine."* London: Athlone Press, 1959.

Hunt, Lynn. *Politics, Culture, and Class in the French Revolution.* Berkeley: University of California Press, 1984.

———. "History beyond Social Theory." In *The States of "Theory": History, Art, and Critical Discourse,* ed. David Carroll, 95–111. New York: Columbia University Press, 1990.

Hunter, Michael. *The Victorian Villas of Hackney.* London: Hackney Society Publication, 1981.

Jackson, Neil. "The Speculative House in London c. 1832–1914." Ph.D. dissertation, the Polytechnic of the South Bank, London, 1982.

Jackson, Rosemary. *Fantasy: The Literature of Subversion.* London: Methuen, 1981.

Jacobs, Jane. *The Death and Life of Great American Cities.* New York: Vintage, 1961.

Jacques, Annie. *La Carrière de l'architecte au XIXe siècle.* Paris: Editions de la réunion des musées nationaux, 1986.

Jallat, Jeannine. "Lieux balzaciens." *Poétique* 64 (1985): 473–481.

Jameson, Fredric. *The Political Unconscious: Narrative as a Socially Symbolic Act.* Ithaca: Cornell University Press, 1981.

Jordan, R. Furneaux. *A Picture History of the English House.* New York: Macmillan, 1959.

Kaenel, Philippe. "Autour de J. J. Grandville: les conditions de production socioprofessionnelles du livre illustré 'romantique.'" *Romantisme* 43 (1984): 45–60.

Kamm, Lewis. "The Structural and Functional Manifestation of Space in Zola's *Rougon-Macquart.*" *Nineteenth-Century French Studies* 3, nos. 3–4 (spring–summer 1975): 224–236.

Kashiwagi, Takao. *La Trilogie des célibataires d'Honoré de Balzac.* Paris: Nizet, 1983.

Kessler, Joan C. Introduction to *Demons of the Night: Tales of the Fantastic, Madness, and the Supernatural from Nineteenth-Century France.* Chicago: University of Chicago Press, 1995.

Klein, Lawrence. "Gender and the Public/Private Distinction in the Eighteenth Century: Some Questions about Evidence and Analytic Procedure." *Eighteenth-Century Studies* 29, no. 1 (1995): 97–109.

Knoepflmacher, U. C., and G. B. Tennyson, eds. *Nature and the Victorian Imagination.* Berkeley: University of California Press, 1977.

Kracauer, Siegfried. *Orpheus in Paris: Offenbach and the Paris of His Time.* Trans. Gwenda David and Eric Mosbacher. New York: Knopf, 1938.

Kruse, Horst. "The Museum Motif in English and American Fiction of the Nineteenth Century." *Amerikastudien* 31, no. 1 (1986): 71–79.

Kudlick, Catherine J. *Cholera in Post-Revolutionary Paris: A Cultural History.* Berkeley: University of California Press, 1996.

Landes, Joan. *Women and the Public Sphere in the Age of the French Revolution.* Ithaca: Cornell University Press, 1988.

Langan, Celeste. *Romantic Vagrancy: Wordsworth and the Simulation of Freedom.* Cambridge: Cambridge University Press, 1995.

Langland, Elizabeth. *Nobody's Angels: Middle-Class Women and Domestic Ideology in Victorian Culture.* Ithaca: Cornell University Press, 1995.

Lapp, John C. "The Watcher Betrayed and the Fatal Woman: Some Recurring Patterns in Zola." *PMLA* 74, no. 3 (1959): 276–284.

Lefebvre, Henri. *The Production of Space.* Trans. D. Nicholson-Smith. Oxford: Blackwell, 1991.

Léon, Paul. "Maisons et rues de Paris." *Revue de Paris* (August 1910): 848–849.

Lethbridge, Robert. "A Visit to the Louvre: *L'Assommoir* Revisited." *Modern Language Review* 87, no. 1 (January 1992): 41–55.

Lewis, R. A. *Edwin Chadwick and the Public Health Movement, 1832–1854.* London: Longmans, Green, 1952.

Lhéritier, Andrée. "*Les Physiologies:* catalogue des collections de la Bibliothèque nationale." *Etudes de Presse,* n.s., 9, no. 17 (1957): 13–58.

Lipstadt, Hélène. "Housing the Bourgeoisie: César Daly and the Ideal Home." *Oppositions* 8 (spring 1977): 35–47.

Loeb, Lori. *Consuming Angels: Advertising and Victorian Women.* New York: Oxford University Press, 1994.

Lorant, André. "*Les Parents pauvres*" *d'Honoré de Balzac.* Geneva: Droz, 1967.

Loyer, François. *Paris: Nineteenth-Century Architecture and Urbanism.* Trans. Charles Lynn Clark. New York: Abbeville Press, 1988.

Lucey, Michael. "Balzac's Queer Cousins and Their Friends." In *Novel Gazing: Queer Readings in Fiction,* ed. Eve Kosofsky Sedgwick, 167–198. Durham: Duke University Press, 1997.

Lukács, Georg. "The Zola Centenary." In *Critical Essays on Emile Zola,* ed. David Baguley, 80–89. Boston: G. K. Hall, 1986.

MacAndrew, Elizabeth. *The Gothic Tradition in Fiction.* New York: Columbia University Press, 1979.

Mackenzie, Compton. *Our Street.* New York: Doubleday, 1932.

McClellan, Andrew. *Inventing the Louvre: Art, Politics, and the Origins of the Modern Museum in Eighteenth-Century Paris.* Cambridge: Cambridge University Press, 1994.

McGuire, James R. "The Feminine Conspiracy in Balzac's *La Cousine Bette.*" *Nineteenth-Century French Studies* 20, nos. 3–4 (spring–summer 1992): 295–304.

McLeod, Mary. "Everyday and 'Other' Spaces." In *Architecture and Feminism,* ed. Debra Coleman, Elizabeth Danze, and Carol Henderson, 1–37. New York: Princeton Architectural Press, 1996.

Marcus, Sharon. Introduction to *The Physiology of Marriage,* by Honoré de Balzac. Baltimore: Johns Hopkins University Press, 1997.

Markus, Thomas. *Buildings and Power: Freedom and Control in the Origin of Modern Building Types.* London: Routledge, 1993.

Martin-Fugier, Anne. *La Vie élégante ou la formation du tout-Paris 1815–1848.* Paris: Fayard, 1990.

Maslan, Susan. "Resisting Representation: Theater and Democracy in Revolutionary France." *Representations* 52 (fall 1995): 27–51.

———. "Representation and Theatricality in French Revolutionary Theater and Politics." Ph.D. dissertation, Johns Hopkins University, 1997.

Massey, Doreen. *Space, Place, and Gender.* Minneapolis: University of Minnesota Press, 1994.

Matlock, Jann. "Censoring the Realist Gaze." In *Spectacles of Realism: Body, Gender, Genre,* ed. Margaret Cohen and Christopher Prendergast, 28–65. Minneapolis: University of Minnesota Press, 1995.

———. *Scenes of Seduction: Prostitution, Hysteria, and Reading Difference in Nineteenth-Century France.* New York: Columbia University Press, 1994.

Maxwell, Richard. *The Mysteries of Paris and London.* Charlottesville: University Press of Virginia, 1992.

Melcher, Edith. *The Life and Times of Henry Monnier: 1799–1877.* Cambridge, Mass.: Harvard University Press, 1950.

Michaels, Walter Benn. "Romance and Real Estate." In *The Gold Standard and the Logic of Naturalism: American Literature at the Turn of the Century,* 85–112. Berkeley: University of California Press, 1987.

Mileham, James W. *The Conspiracy Novel: Structure and Metaphor in Balzac's "Comédie Humaine."* Lexington, Ky.: French Forum, 1982.

Miller, D. A. "Balzac's Illusions Lost and Found." *Yale French Studies* 67 (1984): 164–181.

———. "Body Bildung and Textual Liberation." In *A New History of French Literature,* ed. Denis Hollier, 681–687. Cambridge, Mass.: Harvard University Press, 1989.

———. *The Novel and the Police.* Berkeley: University of California Press, 1988.

Milman, Miriam. *Architectures peintes en trompe-l'oeil.* Geneva: Skira, 1986.

———. *Le Trompe-l'oeil.* Geneva: Skira, 1982.

Mitterand, Henri. "Le Lieu et le sens: l'espace parisien dans *Ferragus.*" In *Le Discours du roman,* 189–212. Paris: Presses universitaires de France, 1980.

———. "*Notice*" to *Pot-Bouille,* by Emile Zola, 456–467. Paris: Gallimard, 1982.

Mollier, Jean-Yves. "Emile Zola et le système éditorial français." *Les Cahiers naturalistes* 67 (1993): 245–262.

Moretti, Franco. *Signs Taken for Wonders: Essays in the Sociology of Literary Forms.* Trans. Susan Fischer, David Forgacs, and David Miller. London: Verso, 1988.

———. *The Way of the World: The Bildungsroman in European Culture.* London: Verso, 1987.

Moses, Claire Goldberg. *French Feminism in the Nineteenth Century.* Albany: State University of New York Press, 1984.

Mount, A. J. *The Physical Setting in Balzac's "Comédie Humaine."* Hull: University of Hull Publications, 1966.

Mozet, Nicole. *"La Cousine Bette" d'Honoré de Balzac.* Paris: Editions pédagogie moderne, 1980.

Muthesius, Hermann. *The English House*. Trans. Janet Seligman. Oxford: BSP Professional Books, 1979.

Muthesius, Stefan. *The English Terraced House*. New Haven: Yale University Press, 1982.

Nelson, Brian. *Zola and the Bourgeoisie: A Study of Themes and Techniques in "Les Rougon-Macquart."* Totowa, N.J.: Barnes and Noble, 1983.

Noiray, Jacques. "La Symbolique de l'espace dans *la Curée*." *L'Information littéraire* 39, no. 1 (1987): 16–20.

Nord, Deborah Epstein. "The City as Theater: From Georgian to Early Victorian London." *Victorian Studies* 31 (winter 1988): 159–188.

———. "The Social Explorer as Anthropologist: Victorian Travellers Among the Urban Poor." In *Visions of the Modern City: Essays in History, Art, and Literature,* ed. William Sharpe and Leonard Wallock, 122–134. Baltimore: Johns Hopkins University Press, 1987.

———. *Walking the Victorian Streets: Women, Representation, and the City.* Ithaca: Cornell University Press, 1995.

Nourissier, François. Introduction to *Oeuvres complètes d'Emile Zola*. Paris: Cercle du livre précieux, 1966.

Olsen, Donald. *The City as a Work of Art: London, Paris, Vienna*. New Haven: Yale University Press, 1986.

———*The Growth of Victorian London*. New York: Penguin, 1976.

Oppenheim, Janet. *The Other World: Spiritualism and Psychical Research in England, 1850–1914*. Cambridge: Cambridge University Press, 1985.

Owen, Alex. *The Darkened Room: Women, Power and Spiritualism in Late Nineteenth-Century England*. London: Virago Press, 1980.

Pardailhé-Galabrun, Annik. *The Birth of Intimacy: Privacy and Domestic Life in Early Modern France*. Trans. Jocelyn Phelps. Cambridge: Polity Press, 1991.

Le Parisien chez lui au XIXe siècle 1814–1914. Paris: Archives nationales, 1976.

Pasco, Allan H. *Balzacian Montage: Configuring the "Comédie Humaine."* Toronto: University of Toronto Press, 1991.

Patten, Robert. "'A Surprising Transformation': Dickens and the Hearth." In *Nature and the Victorian Imagination,* ed. U. C. Knoepflmacher and G. B. Tennyson, 153–170. Berkeley: University of California Press, 1977.

Paulson, Ronald. "Gothic Fiction and the French Revolution." *ELH* 48 (1981): 532–554.

Paulson, William. "Le Cousin parasite: Balzac, Serres, et le démon de Maxwell." *Stanford French Review* 9 (winter 1985): 397–414.

Pelckmans, Paul. *Concurrences au monde: propositions pour une poétique du collectionneur moderne*. Amsterdam: Rodopi, 1990.

Perrot, Michelle. "La ménagère dans l'espace parisien au XIXe siècle." *Annales de la recherche urbaine* 9 (1980): 3–22.

———, ed. *A History of Private Life: From the Fires of Revolution to the Great War*. Trans. Arthur Goldhammer. Vol. 4. Cambridge, Mass.: Belknap Press of Harvard University Press, 1990.

Pichois, Claude. "Le Succès des *Physiologies*." *Etudes de Presse*, n.s., 9, no. 17 (1957): 59–66.

Picon, Antoine. "Du traité à la revue: l'image d'architecture au siècle de l'industrie." In *Usages de l'image au XIXe siècle,* ed. Stéphane Michaud, Jean-Yves Mullier, and Nicole Savy, 153–164. Paris: Créaphis, 1992.

Pinkney, David. *Napoleon III and the Rebuilding of Paris.* Princeton: Princeton University Press, 1958.

Plotz, John. "Jealousy of the Crowd in British Literature, 1800–1850." Ph.D. dissertation, Harvard University, 1997.

Pollock, Griselda. *Vision and Difference: Femininity, Feminism, and Histories of Art.* London: Routledge, 1988.

Pomian, Krzystof. *Collectors and Curiosities: Paris and Venice, 1500–1800.* Trans. Elizabeth Wiles-Portier. London: Polity Press, 1990.

Poovey, Mary. "Anatomical Realism and Social Investigation in Early Nineteenth-Century Manchester." *differences* 5, no. 3 (fall 1993): 1–30.

———. "Domesticity and Class Formation: Chadwick's 1842 *Sanitary Report.*" In *Subject to History: Ideology, Class, Gender,* ed. David Simpson, 65–83. Ithaca: Cornell University Press, 1991.

———. *Making a Social Body: British Cultural Formation, 1830–1864.* Chicago: University of Chicago Press, 1995.

———. *Uneven Developments: The Ideological Work of Gender in Mid-Victorian England.* Chicago: University of Chicago Press, 1988.

Poulet, Georges. *Etudes sur le temps humain: la distance intérieure.* Vol. 2. Paris: Plon, 1952.

Poulot, Dominique. "L'Invention de la bonne volonté culturelle: l'image du musée au XIXe siècle." *Mouvement social* 131 (April–June 1995): 35–64.

———. "Le Louvre imaginaire: essai sur le statut du musée en France, des lumières à la république." *Historical Reflections* 17, no. 2 (1991): 184–203.

Prendergast, Christopher. *Balzac: Fiction and Melodrama.* London: Edward Arnold, 1978.

———. *Paris and the Nineteenth Century.* Oxford: Blackwell, 1992.

Pronteau, Jeanne. "Construction et aménagement des nouveaux quartiers de Paris (1820–1826)." *Histoire des entreprises* 1, no. 2 (November 1958): 8–32.

Rabinow, Paul, ed. *The Foucault Reader.* New York: Pantheon, 1984.

Ragon, Michel. *The Space of Death: A Study of Funerary Architecture, Decoration, and Urbanism.* Trans. Alan Sheridan. Charlottesville: University Press of Virginia, 1983.

Railo, Eino. *The Haunted Castle: A Study of the Elements of English Romanticism.* London: Routledge, 1927.

Reboul, Pierre. "De l'intime à l'intimisme." In *Intime, intimité, intimisme,* 7–12. Lille: Publications de l'université de Lille III, 1976.

Reeder, David A. "Suburbanity and the Victorian City." Second H. J. Dyos Memorial Lecture. Delivered May 20, 1980, at the University of Leicester Victorian Studies Centre.

Regard, Maurice. Preface to *Physiologie du mariage,* by Honoré de Balzac. Paris: Garnier-Flammarion, 1968.

Reid, J. C. *Bucks and Bruisers: Pierce Egan and Regency England.* London: Routledge and Kegan Paul, 1971.

Reid, Roddy. *Families in Jeopardy: Regulating the Social Body in France, 1750–1910*. Stanford: Stanford University Press, 1993.

Richardson, Ruth. "George Godwin of *The Builder*: Indefatigable Journalist and Instigator of a Fine Victorian Visual Resource." *Visual Resources* 6 (1989): 121–140.

Rignall, John. "Benjamin's *Flâneur* and the Problem of Realism." In *The Problems of Modernity: Adorno and Benjamin*, ed. Andrew Benjamin, 112–121. London: Routledge, 1989.

Rivers, Christopher. *Face Value: Physiognomical Thought and the Legible Body in Marivaux, Lavater, Balzac, Gautier, and Zola*. Madison: University of Wisconsin Press, 1994.

Robbins, Bruce. "The Public as Phantom." In *The Phantom Public Sphere*, ed. Bruce Robbins, vii–xvii. Minneapolis: University of Minnesota Press, 1993.

———. *The Servant's Hand: English Fiction from Below*. New York: Columbia University Press, 1986.

———, ed. *The Phantom Public Sphere*. Minneapolis: University of Minnesota Press, 1993.

Rose, Gillian. *Feminism and Geography: The Limits of Geographical Knowledge*. Minneapolis: University of Minnesota Press, 1993.

Ross, Ellen. *Love and Toil: Motherhood in Outcast London, 1870–1918*. New York: Oxford University Press, 1993.

Ross, Kristin. *The Emergence of Social Space: Rimbaud and the Paris Commune*. Foreword by Terry Eagleton. Theory and History of Literature, no. 60. Minneapolis: University of Minnesota Press, 1988.

———. *Fast Cars, Clean Bodies: Decolonization and the Reordering of French Culture*. Cambridge, Mass.: MIT Press, 1995.

Rubinstein, W. D. *Men of Property: The Very Wealthy in Britain Since the Industrial Revolution*. London: Croom Helm, 1981.

Ryan, Mary. *Women in Public: Between Banners and Ballots, 1825–1880*. Baltimore: Johns Hopkins University Press, 1990.

Rykwert, Joseph. *On Adam's House in Paradise: The Idea of the Primitive Hut in Architectural History*. 2d ed. Cambridge, Mass.: MIT Press, 1989.

———. "The Street: The Use of Its History." In *On Streets*, ed. Stanford Anderson, 15–27. Cambridge, Mass.: MIT Press, 1978.

Saboya, Marc. *Presse et architecture au XIXe siècle: César Daly et "la Revue générale de l'architecture et des travaux publics."* Paris: Picard, 1991.

Sack, Robert David. *Place, Modernity, and the Consumer's World: A Relational Framework for Geographical Analysis*. Baltimore: Johns Hopkins University Press, 1992.

Saint, Andrew. "The Building Art of the First Industrial Metropolis." In *London—World City: 1800–1840*, ed. Celina Fox, 51–76. New Haven: Yale University Press, 1992.

———. *The Image of the Architect*. New Haven: Yale University Press, 1983.

Schaffer, Talia. "The Woman's World of British Aestheticism, 1870–1910." Ph.D. dissertation, Cornell University, 1996.

Schivelbusch, Wolfgang. *Disenchanted Night: The Industrialization of Light in the Nineteenth Century.* Trans. Angela Davies. Berkeley: University of California Press, 1988.

Schor, Naomi. "Zola: From Window to Window." *Yale French Studies* 42 (1969): 38–51.

———. *Zola's Crowds.* Baltimore: Johns Hopkins University Press, 1978.

Schuerewegen, Franc. "De la nécessité préfacielle (Balzac, Zola)." *French Forum* 16, no. 2 (May 1991): 178–186.

———. "*Muséum* ou *Crotéum*: Pons, Bouvard, Pécuchet et la collection." *Romantisme* 55 (1987): 42–54.

Schwartz, Vanessa R. "Museums and Mass Spectacle: The Musée Grévin as a Monument to Modern Life." *French Historical Studies* 19, no. 1 (spring 1995): 7–26.

———. *Spectacular Realities: Early Mass Culture in Fin-de-Siècle Paris.* Berkeley: University of California Press, 1998.

Schwarzbach, F. S. "'Terra Incognita'—An Image of the City in English Literature, 1820–1855." *Prose Studies* 5 (1982): 61–84.

Scott, Joan Wallach. *Only Paradoxes to Offer: French Feminists and the Rights of Man.* Cambridge, Mass.: Harvard University Press, 1996.

Scott, Joan Wallach. "A Statistical Representation of Work: *La Statistique de l'industrie à Paris,* 1847–1848." In *Gender and the Politics of History,* 113–138. New York: Columbia University Press, 1988.

Sedgwick, Eve Kosofsky. *The Coherence of Gothic Conventions.* New York: Arno Press, 1980.

Sennett, Richard. *The Fall of Public Man: On the Social Psychology of Capitalism.* 1974. Reprint, New York: Vintage, 1978.

Shapiro, Ann-Louise. *Housing the Poor of Paris, 1850–1902.* Madison: University of Wisconsin Press, 1985.

Sharp, Lynn Louise. "Rational Religion, Irrational Science: Men, Women, and Belief in French Spiritism, 1853–1914." Ph.D. dissertation, University of California, Irvine, 1996.

Shattock, Joanne, and Michael Wolff, eds. *The Victorian Periodical Press: Samplings and Soundings.* Leicester: Leicester University Press, 1982.

Sherman, Daniel J. *Worthy Monuments: Art Museums and the Politics of Culture in Nineteenth-Century France.* Cambridge, Mass.: Harvard University Press, 1989.

Sieburth, Richard. "Une Idéologie du lisible: le phénomène des 'Physiologies.'" *Romantisme* 47 (1985): 39–60.

Silverman, Debora. *Art Nouveau in Fin-de-Siècle France: Politics, Psychology, and Style.* Berkeley: University of California Press, 1989.

Simo, Melanie Louise. *Loudon and the Landscape: From Country Seat to Metropolis, 1783–1843.* New Haven: Yale University Press, 1988.

Simpson, A. W. B. *A History of the Land Law.* Oxford: Clarendon Press, 1986.

Slater, T. R. "Family, Society, and the Ornamental Villa on the Fringes of English Country Towns." *Journal of Historical Geography* 4, no. 2 (1978): 129–144.

Smith, Bonnie. *Ladies of the Leisure Class: The Bourgeoises of Northern France in the Nineteenth Century.* Princeton: Princeton University Press, 1981.

Snyder, Katherine V. *Bachelors, Manhood, and the Novel.* Cambridge: Cambridge University Press, forthcoming.

———. "A Paradise of Bachelors: Remodeling Domesticity and Masculinity in the Turn-of-the-Century New York Bachelor Apartment." *Prospects* (forthcoming).

Soja, Edward. *Postmodern Geographies: The Reassertion of Space in Critical Social Theory.* London: Verso, 1989.

Solomon, Philip. "The Space of Bourgeois Hypocrisy in Zola's *Pot-Bouille.*" *Kentucky Romance Quarterly* 32, no. 3 (1985): 255–264.

Spain, Daphne. *Gendered Spaces.* Chapel Hill: University of North Carolina Press, 1992.

Spencer, Kathleen. "Purity and Danger: *Dracula*, the Urban Gothic, and the Late Victorian Degeneracy Crisis." *ELH* 59 (1992): 197–225.

Stallybrass, Peter, and Allon White. *The Politics and Poetics of Transgression.* Ithaca: Cornell University Press, 1986.

Starobinski, Jean. *Rousseau: la transparence et l'obstacle.* Paris: Gallimard, 1971.

Stein, Richard. "Street Figures: Victorian Urban Iconography." In *Victorian Literature and the Victorian Visual Imagination,* ed. Carol T. Christ and John O. Jordan, 233–263. Berkeley: University of California Press, 1995.

Steiner, Frances H. *French Iron Architecture.* Ann Arbor: UMI Research Press, 1984.

Stone, Judith F. "The Republican Brotherhood: Gender and Ideology." In *Gender and the Politics of Social Reform in France, 1870–1914,* ed. Elinor Accampo, Rachel Fuchs, and Mary Lynn Stewart, 28–58. Baltimore: Johns Hopkins University Press, 1995.

Straus, Erwin. "The Upright Posture." In *Essays in Phenomenology,* ed. Maurice Natanson, 164–192. The Hague: Marhuis Nijhoff, 1966.

Sucksmith, Harvey. *The Narrative Art of Charles Dickens: The Rhetoric of Sympathy and Irony in His Novels.* Oxford: Clarendon Press, 1970.

Summers, Montague. Introduction to *The Supernatural Omnibus.* London: Gollancz, 1931.

Summerson, John. "London, the Artifact." In *The Victorian City: Images and Realities,* ed. H. J. Dyos and Michael Wolff, 1:311–332. London: Routledge and Kegan Paul, 1976.

Sutcliffe, Anthony. *Paris: An Architectural History.* New Haven: Yale University Press, 1993.

———, ed. Preface to *Multi-Storey Living: The British Working Class Experience.* London: Croom Helm, 1974.

Taylor, Nicholas. "The Awful Sublimity of the Victorian City." In *The Victorian City: Images and Realities,* ed. H. J. Dyos and Michael Wolff, 2:431–447. London: Routledge and Kegan Paul, 1976.

Terdiman, Richard. *Discourse/Counter-Discourse: The Theory and Practice of Symbolic Resistance in Nineteenth-Century France.* Ithaca: Cornell University Press, 1985.

Tester, Keith, ed. *The Flâneur.* New York: Routledge, 1994.

Thalamy, Anne. "Réflexions sur la notion d'habitat aux XVIIIe et XIXe siècles." In *Politiques de l'habitat,* ed. François Béguin et al., 5–31. Paris: Corda, 1977.

Thompson, F. M. L. *English Landed Society in the Nineteenth Century.* London: Routledge and Kegan Paul, 1963.

————. *Hampstead: Building a Borough, 1650–1964.* London: Routledge and Kegan Paul, 1974.

————. *The Rise of Respectable Society: A Social History of Victorian Britain 1830–1900.* Cambridge, Mass.: Harvard University Press, 1988.

————. *The Rise of Suburbia.* Leicester: Leicester University Press, 1982.

Thorne, Robert. "George Godwin and Architectural Journalism." *History Today* 37 (August 1987): 11–17.

Todorov, Tzvetan. *The Fantastic: A Structural Approach to a Literary Genre.* Trans. Richard Howard. Cleveland: Case Western Reserve University Press, 1973.

Tyack, Geoffrey. *James Pennethorne and the Making of Victorian London.* Cambridge: Cambridge University Press, 1992.

van Rossum-Guyon, Françoise, and Michiel van Brederode, eds. *Balzac et "les Parents pauvres."* Paris: Societé d'Enseignement supérieur, 1981.

Van Zanten, David. *Building Paris: Architectural Institutions and the Transformation of the French Capital, 1830–1870.* Cambridge: Cambridge University Press, 1994.

————. *Developing Paris: The Architecture of Duban, Labrouste, Duc, and Vaudoyer.* Cambridge, Mass.: MIT Press, 1987.

Vidler, Anthony. *The Architectural Uncanny: Essays in the Modern Unhomely.* Cambridge, Mass.: MIT Press, 1992.

————. "The Scenes of the Street: Transformations in Ideal and Reality, 1750–1871." In *On Streets,* ed. Stanford Anderson, 29–112. Cambridge, Mass.: MIT Press, 1978.

————. *The Writing of the Walls: Architectural Theory in the Late Enlightenment.* Princeton: Princeton Architectural Press, 1987.

Vigier, Philippe. *Nouvelle histoire de Paris: Paris pendant la monarchie de juillet (1830–1848).* Paris: Diffusion Hachette, 1991.

Walker, Philip. "The Mirror, the Window, and the Eye in Zola's Fiction." *Yale French Studies* 42 (1969): 52–67.

Walkowitz, Judith. *City of Dreadful Delight: Narratives of Sexual Danger in Late-Victorian London.* Chicago: University of Chicago Press, 1992.

————. *Prostitution and Victorian Society: Women, Class, and the State.* Cambridge: Cambridge University Press, 1980.

Waller, Margaret. "Disembodiment as a Masquerade: Fashion Journalists and Other 'Realist' Observers in Directory Paris." *L'Esprit créateur* (spring 1997): 44–54.

Warner, Michael. "The Mass Public and the Mass Subject." In *The Phantom Public Sphere,* ed. Bruce Robbins, 234–256. Minneapolis: University of Minnesota Press, 1993.

Welsh, Alexander. *The City of Dickens.* Oxford: Clarendon Press, 1971.

Wigley, Mark. "Untitled: The Housing of Gender." In *Sexuality and Space,* ed. Beatriz Colomina, 327–389. New York: Princeton Architectural Press, 1992.

Williams, Raymond. *The Country and the City.* New York: Oxford University Press, 1973.

Wilson, Elizabeth. "The Invisible *Flâneur.*" *New Left Review* 191 (January–February 1992): 90–110.

Wilton-Ely, John. "The Rise of the Professional Architect in England." In *The Architect: Chapters in the History of a Profession,* ed. Spiro Kostof, 180–208. New York: Oxford University Press, 1977.

Winter, James. *London's Teeming Streets, 1830–1914.* London: Routledge, 1993.

Wohl, Anthony S. *The Eternal Slum: Housing and Social Policy in Victorian London.* London: Edward Arnold, 1977.

———. "Sex and the Single Room: Incest among the Victorian Working Classes." In *The Victorian Family: Structure and Stresses,* ed. Anthony S. Wohl, 197–216. London: Croom Helm, 1978.

Wolff, Janet. "The Invisible *Flâneuse:* Women and the Literature of Modernity." In *Feminine Sentences: Essays on Women and Culture,* 34–50. Berkeley: University of California Press, 1990.

Wright, Gwendolyn. *Building the Dream: A Social History of Housing in America.* New York: Pantheon, 1981.

Yaeger, Patricia. "Introduction: Narrating Space." In *The Geography of Identity,* ed. Patricia Yaeger, 1–38. Ann Arbor: University of Michigan Press, 1996.

Yates, Susan. *Maid and Mistress: Feminine Solidarity and Class Difference in Five Nineteenth-Century French Novels.* New York: Peter Lang, 1991.

Yeo, Eileen. "Mayhew as Social Investigator." In *The Unknown Mayhew,* ed. Eileen Yeo and E. P. Thompson, 51–95. New York: Pantheon, 1975.

Photograph Credits and Permissions

Figures 1–2, 4, 17 reproduced courtesy of the Bibliothèque nationale, Paris.

Figures 12, 19–20 reproduced from Henry-Russell Hitchcock, *Early Victorian Architecture in Britain*, vol. 2 (New Haven: Yale University Press, 1954).

Figure 13 reproduced, by permission, from R. Furneaux Jordan, *A Picture History of the English House* (New York: Macmillan, 1959).

Figures 15 and 16 reproduced, by permission, from Michael Hunter, *The Victorian Villas of Hackney* (London: Hackney Society Publication, 1981). The captions draw on material in Michael Hunter's captions.

Figure 21 reproduced courtesy of the British Library, London.

Figure 22 reproduced, by permission, from Philippe Lefrançois, *Paris à travers les siècles*, vol. 3 (Paris: Calmann-Lévy, 1949).

Figure 23 reproduced, by permission, from David Jordan, *Transforming Paris: The Life and Labors of Baron Haussmann* (New York: Free Press, 1995).

Figure 24 reproduced from Henri Mitterand, *Images d'enquêtes d'Emile Zola de la Goutte-d'or à l'affaire Dreyfus* (Paris: Presses Pocket, 1987).

Thanks to the Library Photographic Service, Doe Library, at the University of California, Berkeley, for reproducing the images in figures 3, 6, 12–16, 18–20, 22–24.

Index

Abléiès, Luce, 62, 225nn.20,22,23
Accampo, Elinor, 271n.56, 272n.73
Adams, Bernard, 244n.55
Addy, Sidney Oldall, 238n.27
Adultery, 59, 167, 171–75, 181–82,
  186; anxieties about female, 40, 53,
  54, 55–57, 59, 184, 187–91
Agrest, Diana, 202n.17, 203n.18
Aguirre, Manuel, 256–57n.130
Air, 84, 105, 147, 153–54, 242n.40,
  268–69n.35, 271nn.59,64
Aisenberg, Andrew, 152, 153, 203n.18,
  206n.6, 270n.53, 271n.56, 272n.73
Alexis, Paul, 193
Anderson, Patricia, 256n.127
Anstey, F., "The Wraith of Barnjum,"
  125
Apartment-house plot, 11–13, 53, 60–
  62, 66, 73, 76, 224nn.17,18
Apartment houses (see also Transparency): 2–5, 8–12, 17–32, 34, 37–40,
  42–50, 70, 71, 72, 157, 214n.48; as
  continuous with street, 2–3, 5, 22, 24,
  38, 53, 153–54, 209n.17; design of,
  in Paris, 19–24; English discourses
  about, 3, 4, 83–85, 86–87, 88; French
  discourses about, 2, 5, 17–19, 25–26,
  136–38, 153–56, 158–65, 209–10
  n.22, 212n.36; and individuality, 160–
  61, 162; as investment, 17, 26–27,

137, 161, 208n.9, 210–11n.28,
  211n.29, 234n.14; lack of privacy in,
  57–58; as modern, 26, 210nn.24,25;
  monumentality of, 28, 211–12n.35,
  212n.36, 266–67n.17; moral effects
  of, 87, 154–55; and naturalist novel,
  166–67, 168–70, 194, 195 fig. 24;
  nomenclature for, 25–27, 98, 210n.23;
  origins of, 21–22, 207n.9; and patriarchy, 162–64; and public health,
  153–56; and realist novel, 52–53; representation of, in tableaux, 33–36;
  separation from street, 53, 55–56,
  140–43, 147–49, 154, 166, 168–70,
  275n.10; and sex, 53, 54–57, 60, 78,
  156, 171–75, 178, 180–82, 185
Archer, Thomas, 106, 107
Architects: in London, 93, 94, 105,
  240n.35; in Paris, 25, 27–28, 138,
  142–43, 155, 158–65, 203n.17
Architectural journals, 25, 85–86, 93–
  94, 111, 158, 159, 240–41n.37
Arendt, Hannah, 201n.8, 205n.28
Ariès, Philippe, 202n.15
Armstrong, Nancy, 90, 201n.12,
  202n.16, 203n.19, 204n.22, 235n.21
Ashpitel, Arthur, 115
Asmodeus, 37, 43, 52, 194, 215n.52,
  267n.22
Auslander, Leora, 6, 201nn.10,11

Babelon, Jean-Pierre, 207n.8
Bachelor (*see also* Domestic couple, homosexual): 53, 59, 63–64, 67, 78, 88, 226n.28, 233–34n.19
Badaud (see also *Flâneur*): 147, 268n.33
Bailey, Colin, 226n.25
Baldick, Chris, 257n.131
Balzac, Honoré de, 51–80, 171, 185, 209n.17, 221–22n.2, 222n.5, 223n.8. Works: *Histoire des treize*, 12, 52; *Illusions Perdues*, 12, 226n.29; *La Cousine Bette*, 58–59; *Le Cousin Pons*, 3, 10, 12, 50, 53, 57–80, 137; *Le Père Goriot*, 11, 51–52, 144, 172, 226n.29, 276n.13; "Philosophie de la vie conjugale à Paris," 57; *Physiologie du mariage*, 53, 54–57, 70; prefaces, 194; *Sarrasine*, 226n.29; *Splendeurs et misères d'une courtisane*, 226n.29
Banfield, Frank, 109–10, 250nn.90,92
Barnes, David S., 206n.6
Barret-Ducrocq, Françoise, 247n.67
Barrow, Logie, 255n.123
Barthes, Roland, 121
Bas-bleu, 41, 220n.91
Basset, Nathalie, 222n.4
Bataille, Georges, 225n.24
Baudelaire, Charles, 144, 266n.28
Beames, Thomas, 105
Becherer, Richard, 211n.33, 213n.47
Becker, Colette, 275n.7, 280n.80
Bédarida, François, 199–200n.5
Beetham, Margaret, 256n.127
Beidler, Peter G., 255n.125
Beizer, Janet, 277n.23
Belèze, Guillaume, 151
Bellet, Victor, 137
Benevolo, Leonardo, 263n.4
Benjamin, Walter, 4, 6, 13–14, 65, 201n.8, 213–14n.48, 227n.30
Bernstein, Carol, 102, 204n.21, 245n.58, 246n.63
Best, Janice, 168, 275n.6, 276n.14
Best, Sue, 200n.6
Betsky, Aaron, 202n.15
Blackmar, Elizabeth, 200n.6, 201n.12, 202n.14
Blanc, Charles, 159, 273n.84
Blankness, 187
Bleiler, E. F., 256n.130
Bloomer, Kent C., and Charles W. Moore, 215n.58
Boden, Deirdre, 202–203n.17
Body, female, 38–39, 55–56, 167, 175–76, 180–88, 196, 197–98, 277nn.26,27; *fêlure*, 184–85; of por-

tière, 42, 43, 49; pregnancy, 34, 172, 176, 180, 276n.17
Body, male, 181, 189–91, 277n.26, 278n.34
Boisson, Daniel, 229–30n.45
Booth, Michael, 243–44n.52
Borie, Jean, 179, 181, 275n.10, 276nn.19,21, 277n.25, 278n.29, 280n.50
Boulevard (*see also* Street): 135, 140, 142 fig. 23, 214n.49
Braddon, Mary. Works: "Charlotte's Inheritance," 12; "The Shadow in the Corner," 126; "The Story of Barbara," 12
Briggs, Asa, 240n.33, 246n.63
Briggs, Julia, 255n.122
Brooke-Rose, Christine, 258n.136
Brooks, Chris, 261nn.164,168, 263n.178
Brothel, 106, 152, 174, 248n.72
Broughton, Rhoda. Works: "The Man with the Nose," 258n.139; "The Truth, the Whole Truth, and Nothing But the Truth," 122–23
Brown, Richard, 93
Builder, The, 86–87, 105, 111, 118, 240–41n.37
Builder's Practical Director, The, 114 fig. 21
Bulwer-Lytton, Edward, "The Haunted and the Haunters," 122, 125, 126
Burke, Edmund, 87
Burney, Fanny, 244n.56
Burton, Elizabeth, 242n.45, 243n.51
Butor, Michel, 58, 203–204n.21, 223n.10, 230n.48

Cacheux, Emile, 156
Cafés, 18, 19, 26, 28–29, 40, 150, 206n.4, 269n.39
Calliat, Victor, 25, 26, 31, 31 fig. 4, 162
Cardon, Emile, 158, 160, 273n.88
"Caroline B.," 2
Castells, Manuel, 201n.7
Castex, Jean, 263n.2, 267n.19
Castle: in English domestic discourse, 3, 91–92, 111, 130, 131, 232n.8, 236nn.23,24, 237n.24, 237–38n.26; in Gothic fiction, 120, 256n.130
Castle, Terry, 253n.114
Céard, Henri, 168–69
Céleste, Patrick, 207nn.7,9
Célibataire. See Bachelor
Cemeteries (*see also* Contagion; Corpses): in England, 89, 127–32, 262nn.172, 174,176,177; in France, 262n.172, 263n.178

Census of 1851, 86, 232n.9
Chadwick, Edwin, 103, 125, 129
Chance, 3, 11, 39, 60
Chartier, Roger, 208n.11
Chemetov, Paul, and Bernard Marrey,
 207n.7
Chevalier, Louis, 199n.5, 206n.6,
 219n.77, 247n.64
Childers, Joseph W., 235n.21
Christ, Carol T., 237n.25
Civil Code, 54, 222n.5
Clark, Anna, 236n.21
Clark, Charles Lynn, 266–67n.17
Clark, T. J., 6, 200n.7, 205n.27, 263n.2,
 265n.14, 266n.15
Clery, E. J., 118
Clubs, 2, 152, 159, 242n.44
Cohen, Margaret, 32, 203n.20, 213n.42,
 215n.52, 258n.139
Cohen, William, 203n.21
Coke, Edmund, 91
Collecting: and bachelor, 59, 66, 67,
 68; cabinets, aristocratic, 62–63,
 226n.25; collector, as type, 63, 64–65,
 227nn.30,32; museums, 62–63, 76–
 77, 226nn.26,27; private, 62–63, 69,
 71, 226n.27
Conrad, Peter, 252n.110
Contagion, 19, 104–5, 115, 125,
 127–29, 152, 206nn.5,6, 241n.40,
 261n.167
Contraction, poetics of (see also Interior-
 ization): 143–44, 173
Corbin, Alain, 201n.12, 223n.7
Cornell, Kenneth, 275n.8
Corpses, 125–26, 128–29, 150,
 261n.167
Corridor plan, 94, 242n.41
Couailhac, Louis, 41
Courtyards, 22, 24, 177
Cox, Alfred, 97
Cox, Michael, and R. A. Gilbert,
 256n.130
Creese, Walter L., 243n.49
Crime, 104, 108, 125
Crook, J. Mordaunt, 243n.49
Crosby, Christina, 238n.30
Cross, Francis, 92, 93
Cruikshank, George, 101, 248n.72
Curl, James Stevens, 261n.168

d'Alq, Louise, 150–52
Daly, César, 159–60, 161, 163, 164–65,
 211–12n.35, 273n.86
Daniel, Malcolm, 274n.95
Daumard, Adeline, 206n.5, 207n.7, 208
 n.9, 219n.77, 264n.8, 265n.9, 274n.91

Daumier, Honoré, 44 fig. 7, 45 fig. 8, 46
 fig. 9, 48 fig. 10, 49 fig. 11
Davidoff, Leonore, 90, 201n.12,
 202nn.14,16, 235n.21, 236n.22,
 237n.25, 239n.33, 242n.44,
 243nn.49,51, 247nn.66,68
Davies, C. Maurice, 119. Works: "A
 Night in a Ghost-Chamber," 120
d'Azincourt, Blondel, 226n.25
Deaucourt, Jean-Louis, 42, 207n.7,
 218nn.75,76, 227–28n.30
de Bassanville, comtesse, 150–51
Debray-Genette, Raymonde, 221n.1
de Kock, Paul, 11. Works: Les Bains à
 domicile, 11, 60, 216n.62, 224n17;
 La Demoiselle du cinquième, 11, 52,
 224n18; La Grande ville, 215n.57;
 Mon Voisin Raymond, 216nn.59,61,
 224n.18
de Lauwe, Chombart, 24
Delord, Taxile, 41, 42
Delvau, Alfred, 148–49
de Maupassant, Guy, 256n.129
Derrida, Jacques, 258n.138
Dessous de Paris, Les, 148–49
Determinism, environmental, 9, 118,
 166, 185, 203nn.18,19, 206n.6
Developers, building, 109
Dickens, Charles. Works: Bleak House,
 12, 116, 253n.110; Great Expecta-
 tions, 12, 91, 237–38n.26, 253n.110;
 "The Lawyer and the Ghost," 123,
 127, 260n.159; Little Dorrit, 12; Mar-
 tin Chuzzlewit, 12; Nicholas Nickleby,
 253n.110; Oliver Twist, 11, 116,
 253n.110; Sketches by Boz, 103; A
 Tale of Two Cities, 12; "To Be Taken
 with a Grain of Salt," 124, 126
Dirt, 46 fig. 9, 104–5, 115, 122, 150,
 177, 270n.45, 277n.23
Disease. See Contagion
Doctor, 183, 191
Domestic complaint, discourse of, 88,
 102, 108–15, 122–29, 252n.105
Domestic couple, heterosexual. See
 Marriage
Domestic couple, homosexual, 64, 68,
 79, 226–27n.29, 248n.72
Domestic ideology, English (see also
 "Home"): 89–101, 235n.21; and
 apartment houses, 3, 83–88, 157; and
 cemeteries, 127–32; and flats, 87,
 233nn.13,15,16, 248n.73; and
 haunted-house stories, 10, 88–89,
 116–17, 120–27; and lodging houses,
 85, 87, 101–2, 104–7, 129, 248n.72,
 252n.106; and middle-class houses,

Domestic ideology, English (*continued*)
1–2, 7, 102, 107–16, 120–27, 128–
29, 252n.106; and national identity,
84–86, 91; opposed to French domestic ideology, 3, 4–5, 27, 83–88, 109,
242n.41; and rural ideal, 4, 90–91,
98–99, 127, 243nn.49,51, 262n.172;
and single-family houses, 1–2, 4, 83–
86, 112–16, 157, 163, 232nn.7,8,
248n.73, 252n.104; and tenancy, 93,
108–11, 122–23, 157, 239–40n.33
Domestic ideology, French, 5, 83, 136–
39, 247n.64, 264n.6, 274nn.98,105;
and English models, 4–5, 26, 135–36,
155–56
Domesticity: viewed as feminine, 1, 8,
18, 89–90, 158; viewed as masculine,
3, 8, 136; and privacy, 1–2, 18, 136,
138, 160
Domestic manuals, 85–86, 90, 92, 139,
149–52, 209–10n.22, 269n.42,
270n.45
Domestic space, 55, 58–59, 73; as urban,
4, 5–6, 11–14, 17, 19, 26, 200–
201n.7
Dubut, Louis-Ambroise, 26–27
Duncan, Carol, 225n.24
Duncan, Nancy, 202n.13
Duverdy, 191–92, 279n.38
Dyos, H. J., 237n.24, 249nn.86,89

Eastlake, Charles, 111
Ecole des Beaux-Arts, 158, 161, 212n.41
Egan, Pierce, 102–3, 244n.56,
245nn.57,58,60
Eleb-Vidal, Monique, and Anne Debarre-
Blanchard, 201n.9, 207nn.7,8,9,
208n.10
Eliot, George, 62, 255n.124
Ellis, William C., 24, 208n.15, 267n.18
Emmet, J. T., 108, 109, 110, 111, 115–16
Encyclopédies, 103
Engels, Friedrich, 157, 244n.54, 272
nn.74,75
Escott, T. H. S., 87
Evans, Robin, 242n.41
Evenson, Norma, 210n.23
Exchange, 3, 50, 65–66, 69
Exteriorization, 148, 181–82, 193–94

Facade, 22, 24, 28, 97, 99 fig. 16, 138,
141 fig. 22, 166, 208–209n.17; and
femininity, 138, 182–87; opacity of,
164–65; transparency of, 37–39; and
trompe-l'oeil, 29, 212n.40; and windows, 22, 97, 208n.13
Faillie, Marie-Henriette, 222n.5

Family (*see also* Domesticity; Marriage):
in apartment-house plot, 11–12, 60–
61; in domestic manuals, 151–52; in
La Cousine Bette, 59; in *Le Cousin
Pons*, 59–61; in Victorian haunted-
house fiction, 123
Fawcett, Jane, 240n.35
Felski, Rita, 201n.13
Feminist scholarship, 5, 6–7, 90
Ferguson, Patricia Parkhurst, 263n.2,
267n.25
Fermigier, 277n.27
Findlen, Paula, 226n.25
Finucane, R. C., 255nn.122,123
Fiorillo, 142 fig. 23
Fitzimons, Raymund, 245n.61
Flâneur, 13, 38, 139, 214n.49, 216n.59
Flats, 233nn.13,15,16; middle-class,
234–36n.19; for wealthy, 87, 88,
235n.20
Flaubert, Gustave, 225n.22
Floor plans, 9, 23 fig. 2, 119
Floors, 143, 159, 273n.84
Fonssagrives, J. B., 155–56
Ford, George H., 243n.49
Foucault, Michel, 73, 202nn.16,17,
203n.18
Fouquier, Henri, 193
Fournel, Victor, 147, 149, 268–69n.35
Frappier-Mazur, Lucienne, 229n.44
Freud, Sigmund, 196
Fried, Michael, 213n.47, 266n.14
Friedland, Roger, 202–3n.17
Frølich, Juliette, 222n.2

Gaillard, Françoise, 230n.45
Gaillard, Jeanne, 139, 263n.2, 265n.14,
266n.15, 267n.19, 270n.55
Gallagher, Catherine, 90, 201n.12,
202n.16, 203n.21, 235–36n.21,
237n.24
Garnier, Charles, 162
Gaskell, Peter, 106
Gautier, Théophile, 148
Gavin, Hector, 86–87, 248n.79
Georgian architecture, 95
Ghosts (*see also* Spiritualism): 4, 9, 116,
117–27, 130–31, 238n.29, 257
nn.137,138,139; and modernity, 117–
18, 254nn.116,118
Ghost story. *See* Haunted-house story
Gil, Biagio Accolti, 207n.7
Girardet, Karl, 30 fig. 3, 37
Girouard, Mark, 201n.7, 236n.21,
237n.25, 243n.51
Glanville, Philippa, 264n.5
Gloag, John, 241n.37

Goncourt brothers, 139, 265–66n.14
Gothic style, 237n.25
Gourlier, Charles, 142–43, 267n.20
Graveyards. *See* Cemeteries
Green, Nicholas, 202n.16, 205n.27, 205n.1, 213n.47, 265n.14
Greg, W. R., 91, 238n.27
Griffin, Andrew, 243n.49
Grisette, 40, 216n.62, 217n.63, 224n.17
Grosz, Elizabeth, 200n.6
Guerrand, Roger-Henri, 271n.55, 272n.65
Guichardet, Jeannine, 221n.1

Habermas, Jürgen, 201n.8, 206n.4
Haine, W. Scott, 206n.4, 266n.15
Hall, Catherine, 90, 201n.12, 202n.16, 235n.21, 236n.22, 237n.25, 239n.33, 243n.49
Hamon, Philippe, 204n.21, 214n.49, 221n.1, 225nn.20,21
Harsin, Jill, 217n.67
Harvey, David, 263n.2
Haunted-house story, 10, 12, 88–89, 116–27, 130–31, 259n.140; compared to French supernatural tale, 120, 256n.129; compared to Gothic fiction, 120–21, 256–57n.130, 257–58n.136, 260n.145
Haussmannization, 3, 19, 137–43, 200n.7, 263n.2, 265n.14, 266n.17; and interiorization, 139–40; and temporality, 135, 146, 148, 161–62, 218n.77; in Zola, 166, 169, 278n.32, 279n.40
Hayden, Dolores, 200n.6, 201n.12
Heller, Geneviève, 270n.45
Hellerstein, Erna Olafson, 205n.4
Hemming, Samuel, 113 fig. 20
Hibbert, Christopher, 264n.5
Hill, Octavia, 87, 131–32, 248n.74, 249–50n.89
Hirsch, Eric, and Michael O'Hanlon, 229n.45
Hobhouse, Hermione, 240n.35
Hollander, John, 200n.5
Hollier, Denis, 278n.32
Hollingshead, John, 106
"Home," 107, 154–55, 156, 201n.8, 210n.23; as English concept, 1, 91, 136, 152, 200n.5, 231n.4, 264n.6
"Home, Sweet Home," 99
Homosexuality: female, 188–89, 248n.72, 278n.33; male, 217–18n.69, 226n.29
Homosociality: female, 49, 50, 75; male, 56–57

Hôtel privé, 59, 65, 161, 207n.9, 211n.35, 222n.6, 273n.86; differences from apartment house, 21–22, 24, 55–56, 63, 70–71
Hugo, Victor, 144
Hulin, Jean-Paul, 243n.51
Hulme, Peter, 223n.12
Humpherys, Anne, 246n.63, 252n.110
Hunt, Lynn, 202n.16, 205n.3
Hunter, Michael, 242n.44, 252n.103
Huysmans, Joris-Karl, 144, 225n.22

Illustration, architectural: in England, 32, 97, 101 fig. 18, 244n.55; in France, 29–32, 37, 212n.41, 214n.50
Immobility, 168, 175, 230n.47
Individuality, 86, 110, 112–13, 144, 160–61, 162, 242n.41
Infidelity. *See* Adultery
Infrastructure, urban, 1, 133, 142, 264n.5, 270–71n.54
Ingram, John, 117
Interior: architectural, 9, 29, 51–52, 138, 142–43, 147–48, 150, 153–54, 168, 174–75; text as, 54, 168
Interiorization, 138–39, 176–85, 198, 266n.14, 268n.28, 275nn.3,10, 278n.36; of apartment house, 138–39, 168–70, 193; of plots in *Pot-Bouille,* 171–76; of urban space, 139–40, 143–47, 166–67, 271–72n.64

Jackson, Neil, 249n.86
Jackson, Rosemary, 257n.133
Jacobs, Jane, 201n.7
Jacques, Annie, 209n.21
Jacquier, Louis, 145–46
Jallat, Jeannine, 222n.2
Jameson, Fredric, 229n.43
Janin, Jules, 37, 43, 47

Kamm, Lewis, 275n.3, 280n.50
Kashiwagi, Takao, 226n.28
Kay, Joseph, 110
Keating, Peter, 246n.63, 253n.110
Kerr, Robert, 94, 97, 160
Kessler, Joan C., 256n.129
Kingsley, Charles, 106
Klein, Lawrence, 202n.13
Knight's London, 107
Krafft, Jean-Charles, 26, 27, 28
Kruse, Horst, 225n.21
Kudlick, Catherine, 152, 206nn.5,6, 247n.64, 270n.53

Lamb, E. B., 101 fig. 18
Lance, Adolphe, 154–55, 156

Land, 93, 97, 108–10, 131–32, 249n.83
Landes, Joan, 205n.4
Landlords, 210–11n.28, 211n.29,
    250n.92; in London, 108–10; in Paris,
    135, 136–37, 153, 265n.9, 270n.55,
    272n.65; in *Pot-Bouille*, 176
Landscaping, 101 fig. 18, 130–32,
    243n.49; garden, 22, 97–98, 242n.44,
    260n.151
Langan, Celeste, 250n.93
"Latest Thing in Ghosts, The," 118, 124
Lazare, Louis, 156
Lee, Vernon, 117
Le Fanu, Sheridan, 257n.132. Works:
    "An Account of Some Strange Distur-
    bances in Aungier Street," 125, 126;
    "The Ghost of a Hand," 127; "Green
    Tea," 259n.140; "The Haunted Gar-
    den," 260n.151
Lefebvre, Henri, 202n.17
Legibility: of urban space, 5, 18, 54, 120,
    145, 185; of women, 38–39, 40, 185,
    277n.24
Le Play, Frédéric, 156
L'Esperance, Jean, 243n.51
Lespès, Léo, 146
Lethbridge, Robert, 225n.21
Lévy, Michel, 154, 212n.35
Lodging houses, 2, 87–88, 104–7, 154,
    248–49n.81; similarities to middle-
    class houses, 115, 125, 128–29
Loeb, Lori, 236n.22
Lorant, André, 223n.11
Lorette, 40, 215n.56, 216n.61
Loudon, John, 93, 97, 99, 101 fig. 18,
    130, 240n.37
Loyer, François, 201n.9, 208n.11,
    211n.34, 266n.17
Lucas, Charles, 136, 156–57
Lucey, Michael, 223n.12, 227n.29
Lukács, Georg, 193

MacAndrew, Elizabeth, 256n.131
Mackenzie, Compton, 117–18
Maison, 25–26, 27, 172–73, 174
Maison à allée, 21
Markus, Thomas A., 203n.17
Marriage (*see also* Adultery): 54–58, 65–
    66, 68, 151, 216n.62, 222n.5, 227n.31;
    of *portière*, 49, 72, 76, 80, 228n.37,
    230n.47; in *Pot-Bouille*, 171, 172–76
Marx, Karl, 220n.89, 251n.95
Masculinity, 237n.25
Maslan, Susan, 205n.3, 206n.4
Massey, Doreen, 200n.6, 201n.12,
    203n.17
Matlock, Jann, 204n.21, 216n.61, 222n.3

Maxwell, Richard, 204n.21
Mayhew, Henry, 103, 236n.24, 246n.63,
    247n.67
McClellan, Andrew, 225n.24
McGuire, James R., 223n.12
McLeod, Mary, 201n.7
Memories, 130–32, 144–45; house as
    repository of, 92, 238n.29, 238–
    39n.30, 254n.120
Michaels, Walter Benn, 251n.96
Mileham, James, 76–77, 230n.48
Miller, D. A., 73, 202n.16, 203nn.18,21,
    226n.29, 229nn.41,42,43
Miller, Thomas, 129, 130, 131, 132
Milman, Miriam, 212n.40
Miniaturization, 47, 170, 178, 213n.43
Mirrors, 29, 68, 77, 78, 170, 212n.39,
    227n.33, 273n.79, 275n.12
Mitterand, Henri, 221n.1, 275n.4
Mobility, 5, 110, 139, 162; female, 3,
    18–19, 38, 40–41, 50, 53, 71, 73,
    103, 217n.67, 230n.47; male, 38,
    246n.63; narratorial, 51, 71; social,
    17–18, 43, 219n.80
Modern, apartment house as,
    210nn.24,25
Modernity, 1, 6–7, 26, 35, 199n.5, 215
    n.5; and ghosts, 117–18, 254nn.116,
    118; Paris as emblem of, 1, 4, 17–18,
    167; *portière* as figure of, 42
Mollier, Jean-Yves, 275n.9
Monnier, Henry, 11, 49, 52, 224n.17.
    Works: *Le Roman chez la portière*,
    43, 60
Monuments, 19, 135, 140, 211–12n.35,
    212n.36, 267n.17, 273n.84
Morality, 87, 115, 158, 255n.121,
    273n.79
Moretti, Franco, 204n.22, 221n.1,
    276n.13
Mount, A. J., 221–22n.2
Mozet, Nicole, 223n.14
Mulock, Dinah, 255n.126
Museum motif, 62, 225n.21
Museum plot, 61–62, 66, 73, 225n.21
Museums. *See* Collecting

Napoleon III, 135–36, 139–40,
    263nn.3,4
Narration, 144–45, 167, 193, 224–
    25n.18, 229n.43; first-person, 111,
    121; omniscient, 10, 52, 53, 71–74,
    80, 127; *portière* as figure for, 43, 53,
    71–74, 79–80, 228n.38
Nash, John, 95, 95 fig. 13, 96 fig. 14
Naturalist novel, 9–10, 166–67, 185,
    192–98, 279n.42

Neighborhoods: of London, 241nn.38,
    39, 242n.44; of Paris, 24, 38, 39–40,
    217nn.64,65
Neighbors, 123–24
Nelson, Brian, 168, 275nn.5,11,
    277n.27
Newly, Howard, 241n.51
Noiray, Jacques, 275n.11
Noise, 37, 94, 113, 122–24, 177–79,
    268n.28, 276n.18
Nord, Deborah Epstein, 90, 102, 205
    n.27, 235n.21, 245n.57, 246n.63
Normand fils, [Louis-Marie], 23 fig. 2,
    27, 28, 100 fig. 17

Observation, urban, discourse of (see also
    Opacity; Transparency): in London, 88,
    94, 101–7, 246n.63, 248–49n.81; and
    male porters, 47–48; and naturalist
    novel, 171, 177, 196–97, 198; in Paris,
    18–19, 37, 143, 146–47, 150, 247
    n.49; portière as figure for, 42–47, 50
Olsen, Donald, 201n.7
Opacity (see also Transparency): 38,
    146–47, 164–65, 170
Oppenheim, Janet, 255nn.123,124
Overcrowding, 19, 104, 105, 129, 261
    nn.168,169, 271n.57
Owen, Alex, 255n.124

Panorama, 213–14n.48, 214n.49
Pardailhé-Galabrun, Annik, 207n.8
Pariset, Mme, 149–50
Parisienne, la, 39–40, 41
Parkes, Mrs. William, 85, 92
Pasco, Allan H., 221n.2
Pater, Walter, 238n.29
Patriarchy, 54, 137, 158, 162–63, 167,
    188–92, 278n.35
Patten, Robert, 253n.110
Pattern books, 8, 25, 27, 28, 93, 100
    fig. 18, 161, 162
Paulson, Ronald, 257n.131
Paulson, William, 227n.30
Pelckmans, Paul, 225n.20
Pelletan, Eugène, 139
Perec, Georges, 12–13
Periodical press, 111, 117, 119–20
Perrot, Michelle, 201n.12, 202n.14,
    205n.4, 266n.15
Personification, 37, 39, 59, 69–70, 106,
    118–19, 254n.120, 255n.121; and
    portière, 19, 42, 43, 76
Physiologies, 32–33, 40–41, 42–50, 54,
    103, 213n.43, 219nn.81, 82; compared
    to realist novel, 51, 64, 76, 226n.28;
    compared to tableaux, 33

Picon, Antoine, 209n.21, 213n.45
Pinckney, David, 263n.2
Piorry, Pierre-Adolphe, 28
Plotz, John, 204n.22
Poe, Edgar Allan, 257n.133
Pollock, Griselda, 7, 201n.13, 204n.25,
    263n.2
Pomian, Krzystof, 225n.24, 226n.25
Poovey, Mary, 90, 199n.4, 201n.12,
    202n.16, 235n.21, 237n.24, 241n.40,
    249n.81
Porter, male, 19, 47, 55–56, 175, 176,
    194, 195 fig. 24, 220nn.87,89; op-
    posed to portière, 42, 47, 53, 63, 70,
    228n.37
Portière, 5, 9, 12, 19, 42–50, 58–59,
    137, 175; in Le Cousin Pons, 52–
    53, 61, 63–80, 137, 227n.33, 227–
    28n.34, 230n.48; lodge of, 42, 47, 49,
    219–20n.85, 228n.37; marriage of,
    49, 72, 76, 80, 228n.37, 230n.47;
    and narration, 53, 71–74, 79–80,
    228n.38; and servants, 42, 221n.92,
    229n.40
Poulot, Dominique, 225n.24, 226n.25
Prendergast, Christopher, 6, 200–201n.7,
    204nn.21,25, 223n.15, 263n.2
Priest, 183, 191
Privacy: and apartment houses, 25, 53,
    57–59, 79–80, 122, 143, 146–47,
    160; and cemeteries, 132; and collec-
    tion, 62–63, 68; and lodging houses,
    85, 87, 101–2, 104–7, 129; and
    middle–class houses, 94, 97, 115,
    126–27, 149–50; narratorial violation
    of, 10, 52, 79–80, 126–27, 146–47,
    167, 197; violation of, by urban ob-
    servers, 107–8, 125, 153
Private sphere, 6, 8, 18, 52, 139, 203n.19,
    237–38n.26
Probyn, Elspeth, 200n.6
Property, 157, 192, 250n.93; in France,
    153, 156–57, 161, 250n.91, 265n.9;
    freehold, 92–93, 108–10, 131, 238–
    39n.30, 239–40n.33, 249n.89,
    250n.95, 262n.177; leasehold, 108–
    11, 115–16, 250n.94, 251nn.96,97;
    literary, 191–92, 279nn.38,40
Propriété, La, 158
Prostitution, 105, 172, 174, 217nn.65,
    67, 246n.63
Public and private (see also Private sphere;
    Public sphere; Separate spheres): 3,
    6–8, 10, 19, 21, 90, 147, 159–60,
    204n.21
Public health, 86–87, 125, 152–57,
    241n.40

Public sphere, 6, 8, 10, 18, 139, 148, 202n.13, 206n.4, 265n.14
Pugin, A. Welby, 238n.30
Puissant, Adolphe, 151

Rabinow, Paul, 203n.17
Raisson, Horace, 54
Rambuteau, Claude, 24
Raphael, Jacques, 2
Realist description, 143, 213n.42; in apartment-house plot, 11, 60, 61; in haunted-house story, 89, 121–22, 126, 257–58n.136
Realist novel, 2, 8, 9–10, 51–52, 76, 80, 116, 203–204n.21, 222n.3, 252–53n.110
Reboul, Pierre, 200n.5
Reeder, David A., 242n.44, 253n.111
Regard, Maurice, 222n.4
Reid, J. C., 244n.56, 245n.60
Reid, Roddy, 204n.21
Renting, 39, 93, 122–23, 135–37, 156–57, 161, 239–40n.33
Revolution, 5, 18, 63, 135, 155, 162, 232–33n.13, 250n.91, 258n.139
Reynaud, Léonce, 159
Richardson, Ruth, 241n.37
Riddell, Charlotte, "The Uninhabited House," 122
Rignall, John, 204n.25
Rivers, Christopher, 277n.24
Robbins, Bruce, 202n.13, 229n.40
Roberts, Henry, 136
Robinet, Dr., 147–48
Romantic friendship. See Domestic couple, homosexual
Rome, 156–57
Rookery, 105
Roqueplan, Nestor, 148
Rose, Gillian, 200n.6, 201n.12, 203n.17
Ross, Ellen, 202n.14
Ross, Kristin, 272n.65
Rousseau, James, 42, 43–46, 44 fig. 7, 45 fig. 8, 48 fig. 10, 49, 49 fig. 11
Roux, L., 26
Royal Institute of British Architects, 83
Rubinstein, W. D., 249n.83
Ruskin, John, 92, 105, 113, 118, 238–39n.30, 254n.120, 255n.121
Ryan, Mary, 200n.6, 201n.12
Rykwert, Joseph, 267n.18, 274n.94

Saboya, Marc, 273n.78
Sack, Robert David, 229n.45
Saint, Andrew, 240n.35
Sala, G. A., 129
Schaffer, Talia, 237n.25

Schivelbusch, Wolfgang, 209n.18
Schor, Naomi, 193, 275n.11, 276n.16, 280n.43
Schuerewegen, Franc, 194, 227n.30, 280n.48
Schwartz, Vanessa R., 205n.27, 225n.24
Schwarzbach, F. S., 245n.57
Scott, Joan Wallach, 202n.16, 206n.4, 207n.6, 270n.53
Scribe, Eugène, 46
Second, Albéric, 38–39
Sedgwick, Eve Kosofsky, 257n.131
Sennett, Richard, 201n.8
Sensation novels, 12
Separate spheres, ideology of, 4–8; in England, 89–90, 235n.21; in France, 18, 150–52, 205–206n.4
Sergent, François, 136–37
Serres, Michel, 227n.30
Servants, 1–2, 94, 174, 176–78, 229n.40, 242n.44, 258n.139
Sewage, 112, 177–78
Shapiro, Ann-Louise, 203n.18, 206n.6, 270n.53
Sharp, Lynn Louise, 256n.129
Shattock, Joanne, and Michael Wolff, 256n.127
Sherman, Daniel J., 225n.24
Sieburth, Richard, 32, 213n.43
Silas, Ferdinand, 135
Silverman, Debora L., 201n.10, 265–66n.14
Simo, Melanie Louise, 241n.37, 243n.51
Simpson, A. W. B., 250n.94
Single-family house, 2, 83–86; nomenclature for, 86, 98–99; semidetached house, 112–13, 112 fig. 19, 113 fig. 20, 114 fig. 21
Sinks of London Laid Open, 104
Slater, T. R., 243n.49, 249n.85
Smells, 94, 242n.42, 260n.151
Smith, Albert, 103, 245–46n.61, 246n.62, 264n.6
Smith, Bonnie, 201n.12, 205n.4
Snyder, Katherine V., 226n.28, 234n.19, 237n.25
Soja, Edward, 203n.17
Solomon, Philip, 275nn.10,12, 276n.20
Soulié, Frédéric, 34, 41
Souvestre, Emile, 144–45, 267n.24
Spain, Daphne, 201–202n.13
Speculation: real-estate, 26–27, 108–9, 137; stock-market, 41, 218n.73
Spencer, Kathleen, 257n.136
Spiritualism, 119, 255nn.123,124,126
Stallybrass, Peter, 258n.139
Starobinski, Jean, 205n.3

Stein, Richard, 253n.110
Steiner, Frances H., 212n.41
Stone, Judith F., 265n.13
"Story of Clifford House, The," 123,
  257n.136, 258n.139
Strangers, 21, 56, 124, 131, 212n.36,
  224n.17; conversion into kin, in
  apartment-house plot, 11–12, 60–61
Straus, Erwin, 229n.45
Streets, 139–43, 147–49, 169, 199–
  200n.5, 237n.24, 267n.18, 271–
  72n.64
Subdivision, 65, 85, 105, 113–15, 116,
  168, 232n.9
Subjectivity, 71, 144–45, 193
Sucksmith, Harvey, 257n.136
Sutcliffe, Anthony, 199–200n.5, 266n.17

Tableaux, 32–43, 47, 48, 50, 53, 57,
  60, 64, 103, 213n.43, 214n.48,
  215nn.52,55,56; compared to litera-
  ture of urban observation, 143–44,
  146; compared to physiologies, 33;
  compared to realist novel, 51, 52, 76,
  213n.42
Taylor, Nicholas, 87
Tenements. See Lodging houses
Terdiman, Richard, 213n.43
Terraces, 95–97, 95 fig. 13, 96 fig. 14,
  98 fig. 15, 99 fig. 16, 113
Tester, Keith, 204n.25
Texier, Edmond, 146–47
Thalamy, Anne, 209n.8
Theatricality, 13, 18, 42, 58, 77–78,
  148
Theobald, F. J., 119
Thiollet, François, 27, 29
Thompson, F. M. L., 239n.33, 251n.96
Thorne, Robert, 241n.37
Transparency (see also Opacity): 18,
  36, 51, 52, 138, 214n.50, 229n.39,
  268n.28; of apartment house, 28, 34,
  38–39, 58
Tristan, Flora, 242n.45
Tyack, Geoffrey, 99, 101, 242n.44,
  244n.53, 264n.5

Vacquer, Théodore, 164
Van Zanten, David, 34, 36, 140, 209n.21,
  211n.33, 215n.53, 263n.2, 266n.16
Verne, Jules, 225n.22
Vidler, Anthony, 211n.33, 214n.48,
  219n.82, 258n.139
Vigier, Philippe, 205n.1, 210n.28
Villars, Emile, 146, 268n.28
Villas, suburban, 86, 98–99, 101 fig. 18,
  136

Viollet-le-Duc, Eugène, 160, 163, 164,
  213n.45, 274nn.101,105
Voyeurism, 58; female, 44 fig. 7, 196–
  97; male, 11, 38, 50, 196

Walker, Philip, 275n.11
Walker, T. L., 112 fig. 19
Walkowitz, Judith, 90, 199n.5, 201n.12,
  202n.14, 235n.21, 246n.63
Waller, Margaret, 205n.2
Wallpaper, 150, 159
Walls, party, 2, 57, 85, 155, 223n.7
Warner, Michael, 203n.21
Webster, Thomas, 85–86
Weill, Alexandre, 137–38
Welsh, Alexander, 253n.110
Whichcord, John, 115
White, Allon, 258n.139
White, William H., 83–89, 113
Wigley, Mark, 202n.15
Williams, Raymond, 204nn.21,22,
  244n.54
Wilson, Elizabeth, 201n.13
Wilton-Ely, John, 240n.35
Windows, 22, 97, 99 fig. 16; in Pot-
  Bouille, 169–70, 173–74, 175,
  208n.13, 228–29n.39, 266n.28
Winter, James, 237n.24
Wohl, Anthony, 238n.27, 248n.72,
  249n.82, 260n.161
Wolff, Albert, 193
Wolff, Janet, 7, 38, 201n.13, 204n.25,
  205n.4, 216n.60, 263n.2
Woman, unmarried, 41
Wood, Mrs. Henry, "Reality or Delu-
  sion?" 121
Working class, 155–57, 249n.81; model
  dwellings for, 88, 234n.19; as tenants,
  153, 176, 219n.77
Wright, Gwendolyn, 200n.6, 201n.12

Yaeger, Patricia, 200n.6
Yates, Susan, 278n.30
Yeo, Eileen, 246n.63
Young, William, 89 fig. 12, 93, 252n.106

Zola, Emile. Works: L'Assommoir, 12, 62,
  169, 225n.21; Au bonheur des dames,
  169; La Curée, 12, 169; Nana, 169,
  174, 277n.24; L'Oeuvre, 169; Une
  Page d'amour, 169; Pot-Bouille, 3, 10,
  12, 165, 166–98, 275n.2, 276n.13,
  277n.24, 278nn.33,42; "La Propriété
  littéraire," 279n.40; "Le Roman expérimental," 193; Thérèse Raquin,
  174; Le Ventre de Paris, 169
Zoning, 241n.39